GLOBAL IMPACT, LOCAL ACTION:

NEW ENVIRONMENTAL POLICY IN LATIN AMERICA

Global Impact, Local Action: New Environmental Policy in Latin America

Edited by
Anthony Hall

Institute for the Study of the Americas
Senate House, Malet Street, London WC1E 7HU
Web: americas.sas.ac.uk

British Library Cataloguing-in-Publication Data
A catalogue record for this book is available
from the British Library

ISBN   1 900039 56 7

INSTITUTE FOR THE STUDY OF THE
A M E R I C A S
UNIVERSITY OF LONDON · SCHOOL OF ADVANCED STUDY

Institute for the Study of the Americas
Senate House
Malet Street
London WC1E 7HU

Telephone: 020 7862 8870
Fax: 020 7862 8886

Email: americas@sas.ac.uk
Web: americas.sas.ac.uk

Dedicated to the memory of
Sister Dorothy Stang, 1931–2005

TABLE OF CONTENTS

ACKNOWLEDGEMENTS

The present collection brings together a series of papers presented at the Third Congress of European Latin Americanists, held in Amsterdam from 3–6 July 2002, organised by the European Research Council on Latin America (CEISAL). 'Crossing Frontiers in Latin America' was its overarching theme, and the chapters in this volume are based on papers presented as part of the Environment Network. Of necessity, this collection had to be highly selective around the theme of Amazonian integration, its environmental consequences and policy responses. The contributions of all those who contributed to the Environment Network are gratefully acknowledged here, as are the efforts of all group coordinators.

Anthony Hall

ABOUT THE AUTHORS

Anthony Hall is Reader in Social Planning, Department of Social Policy, London School of Economics and Political Science. He has been on secondment to the World Bank as Lead Social Development Specialist for Latin America during 2003–05. (**a.l.hall@lse.ac.uk**)

Martin Coy is Professor of Geography, Geographical Institute, University of Innsbruck, Innrain 52, A-6020 Innsbruck, Austria. (**martin.coy@uibk.ac.at**)

Hervé Théry teaches at the Ecole Normale Supérieure, Paris and in the Centre for Sustainable Development (CDS) at the University of Brasília. (**hthery@ens.fr**)

David Cleary is currently with The Nature Conservancy, based in Brazil. (**dcleary@tnc.org**)

Phil Fearnside is a researcher at the National Institute for Amazonian Studies (INPA) in Manaus, Brazil (**pmfearn@inpa.gov.br**)

Neli Aparecida de Mello teaches in the Centre for Sustainable Development (CDS) at the University of Brasília. (**namello@aol.com**)

John Redwood is Director, Environmentally and Socially Sustainable Development (ESSD) for Latin America and the Caribbean, World Bank, Washington, DC. (**jredwood@worldbank.org**)

Martina Neuburger is a researcher in the Department of Geography, University of Tuebingen, Germany. (**martina.neuburger@uni-tuebingen.de**)

Dan Pasca works for GTZ (German Technical Assistance) in Brazil. (**danpasca@ebrnet.com.br**)

Judith Lisansky is Senior Anthropologist at the World Bank, Washington, DC. (**jlisansky@worldbank.org**)

Sergio Rosendo is Senior Research Associate at the Centre for Social and Economic Research on the Global Environment (CSERGE), University of East Anglia, UK. (**s.rosendo@uea.ac.uk**)

Fábio de Castro is an associate researcher at the Anthropological Center for Training and Research on Global Environmental Change (ACT) at Indiana University and Núcleo de Estudos e Pesquisas Ambientais (NEPAM) at the state University of Campinas, Brazil. (**fdecastr@Indiana.edu**)

Larissa Chermont is presently completing her PhD studies at the London School of Economics and Political Science. She is also a research associate with IPAM and teaches at the Federal University of Pará in Belém, Brazil. (**l.chermont@lse.ac.uk**)

LIST OF TABLES

List of Figures

ACRONYMS

APIWATA	*Associação dos Povos Indígenas Waiãpi do Triangulo do Amaparí*
	Association of the Amapari Triangle Waiãpi Indigenous Peoples
ARPA	Amazon Reserves and Protected Areas Project
BNDES	*Banco Nacional do Desenvolvimento Econômico e Social*
	National Economic and Social Development Bank
CAS	Country assistance strategy
CBD	Convention on Biodiversity
CDM	Clean Development Mechanism (of the Kyoto Protocol)
CEISAL	*Consejo Europeo de Investigaciones sobre América Latina*
	European Research Council on Latin America
CIDOB	*Confederación Indígena del Oriente Boliviano*
	Indigenous Federation of Eastern Bolivia
CIFOR	Centre for International Forestry Reseach
CIMI	*Conselho Indigenista Misionário*
	Indigenist Missionary Council
CNPT	*Centro para o Desenvolvimento Sustentável dos Povos Tradicionais*
	Centre for the Sustainable Development of Traditional Populations
CNS	*Conselho Nacional dos Seringueiros*
	National Rubber Tappers Council
COIAB	*Coordenação das Organizações Indígenas da Amazônia*
	Coordination of Indigenous Peoples of Brazilian Amazonia
CPT	*Comissão Pastoral da Terra*
	Church Land Commission

CTI	*Centro de Trabalho Indigenista*
	Centre for Indigenist Work
CVRD	*Companhia Vale do Rio Doce*
	Rio Doce Valley Company
ECOPORE	*Ação Ecológica Vale do Guaporé*
EDF	Environmental Defence Fund
FEMA	*Fundação Estadual do Meio Ambiente de Mato Grosso*
	Environmental Control Agency for Mato Grosso
FETAGRI	*Federação dos Trabalhadores na Agricultura do Estado do Pará*
	Federation of Agricultural Workers of Pará
FLONA	*Floresta Nacional*
	National Forest
FOE	Friends of the Earth
FUNAI	*Fundação Nacional do Índio*
	National Indian Foundation
FUNBIO	*Fundo Brasileiro para a Biodiversidade*
	Brazilian Biodiversity Fund
GEF	Global Environmental Facility
GTA	*Grupo de Trabalho Amazônico*
IBAMA	*Instituto Brasileiro do Meio Ambiente e dos Recursos Naturais Renováveis*
	Brazilian Institute for the Environment and Renewable Natural Resources
IBGE	Instituto Brasileiro de Geografia e Estatística
INCRA	*Instituto Nacional de Colonização e Reforma Agrária*
	National Institute for Colonisation and Agrarian Reform
INPA	*Instituto Nacional de Pesquisas da Amazônia*
	National Institute for Research in the Amazon
IPCC	Intergovernmental Panel on Climate Change
IMAZON	*Instituto do Homem e Meio Ambiente da Amazônia*
	Institute for Man and the Environment in Amazonia

INPE	*Instituto Nacional de Pesquisas Espaciais*
	National Institute for Spatial Research
IPAM	*Instituto de Pesquisa Ambiental da Amazônia*
	Institute for Environmental Research in the Amazon
ISA	*Instituto Socioambiental*
	Socio-environmental Institute
ITERON	*Instituto de Terras de Rondônia*
	Rondônia Land Institute
LBA	Large-Scale Biosphere-Atmosphere Experiment in Amazonia
MCT	*Ministério da Ciência e Tecnologia*
	Minsitry of Science and Technology
MMA	*Ministério do Meio Ambiente*
	Ministry of the Environment
MRE	*Ministério das Relações Exteriores*
	Ministry of Foreign Relations
NGO	Non-governmental organisation
NRDC	Natural Resources Defence Council
OAS	Organization of American States
OSR	*Organização dos Seringueiros de Rondônia*
	Rondônia Rubber Tappers Organisation
OTB	*Organización territorial de base*
PAIC	*Programa de Apoio às Iniciativas Comunitárias*
	Community Project Support Programme
PDPI	*Programa Demonstrativo dos Povos Indígenas*
	Indigenous People's Development Programme
PLANAFLORO	*Plano Agropecuário e Florestal de Rondônia*
	Agro-livestock and Forest programme of Rondônia
PNUD	*Programa das Nações Unidas para o Desenvolvimento*
	United Nations Development Programme (UNDP)

POLONOROESTE   *Programa de Desenvolvimento Integrado do Noroeste*
               Integrated Regional Northwest Development
               Programme

PPA   *Programa Plurianual*
               National Development Plan (Brazil)

PPG7   G7 Pilot Programme to Conserve the Brazilian
               Rain Forest (now known as the RFPP)

PPTAL   *Projeto Integrado de Proteção às Populações e Terras*
               Indígenas da Amazônia Legal
               Integrated Project for the Protection of
               Indigenous Populations and Lands in Legal
               Amazonia (Indigenous Lands Project)

PROARCO   *Programa de Prevenção e Controle de Queimadas e*
               Incêndios Florestais na Amazia Legal
               Programme for the Prevention and Control of
               Forest Fires in the Legal Amazon

PROBIO   *Projeto de Conservação e Utilização Sustentável da*
               Diversidade Biológica Brasileira
               Project for the Conservation and Sustainable
               Use of Brazil's Biological Diversity (National
               Biodiversity Project)

PRODEAGRO   *Projeto de Desenvolvimento Agroambiental de Mato*
               Grosso
               Agro-environmental Development Programme
               for Mato Grosso

PRODESQUE   *Projeto Integrado de Mobilização e Controle de*
               Desmatamento e Queimadas na Floresta Amazônica
               Integrated Project for the Mobilisation and
               Control of Deforestation and Fires in the
               Amazon Forest

PROTEGER   *Projeto de Mobilização e Capacitação de Agricultores*
               Familiares, Extrativistas e Indígenas para a Prevenção
               de Incêndios Florestais na Amazônia
               Project for the Mobilisation and Training of
               Small Farmers, Extractivists and Indians in the
               Prevention of Forest Fires in the Amazon

RFPP	Rain Forest Pilot Programme (formerly known as the PPG7)
SEDAM	*Secretaria para o Desenvolvimento Ambiental*
	State Secretariat for Environmental Development (Rondônia)
SNUC	*Sistema Nacional de Unidades de Conservação*
	National System of Conservation Units
TCA	*Tratado de Cooperação Amazônica*
	Amazon Cooperation Treaty
T-CERs	Temporary certified emissions reductions
TCO	*Tierra Comunitaria de Origen*
	Collective land title
TNC	The Nature Conservancy
UNCED	United Nations Conference on the Environment and Development (Earth Summit)
UN-FCCC	United Nations Framework Convention on Climate Change
WHRC	Woods Hole Research Centre
WWF	Worldwide Fund for Nature

Introduction

Anthony Hall

The contributions to this volume focus on the theme of recent development trends in the Amazon Basin, its increasing international integration and, in particular, new policy responses to the growing environmental pressures that have been generated as a result. Prepared by a range of scholars and specialists from academic, research and development organisations, they point to the emergence of an increasingly tense dynamic in which pressures on the region's delicate ecological balance continue to grow inexorably. This reflects in part a continuation of aggressive economic modernisation and national integration policies for Amazonia, undertaken since the late 1960s and early 1970s with varying degrees of intensity by the governments of Brazil, Venezuela, Colombia, Ecuador, Peru, Bolivia and the Guianas. State-sponsored development and occupation have challenged centuries of physical isolation, myth and political neglect of the rain forest and savanna hinterlands.

Since the 1960s, Amazonia has conveniently served as a vehicle for simultaneously pursuing a number of parallel national development goals.[1] During the 1960s and '70s military governments, especially in Brazil, which occupies about three-quarters of the Amazon Basin, became concerned over potential 'threats' to national sovereignty and sought to physically 'integrate' the region into the national economy and bring it under centralised control. Underpinned by grandiose projects such as construction of the 3,000-kilometre Trans-Amazon Highway and other major roads such as the BR-364 connecting the north-west frontier region of Rondônia, government-sponsored settlement schemes for small farmers sought to populate the region more intensively while alleviating land-scarcity problems in the north-east and south of the country, fulfilling a social 'safety-valve' function. Smaller-scale colonisation programmes have also been implemented in Bolivia, Colombia, Peru and Ecuador.

In a drive to encourage economic development and 'modernise' the region, cattle ranching was strongly encouraged in Brazilian Amazonia through generous official subsidies totalling several billion dollars. Long

---

1   Hall (1989); Mahar (1988).

criticised for being uneconomic and mere fronts for gaining access to cheap money and a commercial failure, livestock enterprises in the Amazon, when properly managed, are now demonstrating more wide-spread profitability.[2] Cattle pastures cover 75 per cent of deforested areas in Brazilian Amazonia. Until recently, Amazonian beef was consumed almost entirely within the region itself. Similarly, over 70 per cent of timber production in Brazilian Amazonia presently serves domestic markets, principally in the industrialised south of the country.[3] The spectre of 'international greed' as a threat to the region's political and environmental integrity has thus remained largely a figment of more fertile nationalistic minds.

In spite of the xenophobic utterances of some observers, it is fair to say most pressures on Amazonia's fragile environment have so far been almost exclusively domestic in origin. Yet this situation is beginning to change significantly. The Amazon Basin has long had international connections, commencing of course with the first incursions of Spanish, Portuguese, Dutch and French colonisers in the sixteenth and seventeenth centuries, and boosted by the exploitation of natural resources such as rubber to serve Europe and North America. Since the 1980s, however, the accelerating forces of globalisation have added a new impetus to the integration of Amazonia into the world market system, opening up economic horizons and bringing new pressures on the environment. Cattle ranching in the Amazon is increasingly geared towards overseas export markets, providing a new 'hamburger connection'.[4] This has been made possible by a series of developments such as devaluation of the *real*, the gradual elimination of foot-and-mouth disease in Brazil and an improved communications infrastructure. Mining of bauxite, iron-ore and associated minerals, alongside the increasingly verticalised production of pig-iron, aluminium and other products in enterprises such as Brazil's Carajás programme, set the stage during the 1980s for a new wave of Amazonian development. Such enclaves as the Carajás mineral complex in southern Pará, while usually enforcing strict controls within their own boundaries, nonetheless act as population magnets, leading to rapidly accelerating forest loss and land conflict over a wide area.[5] Oil exploration in the jungles of Ecuador and Peru has brought new pressures, poisoning the ecosystems upon which in-

2   Margulis (2003).
3   Smeraldi and Veríssimo (1999).
4   Kaimowitz et al. (2004).
5   Hall (1989).

digenous populations depend and giving rise to international legal battles as local groups seek to defend their livelihoods.[6]

The 1990s witnessed a renewed commitment by national and local governments to promoting the regional integration of Amazonia at both domestic and international levels. As Hervé Théry points out in Chapter 3 of this volume, plans have been formulated in Brazil for infrastructure expansion that will, it is hoped, open up new markets within *Mercosur*, stimulate export-led economic growth and break its long-standing relative isolation for good. Although their roots can be traced back to the 'development pole' theories and plans of the 1970s (such as POLAMAZÔNIA) successive Brazilian governments, regardless of political persuasion, have more recently renewed these commitments through ambitious national development plans (PPAs) with suggestive titles. Under President Fernando Henrique Cardoso, 'Forward Brazil' (*Avança Brasil*, 2000–2003) laid out infrastructure expansion plans for the integration of Amazonia with *Mercosul* and ALCA, underpinned by a continuing militaristic and political vision of Amazonia which views such controls as a key part of national defence strategy.[7] The government of Luiz Inácio Lula da Silva in its own plan, 'Brazil, One Country for All' (*Brasil, Um País de Todos*, 2004–2007), is no less adventurous than previous administrations in wanting to develop and modernise the region, earmarking the equivalent of over US$5 billion for transport and energy projects alone,[8] and proving a source of some consternation to environmentalists.

The most striking example of new patterns of economic development in the Amazon Basin is perhaps the rapid expansion of soybean cultivation into central Brazil's savanna or *cerrado*. Confined originally to the *cerrado*, soybean is now expanding north and west, where adapted varieties thrive under favourable conditions which include good quality land, supportive climate and export infrastructure. The northern state of Roraima, for example, had 9,000 hectares under soybean in 2003, a figure predicted to rise to 100,000 hectares by 2006. The Maggi Group's new grain export terminal at Itacoatiara, near Manaus, as well as new highway connections will facilitate exports to the USA, Europe and Venezuela. Around Santarém also, located on the River Amazon at its confluence with the River Tapajós, soybean production is expected to double in the space of just a year from 40,000 to 80,000 hectares by 2004, taking advantage of degraded pasture-

6   Kimmerling (2000).
7   Dreifuss (2000).
8   Brazil (2003a).

lands (whose market value has increased forty-fold in five years). This has been made economically feasible by construction of the Cargill grain facility at the port of Santarém.[9]

However, many environmentalists fear that adapted and genetically modified varieties could in future encourage the destruction of intact forest to make way for the crop, especially if soybean is cultivated in tandem with livestock production in a mutually supportive, symbiotic relationship. Attention is currently focused on the BR-163 highway linking Santarém to Cuiabá, where it is feared that paving of the road could encourage rapid and uncontrolled expansion of production with devastating environmental consequences. In a pioneering attempt to control such impacts, Brazilian government officials, NGOs, indigenous and community representatives have been engaged in a process of consultation to formulate a land-use plan for a 'Sustainable BR-163' that would reconcile much-desired local economic development with the need for natural resource conservation.[10] Proposed measures include the setting up of protected areas, the creation of buffer zones, recuperation of degraded areas and infrastructure for agrarian reform settlements.

In addition to such strictly commercial forces, other factors are also helping to connect the Amazon Basin globally. Widespread concern over the potential consequences of rampant deforestation in the region, for example, has led to the involvement of international organisations in efforts to promote conservation and sustainable development. The United Nations Conference on the Environment and Development (UNCED) or 'Earth Summit', held in Rio de Janeiro in 1992, focused international attention on the growing dangers of uncontrolled forest loss in Amazonia and elsewhere. Calling for the protection of biodiversity and warning against the climatic consequences of unrelenting environmental degradation, new goals and guidelines in the pursuit of more sustainable development were outlined at the UNCED, ideals reaffirmed a decade later in Johannesburg at the 'Rio+10' conference.

A potentially significant initiative for the Amazon Basin to emerge from this process may result from international negotiations relating to the Framework Convention on Climate Change and the Clean Development Mechanism (CDM) of the Kyoto Protocol. As Philip Fearnside describes in Chapter 2, the Amazon rain forest is a critical element in determining patterns of local, regional, national and global climate. Accelerating forest

9   ESP (2004a).
10   ISA (2004).

loss and associated degradation release gases that exacerbate the green-house effect, biodiversity loss and other negative consequences. The pur-suit of development activities that preserve the forest to sequester carbon, either through plantations or by avoiding loss of intact forest, could yield substantial international cash transfers to Brazil and other countries through the CDM. However, this remains a highly controversial debate that has sharply divided domestic and international environmental organi-sations. As Fearnside explains, a range of highly unlikely official and non-governmental bedfellows are united, for a variety of political and institu-tional reasons, in their opposition to the notion of avoided deforestation as generator of carbon credits.

Just as the development of Amazonia is now seen as being influenced by a complex interplay of national and global forces, so the measures required to address the more negative consequences of this process are viewed as having to be equally diverse. Environmental policy for the Amazon Basin has for many years been based heavily on centralised, command-and-control measures, principally the creation of protected areas such as national parks and forests, combined with often relatively ineffective vigilance systems for detecting and punishing the perpetrators of ecological crimes. Nowadays, however, such an approach is regarded as a necessary but not a sufficient precondition for promoting sustainable development. Since the 1990s, new models of decentralised resource management have been introduced which attempt to incorporate local populations and other stakeholders in their co-management, allowing economic development and income generation to take place while conserving the natural resource base upon which these ac-tivities and people's livelihoods depend.[11]

Furthermore, these newer models involve multi-institutional negotia-tion and partnerships, a concept unheard of just a few years ago, in order to forge agreements amongst competing resource users. Increasingly, cen-tral and local government, NGOs, resource-user communities, interna-tional donors and the private sector find themselves involved in particular initiatives which demand that all participants bring their own contributions towards finding solutions. The above brief discussion on sustainable high-way development for the BR-163 is just one reflection of the growing recognition that a degree of cooperation and compromise is necessary in order to avoid irreversible degradation. In Chapter 4, Neli Aparecida de Melo examines this phenomenon in the context of the Pilot Programme to Conserve the Brazilian Rain Forest (PPG7 or RFPP). Set up in 1993 fol-

---

11   Hall (1997, 2000a, 2000b).

lowing an agreement between the G7 countries, led by Germany, and Brazilian government, this US$450 million initiative has sought to stimulate a number of different activities designed to move towards a more sustainable development model for Amazonia. These include support for rubber tappers' extractive reserves, agroforestry schemes, demarcation of indigenous lands, strengthening of local, state-level environmental control institutions and sustainable timber production, amongst others. In a decade, and despite undoubted problems of implementation, the pilot initiatives of the RFPP have had a visible and positive impact on policy dialogue and the emergence of more diverse, negotiated solutions for the region's problems. This is reflected, for example, in efforts by the Lula administration to grapple seriously with the problem of controlling deforestation in Amazonia through a 'transversal', cross-sector inter-ministerial approach, and emerging plans for the sustainable development of the region.[12]

Multilateral aid donors have been actively investing in promoting Amazon development since the 1970s. John Redwood details in Chapter 5 the somewhat chequered history of the World Bank's involvement in Brazilian Amazonia. This started with modest support for official colonisation in Maranhão in 1972, followed by much larger loans for the Carajás iron-ore project (US$305 million) in Pará and the now infamous POLONOROESTE frontier development scheme (US$435 million) in Rondônia, in which paving of the 1,500-kilometre, BR-364 highway between Cuiabá and Porto Velho received the lion's share of funding. Subsequently criticised by many environmentalist bodies and other observers for accelerating the process of frontier occupation and deforestation, this experience prompted a reorganisation of the Bank's structure to incorporate systematic environmental screening of its lending operations. Along with more widespread changes occurring during the 1980s in thinking about the environment and models of 'sustainable development', the lessons of these experiences prompted new integrated projects in the Brazilian Amazon to address issues of natural resource management, local livelihoods and rural poverty, through projects such as PLANAFLORO, PRODEAGRO and the Rain Forest Pilot Programme itself (for which the World Bank was appointed administrator with fiduciary responsibility). As Redwood notes, there has been a marked evolution in the Bank's thinking on Amazonia, which is now far more sensitive to the region's complexity and to the need for diverse policy solutions both within countries and across the Basin as a whole.

12   Brazil (2003b, 2003c).

Although Brazil dominates the Amazon Basin, it is by no means the only country with innovative plans for the region. In Chapter 6, Martina Neuburger analyses Bolivia's policy of decentralised government introduced under the popular participation and decentralisation laws of 1994 and 1995, respectively, and traces their implications for the Amazon (*Oriente*) provinces of Beni and Pando. Municipalities, many of them newly created, now enjoy unprecedented local autonomy, including capitation-based government funding for social services and greater local decision-making powers in key areas such as education and health. New citizens' organisations (OTBs) facilitate local popular participation, including control over budgeting and other areas such as land reform. Despite problems of poor administrative capacity, weak civil society organisations, corruption and elite capture, progress is being made. For example, indigenous groups have been able to push for legal recognition of their collective lands and promote sustainable activities such as certified timber extraction.

More generally in the Amazon Basin, indigenous groups perform an increasingly critical role in conservation policy as custodians of the forest and its associated natural resources and as providers of key environmental services. About one-fifth of Brazil's intact Amazon rain forest is covered by indigenous territories, or twice as much as in nature reserves. From being the passive victims of a few years ago,[13] Amerindians now play a major, active role in resource governance. Dan Pasca notes in Chapter 7 how indians in Brazil are now reasserting themselves to exercise self-determination and control over their natural resources in the face of continued threats to their territories from politicians, land-grabbers, commercial logging, mining and even pharmaceutical interests. Using the Waiãpi of Amapá state as an example, the author shows how new indigenous organisations have emerged to assert control over their mineral resources, to fight off hostile forces and help gain access to the funds necessary for guaranteeing territorial integrity and livelihood support.

Arguably, a fundamental prerequisite for indigenous peoples to acquire such power and influence, reversing the historical trend towards annihilation, is that they secure territorial rights to their ancestral lands. On this basis, legal claims can be pursued in the courts and further development efforts undertaken to build up long-term economic activities. In Chapter 8, Judith Lisansky describes how one component of Brazil's Rain Forest Pilot Programme (RFPP), the Indigenous Lands Project (PPTAL), has significantly strengthened indigenous rights in this respect. Using a participa-

13   Davis (1977).

tory model that involves indians themselves in identification and demarcation procedures, the PPTAL prompted a major acceleration in the legal recognition of indigenous lands in Brazilian Amazonia. From 1996 to 2003, the project facilitated regularisation of some 45 million hectares of indigenous lands, substantially exceeding original targets. This process has empowered indigenous groups, challenging decades of paternalistic dependence on government authorities, it has strengthened grass-roots surveillance and protection in the face of incursions by loggers and land-grabbers, and it has helped indians to begin to plan longer-term development activities, the next major challenge.

One way in which indigenous groups can in theory generate an income flow to support their livelihoods in newly secured territories is to seek payment for environmental services rendered, such as those contemplated under the CDM of the Kyoto Protocol. As already noted, indigenous reserves occupy 20 per cent of Brazil's Amazon rain forest, forming unusually well preserved islands of conservation in an encroaching sea of destruction. By avoiding deforestation, valuable services to humanity are provided, ranging from biodiversity conservation to carbon sequestration and climate regulation. Yet as Philip Fearnside warns in Chapter 9, deforestation data from the state of Mato Grosso show that indigenous peoples are not necessarily as inherently conservationist as many outsiders believe and there are signs of increased forest loss even in their hitherto pristine reserves. Like any other group, indians may succumb to economic pressures and be tempted to collude in destructive activities such as commercial logging unless provided with an alternative income source to support their conservationist role.

Protected areas, including indigenous territories, play a vital role in preserving Amazonia against the ravages of mainstream development based on resource exploitation. As David Cleary demonstrates in Chapter 10, protected area policy has been obliged to cast aside questionable scientific arguments based on notions such as 'refugium theory', originally used to justify total conservation at the expense of all human activity. Increasingly active political representation of indigenous groups, extractivists such as rubber tappers and traditional fisher people, has forced governments to acknowledge the need for more realistic models of conservation and development in the design of protected area systems. This signifies creating new areas where necessary but, above all, consolidating those which already exist and providing their populations with the means to become more self-reliant. The significance and potential of this approach is underlined by the fact that legally protected areas, including indian lands and nature reserves, occupy fully one-third of Brazil's Amazon region.

If for many years the idealised concept of unpopulated, pristine, fully protected areas dominated scientific thinking as the basis for environmental policy in Amazonia, events during the 1980s and 1990s provided policy-makers with a rude awakening. During this period, proactive groups such as the rubber tappers, indians and riverine communities started to seriously press their claims for the right to govern their local habitats. Deviating from the scientific notion of pure conservation, this new environmental agenda involved preserving the natural resource base upon which local people's livelihoods depended; that is, one of 'productive conservation'.[14] Thus, perhaps the biggest challenge in this new era of sustainable development is the absolute need to establish systems of joint resource management involving local user populations and a range of other organisations; these include institutions of local and central government, NGOs, international donors and the private sector. Several new models are being tried, including extractive reserves for both terrestrial and riverine resource-users. Brazil's ARPA project, for example, aims to significantly expand the area of Amazon rain forest under sustainable management.

In Chapter 11, Sérgio Rosendo investigates the specific problems of trying to set up partnerships for the collaborative management of extractive reserves in the north-west state of Rondônia. Extractive reserves comprise a policy instrument introduced in 1990 by the Brazilian government as a result of pressure from the rubber tappers' movement led by Francisco 'Chico' Mendes. Rightly hailed as a major new policy instrument for supporting conservation-based development, the author highlights many of the problems inherent in trying to convert theory into practice. These include institutional inertia in the setting up of reserves, conflicts between state and federal governments over territorial jurisdiction, lack of effective vigilance mechanisms, the poor economic feasibility of development projects, inadequate local organisational capacity and the difficulties of inducing local 'participation' where no such collaborative traditions exist. He pointedly warns against the dangers of assuming too great a propensity for inter-institutional harmony in these 'partnerships' and of the dangers of co-optation of local organisations by outside agencies with their own self-serving interests.

Many of the problems currently being experienced in the implementation of models such as extractive reserves are due to a combination of several factors. In part, they are the result of sometimes over-zealous wishful thinking by well-meaning donors and other stakeholders desperate to

14   Hall (1997).

prove that a sustainable alternative to deforestation is viable. Other causes relate to the 'Amazon factor', that combination of hostile climate, natural hazards, lack of appropriate infrastructure and organisational capacity that has bedevilled so many ambitious enterprises in the region. However, these problems are in turn also due to a reluctance to properly evaluate past experience and learn lessons that might better inform future ventures. International donors, who provide most of the funds supporting such resource co-management, at least in the initial years, are no less guilty of this than local beneficiaries themselves. Much planning in this sector is based on idealised and misleading notions of community homogeneity, local harmony and effective stakeholder participation, which ignore the large diversity of participatory resource management systems and their complex realities.

This lacunae is highlighted in Chapter 12 by Fábio de Castro, who proposes a 'participatory management assessment framework' (PMA) for evaluating six very different experiences along the Amazon and its tributaries, each with its own distinctive geographical, ecological, economic, social and political characteristics. By applying this rapid assessment methodology to a range of diverse situations, the proposed research will, it is hoped, inform future actions in this expanding sector of environmental policy. All that will then remain is for such lessons to be actually applied.

The final chapter comprises another piece of applied research designed to support environmental policy-making for the Amazon, in the area of fire prevention and control. Larissa Chermont points out that, although the controlled use of fire is important for agricultural production and ecosystem sustainability, wildfires can cause potentially catastrophic damage. In 1998, fires destroyed 14,000 hectares in the states of Roraima and Pará, provoking an emergency government response. Data from the LBA climate project suggests that wildfires may exacerbate forest loss, reduce rainfall levels in the Amazon and catalyse the spread of savanna.[15] The author's purpose in Chapter 13 is to understand the logic behind rural household adoption of fire as a management tool in agriculture and cattle ranching, and the implications of the growing spread of accidental fires in Amazonia. Econometric models will be constructed to explain decision-making by different groups of fire-using producers. This research will, it is hoped, produce valuable lessons for informing government policies on fire prevention and control, particularly with regard to the provision of appropriate financial incentives and educational messages as part of an integrated approach.

15   ESP (2004).

Surveying Amazonia today, there is cause for both optimism and pessimism. Undoubtedly, there has been much innovative thinking in the development of new policy instruments and models for promoting more sustainable development. There has been undeniable progress on this front since the early 1990s, as the present volume and other studies have demonstrated.[16] In the Brazil of President Lula, there have been encouraging attempts to at least begin to adopt the long-called-for cross-sector approach (*transversalidade*) to dealing with environmental problems in Amazonia. The 'Plan for a Sustainable Amazon',[17] although still at the discussion stage in mid-2004, represents a step in this direction. The aforementioned 'Sustainable BR-163' highway project will be a decisive test case for this approach. Even more significant perhaps is Brazil's inter-ministerial 'Action Plan to Prevent and Control Deforestation in the Amazon', published in March 2004, which allocates US$135 million to anti-deforestation measures in specific key areas.[18]

Paradoxically, however, even while such commendable efforts gain force, deforestation rates continue to rise. During 2002–03, Brazilian Amazonia lost 23,750 square kilometres of forest, the second highest annual figure ever recorded, the peak year having been 1994–95, when 29,000 square kilometres of trees were cut down.[19] Most destruction has been concentrated along the now infamous 'deforestation arc', running across the southern borders of Amazonia, the champion states being Mato Grosso, Pará and Rondônia. Recent research, however, warns against accelerating deforestation even along international borders with Colombia, Peru and Bolivia as the result of *coca* production. Scientific studies have pointed to steadily increasing rates of deforestation due to infrastructure developments such as highway construction, soybean expansion, rampant illegal logging and gold mining, as well as cattle ranching.[20]

It is thus a moot point whether the forces driving deforestation respond to changes in environmental policy, compared with the pressures exerted by other overwhelming macroeconomic, social and political forces. The experience of Mato Grosso with its widely praised system of environmental licensing for forest clearance suggests that such controls are feasible provided that there is political commitment and appropriate tech-

---

16 See, for example, Goodman and Hall (1990); Hall (1997); Hall (ed.) (2000).
17 Brazil (2003b).
18 Brazil (2003c); Kaimowitz et al. (2004).
19 FOE (2003).
20 Nepstad et al. (2000); Margulis (2003).

nical as well as financial support.[21] Yet the same example also demonstrates how such efforts can be undermined by the withdrawal of political support. In 2002–03, deforestation in that state increased by no less than 133 per cent over the previous year, accounting for 44 per cent of total forest loss in the region as a whole. Of this forest removal, two-thirds was illegal in spite of the state's supposedly stringent environmental licensing system.[22]

The Mato Grosso example begs the question of whether official environmental controls can ever make a significant dent in rates of Amazonian deforestation. Efforts in this direction must continue, since only now has the government made a serious commitment to implementing a cross-sector, integrated approach to tackling the problem. At the same time, however, the knee-jerk reaction to record deforestation levels still tends to be one of crisis management to assuage international opinion. This was apparent once more in April 2004 following publication of rates for 2002–03.[23] Although such 'emergency measures' are necessary in the short term, along with improvements in the effectiveness of longer-term environmental policy itself, these should not substitute for sustainable forms of development. There is, in addition, a less publicised but more politically sensitive need to influence the wider macroeconomic context in terms of influencing the pace and pattern of potentially destructive forms of development, such as uncontrolled agribusiness and infrastructure expansion, rather than treating them as inevitable indicators of progress. This is perhaps the hardest challenge of all.

21   Fearnside (2003b).
22   FOE (2004); *Gazeta de Cuiabá* (2004).
23   Greenpeace (2004).

1

Between Globalisation and Regionalisation: The Political Ecology of Pioneer Fronts in the South-west Amazon

Martin Coy

Introduction: Frictions between Globalisation and Regionalisation and their Effects on Brazil

Globalisation is not an abstract problem. For the individual, it can be experienced — not only in industrial countries but also in developing countries — in changes in work and daily life, since events and decisions in supposedly far away places more and more often have local consequences. Thus, actors or regions are more than ever confronted with the problem of finding answers to the challenges of globalisation in their respective situations. In either case, globalisation has a growing impact on their respective space. This affects not only the change of economic location patterns but also the decision to act and the options open to social actors. Regions both at the global scale as well as within individual countries have, due to their structures and potential, enjoyed diverse forms of participation in the process of globalisation. Globalisation is generally linked to economic and socio-spatial fragmentations between 'winners' and 'losers' at different scales.[1] This is also true of today's Brazil, where political decisions, socio-economic change and spatial processes are increasingly influenced by the country's incorporation into the globalisation process (Figure 1.1). Modification of the political framework of the 1990s has been largely responsible for this, as retrenchment in public social and regional policies during the last few years has led to a substantial intensification of the socio-economic disparities and to a strengthening of socio-spatial fragmentation.

---

1   Scholz (2002).

Figure 1.1: Consequences of Globalisation in Brazil

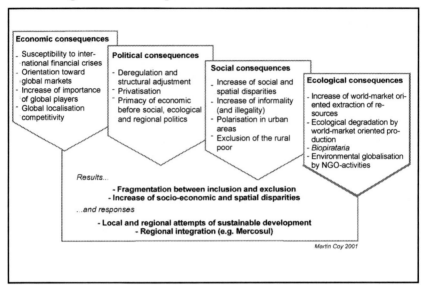

Brazil's central regions, especially its peripheral areas, are currently experiencing the economic and social consequences of globalisation in a very severe way. At the same time, sharp contrasts between inclusion and exclusion have come to characterise the current pattern of regional development in the south-west Amazon. This has affected the feasibility of alternative development concepts. South-west Amazonia is understood as the three states of Mato Grosso, Rondônia, and Acre. This chapter will above all, however, concentrate on developments in Mato Grosso during the 1990s.[2]

Politicians and planners in Brazil and all over the world have, since the 1992 UN Conference on Environment and Development ('Earth Summit') in Rio de Janeiro, considered sustainable development the model for a lasting compromise between the economy, social need and ecological necessities. At the very least, sustainable development is meant to serve the purpose of pursuing a resource-saving and socially balanced style of development that does not preclude economic growth. It is meant to guarantee current generations the supply of their basic needs without endangering future generations' needs satisfaction. However, if 'sustainable development' is not meant to become merely hollow words, and with glob-

2   Coy and Neuburger (2002b).

alisation on the advance, strategies to realise it must be defined for the local/regional level in particular. This level is crucial for people's everyday lives. However, in order to make a local/regional realisation possible in the first place, sustainable development calls for new types of regulation at different levels. Here the general framework for the often-quoted claim to 'think globally and act locally' must be created.[3] In the face of a reality marked by deregulation and increased flexibility this is no doubt a distant utopia. However, a public change in consciousness as well as positive examples of alternative development have been observed in Brazil within the last few years. Hence, it may be hoped that sustainability will become effective not only in political discourse but also, increasingly, in development practice.

Pioneer Frontier Development in the Amazon: A Political-Ecological Analysis

Since the 1970s, Brazilian Amazonia, as one of South America's last frontier settlement regions, has experienced a development boom of an as yet unknown dimension. This is characterised by the construction of highways, agrarian colonisation and huge cattle ranches, the exploitation of raw materials (iron ore, gold, oil, natural gas) as well as the construction of large hydroelectric power plants. The consequences are numerous conflicts over land, intensive urbanisation, displacement of indigenous population as well as increasing destruction of the rain forest. Thus the development of the pioneer front in the world's largest rain forest is, in terms of its background, influencing factors, consequences and tendencies, an example of the socio-economic and political complexity of concrete environmental problems. From a political-ecological perspective, such environmental changes are the expression of a 'politicised environment'.[4] It represents a scenario of conflicting interests amongst various actors. In the sense of an actor-oriented multilevel analysis, so-called place-based actors (local actors) are contrasted with the non-place-based actors, who are involved in a much wider range of activity.[5]

The development of the pioneer front can be divided into different phases (Figure 1.2) in which clearly identifiable shifts in importance between the main actors and their interests can be observed.[6] Until well into

3   Coy (1998).
4   Bryant and Bailey (1997).
5   Coy and Krings (2000).
6   Coy and Neuburger (2002b).

the 1960s, the Amazon and the mid-west were to a large extent development laggards in Brazil, not least because of their spatial isolation. Cyclical
boom phases, such as the extraction of rubber in connection with immigration and temporary prosperity in a few cities were superseded by continuous bearish phases. However, around the mid-1960s, and especially
since 1970, a far-reaching regional change began, which accompanied
basic change in economic and socio-spatial structures, bringing about profound environmental changes. Against the background of pioneer front
development, the destruction of the rain forest, which had at that point
already been initiated, must be called survival oriented. In many places,
traditional forest peoples were the victims of pioneer front development.
They had no opportunity to realise their property rights.[7]

Figure 1.2: Phases of Incorporation of the Amazonian Periphery

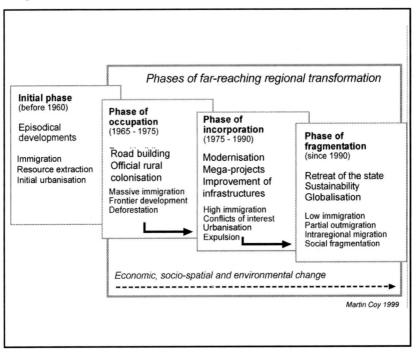

The change was triggered primarily by spatially effective projects undertaken by the State. The construction of highways and the establishment

7   Pasca (2002).

of peasant settlement projects were the main instruments of the development and control of the periphery. In the background throughout all of this
were geo-strategic motives on the one side and, on the other, the attempt to
avoid social tensions under the motto 'land without people for people without land'. Typical pioneer fronts emerged similar to those in various parts of
southern Brazil in earlier times. Displaced migrants from southern and
north-eastern Brazil were the new place-based actors of the emerging pioneer fronts, which thus fulfilled the function of a breeding ground for the
powerless. However, due to the very dynamic and spontaneous nature of
these processes, the State rapidly lost control of regional development.

Priorities have changed since the mid-1970s, when modernisation of
the regional economy and society in connection with tax concessions were
at the forefront. Agribusinesses (for example, extensive and largely speculative cattle ranches) profited the most. Moreover, major projects for the
production of energy and the exploitation of raw materials as well as infrastructure expansion were advanced, such as the Greater Carajás
Programme.[8] Although survival-oriented pioneer front development proceeded simultaneously, the appearance of new actors led to clear shifts in
regional power conditions, to increasing conflicts of interests and to repeated displacement of the less powerful. The prospect of profit or the interest in speculation has led to increased destruction of the rain forest. At
the same time, regional urbanisation began to intensify. As a result, the degree of urbanisation in Amazonia and the mid-west exceeded 50 per cent
in the year 2000 and, in some parts, 75 per cent or more.

The 1990s were even more than these earlier phases characterised by
contradictory development trends. The dynamic of the pioneer front development of earlier phases is weakening, yet the number of conflicts has
not diminished. Today the former omnipresence of the central State can
hardly be felt as a result of deregulation and increased flexibility in peripheral regions. Formerly powerful institutions of the central State such
as the colonisation agency INCRA or the public agrarian advisory boards
have largely lost their influence. Local and regional authorities advance into
the emerging vacuum as do national and international non-governmental
organisations or different private bodies. Moreover, new ambivalences
concerning regional development targets cannot be ignored. Sustainability
targets have since come to determine regional political discourse. For this
purpose, it is important that environmental changes in the Amazon are in
creasingly chosen in the international arena as a global problem. This

8   Kohlhepp (1987).

brings forth new actors, non-place-based actors in the political-ecological sense; above all, international NGOs and the multilateral development agencies. They emphasise the protection of indigenous groups as well as conservation of the environment, and they propagate adapted forms of resource of utilisation. New opportunities are thus opened up to the traditionally powerless place-based actors, forest peoples, peasants and the landless. At the same time, the central State backs out of many realms of influence at the regional level in the course of deregulation and increased flexibility, leaving the field open to private capital and global players as the new actors, for whom the world market represents the crucial point of reference to which new risks are tied.

Figure 1.3: Types of Pioneer Fronts in the Amazon

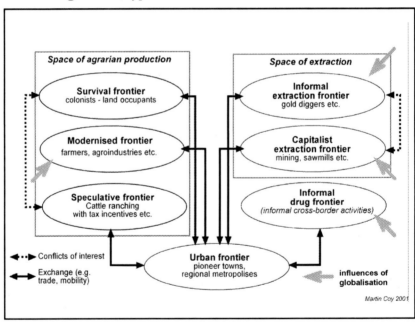

The development phases described above have in each case created specific options open to different groups of actors. These pursue diverging economic interests, they perceive regional resources in different ways and their action is often oriented toward contradictory aims (for example, survival versus profit-orientation, or extraction of raw materials versus agricultural production). In this manner, different types of pioneer fronts are formed, and they represent the recent socio-economic differentiation processes in the Amazon (Figure 1.3). In different parts of the region, different types of pioneer fronts may dominate, at least temporarily. Yet, by the same token, different types of pioneer fronts can overlap in the same space at the same time. Moreover, in the course of displacement processes, diversely structured pioneer fronts can succeed each other. A rapid change in social and economic structures is characteristic of all pioneer fronts in the Amazon. The change involves conflicts of interest between the different actors expressed in unequal competition over the utilisation and the control of space. In the reality of power structures in the Amazon, this usually means that the well funded have their way and the socially weak are again displaced.

Thus, spatial structures at the beginning of the twenty-first century and current processes in the Amazon are the result of a combination of public regional development planning and pioneer front development. Those regions with the most severe environmental degradation, known as the 'arc of deforestation', have the greatest number of different types of pioneer fronts (Figure 1.4). Due to their overlapping, succession and competition over land utilisation, these regions are characterised by socio-economic changes as well as by spatial instability. Hence, because of displacement processes in the rural area, intra-regional migration, particularly into the regional metropolises and new pioneer towns, leads to a growth of impoverishment and fragmentation processes there. At the same time, spurred by a sound economic environment, the land claims of world market-oriented actors and the pioneer fronts established by assertive actors, above all for the production of soybeans, have expanded in many rural areas. The number of land conflicts has increased in places where different types of pioneer fronts — and thus powerful and powerless, place-based and non-place-based actors — come into contact with one another. For instance, many indigenous territories in the Amazon region are, to an increasing extent, 'surrounded' by claims to utilisation of the different groups of actors. Unlike in earlier years, the 'overrunning' of indigenous territories by the different pioneer fronts is made difficult today. New difficulties accrue from the strengthened self-confidence of indigenous peoples, who are better organised, as well as from alliances of shared interest with NGOs. Moreover, international pressure has forced the government to react as well.[9]

9   Pasca (2002).

Figure 1.4: Spatial Structures in the Amazon and Recent Processes

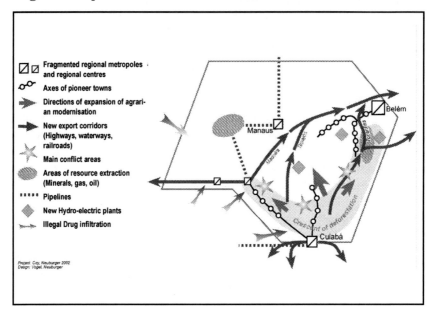

In spite of deregulation, the State still has a lot of influence on regional development in the Amazon. Today, however, regional policy for the Amazon stands more than ever in the conflict between continued development and incorporation, with their associated ecological danger on the one hand and sustainability targets on the other. In the face of the continuation of the classic policy of modernisation, a more detailed analysis of current capital spending programmes leads to suspicions that the political discourse of sustainability still has little practical relevance, since the most important fields of action on the part of investments made by the central State in the Amazon are currently as follows (Figure 1.4):

- Expansion of new export corridors (waterways and highways) in order to improve the international competitiveness of modern agribusiness (above all the production of soybeans).

- Expansion of the energy industry (new hydroelectric plants, the development of natural gas deposits in the western Amazon and the construction of large oil and gas pipelines) and of the telecommunications system.

- Promotion of biotechnology (among other things through increasing the value of tropical rain forest gene potential).

- Promotion of rural development through the distribution of land.

- Measures that aim at an increased incorporation of peripheral areas and, according to previous experiences, may involve a growing number of socio-economic and ecological conflicts are thus clearly predominating.

In terms of the central environmental question, namely conflicts over conservation versus further development of the forests,[10] against the background of the differentiation processes and development trends from a political-ecological perspective, a complex network of groups of actors with different degrees of assertiveness has appeared. On one side, they plead for a continuation of the development of the forest, and on the other they defend its conservation (Figure 1.5). In this context, respective interests in the pursuit of similar targets are often contradictory. The conservation idea is to a large extent brought to the region from outside. The interest of further 'development' of the forest prevails with locally anchored actors. The legitimisation of actions typical of pioneer fronts is reflected herein. They are the expression of a 'pioneer front mentality' in which short-term interests (to secure survival or commercial profit) combine with the perception of an unlimited availability of natural resources.

The Amazon as a 'politicised environment' is thus characterised by a contradiction between pioneer front development, on the one hand, and the move towards sustainable development, on the other hand. Here, conservation of the rain forest and the rights of forest-dwellers are at the forefront. This discrepancy forms the backdrop for areas of conflict at different levels to which the varied groups of actors can be related. This extends all the way from their incorporation into localised conflicts for land up to political disputes at higher levels. In this context, the actors differ with regard to their respective positions following the principle of the place-based- and the non-place-based-approach. Connected with that are different degrees of susceptibility (or vulnerability) as well as, depending on their respective position of power, different strategies of action and implementation. In order to reach their targets, groups of actors enter into communities of interest. They can change, depending on the context.

---

10   Kohlhepp (1998a).

Figure 1.5: Different Actor Interests in the Conflict over Land and Rain Forest Conservation

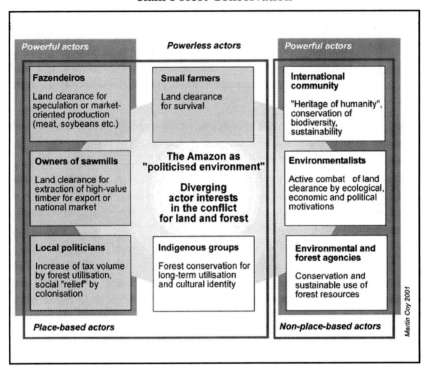

Regional Development in the South-west Amazon: An Example of the Incorporation of the Brazilian Periphery into Globalisation

The example of Mato Grosso (900,000 square kilometres), situated in the transitional region between the tree savannas or *cerrado* and the Amazon rain forest, serves to illustrate the fragmentation between inclusion and exclusion, exacerbated through globalisation, of the social and spatial structures of peripheral areas (Figure 1.6). Regional development has boomed since the 1970s. It has led to a growth in population from 700,000 in 1970 to more than 2.5 million in 2000, and it has allowed for the emergence of a non-sustainable milieu in terms of ecology and of socio-economy.[11] The following factors are responsible for this growth: highway construction, low land prices, colonisation activities of private companies exclusively

11   Coy and Lücker (1993); Kohlhepp (1995).

from southern Brazil and, above all, the rapidly increasing immigration of settler families, also from the south. Large areas of rain forest and savanna were cleared in the course of the development process. In the meantime, different economic and social spaces of inclusion or exclusion respectively have come to overlap in the pioneer regions. Their actors follow different paths of action and come into conflict with each other (Figure 1.6).

Figure 1.6: Spatial Structure of Mato Grosso under the Banner of Globalisation

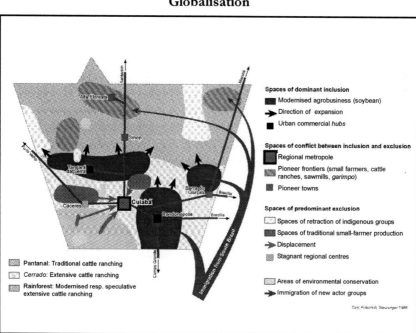

Thus the peasant, in the main subsistence-oriented, traditional production spaces are to be described as stagnant spaces. Here, the rural exodus has reached a high degree of intensity. These spaces and the settlement areas of the indigenous groups are the 'loser regions' of the regional development boom.

Migrants with few financial resources have also embarked upon a subsistence-oriented form of agriculture and settled down in the northern forest areas.[12] In addition, numerous gold-prospector camps came into

12   Coy and Lücker (1993).

being in this region. During the boom phase of the 1980s, more than 100,000 *garimpeiros* tried their luck (while many of these camps have since been abandoned). In the immediate neighbourhood of the peasant settlement areas and the *garimpos*, there are sometimes huge cattle ranches that have been set up by big national and international companies with the help of public tax concessions.

Land conflicts amongst the few indigenous groups left, *garimpeiros*, settlers and large landowners are the order of the day. Moreover, due to a lack of State support as well as land concentration, peasant farmers come under displacement pressure. Several of the author's own empirical studies have shown that, in many cases, more than 50 per cent of the settlers in the colonisation projects of the south-western Amazon have already sold their land after a short period of time.[13] The socio-economic vulnerability of the pioneer regions is reflected herein.

Within the last 20 years, numerous pioneer towns have developed in these areas. After only a short period, they have become important as supply and market centres and for receiving those displaced from the land.[14] With many sawmills and agro-industries, they have become the current focal points of dynamic regional development, a good example being Sinop, the regional centre of North Mato Grosso on the Cuiabá-Santarém highway, the BR-163 (Figure 1.6).

Development in the *cerrado* has been quite different. On its plateaux, areas of modernised agriculture have been established. Today Mato Grosso is among the biggest soybean producers of Brazil and the world. Thus, in fiscal year 2000–01, about ten million tons of soybean were produced on about three million hectares. This represented 33 per cent of Brazilian production and about six per cent of world soybean production. The soybean farmers of Mato Grosso usually work on large properties over several hundred hectares. Growing islands of modernisation have emerged in the form of southern-Brazilian enclaves, spaces of inclusion, which have come to shape Mato Grosso's economy and society and which can be called 'winner regions' in the regional context. However, the ecological costs (clearing of large areas, soil erosion and pollution by agro-toxics) and socio-economic vulnerabilities (market risks, indebtedness, closing down of farms) of this extraordinary boom are enormous.

The Brazilian soybean boom commenced in the three states of the south during the 1960s and '70s. Within the last 30 years, it has expanded to the

13   Coy (1988); Coy and Lücker (1993).
14   Coy (1990).

southern mid-west and during the 1980s and '90s to the most extensive sections of the tree savanna (Figure 1.7). At the same time, the formerly peripheral inland spaces of the Brazilian mid-west in the transitional area towards the Amazon have joined the top group of soybean producer regions.[15]

Figure 1.7: The Globalisation of the Periphery

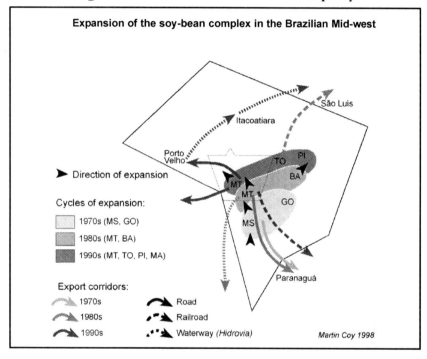

This cyclical expansion of soybean cultivation in the *cerrado* is due to the following location factors:

- the availability of large land areas;

- much lower land prices in comparison with southern Brazil;

- favourable conditions for the clearing and mechanisation on the plateaux of the so-called *chapadões*;

---

15   Coy and Neuburger (2002a).

- the breeding of new crops adapted to climatic conditions, and above all;

- the immigration of farmers from southern Brazil who could purchase much more land in the *cerrado* with the money from the sale of their properties.

'Orientation of the periphery towards the globalisation process under basic conditions of deregulation'. Thus could be headlined the latest developments in the modernisation enclaves of the *cerrado*. After the initially strong commitment of the State, private capital from national and international sources has since come to take the initiative. Multinational agribusiness companies commit themselves to the production of seeds and in biotechnology. The improvement of the communications infrastructure (cellular phones, internet, satellite TV channels for the 'despaced' boundless trade with agricultural products) is meant to help compensate for the disadvantage due to location of producers in peripheral areas in global competition.

The high cost to agro-industries of road haulage and the distance of southern ports were a disadvantage for the *cerrado* from the beginning. Therefore, regional pressure groups called for the creation of new export corridors in order to be able to survive in the face of global competition (Figure 1.7). Since the late 1980s, besides other waterway projects in the Amazon, transformation of the Rio Paraguai into an international waterway within *Mercosul*[16] as well as construction of a highway to the Pacific via Bolivia are projects designed to improve links between the periphery and the world market. Another major project was construction of an east–west railroad. In parallel, another export corridor via road and river has come into being.[17] What is new about the last two projects is that they were largely privately funded by the most important soybean producers. Private initiative thus rapidly assumes the regulating function of the State and leads the orientation of the periphery toward globalisation.

The specific connection between soy cultivation and regional development can be summarised in a simple three-phase model (Figure 1.8). Although orientation towards the world market predominates in each phase, structural changes come with the embedding of soybean cultivation into the regional context. In a first phase, the processing and marketing structures are unilaterally directed from the periphery toward central regions (large agro-industries in southern Brazil, ports for export). There are

16   Friedrich (1995).
17   Pasca and Friedrich (1998).

virtually no intra-regional connections in the periphery, and the intra-regional relationships are similar to unilateral, functional dependencies. In a second
phase, this changes insofar as, due to an increase in importance of production in the periphery, regional centres develop their own marketing and sometimes also processing infrastructures (for example, Cuiabá, the capital of
Mato Grosso). These, however, are only branches of the big national or international companies. These regional centres thus assume the functions of
an 'entrepôt', channelling portions of local production. In the third phase,
which has already become a reality in some soybean areas, new networks finally develop, mostly as a reaction to the disadvantages and peculiarities of
the peripheral location. They are aimed at improving the market position (for
example, through the joint use of warehouses) and development of new possibilities for sale, the generation and diffusion of regionally adapted knowledge (by means of joint agricultural research and advisory services) and also
through the representation of political interests and the work of lobbies.

**Figure 1.8: The Soybean Economy and Regional Development in
the South-western Amazon**

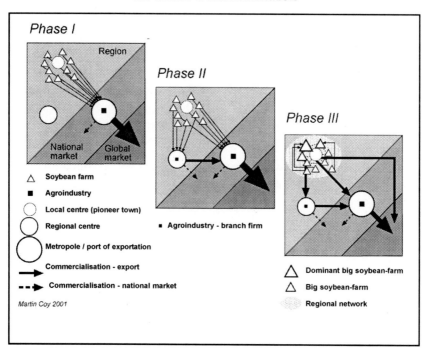

The basis is formed by differentiation in terms of the size of farms, position in the market and the target of a leading position in the network. Thus, new dependencies can develop within a network. Such networks can exhibit informal organisational structures or constitute themselves as formal partnerships of convenience. Newly developing networks are usually embedded in territorially based milieux. For the makeup of such specific conditions, socio-cultural factors are especially important. These factors include, for example, a common regional and cultural origin of the actors and thus well-founded trust, common experience in the development of the region for the cultivation of soybean and, at the same time, deliberate separation from the traditional inhabitants of the region. However, private capital interests are not very considerate of ecological dangers, of indigenous groups or of peasants' survival strategies.

Within the last few years, internal differentiation of the pioneer regions has led to a fundamental change in migration patterns. In the 1970s and early 1980s, interregional migration into the diversely structured pioneer front regions predominated. Migrant groups did not only differ in regard to their region origin but also their target areas, capital endowment and survival strategies. In most of the pioneer areas, processes of land concentration, difficult living conditions and economic failure lead to renewed migration after a short period. Four basic alternatives can be observed which characterise migration patterns in the south-west Amazon:

- Migration to the pioneer towns, which undergo a development boom. Due to their growth the degree of urbanisation in Mato Grosso now exceeds 70 per cent. Despite their economic dynamics, they are characterised by increasing marginalisation as a consequence of displacement migration from the rural areas.

- Further migration into even younger pioneer areas, where the purchase of land is still possible.

- Migration back to the regions of origin, such as southern Brazil, a phenomenon which was still unknown in the 1980s.[18]

- Migration to regional centres and metropolises such as Cuiabá, which now functions as an economic hub between production areas at the periphery and the national and international market. Migrants of the pioneer areas expect employment alternatives and better living conditions from the urban dynamics of growth.

18   Santos (1993).

Thus the development boom of the capital of Mato Grosso is directly related to the processes of differentiation and change in rural areas. For generations, Cuiabá was a largely stagnating provincial town. In 1970, it had barely 100,000 inhabitants. Yet it has now merged with the neighbouring town of Várzea Grande and grown to more than 700,000 inhabitants. Within the last 30 years and with annual growth rates of up to eight per cent, it belongs to the group of rapidly expanding regional metropolises of Brazil. About 60 per cent of immigrants are rural in origin from Mato Grosso, some from the pioneer areas of the north.[19]

Comparing the traditional and the modern town of Cuiabá, the most important physical, functional and socio-spatial conversion factors over the past 30 years have been as follows:

- Firstly, the traditional quarters undergo fundamental physical and social change. On the one hand, this means decay through construction and social degradation as well as an increase in marginalisation. On the other hand, the centre undergoes a functional conversion due to the concentration of trade and services as well as to the disappearance of residential zones. As a consequence, central anchors of traditional local identity are, sometimes deliberately, destroyed in the interest of an uncritically pursued ideal of modernisation.

- Secondly, horizontal expansion of the town occurs together with a vertical expansion of some areas. New lifestyles, perceived as modern and urban, prevail. Physically, this can be perceived in the rapid emergence of high-rise buildings and gated communities of the middle and upper classes as well as in shopping malls.

- Thirdly, major social housing projects come into existence. They cannot, however, satisfy the growing demand for housing. New quarters and sub-centre structures develop, which affect the fragmentation of city-dwellers' spaces.

- Fourthly, for the most part illegal marginal quarters expand at the fringes of town, where more than a third of the urban population lives. In many cases, these people have been displaced into the metropolitan periphery by rural modernisation and land concentration processes.

Thus the result of urban change under the banner of modernisation is a socio-spatial fragmentation of the town that considerably increases the po-

19   Coy (1996, 1997, 1999).

tential for social conflict. Moreover, these changes lead to a hopeless overload of the social and sanitation infrastructure, as a consequence of which local politics and planning institutions face enormous problems in the creation of basic conditions for a sustainable stabilisation of urban development.[20]

The economic basis of the town is also directly and indirectly related to the processes of differentiation and change in rural areas, especially that of modernised agriculture. In the urban tertiary sector, banks which are financing the production of soybeans, distributors, trade with agrochemicals and agricultural machinery and business consultancies as well as the haulage industry play a special role. The generally little developed industrial activities are also unilaterally aimed at the production of soybean. This can be clearly identified in the spectrum of industries of the industrial district of Cuiabá, implemented in 1978. Of the around 120 farms existing in the mid-1990s, most can be classed as part of the agro-industrial sector in a broad sense. Within the last few years, one of the largest soybean processing and transhipment centres of the Brazilian mid-west has come into existence there. Four soy mills with 300–400 employees each are by far the largest in terms of number of employees and business volume. They are all branches of agro-industries from southern Brazil. Cuiabá industrialists expect a further expansion of the agro-industrial sector from expansion of the production of energy using Bolivian natural gas deposits, hitherto a bottleneck, and from improved transport connections.

The tight spectrum of industries of the Cuiabá industrial district reflects the 'hub-function' of the town in the exchange of goods between centre and periphery. The emphasis is laid upon simple processing of agricultural raw materials. These products play a decisive role in regional exports. Thus, in the course of the incorporation of the periphery into the national and global market, the industrial district with its branch structure represents the dependent, functionally extroverted and little diversified development style of Mato Grosso.

Alternative Approaches to Sustainable Development in the South-west Amazon

Despite the above-mentioned processes of incorporation, alternative development approaches can also be observed in the south-west Amazon which are meant to be based on the principle of sustainability. In this context, the importance of regional actors for the promotion and realisation

---

20   Coy (1997).

of sustainable regional development, aside from international development cooperation and the development programmes of the central government, must not be underestimated.[21] Thus, the importance of Amazon states has rather increased over the last few years. At this level, there are still problems with regard to their competence in pioneering a model of sustainable regional development. The problems are, amongst others, institutional weakness and clientelistic structures, or rather the direct exertion of influence by economic interest groups or regional elites. However, among the nine Amazonian states, Acre and Amapá have recently shown that a political orientation toward sustainability targets is feasible at the local level. In both cases, progressive and very committed politicians pursue a new style of politics with popular support and backed by NGOs. In both states, the main objectives are the participation of all regional actors (especially of the previously rather marginalised traditional population groups) in the planning and realisation of alternative measures and the easing of regional conflicts of interest between further development and conservation targets, as well as the promotion of the production, processing and marketing of ecologically adapted products. In this respect, support from agri- and silvicultural production and from traditional extractivists are fundamental. In Acre, whose current administration calls itself the 'government of the forest', a zoning plan has been implemented as an instrument of coordination for single measures of sustainable regional development since the end of the 1990s. Zoning, however, is understood within the regional context as a participatory process contributing to the creation of awareness. Through zoning, the principles of sustainability in terms of considering ecological vulnerability, social potential and the requirements of spatial structures, can be systematically considered.

Historically, extractivism (especially of rubber) has had special significance for the economy and society of the state of Acre. During the rubber boom at the end of the nineteenth and the beginning of the twentieth centuries, this area which originally belonged to Bolivia and was then ceded to Brazil following the Petrópolis agreement (1903) was settled by migrants from north-east Brazil. They used to live as rubber tappers (*seringueiros*) on the forest estates of the rubber barons, rather like indentured labourers.[22] Rubber extraction is still an integral part of the regional identity. According to IBAMA, about 120,000 people (this corresponds to about one-quarter of the total population of the state) are likely to have worked in

21   Kohlhepp (1998b).
22   Assies (1997).

rubber extraction.[23] Economic and social forms of organisation, as well as the self-perception of the rubber tappers, have changed drastically within the last 20 years. Due to expansion of the pioneer front to Acre, pressure on the forests, especially for their conversion into pastureland, increased substantially during in the 1970s. The *seringueiros* efficiently defended themselves through collective action or stand-offs (*empates*), as a consequence of which they received much international publicity. The common struggle for survival, led in Xapurí by Chico Mendes, leader of the *seringueiros* and later murdered in 1988, led to the formation of local and regional support groups as well as to the formation of the national council of rubber tappers (*Conselho Nacional dos Seringeiros* — CNS). Moreover, it led to the intensification of discussions about survival strategies for this marginalised population group. The original idea of distributing individual plots of land within the framework of settlement projects soon proved unsuitable for the specific circumstances of the extractive economy.

Out of this discussion, the concept of extractive reserves (*Reservas Extrativistas* — RESEX) emerged.[24] These are large forested areas with resident populations of extractivists (Figure 1.9). The responsibility for setting them up, fostering social organisation and drawing up management plans for the sustainable use and supervision of these territories falls upon the national environmental agency, IBAMA. The population, which is entitled to collective use rights, is meant to organise in small-scale cooperatives, through which forest products are prepared, processed and marketed. While at the beginning of this new movement the question of land as a basis for survival was clearly at the forefront, since then the connection of nature conservation and sustainable forest cultivation has been emphasised.

Extractive reserves are put forward as examples of sustainable regional development. Presently, there are 12 such extractive reserves with a total area of 3,300 square kilometres and a population of about 22,400 families. The largest in terms of area and population are situated in Acre, Amapá and Pará (Figure1.9) and more are due to be established. Rubber, Brazil nuts, tree oils, resin, palm fruits and fishing form the basis of their extractive economy. However, there are several factors inhibiting their economic success: the uncertain marketing situation of the extractive products (low and fluctuating prices, low market volume), the often poor quality of the products and the 'competition' which exists in the reservations between the continuation of extractive activities and the transition to commercial activities such as farming and logging.

23   http//:www.ibama.gov.br/resex/...
24   Arnt (1994).

Figure 1.9: Extractive Reserves in the Amazon

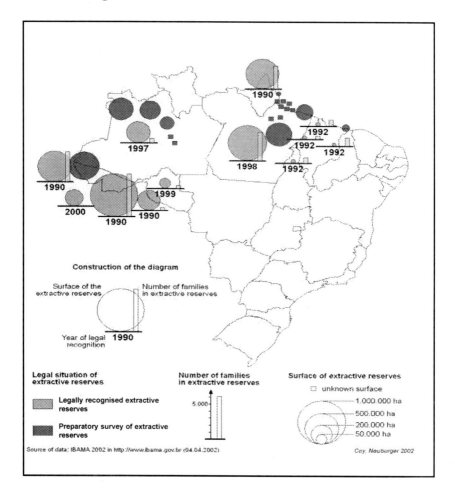

The latter could eventually threaten the ecological character of the reserve concept. Studies conducted on Acre extractive reserves show that the extractive products represent only 30 per cent of rubber tapper family incomes. Thus, the economic potential of the extractive economy should not be overestimated. Considering the total export value of forest products in the Amazon for 1998, non timber products (rubber, Brazil nut, oils) comprise just eight per cent and timber products 87 per cent.[25] Moreover,

25   http//www.ibama.gov.br/resex/

one must not overlook the fact that extractivists are abandoning their activities because of the difficult market situation and isolation. To make the model sustainable, reserves need to be consolidated. Conditions on the mostly isolated reservations must be improved; an economic foundation must be secured through improved extractive activities as well as alternative employment possibilities that are not harmful to the environment. In respect of the extractive economy, local preparation and processing must be promoted in particular, market opportunities must be opened up, while management capacity of rubber tappers' organisations has to be strengthened.

Conclusion

Regional development trends in the Brazilian Amazon are highly contradictory. Following the development processes over the last 30 years, the socio-spatial and market structures in the pioneer front regions of the southern and south-western part of the Amazon in particular have changed radically. The hopes of many migrants who, believing government propaganda, came to the Amazon to secure sound economic opportunities have often been disappointed. The rapidly expanding pioneer towns and regional metropolises of the Amazon have turned out to be the final destination for many settlers.

Regional development politics has undoubtedly drawn its conclusions from these negative experiences. Under the banner of sustainable development, it has initiated a move toward the observance of nature conservation targets, the securing of indigenous territories and the promotion of adapted production models. Public and private activities are nowadays much more differentiated than in the past. A special challenge for regional development in the Amazon lies in the inherent contradictions of public regional policy itself. Nature conservation and adapted development, on the one hand; on the other, continuation of development and valuing of regional resources through export corridors, promotion of the agribusiness and the orientation of the region toward private, regional and international interests. Zoning, area protection, promotion of local initiatives and securing of the interests of traditional populations are certainly essential steps towards sustainable regional development. However, defining a permanent focus on sustainable development for problematic areas of the Amazon remains an elusive prospect. Such problematic areas include those of peasant settlement, regions with extensive, large-scale cattle farming, advancing areas of export-oriented soybean cultivation and especially the towns housing three quarters of the regional population. In the search for solutions to these pressing problems, it remains to be seen whether the Amazon can become an example of an ecologically compatible and socially acceptable sustainable model of tropical rain forest development, or whether it will remain an example of ecologically and socially misguided and destructive development.

2

Global Implications of Amazon Frontier Settlement: Carbon, Kyoto and the Role of Amazonian Deforestation

Philip M. Fearnside[*]

Introduction

Land-use and land-use change in Amazonia contribute to global climatic change in several ways. Climatic changes affected by deforestation include reduced rainfall due to a decrease in the recycling of water, especially in the dry season. Water recycled by the Amazon forest makes a substantial contribution to rainfall in the central and southern parts of the country during December and January, a critical time for refilling hydroelectric reservoirs in that area.[1] Deforestation contributes to global warming. Brazil's Amazonian deforestation released net committed emissions of 258–270 million tonnes of CO_2-equivalent carbon annually during 1988–94. In 2002, considering the preliminary official estimate of deforestation at 25,500 square kilometres per annum and median values for trace gases, the net committed emissions (i.e., with the re-growth of secondary vegetation already deducted) totalled 442 million tons of carbon, an astronomical amount. Gases are released by deforestation through burning and decomposition of biomass, from soil, logging, hydroelectric dams, cattle and the repeated burning of pasture and secondary forests.

Burning also affects the formation of clouds and affects the chemistry of the atmosphere in several ways in addition to the greenhouse effect. The contribution of forest loss to these climatic changes, together with other global changes such as biodiversity loss, provides the basis for a new strategy to sustain the population of the area. Instead of destroying the forest to produce some kind of merchandise, as is the current pattern, this

*   Instituto Nacional de Pesquisas da Amazônia (INPA), Av. André Araújo, 2936, Caixa Postal 478, 69011-970 Manaus, Brazil (pmfearn@inpa.gov.br). The author's work is supported by the National Council for Scientific and Technological Development, CNPq (Proc. 470765/01-1).

1   Fearnside (2004a).

alternative strategy would use forest maintenance to generate cash flows based on environmental services provided by the forest; in other words, the value of avoiding the impacts that result from forest destruction.[2] The value of avoided deforestation in combating global warming is closer than other environmental services to becoming an alternative to deforestation in the region's economy. However, controversies surround the inclusion of avoided deforestation in the Kyoto Protocol's Clean Development Mechanism (CDM), and credit for this measure has now been barred until 2013. As a matter of disclosure, I have been arguing since 1982 for reducing deforestation as a means of mitigating global warming. Since 1983, a large part of my professional efforts have been devoted to filling the gaps in data and analysis needed to quantify deforestation emissions and make avoided deforestation a source of value for supporting the Amazonian population. Therefore, although I will attempt to explain the positions of all sides, readers should not expect neutrality.

Saving tropical forests as a means of mitigating the greenhouse effect divides the environmental movement politically. Divisions among non-governmental organisations (NGOs) are as large as the differences among national governments. While the debate is frequently couched in scientific terms with appeals to high universal principles, the positions of the different parties are better understood in terms of hidden agendas. In the case of European governments, which have opposed inclusion of forests in the CDM in the first commitment period (2008–12), the exclusion of the forests would force the USA to meet its Kyoto commitments almost exclusively from domestic measures. Most importantly, this would imply an increase in the price of gasoline, improving Europe's industrial competitiveness in relation to the United States. This is due to the fact that the emission quota for each industrialised country during the first commitment period was fixed in the Kyoto conference in December 1997; in other words, before reaching an agreement on the rules of the game, mainly on the inclusion (or not) of tropical forests in the CDM.

In the case of Brazil's Ministry of Foreign Relations, opposition to including avoided deforestation derives from fear of threats to Brazil's sovereignty in Amazonia, combined with a vision of the process of deforestation as inherently beyond the government's control. Other sections of Brazilian society, including state governments in the Amazon region, do not share the interpretation of the Ministry of Foreign Relations. The best news with regard to the opposition of Brazilian diplomats is the experience of deforesta-

2   Fearnside (1997a).

tion control in Mato Grosso from 1999 to 2001, indicating the government's capacity to control the process when it so chooses (although there is still discrepancy with INPE data regarding 2001 deforestation in Mato Grosso).

For NGOs headquartered in Europe, opposition to inclusion of forests follows logic parallel to that of the European governments. It is best explained as a blow against the United States, which is seen as deserving punishment for its many sins in the world, including its place as the largest single emitter of greenhouse gases and its role as an obstacle to international negotiations on climate change. From the point of view of Brazilian NGOs interested in maintaining the Amazon forest, these alternative agendas are side issues that, although they may have merit, do not justify throwing away a major opportunity for maintaining the forest. The technical arguments presented by critics of avoided deforestation contain great distortions of the climatic consequences of projects in this area. Proposals exist to deal with issues such as uncertainty and the permanence of carbon. Adoption of these measures would make the climatic benefits of the avoided deforestation become a reality, allowing carbon mitigation activities to provide a gain both for the climate, for biodiversity and other values.

In July 2001 the Bonn agreement excluded avoided deforestation from the CDM for the first commitment period, but the chances of this type of mitigation entering in the CDM are much better for the second period (2013–17). This is because emission quotas for industrial countries have not yet been negotiated and, if forests are not included, these countries will simply agree to smaller decreases in their emissions. Decisions for the second period will be negotiated in 2005. In the same year the level for 'stabilisation' of the concentration of CO_2 in the atmosphere will also be negotiated. The United Kingdom's Hadley Centre has made catastrophic forecasts concerning the survival of the Amazon forest from climate changes that are expected without mitigation.[3] These simulations indicate that the stabilisation level should be below 550 parts per million by volume (ppmv) of CO_2 to avoid massive mortality of trees in the twenty-first century.[4] The future of the Amazon forest depends on human decisions.

Amazonian Deforestation

On 25 June 2003, Brazil's National Institute for Spatial Research (INPE) released data on its website[5] indicating two significant changes in

3   Cox et al. (2000, 2003).
4   Arnell et al. (2002).
5   INPE (2003).

Amazonian deforestation. First, a large revision of estimated deforestation for 2001 (a 15 per cent increase over the preliminary 2001 estimate released in 2002); second, a preliminary estimate for deforestation in 2002 indicating a tremendous leap in the annual rate (a 40 per cent increase over the revised 2001 estimate). Anecdotal evidence indicates that the rate for 2003 will also be high. Among the disturbing features of the 2002 data is an explosion of clearing activity around Novo Progresso, located on the BR163 highway. In the 185 × 185 kilometre LANDSAT scene (227-65) cantered on Novo Progresso the deforestation rate more than tripled in 2002 relative to the previous year. This area has been the scene of a frenetic migration of sawmills, ranchers and hopeful soybean planters in anticipation of paving the highway under the 2004–07 regional development plan (*Programa Plurianual* — PPA), successor to *Avança Brasil*.[6]

A critical issue here relates to the meaning of deforestation data for evaluating the success of the deforestation licensing and control programme in Mato Grosso. The new results from INPE contain significant discrepancies with those from LANDSAT imagery interpreted by the State Foundation for the Environment (FEMA) of the Mato Grosso state government. These need to be clarified before firm conclusions can be drawn.[7] Data through 2000 offer several indications that the control and licensing programme has had an effect on clearing rates.[8] At the state level, INPE data indicate that the annual deforestation rate in Mato Grosso declined during 1999–2000, while the rest of Amazonia experienced an upward trend over the same period. However, the annual rate of deforestation in Mato Grosso was already beginning to drop before the control programme started in 1999, indicating that at least part of the decline probably reflected forest disappearance in some parts of the state. However, the decline in deforestation was sharper after 1999, which is consistent with an effect from the programme. In order to separate the effect of dwindling forest from the enforcement programme itself, FEMA data were examined from a series of counties (*municípios*) with a range of levels of previous clearing and with different dominant land uses; soybean, ranching and small farmer settlement (mixed with ranching), as well as locations where enforcement effort was concentrated or otherwise. The FEMA data used in these comparisons are for clearing in all vegetation types, including *cerrado* (savanna) as well as forest 'transition'.[9] For counties with little previous clearing, the FEMA data

6   Fearnside (2002a).
7   Fearnside and Barbosa (2004).
8   Fearnside (2003b).
9   This differs from INPE data, which do not include clearing in *cerrado*.

show the clearing rate increasing until 1999, after which the trend reverses direction and declines. In contrast, in areas where clearing was already well advanced, the annual rate declines (beginning before 1999) and is unaffected by the control programme. This pattern suggests that at least some of the decline at state level is a result of the programme. Also consistent with this is a stronger effect where enforcement efforts were concentrated.

County-level data for 2002 from FEMA indicate a generalised upsurge in deforestation throughout Mato Grosso, independent of dominant land-use, the degree of previous clearing or the level of enforcement. This may be a reflection of anticipation among large landholders that Blairo Maggi would be elected governor in the October 2002 elections, and that all previous deforestation sins would be forgiven. Maggi is the world's largest individual soybean entrepreneur and easily won the 2002 election with a self-financed campaign.[10] The effort and sophistication of the enforcement programme increased progressively after its inception in 1999, making the deforestation upsurge in 2002 a disappointment. In 2002, enforcement increased substantially, with fines applied to 94 per cent of the area detected with illegal clearings larger than 200 hectares (clearings subject to control by FEMA). However, this finding would have little effect in 2002 since the clearing was almost always already completed by the time of inspection.

With the entry of the Maggi administration in 2003, the enforcement programme went into decline (although it has not been officially abolished). Among the changes introduced was the disappearance of the website containing the list of registered properties, to which public access had been provided from 2001, indicating which were in violation of environmental legislation. The site provided maps and measurements of clearings in legal reserves and permanently protected areas in each property, together with the names, addresses and identity of the property owners.

The significance for climate mitigation of the Mato Grosso programme is considerable. As an illustration, if one uses the clearing rate in 1999 as the baseline (i.e., taking credit for all reduction in the rate below the 1999 level), the average annual reduction in clearing through 2000 was 319,393 hectares, of which 223,559 hectares was in forest and transition. Considering the biomass of each vegetation type and soil changes to a depth of one metre, this reduction avoided an emission of 36 million tonnes of carbon annually.[11] An idea of the potential economic significance can be gained by considering a carbon value of US$20/tonne. What

10   Edward (2003).
11   Fearnside and Barbosa (2003).

the price will actually be (i.e., what the supply and demand will be for CDM carbon credits) and what percentage of avoided deforestation carbon can be claimed as credit will, of course, depend on future decisions. At US$20/tonne, the programme would be producing a carbon value of US$722 million annually. This would represent a maximum value, as it assumes that all carbon is credited in full, without adjustments for such factors as permanence, uncertainty and leakage that are advocated by this author.[12] Note that for the first commitment period, with no US participation and with avoided deforestation excluded by the Bonn Agreement, the price of carbon is expected to be only US$9/tonne C.[13]

If avoided deforestation is eventually included in the CDM, the bulk of the profit from sale of carbon credit generated will go to project developers. These might be federal bodies (such as the environmental control agency, IBAMA), state governments, private landowners, or cooperatives and citizens' groups. A five per cent tax on the proceeds will go to the climate convention's adaptation fund and for activities related to biodiversity conservation. Some of this smaller stream of funding may also become available to Brazilian government and non-government organisations. Prospects for the use of funding generated by avoided deforestation during the second commitment period will depend heavily on experience gained with the more modest amounts of money expected from the CDM during the first commitment period, when only projects for plantations and energy-sector mitigation will be eligible credit. However, the difficulties in actually spending the money in a timely and effective fashion to promote sustainable development and conservation are tremendous.[14] The great effort that has been needed to spend significantly smaller sums under the Rain Forest Pilot Programme (RFPP) makes this all too clear. Yet, notwithstanding these problems, this source of value must be maintained if the transition to an economy based on environmental services is ever to take place. This means both recognising the value of avoiding deforestation and having a forest left to maintain.

Greenhouse Gas Emissions from Deforestation

Amazonian deforestation makes a significant contribution to global warming, but the amount of this contribution has been the subject of extended

12   See, for example, Fearnside (2001a).
13   den Elzen and de Moor (2001).
14   Fearnside (1997a).

controversies and strong political divisions underlie the debate. Half of the dry weight of wood is carbon. Both burning and decay release this carbon as greenhouse gases such as carbon dioxide (CO_2) and methane (CH_4), in addition to releasing non-carbon greenhouse gases such as nitrous oxide (N_2O). The magnitude of greenhouse gas emissions from deforestation in Brazil's Amazon forest is the subject of longstanding debate both inside and outside the country. The range of estimates is very large.[15] Only a relatively small part of this range is the result of genuine differences in data for forest biomass and other relevant factors. Most derives from the choice of what items to include in the estimates. The choices made have direct impact on policy questions, about which opinions are sharply divided for non-scientific reasons. Close examination of the effect of choices is therefore necessary. The goal should be to base all policies on complete accounting.

The Brazilian government has long had a pattern of announcing lower deforestation and emissions estimates than those suggested by other evidence.[16] Just before the Kyoto conference, the government even announced that the country produces *zero* net emissions from Amazonian deforestation![17] In recent years, official deforestation rate estimates have been free of the crude errors that led to the understating of deforestation contained in earlier estimates, but emissions calculations continue to minimise the impact of deforestation on global warming.

The political context in Brazil was made clear by José Domingos Gonzalez Miguez, head of the climate sector of the Ministry of Science and Technology (MCT), in the transcript of a February 2002 workshop on the greenhouse gas emissions from reservoirs held at MCT's Centre for the Management of Strategic Studies in Brasília. Although this 'smoking gun' relates to the question of emissions by hydroelectric dams[18] rather than deforestation for ranching and agriculture, the political context is the same:

> I asked for the help of ELETROBRÁS [on the subject of greenhouse gas emissions from dams]; actually, it was ELETROBRÁS that coordinated this work exactly because of this, because this subject was becoming political. It has a very great impact at the world level; we are going to suffer pressure from the developed countries because of this subject. And, this subject was little known. It is mistreated. It is mistreated and continues to be mistreated by Philip Fearnside himself, and we have to be very careful. The debate that is taking place now in the

15   R.J.A. Houghton et al. (2001).
16   Fearnside (1997b, 2000a).
17   *IstoÉ* (1997).
18   Fearnside (2002b).

press shows this clearly; that is to say, you can take any one-sided statement to show that Brazil is not clean, that Brazil is very remiss, that
Brazil, implicitly, will have to take on a commitment [to reduce emis-
sions] in the future. This is a great political debate and we are preparing ourselves for it.[19]

This confession is maintained on a public website administered by the
MCT climate sector itself. Needless to say, the idea that research on emissions must be carefully 'coordinated' in order to assure that only politically palatable conclusions are reached is not the only viewpoint. As unpop-
ular as it may be, I defend the position that *all* sources and sinks of greenhouse gases must be quantified and taken into account in policy-making.

Brazil is preparing its first national inventory of greenhouse gas emissions, as required by the 1992 United Nations Framework Convention on
Climate Change, or UN–FCCC (1992). The inventory was finally completed in 2004. The current Brazilian inventory covers the 1988–94 period,
when the average annual deforestation rate in Amazonia was 15,200 square
kilometres. Estimates for the deforestation portion of the report have
evolved over time. In August 2002, a preliminary estimate for this component totalled 90 million t C, a value that was increased to 117 million t C
in September 2003, but may undergo further revision. My estimates for the
same period are 56 per cent higher (Table 2.1). Differences include count-
ing below ground biomass, dead trees and trace gases. The upsurge in the
deforestation rate in 2002 implies astronomical emissions — in the neighbourhood of 450 million tonnes of carbon annually (Table 2.1).

Controversies over numbers for emissions from Amazonian deforestation are also common within the academic community. A recent estimate
by researchers at the European Union's Joint Research Centre in Ispra,
Italy, concluded that emissions are much lower than those detected by others.[20] However, a series of omissions in this low estimate adds up to an un-
derstatement of the global-warming impact of deforestation by more than
a factor of two.[21] Outside observers often react to differing results among
scientific groups by assuming that the truth must lie somewhere between
the two extremes, presumably at the midpoint. Unfortunately, this kind of
shortcut methodology is utterly insufficient: there is no substitute for read-
ing the original literature on these controversies and tracing the origin of
each item back to its source. Entering into this literature will quickly reveal

19   MCT (2002).
20   Achard et al. (2002); Eva et al. (2003).
21   Fearnside and Laurance (2003, 2004).

that many of the published estimates are little more than guesses. The reliability of an estimate depends on three basic factors: the quality of the data, the quantity (and representativeness) of the data and the consistency of the interpretation.

Table 2.1: Emissions from Amazonian Deforestation

	1988-1994	2002
Deforestation rate in Legal Amazon (thousand km²/year)	15.2	25.5
Net Committed Emissions from deforestation in Legal Amazon (million t CO_2-equiv. C/year)		
Low trace-gas scenario	258	432
Midpoint	264	442
High trace-gas scenario	270	451
Brazilian inventory (Amazon deforestation)	117	
Approximate discrepancy	56 %	

Some values for input parameters in emissions calculations are much better than others in terms of the underlying data and in terms of the interpretation of those data. Great care must be taken that all components of the carbon stock are included. Values for the percentage of above-ground live biomass (AGLB) for frequently omitted components include: trees less than ten centimetres in diameter (12 per cent), vines (4.3 per cent), palms (3.5 per cent) and strangler figs and other 'non-tree' components (0.2 per cent).[22] A valid estimate must include below ground biomass, which averages 19.3 per cent expressed as a percentage of AGLB for all Amazonian forests[23] and dead biomass (necromass), which is typically 9–12 per cent of AGLB.[24] The full emission must include either the 'committed emissions' after the year (or multi-year time period) used for the estimate, or the 'inherited emissions' from decay or combustion of biomass that remains un-

22   Fearnside (1994, 1997c, 2000c).
23   Fearnside et al. (1993).
24   Nascimento and Laurance (2002).

oxidised from deforestation in the years prior to the year or period of interest. Re-growth in the deforested landscape is often overestimated by using data on secondary forests that are not derived from cattle pasture, which predominates overwhelmingly as a land-use history and which produces secondary vegetation that grows only slowly.[25] Soil carbon release from the top metre of soil (9.6 per cent of the impact)[26] is often an additional omission. To fully reflect the global-warming impact of deforestation, emissions of trace gases such as CH_4 and N_2O must be included, as well as carbon (CO_2). Inclusion of trace gases increases the impact of deforestation by 15.5±9.5 per cent over calculations that consider only carbon.[27] All of the above factors are omitted in varying degrees from a number of widely used emissions estimates for Amazonian deforestation.[28]

Tropical Deforestation in the Kyoto Protocol

International negotiations on climate change have been underway since the preparatory conferences for the 1992 'Earth Summit' (UNCED or ECO–92), held in Rio de Janeiro. Tropical deforestation was considered a major contributor to global warming both by European governments and by European-headquartered NGOs. A report published by Friends of the Earth–UK[29] and another by Greenpeace[30] made similar claims. This widespread agreement on the importance of tropical deforestation would evaporate abruptly with the Kyoto Protocol in December 1997, after which European governments and European-based NGOs would turn against avoiding tropical deforestation as a form of mitigation.

The Kyoto Protocol established an 'assigned amount' (quota) for the emissions of each of the countries in Annex I of the Climate Convention and Annex B of the Kyoto Protocol.[31] These are currently the developed countries. The amount that each of these countries could emit without penalty in the Kyoto Protocol's first commitment period (2008–12) was fixed in Kyoto — but the rules of the game had not yet been settled. Especially important was the question of whether tropical forests would be included for credit under the Protocol's Clean Development Mechanism.

25   Fearnside (1996a); Fearnside and Guimarães (1996).
26   Fearnside (2000c); Fearnside and Barbosa (1998).
27   Fearnside (2000b), pp. 143–5.
28   Fearnside and Laurance (2003).
29   Myers (1989), p. 73.
30   Leggett (1990), p. 399.
31   UN–FCCC (1997).

Blocks of countries formed with distinct positions on credit for different types of forest-sector projects in the CDM, as shown in Table 2.2.

Table 2.2: Government Positions on the Clean Development Mechanism(a)

	Plantations	Agro-forestry	Avoided deforestation
Brazil	+	+	-
Umbrella Group	+	+	+
(USA, Canada, Japan, Australia, New Zealand)			
European Union	-	-	-
AOSIS (Association of Small Island States)	-	-	-
G-77 + China	?	?	?

(a) Plus sign indicates favouring inclusion, minus sign opposing, and blank indicates no position.

Government Positions

BRAZIL

The Brazilian Ministry of Foreign Relations (MRE) has opposed inclusion of avoided deforestation in the Clean Development Mechanism, but at the same time has supported credit for silvicultural plantations (i.e., afforestation and reforestation). This split position makes Brazil unusual. It should be emphasised that the official position of the portions of government responsible for the negotiation (the Ministry of Foreign Relations and the Minister of Science and Technology) differed sharply from that of other parts of the government, such as the Ministry of the Environment. It is also significant that the Minister of Science and Technology during the presidential administration of Fernando Henrique Cardoso (1995–2002) was a high-ranking diplomat from the Ministry of Foreign Relations.

In June 1999, the divergent opinion of the Ministry of the Environment became a matter of public record. At the meeting of environment ministers of Amazonian countries held in Cochabamba, Bolivia, the Brazilian minister of the environment (José Sarney Filho) signed a joint declaration calling for approval of credit under the CDM for avoided deforestation.[32] Sarney Filho signed the document despite objections from the envoy from the Ministry of Foreign Relations. The disagreement even took on the form of a physical struggle, with Sarney Filho and the MRE representative engaged in a tug-of-war for the microphone, to the amazement of the audience.[33] Sarney Filho, who was physically much more imposing than the slender young man who represented MRE, easily won the contest. However, by the time of the next meeting of the environment ministers, held in Quito, Ecuador in October 1999, the Ministry of the Environment had been forbidden to say anything related to the Kyoto negotiations.

It should be emphasised that Brazilian negotiating policy for Kyoto has been set by a handful of individuals, and the result is very much tied to the opinions of those individuals, rather than to a logical argument on which there is wide agreement. Each new set of individuals represents a toss of the coin, and the probability is significant that key positions will eventually be occupied by individuals who favour forests.

A sort of allergy has developed to discussion of the role of avoiding tropical deforestation as a means of mitigating climate change, stemming from fear of 'international greed', or the belief that the world at large is engaged in a permanent conspiracy to take Amazonia away from Brazil. The key individuals who determine Brazil's negotiating stance all believe piously in the threat of internationalisation. The fear that carbon could lead to international interference with Brazilian sovereignty in Amazonia is at the root of the aversion of the Ministry of Foreign Affairs and the Minister of Science and Technology to the notion of obtaining credit for avoided deforestation.

Yet as important as the internationalisation theory is in this arena,[34] it is not in itself enough to explain the aversion to carbon credit for avoided deforestation. This is best illustrated by the case of the governors of the Amazonian states, who have traditionally embraced both positions. These include Amazonino Mendes, governor of Amazonas until 2002. In his po-

32 Environment Ministers of the Amazonian Countries (1999).
33 Luis Castello, personal communication (2000).
34 Council on Foreign Relations Independent Task Force (2001); Fearnside (2001b).

litical discourse, Mendes constantly raises the threat of international threats to Amazonia, yet at the same time he has been voluble in support of carbon credits and even travelled to Chicago to try to sell Amazonian forest carbon on international commodities markets.

The essential question is whether one believes that Amazonian deforestation is at all controllable. The key individuals in Brazil's negotiating position believe that deforestation is inherently uncontrollable. If this is accepted as a starting point, then if Brazil were to commit itself to reduce deforestation and then not actually do so, the country could be open to international pressures. Although Article 12 (paragraph 5a) of the Kyoto Protocol makes clear that the CDM is entirely voluntary, the fear persists that Brazil could be threatened with economic sanctions such as tariffs on Brazilian exports ranging from orange juice to shoes unless the country agrees to accept carbon projects that are in the interest of major economic powers, especially the United States.

If the impediment to using forest conservation as a global-warming mitigation measure is concern over national sovereignty, then it is national sovereignty that must be discussed and examined, rather than debating the sources of climate change or the moral value of changes in this century versus the next. Admitting that sovereignty is the issue implies the need to subject this problem to the same level of critical scrutiny as that applied to the technical aspects of mitigation proposals. The notion that the world is permanently conspiring to take Amazonia away from Brazil is not likely to stand up to such scrutiny. Nevertheless, it is important to remember that no amount of evidence is likely to change the opinion of the individual diplomats involved, since the internationalisation theory rests directly on their 'pre-analytical vision'.[35] Even the most intelligent people only draw conclusions from the experiences that their prejudices allow.

While the internationalisation theory is directly analogous to religion in terms of its means of acquisition of belief, its immunity to 'reason' and the need for respecting a diversity of opinions, it is also analogous in another way. This is in the proper relationship with government decision-making. With the exception of a few countries under Islamic law, most present-day governments operate on the principle that Church and State should be separate. The same principle should be applied to the internationalisation creed.

35   Daly and Cobb (1989).

REST OF LATIN AMERICA

The Latin-American countries most active in the effort to get rules approved for the CDM to allow credit for avoided deforestation under the CDM were Bolivia, Costa Rica, Colombia and Mexico. Besides Brazil, only Peru (under President Alberto Fujimori) opposed granting credit for avoided deforestation. Peru has since reversed its position.[36] The question arises as to why the Fujimori government in Peru opposed credit for forests in the Kyoto negotiations, a stance that appears to be contrary to Peru's national interest as a country with substantial areas of tropical forest that could potentially generate revenues through avoided deforestation projects under the CDM. The timing of Peru's adoption of this position is intriguing. Peru's opposition was made known at the Intergovernmental Panel on Climate Change (IPCC) plenary session in Montreal in February 2000, just weeks before the 9 April first round of Fujimori's 're-re-election'. Peru's opposition to avoided deforestation represented a reversal of its previous position.[37] During the 'crisis' between the allegedly fraudulent 9 April first round and the 28 May runoff election, Brazil showed support for Fujimori by granting Order of the Southern Cross medals to three of Fujimori's cabinet ministers and, perhaps more importantly, by receiving a secret delegation of Peruvian diplomats and informally agreeing to support the official results of the upcoming runoff election even if the validity of the election were to be questioned by the international community.[38] The runoff election, in which Fujimori ran unopposed, was questioned by the Organization of American States (OEA), but Brazil was decisive in blocking sanctions against Peru by the OEA.[39] The tilt towards Fujimori was unexpected in light of Brazil's customary discourse in favour of democratic institutions. Fujimori was eventually forced from office in November 2000, by which time Brazil had discretely ceased to support him. Conclusions about whether there was a causal link between the Fujimori government's positions on Kyoto and Brazil's suggestively timed support in the first half of 2000 will necessarily remain speculative until such time as the diplomatic records of Brazil and/or Peru are released to the academic community.

36   Ambassador Armando Lecaros-de-Cossío, public statement (31 October 2002).
37   Environment Ministers of the Amazonian Countries (1999).
38   *Folha de São Paulo* (2000).
39   Cantanhêde (2000).

CHINA AND INDIA

China and India are key countries in discussions regarding global warming because they are likely to greatly increase their emissions in the coming decades, as a result both of population growth and increased consumption. These countries have little forest left to destroy and have tremendous emissions from inefficient fossil fuel combustion. China and India therefore see allowing inexpensive credit from avoided deforestation as competition that would reduce their chance to profit from energy-related CDM projects.[40] It is worth noting that Brazilian diplomats have cultivated China and India as potential allies in climate negotiations.

USA

The United States is the world's largest single emitter of greenhouse gases, with a baseline emission of 1.6 billion tonnes of carbon in 1990 from fossil fuel and cement. Prior to the Kyoto Conference, the US Senate approved a motion by a vote of 95 to zero advising the president that no agreement would be ratified unless it included a significant commitment by developing countries to reduce emissions. In the weeks before the Kyoto conference, and during the three months leading up to the conference, the fossil fuel industry spent US$13 million in advertising in the US to convince the public that global warming is scientifically unfounded.[41] Public understanding of the problem is still low in the US, a feature that extends to the country's current president (George W. Bush), who has made a variety of statements indicating his scepticism about climate science. On 13 March 2001, only two months after taking office and before he had appointed any science advisors, Bush withdrew the US from Kyoto negotiations over the first commitment period. The US has not withdrawn is participation in the 1992 Climate Convention, and continues to send representatives to negotiating meetings.

During the period when the US was engaged in the Kyoto negotiations the country supported granting credit for avoided deforestation, as did other members of the 'Umbrella Group' such as Canada, Japan and New Zealand. It should be emphasised that this position cannot be interpreted as a sign of environmental concern, but rather as a means of minimising the cost of compliance with the Kyoto agreement. It could, nevertheless, be used to environmental advantage to obtain resources for maintaining tropical forests.

40   Dutschke (2002), p. 385.
41   Beder (1999).

EUROPE

In 1989 Germany held a series of parliamentary hearings on tropical deforestation and climate change (in two of which this author testified), and
the resulting report identified reducing deforestation as a top priority to
avoid global warming.[42] The Pilot Programme to Conserve the Brazilian
Rain Forest (PPG7) was negotiated in the lead-up to the 1992 United
Nations Convention on Environment and Development (UNCED, or
ECO–92) in Rio de Janeiro. This author served for nine years (1993–2001)
as a member of the PPG7's International Advisory Group, during which
time the G7 countries (primarily European countries) contributed over
US$250 million to the Programme. Among the objectives of the PPG7
was to reduce the emission of carbon dioxide from tropical deforestation.[43] In fact, of the four supposedly equal objectives of the programme,
this was undoubtedly the 'most equal' from the point of view of the
PPG7's European donor countries at that time. Germany was, and remains, the largest funder of the PPG7. Needless to say, this echoes from
a previous age, given that the European countries, especially Germany,
suddenly turned against forests as evil 'sinks' in the Kyoto negotiations
from December 1997 until the Bonn Agreement in July 2001.

In the negotiations following on from Kyoto, the theoretical argument
adopted by these European countries against assigning any value to avoided deforestation is based on the notion that only the very long term (i.e.
equilibrium) composition of the atmosphere matters and that combating
tropical deforestation is therefore unimportant because forests are likely to
be cut and/or burned anyway for one reason or another over the course
of a few centuries. Obviously, in the context of the PPG7, the European
countries think that avoided deforestation has a real value for climate, even
though the impossibility of controlling history over a timescale of centuries means that the carbon in the forests might eventually be emitted to
the atmosphere. The European counties were not wrong in 1991 or in the
years since then over which they have supported this ongoing programme.
Instead, they are being hypocritical now in claiming that emissions avoidance only has value if it is permanent and certain.

The geographical distribution of national positions on the issue of
crediting avoided deforestation could not be more striking, with opposition concentrated in Europe and North America favouring credit The pa-

---

42   Deutscher Bundestag (1990).
43   World Bank (1992).

rameter that matches this distribution most perfectly is that of gasoline prices (Table 2.3). In virtually any European country a litre of gasoline costs at least double that in the USA.[44]

Table 2.3: Gasoline Prices (a)

Country	Price (US$/litre)
Brazil	0.92
USA	0.41
Canada	0.50
UK	1.13
France	0.96
Italy	0.95
Germany	0.92
Spain	0.73

(a) Prices in October 2000 from Sheehan (2001).

NGO Positions

NGO positions on the Clean Development Mechanism are listed in Table 2.4. Some obvious patterns emerge. Brazilian grass-roots NGOs universally support credit for avoided deforestation, including groups throughout Brazil's Amazon region. These include the National Council of Rubber Tappers (CNS — founded by Chico Mendes and his allies), the largest organisation of indigenous peoples in the region (COIAB) and groups representing hundreds of small-farmer organisations (GTA, FETAGRI and CPT).[45] Brazilian research NGOs such as ISA, IPAM and IMAZON adopt a similar position, although there is one exception, *Vitae Civilis*.[46] Brazilian branches and affiliates of European-headquartered 'internation-

---

44   Sheehan (2001), p. 48.
45   Manifestação (2000).
46   'A Brazilian NGO Declaration' (2000).

al' NGOs such as WWF, Greenpeace and FOE–Porto Alegre have opposed credit for forests in line with their European headquarters. An important exception has been FOE–Brazilian Amazonia, which has resisted pressure from Europe and assumed a leading role in promoting credit for forest carbon.[47] The pattern in the United States is exactly parallel to that in Brazil, with US-headquartered NGOs (EDF, TNC, NRDC and UCS) supporting credit for forests and US branches and affiliates of European-based NGOs such as WWF, Greenpeace and FOE, opposing it.

Table 2.4: NGO Positions on the Clean Development Mechanism

	Plantations	Agro-forestry	Avoided deforestation
A.) International NGOs			
Greenpeace-International	-	-	-
WWF-International	-	-	-
FOE-International	-	-	-
Birdlife International	-	-	-
Climate Action Network	-	-	-
Indigenous People's Forum on Climate Change	-	-	-
B.) US NGOs			
National and US-headquartered NGOs			
EDF (Environmental Defense)	+	+	
CI (Conservation International)	+	+	
TNC (The Nature Conservancy)	+	+	
NRDC (Natural Resources Defense Council)	+	+	
UCS (Union of Concerned Scientists)	+	+	

47   Monzoni et al. (2000).

Table 2.4 continued

	Plantations	Agro-forestry	Avoided deforestation
Branches or affiliates of International NGOs			
WWF-US	-	-	-
FOE-US	-	-	-
C.) Brazilian NGOs *National NGOs*			
CNS (National Council of Rubber Tappers)		+	+
GTA (Amazonian Working Group)		+	+
COIAB (Coordinating Body of Indigenous Peoples of Brazilian Amazonia)		+	+
FETAGRI (Federation of Agricultural Workers of Pará)		+	+
CPT (Pastoral Land Commission)		+	+
IMAZON (Institute for Man and the Environment in Amazonia)		+	+
IPAM (Institute of Environmental Research of Amazonia)		+	+
ISA (Socio-Environmental Institute)		+	+
Vitae Civilis (Institute for Development, Environment and Peace	-	-	-
Branches or affiliates of International NGOs			
Friends of the Earth – Brazilian Amazonia		+	+
Friends of the Earth –Porto Alegre		+	+
Greenpeace-São Paulo		+	+
WWF-Brazil	-	-	-

(a) Plus sign indicates favouring inclusion, minus sign opposing, and blank indicates no position. Often, NGOs that support avoided deforestation and agro-forestry and do not have positions on silvicultural plantations would be likely to oppose many plantation projects on the basis of their environmental and social impacts (not on the basis of carbon accounting). The G-77 + China does not have a unified position.

The positions of European NGOs underwent an abrupt turnaround at the time of the December 1997 Kyoto Protocol. Before then, the same NGOs had argued strongly in favour of using forests as a tool to combat global warming; for example, in a 1989 report by Friends of the Earth-UK[48] and in the 1990 Greenpeace report on global warming:

> It now appears that one of the most cost-effective and technically fea-sible ways to counter the greenhouse effect lies with grand-scale refor-estation in the tropics as a means to sequester carbon dioxide from the global atmosphere —provided, of course, that the strategy is accom-panied by greatly increased efforts to slow deforestation.[49]

Such statements would be considered absolute heresy by Greenpeace and other European NGOs after 1997. Carbon sequestration through refor-estation (i.e. plantations) became anathema to those NGOs and, unfortu-nately for tropical forests, these NGOs chose to lump avoided emissions through forest conservation under the same catchword as 'sinks'.

The reasoning, as described in the various publications and websites of those organisations, is well represented by the following quotation from WWF: '… every tonne of carbon absorbed by a sink allows a tonne of car-bon to be emitted from burning fossil fuels'.[50] Taking such statements at face value for the moment, it is important to recognise that this interpre-tation of the Kyoto Protocol is in error. It is not every tonne of carbon 'absorbed' but every tonne of credit that is granted that permits a tonne of fossil fuel carbon to be emitted. The credit is very different from the physical tonne of carbon present in the trees. Credit is a piece of paper that will be negotiated on international commodity exchanges. Nothing in the Kyoto Protocol specifies a one-to-one ratio between the physical car-bon and the credit. One could easily grant substantially less credit for each tonne of physical carbon in order to more than compensate for concerns regarding permanence of carbon, leakage (indirect effects outside of the project boundaries that nullify the climatic benefit) and uncertainty. Throwing out the forest option is foolhardy for various reasons, including the obvious fact that the task of combating global warming so greatly ex-ceeds the capacity of different individual mitigation measures that one must use all available measures to confront the problem.

48   Myers (1989).
49   Myers (1990), p. 399.
50   WWF Climate Action Campaign (2000).

European NGOs seized upon the question of permanence as a defect of forests and dismissed forest carbon as a 'loophole' or a 'dangerous distraction'.[51] Permanence is falsely portrayed as an all-or-nothing proposition; either carbon is permanent or it is worthless by this view. Greenpeace drafted a document explaining how a tonne of carbon might be sequestered by a forest project for 100 years, after which the carbon is released when the forest burns down or is otherwise destroyed.[52] The atmosphere thereby winds up with two tonnes of emitted carbon; one from fossil fuels that were allowed to be emitted by the carbon credit, and the other from the trees destroyed at the end of 100 years. The argument has two problems; the assumption of a one-to-one ratio between carbon credit and physical carbon in the forestry project, and the assumption that holding a tonne of carbon out of the atmosphere for 100 years has no value to human society. In fact, holding carbon out of the atmosphere for finite periods has substantial value in that a corresponding quantity of impacts (including human deaths) would be averted over the period that the carbon remains out of the atmosphere.[53]

Greenpeace lawyers stress two clauses to bolster their rejection of carbon that is less-than-permanent. One is Article 2 of the UN Framework Convention on Climate Change (UN–FCCC), which defines the purpose of the Convention in terms of 'stabilisation' of atmospheric concentrations of greenhouse gases. Because emissions changes require around 200 years to be reflected in a new equilibrium of atmospheric gases, the transient course of our pathway to reaching stabilisation would have no importance under the UN–FCCC. Unfortunately, this grossly misrepresents the interests of human society, which will be greatly affected by climate changes over the coming decades and not only by the situation 200 or more years into the future. The other legal argument used is that Article 12 of the Kyoto Protocol, which creates the Clean Development Mechanism and specifies that the benefits must be 'long term' — leaving the question of what constitutes 'long term' up to future negotiations. Greenpeace has even gone so far as to demand that carbon be held for 'geological time'. Luis Gylvan Meira Filho, one of the most influential voices shaping the Brazilian negotiating position, has argued for considering events as long as 35,000 years into the future.[54] Needless to say, these positions would render any kind of forest project unviable.

51   Greenpeace (2000); WWF Climate Action Campaign (2000).
52   Meinshausen and Hare (2000).
53   Fearnside (2002c).
54   See Fearnside (2002d).

The intellectual argument for dismissing forests as an option based on infinite or very long time horizons runs counter to the interests of human society and the way that decisions are made in virtually all other spheres. The twenty-first century must not be dismissed as unimportant in order to try for presumed climatic gains several centuries or millennia in the future. Projections of global warming over the course of the twenty-first century imply catastrophic changes in this time frame.[55] This century will be critical both for the climate and for the fate of Brazil's Amazon forest.

As indicated earlier, there are strong reasons *not* to believe that intellectual arguments regarding such issues as permanence represent the real reason for the positions adopted by the European NGOs. The geographical distribution of the positions of the different groups and governments makes the probability of this explanation being correct vanishingly small. People in Europe are not more concerned with distant generations than are people in South America, Central America or North America. Basically, the intellectual structure that the European NGOs have erected is best viewed as a smokescreen of sophistry that has been built for the purpose of justifying a position that is based on a hidden agenda. Most rank-and-file members of European NGOs would probably be hard pressed to explain the intellectual rationale of their opposition to avoided deforestation, but simply accept without question that all 'sinks' must be bad if WWF, Greenpeace and Friends of the Earth say so.

The underlying motivation of the European NGOs is parallel, but not identical, to that of the European governments. Unlike governments, NGOs are not much concerned with economic competitiveness and terms of trade, but the opportunity to strike a blow at the United States, drawing together governments and NGOs in a common position. NGO members, as with much of the European population, dislike the US for a variety of reasons.[56] In the area of climate, the US is, in fact, the principal villain, being the largest single emitter of greenhouse gases on the planet and having repeatedly manoeuvred to block or weaken international efforts to contain global warming. The March 2001 decision by US President George W. Bush to withdraw from negotiations for the first commitment period of the Kyoto Protocol was only the crowning incident in a long series of diplomatic efforts to weaken international agreements on climate change, dating from the preparatory meetings leading

55   J.T. Houghton et al. (2001).
56   See Fearnside (2001c).

up to the 1992 UNCED (ECO–92) meeting that approved the UN–FCCC.[57] Punishing the US is the European NGOs' primary reason for opposing credit for forests in the CDM.

It is difficult to converse with European NGO campaigners for more than a few seconds on the subject of credit for forest carbon without hearing the opinion that that we 'can't let the US off cheap'. Two considerations are relevant. First, the cost of the mitigation is irrelevant to climate change, as a tonne of carbon emission avoided has the same effect, whether it was achieved by cheap or expensive means. In fact, low cost is beneficial for climate change in that it encourages willingness to make deeper cuts in emissions in future commitment periods. Second, nobody is suggesting that the US or any other country should be 'let off' and allowed not to meet the commitments agreed to in Kyoto. By appropriate assignment of credit, allowing projects for avoided deforestation would fully meet (and, in reality, exceed) the emissions reductions promised in Kyoto.

The debate over the role of tropical forests in mitigating global warming has revealed with unprecedented clarity the undemocratic nature of many 'international' NGOs. These organisations function well when all are in basic agreement, for example on issues such as saving whales. This changes dramatically when issues divide along geographical lines, as in the question of forests in the CDM. While NGO branches are allowed to have some differences of opinion on minor issues, on 'key issues' all branches and employees are expected to close ranks around a single position. The question of forests in the CDM has been considered to be such a 'key issue'. The positions adopted on key issues are virtually always those of the European branches, which are more numerous than those from any other part of the world, including North America. Employees of Brazilian branches of European NGOs suffered a long series of subtle and not-so-subtle pressures, with several notable casualties on the Brazilian side.[58]

European NGO reaction to the existence of a different viewpoint in Brazil has been the suggestion that Brazilian NGOs are under the influence of North Americans because few European NGO staff speak Portuguese and they lack a tradition of working in Brazil. Needless to say, the implication that Brazilian NGOs have been tricked by NGOs from North America, and that they are mere pawns in a game masterminded from the US, would not be well received in Brazil. Brazilian NGOs are fully capable of thinking for themselves and arriving at their own conclu-

57   Carvalho (1992).
58   See Fearnside (2001a).

sions. The other theory presented to explain the difference is that Brazilian NGOs have favoured credit for forests because they want money from carbon credits. The prospect of monetary flows is, indeed, a reason for interest in carbon credits. However, this in no way can be construed as a sin. The desire to use the environmental services of the forest as a new basis for economic development in the region is a healthy shift, and very much furthers the environmental objectives of NGOs.

It is very important to distinguish between avoided deforestation and plantation silviculture, despite the two being frequently lumped together as 'sinks' in European NGO discourse. They are very different, both in terms of carbon benefits and in terms of their impacts and benefits for biodiversity and social concerns.[59] Avoided deforestation almost always is more beneficial. It is also important to understand that the reasons for the different positions on forest carbon are *not* scientific, despite the debate frequently being couched in scientific terms. The NGOs have a scientific argument that, combined with moral choices regarding time horizon, time preference and 'ancillary' effects, leads to their conclusion of rejecting avoided deforestation. However, an equally sound scientific argument, combined with different moral choices on the other critical factors, leads to the opposite conclusion.

We must also be able to distinguish between conclusions based purely on scientific evidence and a moral judgment. Science can provide answers to questions such as: 'How much carbon will a given project hold out of the atmosphere, for how long and with what degree of certainty?' It cannot tell us whether that answer means that the CDM should include or exclude avoided deforestation. Such a conclusion requires moral choices to be made. We must have the courage to admit that we are making moral decisions, and to go ahead and make them. It would be an act of consummate foolishness to throw away the Amazon rain forest in exchange for a climate benefit several centuries or millennia in the future. Despite the discourse of European NGOs justifying their positions in terms of the interests of generations in the [far] future, we would be advised to bear in mind the famous words of E.O. Wilson that allowing the Earth's wealth of species to be lost is 'the folly that our descendants are least likely to forgive us'.[60]

The forces driving deforestation in Amazonia have evolved continuously over the past three decades. Today, powerful economic pressures such as those fuelled by soybean cultivation represent much greater threats

59   Fearnside (1996b).
60   Wilson (1992).

than in the past, when a larger share of clearing and its underlying infrastructure were driven by an economically weaker lobby of ranchers and
land speculators.[61] Substantial funds will be necessary to alter some of
these trends. The hard fact is that there is presently no other money on the
table likely to fill this role. The Convention on Biological Diversity, for example, is well behind the UN–FCCC in terms of having billions of dollars
of potential funding in the coming years.

The common European NGO response that tropical forests should be
protected with money from other sources such as the Biodiversity
Convention is only a diversion, since significant amounts of money simply
do not exist in these 'other' sources. None of the countries (or NGOs) suggesting that these sources be used is offering to put up billions of dollars.
The same applies to calls for using the Kyoto Protocol's adaptation fund
(Article 4.8) for saving tropical forests. Needless to say, countries in which
the human population will soon be facing heavy impacts from climate
change would not take kindly to having the scant adaptation resources provided by the Protocol diverted to conservation projects elsewhere.

The funds potentially available through climate mitigation could make a
tremendous difference for tropical forest conservation, in addition to generating real carbon benefits at a highly competitive cost. An illustration of
scale is offered by the expectations of State Department planners during the
Clinton administration in the US. Over the 2008–12 first commitment period a gap of 600 million tonnes of carbon was expected annually above domestic energy-sector mitigation results. If all had been purchased abroad
through the various 'flexibility mechanisms' in the Kyoto Protocol, the total
for the US would have been US$12 billion/year at the US$20/t C carbon
price projected at that time. The US wanted to obtain 300 million t C of
credit from Articles 3.3 and 3.4 (domestic afforestation, reforestation and
deforestation activities, plus 'other' activities such as forest and soil management), leaving a shortfall of 300 million t C for mechanisms such as the
CDM. This 300 million t C corresponds to an expected cost of US$6 bil-
lion/year. Prior to its withdrawal from Kyoto negotiations, the US represented approximately half of the expected total demand for carbon credits.

NGOs that oppose using carbon funds to maintain forests seem to
have forgotten that some urgency is appropriate with respect to combating biodiversity loss. If we wait until the second commitment period begins in 2013, there will not be nearly as much tropical forest left to save.
Not taking advantage of the carbon value of tropical forests in the efforts

61   Fearnside (2001c).

to save them, claiming as an excuse that saving tropical forests is an objective that is doomed to failure, is inappropriate as a stand for environmental NGOs. This is no time to throw in the towel on Brazil's Amazonian deforestation when only 16 per cent of the forest has been cleared. Instead, environmental NGOs should be committed to fighting deforestation tree by tree. International NGOs should take stock of what they are trying to accomplish. Organisations such as WWF represent their stakeholders, who are a contributing membership composed of people who are primarily concerned about biodiversity. In the twenty-first century habitat loss and especially tropical deforestation is likely to be the greatest threat to biodiversity. Over a longer timescale, climate change would increase in importance, and in this case would act mainly in finishing off species that had escaped a century of direct habitat destruction. In keeping biodiversity and carbon issues in perspective, it should be remembered that carbon is more reversible than most environmental problems such as biodiversity loss, toxic and nuclear wastes, or ozone loss. This is also true of underlying forces such as population growth and rising per-capita consumption.

European NGOs take great pains to find weaknesses in avoided deforestation projects (as well as with plantation projects). This 'watch-dogging' effort certainly provides a valuable service. However, the same information on project defects can be used for two distinct purposes. One is to suggest improvements to the system that will help to make the CDM work. The other is to provide ammunition to efforts designed to torpedo the entire process. The first use is an appropriate goal of environmental NGOs, while the second is counterproductive for both climate and biodiversity objectives of these organisations.

The process of developing carbon mitigation projects is inherently difficult, with multiple opportunities for some portion of the credit granted for activities that have less climatic benefit in reality than in the official accounting.[62] This applies both to energy and forest sector projects.[63] The important question here is what should be done; that is, should one work to solve or at least minimise the various problems as they are identified, or should one simply oppose all credit *a priori*. I would argue that it is essential to try and make the credit mechanism work.

In going forward, it is essential that focus be maintained on the second commitment period (2013–17). Negotiations for this period begin in 2005, making the issues extremely current. All environmental NGOs concerned

62   Fearnside (1999a, 2003, 2004b); Van Vliet et al. (2003).
63   Herzog et al. (2003).

with climate, including those based in Europe, will have to reach out to grass-roots NGOs if effective alliances are to be built to conserve tropical forests. The history of European NGOs having turned their back on over 500 grass-roots groups in the Brazilian Amazon is an unfortunate backdrop, but it must be overcome if the common goals of maintaining forests are to be achieved.

Likely Changes

The Bonn and Marrakech accords of 2001 ruled out avoided deforestation for the first commitment period (2008–12), but the question remains open for the second and subsequent commitment periods. Final decisions on the first commitment period change the underlying motivations of the opposition that has existed and open the way for the various groups to make peace with each other.

Another change has been European NGO positions on temporary certified emissions reductions (T-CERs). This proposal,[64] known as the 'Colombian proposal', was rejected prior to the July 2001 Bonn agreement. The European Union (EU) also rejected the proposal. After plantation silviculture was included in the CDM under the Bonn agreement, T-CERs were seen by both the EU and the European NGOs as the best way to undertake carbon accounting, which is a healthy change. However, it is worth asking whether, if T-CERs are now perceived as the best accounting method for forestry projects, why they were not supported before the inclusion of forestry became a *fait accompli*. The obvious answer is that this would have been an admission that the 'permanence problem', which was constantly presented as an insurmountable obstacle to having meaningful climate benefits from forestry, could indeed be solved. The sudden switch in positions on T-CERs was essentially a confession of hypocrisy indicating that, before the Bonn agreement, European governments and NGOs had simply been manoeuvring to block all forest projects by thwarting any efforts to solve the problems associated with them. Adoption of T-CERs effectively removes any intellectual foundation for future opposition to avoided deforestation on the basis of permanence. Yet intellectual consistency has clearly not always characterised past efforts of European NGOs to block inclusion of forests in the CDM. The good news in this arena is that for the second commitment period there is no motive to keep forests out. The fact that the assigned amounts (emissions quotas) will be renego-

---

64   Blanco and Forner (2000).

tiated means that keeping forests out of the CDM would only result in the various countries agreeing to reduce their national emissions by more modest amounts than they would if forests are included for credit.

Article 17: Emissions Trading

While the CDM, namely Article 12 of the Kyoto Protocol, is the focus for the vast majority of discussion regarding forests in the Protocol, it should be remembered that this is not the only way that the Protocol could provide carbon credit for maintaining tropical forests. Article 17 (Emissions Trading) also offers this possibility to members of Annex I of the UN–FCCC and Annex B of the Kyoto Protocol, those countries that have accepted caps on their national emissions totals. Article 3.7 of the Protocol (the 'Australia clause') specifies that any Annex B country that had a positive emission of carbon from its forests in 1990 can trade any difference below the baseline established in the initial national inventory through the 'emissions trading' provisions of Article 17. With the exception of Australia the current members of Annex B, such as the United States, are thereby excluded from trading forest carbon based on their national inventories. But Brazil, were it to join Annex I and Annex B, could trade this carbon at will. This represents a substantial opportunity for Brazil, and would suffer much less loss of credit than would be the case for the project-based mitigation allowed under the CDM.[65] All emissions reductions below the baseline can be traded without need to show a causal link to the results of any given mitigation project.

The major questions for this option relate to whether the Brazilian government could, in fact, reduce deforestation rates to levels below those in the period chosen as the baseline for the national inventory (1988–94). The *Brasil em Ação* (Brazil in Action) and *Avança Brasil* (Forward Brazil) plans of the Fernando Henrique Cardoso government have been succeeded by the *Plano Plurianual* (Pluriannual Plan–PPA) of the Luiz Inácio Lula da Silva government, but the current plan is just as ambitious as its predecessors in proposing extensive highway paving and other infrastructure projects that make slowing deforestation more difficult. Despite the great reversal represented by the upsurge in deforestation in 2002 to 25.5 thousand square kilometres per year (versus 15.2 thousand square kilometres per year in the baseline period), the process could still be brought under control if the government so decided.[66]

65   Fearnside (1999b, 2001d.)
66   Fearnside (2003b); Fearnside and Barbosa (2004).

Conclusions

Amazonian deforestation makes a significant contribution to global warming. Complete accounting of emissions and uptakes is needed to reflect the climatic impact of deforestation and the consequent benefits of avoiding it. Gaining credit for avoided deforestation could provide substantial potential environmental and economic benefit to Brazil, particularly for Amazonia. Changes in the way that Kyoto negotiations fit into the wider geopolitical context greatly increase the chances of avoided deforestation becoming eligible for credit under the Clean Development Mechanism (Kyoto Protocol Article 12) in the second commitment period (2013–17). Credit for avoided deforestation through emissions trading (Kyoto Protocol Article 17) remains a possibility with substantially greater potential gains, but is threatened by continued plans in the latest development plan (PPA), which involves extensive highway paving and other infrastructure projects that make slowing deforestation far more difficult. The most positive sign is the experience with deforestation control in Mato Grosso during 1999–2001, providing a concrete example that is possible for government to prevent landholders from clearing if it has the commitment to do so. The substantial value of avoided deforestation is the most likely source of the political will required for this to happen in a sustained fashion and on a large scale.

3

New Frontiers in the Amazon

Hervé Théry

Images produced from recent statistics can contribute significantly to the debate on the evolution of the Brazilian Amazon. Those images shed a cruel light on the current status of the region, since they show how little concern there seems to be in the context of national planning compared with other regions and point to probable conflicts over land-use in the near future. A selection of some pointers (see Figure 3.1) shows the clear imbalance that exists between the size of the Amazon region on the one hand and its economic and social importance on the other. While it represents 60 per cent of Brazil's area, its GNP is but five per cent of the national figure. Only 12 per cent of the national population and ten per cent of the urban population live there, while it has received a slightly larger proportion of recent migrants (14 per cent). In terms of highways and number of municipalities the region is comparable with others. The only area in which Amazonia excels is, unfortunately, the number of people killed in land conflicts.

In demographic terms, the 'Legal Amazon' continues to be the least densely populated part of the country. The region has grown by 13 million inhabitants since 1970, an increase of 172 per cent and double the rate for the rest of Brazil (82 per cent). However, the regional population represents 12 per cent of the national total (as against eight per cent in 1970). Densities continue very low, with 4.18 inhabitants per square kilometre for the Legal Amazon region compared with a national average of 20. Amazonia's population density is itself, of course, an average including states of much lower densities such as Amazonas, with just 1.83 inhabitants per square kilometre. Figure 3.2 illustrates the contrast between the concentration of population in the south-south-east and the demographic sparsity of the Amazon, with few concentrations in urban areas as well as along rivers and roads. The Amazon region continues to be, therefore, a spatial reserve and Brazil's last frontier of migration and settlement.

Figure 3.1: The Weight of the Amazon Region inside Brazil

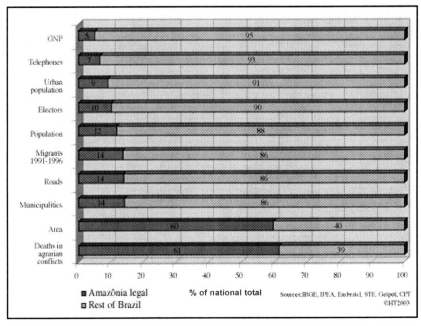

Sources: *Censo Demográfico*, IBGE, 2000; *Contas Regionais*, IPEA, 2003; *Anuário*, Embratel, 2003; *Anuário*, Geipot, 2003; Supremo Tribunal Eleitoral, *Dados Eleitorais*, Comissão Pastoral da Terra, 2003.

Moreover, the region continues as a resource frontier especially for timber, a key product for which there is an increasingly strong demand in international markets as Asian reserves are depleted. Until recently, conventional opinion held that most Amazon timber was exported overseas. However, the research carried through by IMAZON and Friends of the Earth (see Figure 3.3) demonstrated that timber from Amazonia was sold principally within Brazil, and São Paulo in particular. Overseas exports are only significant in the cases of Amazonas and Pará states. In the latter, exports are less than the quantities sold to the south-east and north-east of Brazil. Those regions also form the main market for logs supplied by the states of Rondônia and Mato Grosso. This is a highly promising market, provided that investment is undertaken in the technology to set up sustainable forest management systems to replace the current activities either of clear felling or the selective extraction of valuable species with no regard for regeneration.

Figure 3.2: Population of Legal Amazonia and Brazil, 2000

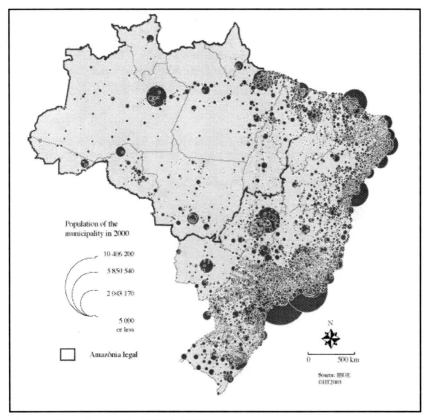

Source: *Censo Demográfico*, IBGE, 2000.

Amazonia is the main source of timber for Brazil, but could the region also supply more food products? For specific products such as Brazil nuts, rubber or pepper, the Amazon plays a leading role. However, for fruits such as *urucum* and *guaraná*, which are Amazonian in origin, the region has ceded first place to the north-east, which has managed to successfully cultivate them in its drier ecosystems. This process had already occurred with the rubber tree, and could well happen again with other plants. The reverse process is rare, the only significant exception being the *dendê* (oil palm), one of the rare exotic species that has adapted well in the Amazon. With the exception of those products, Amazonia's contribution to national agricultural production is modest. The region has a reasonable output of cassava, a staple base in the regional diet but its success with rice, livestock and soybean is due to production in the states of Maranhão and Mato Grosso, which are situated outside of the principal Amazonian ecosystems. Beef cattle and soybean (Figure 3.4) are without doubt the products that have expanded fastest since the 1970s. The drive towards the north-west of both activities has constituted a powerful frontier that has brought about massive changes in the region. Huge, highly capitalised and (in the case of the soybean) highly mechanised farms are expanding rapidly, penetrating open savannas and intact forest.

Figure 3.3: Timber Commercialisation in the Brazilian Amazon

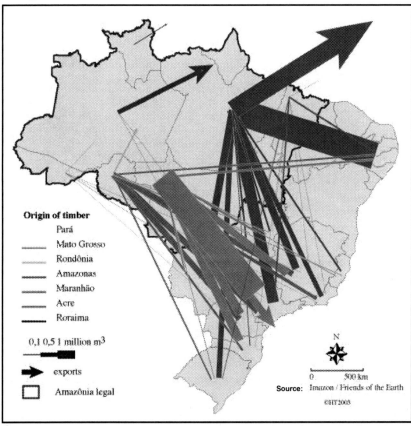

Source: R. Smeraldi and A. Veríssimo (1999) *Açertando o Alvo* (São Paulo: Friends of the Earth).

Figure 3.4: Progress of the Soybean Front, 1977–99

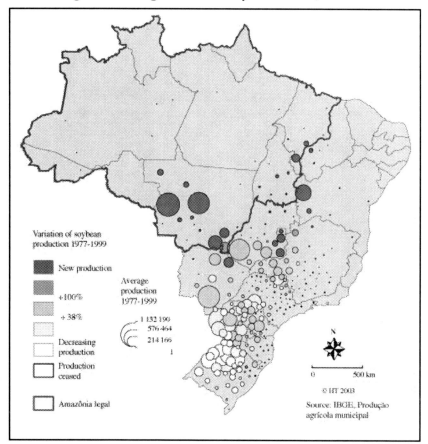

Source: *Produção Agrícola Municipal*, IBGE, 1999.

This rapid process of occupation started with the building of the first highways across Amazonia during the 1960s and continues today catalysed by substantial economic and social infrastructure investments under the national development plan, the *Programa Plurianual* (PPA) for 2000–03 (Figure 3.5). Highways facilitated settlement by migrants from other regions whose arrival produced both positive and negative impacts. Improvements in waterways and telecommunications networks together with expansion of the energy sector are bringing about major economic and strategic changes in the Amazon region. These changes generate new imbalances. They may also be the source of a new regional development impetus or lead to Amazonia's subordination to external interests. Housing one of the world's richest areas in terms of biodiversity, the Amazon might find in the sustainable use and valorisation of these natural assets the basis of a new development model.

Figure 3.5: Pluriannual Plan Infrastructure Development

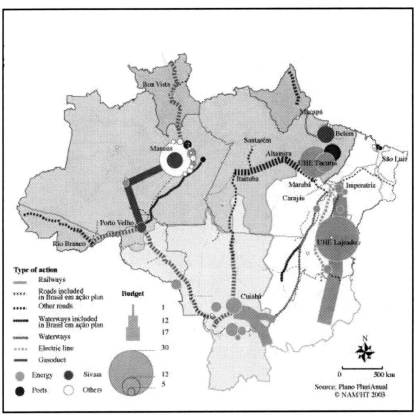

Source: *Plano Plurianual, 2000–2003*, Ministério do Planejamento, Brasília, 2000.

Amongst the factors that could produce the deepest impact in the region is the opening of links with neighbouring countries, until now impossible given the distances and the difficulties of penetrating dense forest. Today, one can travel by road between Manaus and Caracas via Boa Vista, while completion of the stretch between Saint Georges de l'Oyapock and Regina in French Guyana will connect Macapá with the three Guyanas. With a link to Bolivia already in existence through Mato Grosso, others are being established by way of Rondônia. Access to Peru and the Pacific Ocean is possible via Assis Brazil in the southern Acre, even without waiting for the long-expected access route through Cruzeiro do Sul. Of Brazil's Amazon neighbours, road access is lacking only to Colombia because the *Perimetral Norte* (northern perimeter) highway project was never concluded.

Figure 3.6: Protected Areas in the Brazilian Amazon

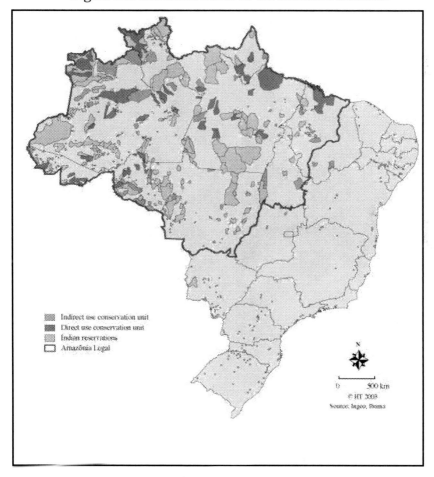

Sources: Ingeo Consortium, IBAMA.

Figure 3.7: Typology of Tendencies and Probable Conflicts in the Amazon

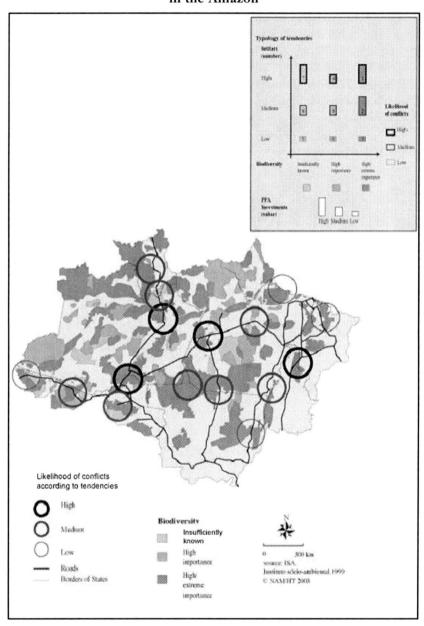

Completion of those road links and of the public and private investments associated with them will lead to changes that will deeply alter the situation of the Amazon region, or at least of some corridors that cross it, while other parts will remain relatively untouched. These investments create a *de facto* zoning, rendering irrelevant the long theoretical discussions on the subject. The attention of planners and policy-makers should instead be focused on critical areas, those where the new axes cross protected territories, important conservation units and indigenous reservations or zones of interest for the conservation of biodiversity (Figure 3.6). Conflicts over land and access to key natural resources are likely to occur at those points where areas of ecological importance, heavy capital investment and agrarian reform settlements coincide (Fig. 3.7).

It should be pointed out that the development axes projected by military geopolitical strategists during the late 1970s and early 1980s have been almost all been realised, even if the context has changed radically from dreams of conquest and domination toward policies of cross-boundary cooperation and continental integration. Some axes have benefited from planned infrastructure concentrated along two major lines. These are (a) south–north — the Araguaia-Tocantins axis, and (b) south-east–north-west — linking via Cuiabá, Manaus and Boa Vista to São Paulo (and therefore the *Mercosul*) and the Caribbean. Planned investments are generating a trans-continental axis that offers an alternative for traversing Brazil to the current north-south highway (*Carretera Panamericana*) that runs from Tierra del Fuego to Panama. The works currently underway, a continuation of those initiated in the 1970s, are literally changing the situation of Amazonia. Instead of Amazonia forming a cul-de-sac or marginal territory, it will form the heart of the continent, a junction for various networks linking and bringing together countries that used to ignore each other. Treaties and agreements in matters of environment made by countries of the Great Amazon region (through the Amazon Cooperation Treaty — TCA) suggest that the moment of integration may have arrived. It is by no means evident that such changes will bring advantages only for the Amazon region but, without doubt, they will focus attention on a region that has long suffered and still suffers from the effects of its marginalisation.

4

Between Conservation and Development: Innovations and Paradox in Amazon Environmental Policy

Neli Aparecida de Mello

In Amazonia today multiple environmental objectives are pursued deriving from distinctive chains of thought originating in global debates. These range from a quest for 'pure' preservation to business-oriented environmentalism and alternative sustainable systems of production. Current social groups have substituted the old *posseiros* and *caboclos*, attaining the status of partners in the decisions of the government environmental sector.[1] New regulations extend the possibilities of conservation, protection and control of the use of natural resources, while new organisations are mobilised to implement alternative strategies.[2] The current dynamic of this region involves more sophisticated technological vectors, scientific and technological knowledge, the linking of areas by means of communication and information networks, certification of natural resources and industrial processes (FSC and ISO 14000) and new economic sectors for the exploitation of biodiversity, ecological tourism and agroforestry.

These new conditions are already being incorporated into the process of regional development and, despite the changed political context, matters of national and continental integration are still the order of the day, making the diverse Amazonias objects of political strategy. Current policies in Brazil for the integration of physical communications networks, mostly through transcontinental corridors, become more concrete each day and lay the foundations for the intensification of economic activities.[3] Other countries that share the Amazon Basin also stimulate the building of regional infrastructure networks, at the same time driving the consolidation of their 'national' territories in 'their' Amazonias.

1   Andrade (1996).
2   Pouyllau (1997); Runyan (1999).
3   Becker (2001); Costa (1999).

These different Amazon territories continue to be the locus of pioneering frontiers, currently embracing environmental initiatives through the setting up of legally protected areas. At a continental level, collaboration amongst members of the Amazon Cooperation Treaty (TCA) strengthens this process, especially when it reinforces the principles of environmental conservation and respect for local populations. Commitments towards joint implementation of ecological-economic zoning along border areas, Agenda 21 for Greater Amazônia, the regional strategy for use and conservation of biodiversity and a common regional position on forests illustrate such cooperation within the region.[4] They also serve to re-ignite old rivalries and disputes between Brazil, Venezuela and Peru for hegemony over the Amazon Basin. These dynamics illustrate the contradictory nature of national and continental public policies, between development, integration and imperious conservation.

There were major changes in political behaviour and commitments between the 1970s and 2000. The inflamed speeches of the 1970s underlined the imperative to integrate through planning in order to resolve the conflict between environment and development. Thirty years later, many methods, parameters and policy directives are available which now promise a range of production models based on traditional methods.[5] During the 1970s the State was the main implementing agency in development, underpinned by geopolitical and frontier occupation strategies.[6] Today, new actors have taken up positions to defend themselves and their territories while ameliorating the impacts of authoritarian decisions. Yet this new strength that derives from the presence and actions of local populations and communities only occurs as a means of legitimising rules imposed by international financial organisations.

Since that period, there has been an increase in the number of areas under legal protection (conservation units and indigenous lands) in both Amazonia and other regions of the country, along with projects for conservation, protection and sustainable development. The political situation allowed the Brazilian government to neutralise critics by accepting the G7 Pilot Programme to Conserve the Brazilian Rain Forest (PPG7), launched at the Houston Summit of 1990 under German government initiative. Yet the virtue of the proposal and the German government's role should be seen within the context of strong mobilisation by German environmental

4   Amigos da Terra (1994); Clusener-Godt and Sachs (1995); Roux (2001).
5   Teniere-Buchot (2001).
6   Eglin and Théry (1982); Théry (1995).

NGOs working together with some international and Brazilian agencies in their critique of Amazonian deforestation during the 1980s.[7] As a consequence, the two most important objectives of the PPG7 were defined as the reduction of deforestation in Amazonia and the conservation of biodiversity.[8]

In the relatively short period since the PPG7 was launched in 1990, it has stimulated significant change, introducing new experiences and models. Not long enough to promote structural changes but long enough for the attainment of some results and for it to have an influence in other governmental spheres. Institutions that supported contradictory policies and competed for the use of Amazonian space have become partners in the construction of more coherent policies. However, disputes over leadership, power and spheres of influence amongst participant institutions within the programme have been the great obstacle to its broader implementation. Other problems have included technical disagreements, lack of clarity regarding the concepts of protection, conservation and development, the delayed project cycle and tough preconditions for disbursement.[9]

There have been notable positive results. In the Demonstration Projects (PD/A) component, 181 small projects have been funded, nearly three-quarters of which are community-based. The Indigenous Lands component (PPTAL) has resulted in the demarcation of over 45 million hectares with another ten million hectares identified. The 'extractive reserve' (Resex) land management model has been developed on four federal units and now faces the challenge of establishing continuity. State-level environmental management institutions have been strengthened, harnessing improved surveillance technology while promoting cooperation and sharing of intra-regional experiences on environmental management.[10]

One of the most positive results of the Pilot Programme has been the stimulation offered to central government by diverse regional social groups investing in high-profile demonstration experiences. The immediate positive response to demonstration projects in the states of Maranhão, Acre and Mato Grosso has been due to the construction of a solid community base amongst some groups. These grass-roots organisations have contributed significantly to the less conflict-ridden implementation of projects, alternative production and organisational experiences. Their great

7   Rossi (1997).
8   Mello (1999).
9   Brazil (1998); PPG7 (1991–2001).
10   Mello (2002).

contribution has been the democratisation of resource-use for a population that previously had little or no access due to the restrictive rules and conditions imposed by the banking system. Innumerable projects reproduce traditional methods and techniques, already tried in community-based projects, such as agroforestry and mixed cropping.

Researchers from federal universities and local institutes have been active in providing alternative proposals rather than as critics. In the context of the PPG7, the science and technology component evolved from the idea of strengthening 'centres of excellence' and promoting 'directed research' based on the wish for a new organisational model that would enhance thematic networks. This offers promise to local scientific groups while facilitating the increased participation and power of NGOs within the scientific community.[11]

State governments such as those of Amapá and Acre have also contributed to the policy options for sustainable development, feeding the lessons acquired from grass-roots action into public policies. Legislative advances, financing and planning mechanisms have been introduced. These include the first law on the protection of biodiversity in Amapá, ecological-economic zoning, the development agencies and the scientific-technical cooperation behind them. But concrete results are still limited. New local products have made little market penetration, the use of Amazonia's ecologically friendly image has seen technological progress but this has not yet been properly harnessed as a basis for alternative economic development. Furthermore, support for this model is not unconditional, still lacks the full backing of all elements in the state machine and has by no means been replicated in all parts of Amazonia.[12]

The use of improved communications technology has substantially strengthened the international presence in national and local debates along with its potential for active influence over processes and projects. Global networking facilitates the monitoring of Amazonia and condemnation of environmentally harmful policies, enhancing public participation in real time in such debates. The environmental sector is caught up in this battle, with information about the retreat and the advances of these policies circulating over the worldwide networks. They constitute permanent pressures on governmental actions that may constrain and slow down the impacts of infrastructure development schemes. The actions and performance of federal and state public ministries add to these pressures, as representatives of the State, based on laws that support the public interest.

11   PPG7 (2000b).
12   Molin (2001).

Public participation adds new social groups to the equation. We now have to ask about the territorial interests of these new groups and about their stake in environmental protection and development. Proposals for new models of sustainable development will have to compete not just with local and regional interests. They will be the subject of disputes among the new social actors themselves, strengthened by the feelings of participation and citizenship, demanding recognition of their territorial rights.[13]

In this context, development options for Amazonia continue to be problematic in terms of reconciling conservation and development. The rational exploitation of natural resources or new techniques based on biotechnology and certification are in the early phase of development. Yet they enjoy little representation in national plans and budgets, in which the environment, information and knowledge correspond only to six per cent of the national budget compared with 58 per cent for infrastructure investment.[14]

In this competition over physical space, fully protected conservation areas will tend to be reduced to isolated islands, vulnerable to land invasions and areas increasingly being converted to areas of sustainable resource use. The evolution from pure conservation towards sustainable land use policy seems to represent a step forward but it also presents a contradiction. We must ask whether this signifies the abandonment of limits and restrictions on resource use and, if not, who will be responsible for exerting more direct controls on degradation and pollution?

The future of Brazilian environmental policy will have to be supported through bolder proposals to deepen methods and models.[15] Greater knowledge is available on the functioning of local ecosystems but this on its own is insufficient and it needs to be fed into the process of improving and streamlining public policy. Increasing investments in resource inventories, social and cultural initiatives, adding value to forest products and environmental services, and biodiversity knowledge can represent the future economic base for the region as well as for its scientific creativity. In their absence, there will still be different speeds in terms of economic and environmental-partner processes, the environmental arguments serving only to versify impacts. These proposals will depend on regulation, financing and credit alternatives, information and the promotion of effective and continuous social controls.[16]

13   Almeida (2000).
14   Brazil (1999); Nepstad et al. (2000); Kohlhepp (2001); Mello (2002).
15   Hall (1997a); Brazil (1997).
16   Brazil (1995); Garay and Dias (2001).

Development planning tools would also have to be adventurous. The modernity of incorporating the environmental dimension into the development process and the analysis of macro vectors of national development is reflected in the new theoretical-conceptual landmark that formed the basis for reaffirming the discourse of government planning, strengthened by the distribution of programmes and resources contained in the national plan (PPA) for 2000–03. Again, it is possible to identify a large gap between stated intentions and allocated resources. Even though the federal government's current discourse relates to the future, the old processes are repeated. The marginal consideration of environmental problems is highlighted by the huge discrepancy between economic investments and spending on the environment, information and knowledge. Yet even though funding for science, technology and development could be increased, this would never be enough to counterbalance the impacts of economic growth at any cost.[17]

It is interesting to consider what territorial dynamics will result from these policies. Would both dimensions develop at distinct speeds? Numerous arguments supporting the study of 'National Integration and Development Axes' are based on the potential for stimulating growth in these regions, making them competitive in global markets. These arguments are not universally applied in Amazonia as a whole, but only to the spaces that respond quickly to the requirements of worldwide competition. Investments in waterways only transform the space-time of rivers in terms of whether they can be used as corridors for transporting products for export. The sub-products of these investments will probably be of benefit to traditional populations that depend on fluvial transportation or the landless recently installed in the settlement projects and complaining of the lack of roads for the marketing of their production.

Despite the environmental discourse propagated by international bodies, territorial strategies for implementing the road and energy infrastructure in the *Avança Brasil* programme are linked to the rate of execution of conservation policies. The determination of conservation areas is dependent on the results of scientific research, the systematisation of traditional knowledge and relevant technologies. Infrastructure development depends on the availability of investment once a database and set of development strategies are already determined. These encourage the incorporation of new lands along a new arc in western Amazonia which links the state capitals of Porto Velho, Manaus and Boa Vista, repeating the pattern of the

17   Brazil (1999); Dourojeanni and Padua (2001).

1960s when the Belém-Brasília highway marked the arrival of the agricultural front in the central Brazilian savanna (*cerrado*). This arc binds the north of the country to the south and its consolidation can be easily observed as a function of the volume of foreseen investments. This process is positive on the one hand, since it integrates the main cities of this immense region, providing access to international borders. On the other hand, and less positively, it will also accelerate the appearance or the revival of small cities, stimulate new migrations, create new spaces suitable for agricultural export production, speed up deforestation and put pressure on areas which are still intact and home to valuable biological assets.

These dynamics can generate two models of spatial organisation. First, marginal sustainable experiences in a few places and integrated to national and local markets, often stimulated by resources, technologies and forms of management such as those provided under the demonstration projects of the PPG7 or other international projects. Second, in regions where activity is stimulated by competition within international markets. Major questions of this nature cannot yet be answered for several reasons. Many new experiences have not had time to prove themselves. Groups previously excluded from access to information are now fighting for such access and their rights to citizenship, while many large-scale projects are being actively resisted. These issues complicate our understanding of the territorial dynamic that characterises the western extremity of the region with the consolidation of Porto Velho–Manaus–Boa Vista links, and the integration with other Amazon Basin countries. Construction of a new model of development and conservation model for Amazonia will require the inclusion of a diverse range of social actors in a process capable of regulating territorial occupation to reconcile wider interests with those of local communities.

5

World Bank Approaches to the Brazilian Amazon: The Bumpy Road towards Sustainable Development

John Redwood*

Introduction

Over the past several decades, environmental sustainability, and following the Brundtland Report in 1987, sustainable development, has become increasingly central to the World Bank's mission.[1] A central Environment Department and environment divisions in each of the Bank's six operational regions were established as part of a major reorganisation in 1987. A central Vice Presidency for Environmentally (later Environmentally and Socially) Sustainable Development (ESSD) was created in 1992. That same year, the Bank's *World Development Report* (WDR) on development and the environment constituted its principal contribution to the Rio Earth Summit.[2] Ten years later, a new WDR on sustainable

---

[*] I would like to thank Robert Goodland, Anthony Hall, Josef Leitmann, Dennis Mahar, Sergio Margulis and Robert Schneider for their helpful comments on an earlier draft and Stael Baltar, Hans Binswanger, Kenneth Chomitz, Christoph Diewald, Philip Fearnside, Josef Leitmann, Judith Lisansky, Kenia Parsons, Robert Schneider, Claudia Sobrevila, Loretta Sprissler and Nils Tcheyan for helping me access some of the information cited in this chapter. The paper was initially presented in a workshop on environment and sustainable development at the Third European Congress of Latin American Scholars in Amsterdam in July 2002 and I am grateful to the participants for their helpful observations.
[1] The Bank's current mission statement reads in part, 'to fight poverty with passion and professionalism for lasting results; to help people help themselves and their environment by providing resources, sharing knowledge, building capacity and forging partnerships in the public and private sectors'.
[2] One key message of the 1992 WDR was that, '...protection of the environment is an essential part of development. Without adequate environmental protection, development is undermined; without development, resources will be inadequate for needed investments, and environmental protection will fail' (World Bank, 1992b, p. 2).

development formed the Bank's flagship document for the Johannesburg Summit.[3] The Bank's first explicit environmental strategy, *Making Sustainable Commitments*, has also recently been published.[4]

The growing importance of sustainable development is reflected in the evolution in the Bank's country policy dialogue, analytical work and lending operations on poverty and the environment. This can be illustrated with reference to the vast and ecologically sensitive 'Legal Amazon'[5] region in Brazil, an area covering over five million square kilometres with a population of some 21 million, more than two-thirds of whom are urban.[6] This paper will review a number of significant Bank-supported activities in (or, in the case of analytical work, on) the region,[7] identifying the principal changes in focus and approaches to development over time and drawing some preliminary conclusions and lessons from this rich and diverse experience.[8]

3   World Bank (2002c).

4   World Bank (2001).

5   'Legal Amazonia' refers to the areas in the Amazon Basin formerly entitled to receive fiscal incentives under the 34/18–FINAM system (see footnote 15 below), including all of the present states of Acre, Amapá, Amazonas, Pará, Rondônia, Roraima and Tocantins (formerly the northern part of the state of Goias) and the western part of Maranhão and northern part of Mato Grosso.

6   For non-Bank discussions of sustainable development issues in the Brazilian Amazon, see Bierregaard et al. (2001); Browder and Godfrey (1997); Bunker (1985); Cardoso and Muller (1977); Davies de Freitas (1998); Fearnside (1986a); Goodman and Hall (1990); Goulding, Smith and Mahar (1986); Hall (2000a); Hecht and Cockburn (1989); Nitsch (2000); Schmink and Wood (1984); Smith et al. (1995); Smith (1999); and UNAMAZ (1998).

7   While not specifically considered in this chapter, many of the observations below may also be of direct relevance and applicability to the Amazon portions of the other countries — Bolivia, Peru, Ecuador, Colombia, Venezuela, Guyana and Suriname — in the broader Amazon River Basin. For an example of Bank analytical work done elsewhere in the Amazon region (Ecuador), see Hicks et al. (1990).

8   All Bank lending and GEF (Global Environment Facility, for which the Bank is one of the executors) and Rainforest Trust Fund (see text below) grant operations in the region were in support of federal or state government investment programmes, projects or other initiatives, and much of the credit for their positive evolution from a sustainable development standpoint belongs to the Bank's government and, increasingly, civil society partners in Amazonia and elsewhere in Brazil.

The 1970s and '80s: Mining, Infrastructure and Integrated Regional Development[9]

No formal Bank sector or strategic work on Amazonia as a whole was undertaken in the 1970s. However, during a period of leave from the Bank, the then chief of the Programmes Division for Brazil and a graduate student (who later became a Bank staff member) carried out a survey of the economic development prospects of the region which helped orient the Bank's involvement in Amazonia in the late 1970s and 1980s. The resulting paper covered a broad range of issues including the regional economic base, regional development objectives, constraints on development (specifically, the weak data base; high costs, especially of transport infrastructure; the scarcity of entrepreneurial, managerial and technical talent; the narrow regional market; limited fiscal resources; and the confused land tenure situation in many places), environmental issues, indigenous peoples, major productive projects, industry (including mining) and industrial policy, the livestock sector, land settlement, forestry and forest policy, amongst others. From the very beginning, therefore, the Bank has given attention to environmental and (what at the time were generally referred to as) 'Amerindian' issues in the region. The survey concluded, for example, by affirming:

> The question has been asked: should the Amazon be regarded as a resource frontier or as an underdeveloped area requiring special assistance? In fact, it is both. There are important new production possibilities that deserve vigorous development. At the same time, the region is poor, with only half of the country's per capita national income, and needs special measures to redress the inequality. In both perspectives the possibilities are great — as are the difficulties. The Amazon is very small economically, and by devoting resources to its development, Brazil may not only forego faster growth in the south, but also deprive a far more populous (eight times more), but equally poor region, the north-east, of development resources. Finally, the Amazon is unique in one respect. It possesses a natural environment that does not exist elsewhere in the world, but which Brazil and the world wish to preserve. Respect for this fact may prove to be the greatest constraint of all when planning Amazon development.[10]

9   Contrary to what is sometimes alleged, the Bank had no role in the most significant and environmentally damaging infrastructure investments in the Brazilian Amazon in the 1970s and '80s, including the Belém–Brasília (construction and subsequent paving), Transamazon and Cuiabá-Santarém highways, and Tucurui Hydroelectric project, nor, other than through the Iron Ore Project discussed below, in the Greater Carajás Programme.

10   Skillings and Tcheyan (1979), pp. 126–7.

The Bank's first loan in the region (US$ 6.7 million for the Alto Turi Land Settlement Project, approved in July 1972), however, was intended, with mixed results, to support a directed rural 'colonisation' project in northwestern Maranhao.[11] Much larger lending operations were those to help install major mining, rail and port facilities, involving US$2.8 billion in total investments, through the Carajás Iron Ore Project (Bank loan for US$304.5 million, approved in August 1982) and to help implement the Northwest Integrated Development Programme (POLONOROESTE). This programme, with an estimated total cost of US$1.55 billion, was partially financed by six interconnected Bank loans totalling US$434.4 million, approved between December 1981 and December 1983, for road improvements (especially paving of the BR–364 highway), integrated rural development, health (particularly malaria control) and environmental and indigenous peoples protection in Mato Grosso and Rondônia.[12]

Carajás

The Carajás project involved construction of a 900-kilometre railway, connecting iron and manganese mining facilities in the Carajás highlands in eastern Pará (which contain one of the world's largest ore deposits, first discovered in 1967) and a deepwater port near the capital city of São Luis, Maranhão. At the Bank's insistence, it also included components for urban development (two townships), environmental protection and an 'Amerindian Special Project'.[13] Much of the 'Carajás corridor' was originally covered by dense tropical forest, although the easternmost part of the area contains extensive coastal marshlands and other subregions consist of drier savanna grasslands. At the time the Bank loan was approved, much of the project's area of influence was already undergoing the rapid rural and urban settle-

11   Annex I contains a complete chronological list of all Bank/GEF/Rain Forest Pilot Programme loans and grants in support of development and environmental management activities in the Brazilian Amazon region.
12   The discussion of Carajás and POLONOROESTE below is further elaborated in Redwood (1993) and World Bank/OED (1992a; 1992b). The Brazilian counterpart team also published the results of this study (see IPEA, 1990). For non-Bank, and largely critical, views on Carajas, see Hall (1989) and on POLONOROESTE, see Cowell (1990); Price (1989); and Rich (1994). At the time the first loans for POLONOROESTE were prepared Rondônia was a federal Territory, becoming a state in December 1981.
13   The 'Special Project' was implemented by the National Indian Foundation (FUNAI) with, at the insistence of the Brazilian government, no Bank funding.

ment, productive occupation and environmental degradation typical of frontier expansion in central and northern Brazil. The Bank was first approached in connection with Carajás in late 1972, but did not become actively involved until the Rio Doce Valley Company (CVRD)[14] received authorisation to seek external financing in October 1980. The much broader Greater Carajás Programme was created one month later with power to grant fiscal and other incentives to private investors and state enterprises for productive activities in the Carajás corridor.[15]

When the Bank's only preparation mission took place in February 1981, CVRD was already pressing ahead with construction on several fronts. As a result, most design decisions had already been taken. Because of the Bank's comparatively late engagement, the environmental and indigenous people's components were not introduced until the overall project preparation process was well advanced.[16] Except for the indigenous and urban components, project execution was relatively problem-free. Iron-ore mining and export activities began in May 1985 and the railway was completed ten months ahead of schedule at a considerable cost saving.

Important economic and social benefits have accrued to the Carajás region as a result of the project. These include substantial short and longer-term employment in construction, mining and metallurgical (mostly pig iron) industries and related commercial and service activities. They also include passenger and freight rail and road transport, together with other infrastructure improvements at Carajás, Parauapebas[17] (the two project-cre-

---

14   At that time, CVRD, whose main activities were in the south-eastern states of Minas Gerais and Espirito Santo, was Brazil's largest state-owned mining company. It was privatised in 1997.

15   Hall (1989).

16   The Bank's experience with major infrastructure investments affecting indigenous peoples both in the Carajás corridor and north-west Brazil (POLONOROESTE), however, provided the stimulus for elaboration of its indigenous peoples' safeguard policy, which has been in effect since 1991 and is now undergoing revision. For the study that underlay the original policy on vulnerable ethnic minorities, see World Bank (1983). The first draft of this publication was available in July 1981 and formed the basis for the Bank's intervention regarding indigenous peoples' protection in the case of Carajás. On the plight of Brazil's indigenous peoples in Amazonia in the 1960s and '70s, see Davis (1977), and on their current status, see ISA (2000).

17   Additional infrastructure improvements at Parauapebas and elsewhere in the Carajás corridor were implemented under the follow-up CVRD Environmental Conservation and Rehabilitation Project, partially financed with a Bank loan of US$50 million, approved in July 1995. Most of the activities supported by this project, however, were in CVRD's 'southern system' in Minas Gerais and Espirito Santo.

ated townships), São Luis and other urban centres along the corridor. However, the project also had significant indirect adverse environmental and social consequences, although many of these were by-products of tendencies already underway in its broader area of influence that Carajás helped to accelerate or exacerbate.

Both CVRD and the Bank foresaw that the operation would have a considerable catalytic effect on agricultural and industrial development in the region. However, the combined impacts of the project and other public and private interventions, especially roadbuilding and fiscal incentive-induced cattle ranching,[18] were underestimated. In rural areas, there was a significant increase in property values and concentration in land ownership, especially near urban-industrial 'growth poles' such as Marabá, Açailândia and Santa Inês. Rising landlessness with a shift to wage labour and land-related conflicts,[19] together with increasing conversion of forest to pasture, have accompanied this process. Growth of a charcoal industry to support pig iron and other metallurgical industries along the Carajás railway line has further increased pressure on the native forest.[20] Towns and cities throughout the Carajás corridor also experienced accelerated growth, resulting in a substantial disparity between rapidly expanding demand for urban services and the ability of state and municipal authorities to provide them.

In short, while the Carajás project successfully implemented its internal environmental protection measures (including air and water pollution control at the mine and port sites, soil erosion control along the railway, environmental education and ecological research, and establishment of conservation tracts, greenbelt buffer zones, ecological stations and biotic invento-

---

18 From 1961 through the early 1990s, the Brazilian federal government maintained a programme of fiscal incentives to stimulate productive private sector occupation of Amazonia, known popularly as the '34/18 — FINAM' system. Most of the incentives in Amazonia were utilised to support the installation of extensive cattle ranches, which had a very significant adverse environmental (and social) impact. See Binswanger (1987; 1989); Gasques and Yokomizo (1986); Hecht (1984); Mahar (1979; 1989); and Redwood (1979) for evaluations of this programme and other environmentally detrimental government policies.

19 The most tragic of which took place at Eldorado dos Carajás in April 1996 when 19 small farmers were killed by the military police.

20 For further discussion, see Anderson (1990); Hall (1989); and Redwood (1996). Dealing with these pressures, but with mixed success, was one of the objectives of the 'northern system' component of the CVRD Environmental Conservation and Rehabilitation Project cited above (see World Bank/ICR, 2001).

ries), the government[21] did not adequately anticipate or address the broader regional environmental and social impacts[22] to which the project contributed in conjunction with other public investments and policies.[23] Similarly, while the 'Amerindian Special Project' resulted in significant improvements in the living conditions of indigenous communities in the project's broader area of influence, particularly with respect to health and land demarcation, several key issues remained unresolved at the time the project closed. As a result, the longer-term sustainability of efforts to protect local indigenous populations under the 'Special Project' (and similar actions under the subsequent CVRD Project, which has now also closed) is uncertain.

POLONOROESTE

As suggested above, during the 1960s and '70s, Brazil adopted ambitious measures to better integrate Amazonia into its rapidly expanding economy. Major highways were built and/or paved, rural settlement programmes were implemented, and 'growth pole' strategies and fiscal incentives attracted private investment to the region.[24] Large-scale hydroelectric and mining projects, such as Tucuruí and Carajás, were undertaken in eastern

21 One senior Bank economist did, in fact, raise the issue of the potential broader economic, environmental and social impacts of Carajás on several occasions, but his government interlocutors showed no real interest in the subject or in additional Bank support to help address such impacts at that time.

22 For more on the broader environmental and social issues and impacts related to the Carajás undertaking, in addition to Hall (1989), see Gonçalves de Almeida (1986) and Secretaria Especial do Meio Ambiente et al. (1987).

23 In fairness to CVRD, dealing with their impacts is not its responsibility alone, but rather that of the public sector at all levels — federal, state and municipal — more generally, and CVRD does periodically channel a portion of its profits from mining operations at Carajás back to the municipalities in the corridor to finance physical and social infrastructure priorities. In addition, Parauapebas, as the municipal jurisdiction where the mining complex is located, receives considerable tax transfers. However, with privatisation, it is unclear to what extent the annual transfers to corridor municipalities from CVRD will be maintained (Redwood, 1998).

24 For an interesting analysis by the Bank's first staff ecologist of the comparative environmental impacts of the various types of public and private investments in Amazonia at the time, see Goodland (1980). Like Dennis Mahar, who coordinated the Bank's sector work in north west Brazil, Robert Goodland had previously written about Brazilian Amazonia before joining the Bank in the late 1970s (see Mahar, 1978; Goodland and Irwin, 1975). Goodland was also a member of the north-west sector study mission and wrote the environmental and Amerindian chapters of the report (World Bank, 1983).

Amazonia. At the same time, increasing numbers of small farmers and
rural workers were being expelled by agricultural modernisation and associated land concentration in south-central Brazil (especially northern and
western Paraná) and by demographic pressures and recurrent droughts in
the impoverished north-east. The need to absorb these migrants lent additional impetus to attempts at directed Amazonian settlement.[25]

Colonisation projects along the Transamazon Highway in Pará in the early
1970s, however, fell well short of their targets as complex settlement schemes
proved incapable of developing sustainable agriculture in a poorly known
tropical environment.[26] The discovery of fertile lands under public domain
in Rondônia in western Amazonia appeared to provide a more promising
outlet for the growing number of people drawn to the region.[27] By the late
1970s, Rondônia's population had more than quadrupled,[28] socio-economic
problems were mounting, deforestation was increasing and the security of
Rondônia's indigenous inhabitants was seriously threatened. These problems
were all clearly identified in the pioneering Bank sector study on the 'north-
west region' undertaken in late 1979. POLONOROESTE was the Brazilian
government's and the Bank's response. Nevertheless, the Bank's sector report
identified a number of major risks:

> ...the north-west has the potential to become an important agricul-
> tural and timber-producing region ... and a place where migrants from
> other parts of the country may be productively and permanently set-
> tled on small-scale farms. Thus, the measures proposed under
> POLONOROESTE in support of future settlement and development
> of the region seem justified on both economic and social grounds.
> Such measures also seem justified on the grounds that a sizeable pop-
> ulation already exists in the region — a significant portion of which

25   For the history of public sector development strategies and associated inter-
      ventions in Amazonia through the late 1970s, see Mahar (1978; 1979) and
      Redwood (1979).
26   On the Transamazon colonisation experience, see Smith (1982) and Moran
      (1984); and on that elsewhere in Amazonia, see Lisansky (1990); Ozório de
      Almeida (1992); and Ozório de Almeida and Campari (1995).
27   However, even in Rondônia, poor soil fertility in parts of the state contributed
      directly to the subsequent failure of some new land settlement projects and, in
      preparing and appraising POLONOROESTE, the Bank gave insufficient atten-
      tion to these significant constraints on sustainable rural development.
28   On population movements, including frontier expansion in Brazil through the
      1970s, see Katzman (1977); Martine (1990); Merrick and Graham (1979);
      Redwood (1972); and Wood and Wilson (1984).

now finds itself in insecure land tenure situations and without access to basic services.

Though the measures contemplated in POLONOROESTE deal with most of the region's major problem areas, it may be concluded that execution of this programme will entail a higher-than-normal degree of risks. Most of these risks emanate from the basic characteristics of the northwest: (i) its huge land area [600,000 square kilometres] and frontier status; (ii) its rapidly growing population; (iii) its confused land tenure situation; (iv) its fragile, and imperfectly known, natural environment; (v) its Amerindian population, now in the early stages of contact with modern society; and (vi) its thin administrative structure.

> Perhaps the greatest risk is that the administration of POLONOROESTE and those of the executing agencies may be unable to fully control and monitor the future occupation and development of the north-west. Thus, the government should be prepared to accept some of the negative effects frequently associated with accelerated development in frontier areas. Included in these negative effects are likely to be: (i) continued conflicts over land-related issues, including some invasions of indian lands; (ii) some indiscriminate deforestation and unsound farming practices; and (iii) instances of general lawlessness. While such effects are to some extent inevitable, they would certainly be more widespread and serious in the absence of the special measures contemplated under POLONOROESTE.[29]

Unfortunately, this proved to be highly prophetic and much subsequent debate has occurred both in the NGO community and elsewhere as to whether the adverse environmental and social impacts associated with POLONOROESTE were in fact less widespread and serious than they would have been in its absence and that of the Bank's support. Be that as it may, the Brazilian government formally launched the programme in May 1981, having as its primary objective, 'to promote the orderly human occupation and development of the north-west region.' Its principal components were the paving of the 1,500 kilometre federal highway (initially built in the 1950s and '60s) between Cuiabá and Porto Velho, extension of the feeder road network, consolidation of existing rural settlement schemes and support for the establishment of new ones, improvement of social (especially health) services in rural areas and measures to protect the natural environment and indigenous communities.

29   World Bank (1983), pp. v-vi.

Even though reconstruction of the BR-364 highway was subsumed under a broader 'integrated' regional development concept, combining physical infrastructure, social services, rural development and environmental protection, the execution of POLONOROESTE's various components was seriously imbalanced. The trunk highway was completed ahead of schedule and other physical infrastructure investments were executed satisfactorily. However, agricultural support services, community facilities and environmental and indigenous peoples protection lagged seriously behind.[30] Moreover, an economic stabilisation programme adopted in 1982 led to serious cutbacks in official agricultural investment credit, an essential input for the establishment of ecologically more friendly tree crops such as coffee and cocoa. Transforming the government's original proposal for road improvement into a more complex regional development initiative (largely at the Bank's insistence) challenged and strained the borrower's capacity, not to mention their political will, to achieve the programme's production, environmental and social objectives. However, insufficient attention was given by the Bank and other stakeholders either to the underlying ecological constraints or the political economy of frontier occupation in the region.

Uneven implementation also exacerbated several other problems. Enhanced access to and within the region for a wide variety of economic actors in addition to the programme's small farmer target population, together with subsidised credit and infrastructure investments not financed by the programme, helped to increase the profitability of logging, ranching and (primarily gold) prospecting activities.[31] This further stimulated inmigration during the 1980s, well beyond the levels initially expected and at a time when the public sector was increasingly unable to ensure environmental protection or respond to growing local demands for productive support and community services. As feared, the institutional mechanisms initially established for the implementation of POLONOROESTE proved inadequate. Moreover, as most of the Bank's funds had been allo-

---

30 The paving of BR–364 was originally to be financed as part of a broader Bank highway project for Brazil. Only later was it incorporated into a broader regional development programme at the Bank's insistence, but without real government 'ownership' of the non-transport components. As a result, road improvements were implemented expeditiously, while the agricultural, environmental and indigenous components lagged.

31 For more detailed discussions of the human occupation of Rondônia in the 1970s and '80s and its causes and effects, see Browder (1989); Martine (1990); Millikan (1988); Mueller (1990); and Wilson (1985).

cated to the programme's transport components, these resources were largely disbursed before the distortions in the programme's overall execution became fully known, thus considerably reducing the Bank's leverage.

Partly in response to increasing criticism by international environmental NGOs, POLONOROESTE was restructured in the mid-1980s. A mid-term review (MTR) in late 1984 highlighted the differences between the assumptions under which the programme had originally been planned and the actual circumstances under which it was being implemented,[32] while problems with several key components led the Bank to suspend disbursements in March 1985. Bank funding was resumed in August 1985 after federal authorities took steps to resolve the problems identified by the MTR, including protection of several indigenous areas. Agreement was also reached on an agenda for redirection of the programme, improving performance of its environmental and Amerindian components and highlighting the need for a different approach to productive settlement and natural resource management, which the Bank would support, again with very mixed results, over the next decade.

Other Projects and Analytical Work

The 1980s witnessed other important Bank-supported activities involving the Brazilian Amazon. One was implementation of the Amazonas Agricultural Development Project, approved in May 1982, which modified the centralised, technocratic 'integrated' rural development approach the Bank was pursuing, with lacklustre results, in north-east Brazil (including Maranhão, the western part of which is also in 'Legal Amazonia') and, through POLONOROESTE, in Mato Grosso and Rondônia. The Amazonas Project, which sought to assist existing rural residents to achieve sustainable agricultural production in riverine areas, successfully piloted a more decentralised, community-based approach, in part through establishment of a revolving credit fund.[33] This now forms the central

32 By 1985, migration into Rondônia was roughly 150,000 a year (as compared with a total population in 1980 in the order of 490,000), while largely uncontrolled rural settlement and environmentally damaging logging, ranching and prospecting activities were spreading in various parts of the state, bringing increasing pressure on lands with soils incapable of supporting sustained agricultural production and on official indigenous and ecological reserves.

33 For pointing out this connection, I am indebted to my colleague Antonio Rocha Magalhaes, who has also spearheaded important sustainable development planning exercises both in north-east Brazil (*Projeto Aridas*, Ministry of Planning and Budget, 1995; and Gomes et al. 1995) and Rondônia (*Projeto Umidas*, Governo do Estado de Rondônia, 1998) before and after joining the World Bank office in Brasília in 1996. See also World Bank/PCR (1992).

thrust of the Bank's rural poverty reduction activities throughout Brazil, especially in the north-east.[34]

A second major area of Bank concern was public health, particularly malaria control. One of the POLONOROESTE loans was designed to address this problem, but with limited success. Despite this loan and due to the rapid human occupation of the state, the number of reported cases of malaria in Rondônia rose from 59,000 in 1980 to nearly 280,000 in 1988.[35] Recognising the increasing presence of this disease throughout the region, due in part to the rapid spread of prospecting (*garimpo*) activities, the Bank approved a US$99 million loan for the Amazon Basin Malaria Control Programme in May 1989. This scheme was subsequently estimated to have reduced the incidence of malaria in the region by some 45 per cent in relation to what it otherwise would have been, while improved diagnosis and treatment helped diminish the severity and fatality of the disease, saving an estimated 5.7 million disability-adjusted life years (DALYs).[36]

The third major area of Bank attention in the late 1980s, largely in response to its unhappy experience with POLONOROESTE,[37] was the extent and causes of deforestation. This led to two sector studies exploring the relationship between government policies and deforestation in the Brazilian Amazon. The first, by Hans Binswanger, focused on the adverse

---

34   See World Bank/OED (1991) for an evaluation of the older, and only partly successful, supply-driven 'top-down' approach to rural development in northeast Brazil in the 1970s and '80s and World Bank/OED (1988) for the experience worldwide. See Wiens and Guadagni (1998) for a description and comparative assessment of current approach in Brazil, Colombia and Mexico and the Bank's new rural development strategy for its proposed future application in all regions (World Bank, 2002b).

35   In the latter year, Rondônia accounted for almost half of the reported malaria cases in Amazonia, which, in turn, accounted for 95 per cent of all such cases in Brazil, giving it one of the highest incidences of this disease in the world. This phenomenon was described in one Bank report as 'frontier malaria'; see Wilson and Alicbusan-Schwab (1989) for details. For more on this project, see World Bank/PCR (1997).

36   World Bank/PCR (1997).

37   In a speech at the World Resources Institute in May 1987, then Bank president Barber Conable affirmed: 'POLONOROESTE is a sobering example of an environmentally sound effort which went wrong. The Bank misread the human, institutional and physical realities of the jungle and the frontier. In some cases, the dynamics of the frontier got out of control. Productive measures to shelter fragile land and tribal peoples were included; they were not, however, carefully timed or adequately monitored.'

environmental effects of fiscal and legal incentives.[38] It showed that general tax policies, special tax incentives, the rules of land allocation and the agricultural credit system all accelerated deforestation in the Amazon by stimulating an increase in the size of land holdings and reducing the chances of the poor to become farmers.[39] Binswanger concluded that: (i) these distorting provisions must be removed before afforestation projects and programmes could succeed; and (ii) a coherent system of land-use planning that sets aside more marginal lands in forest reserves and establishes biological reserves is also required.[40]

The second study, by Dennis Mahar, estimated that forest clearing in Legal Amazonia had increased from 28,600 square kilometres in 1975 to about 600,000 square kilometres in 1988, with the most extensive deforestation occurring in Rondônia, Mato Grosso, Maranhão and Pará. Its 'proximate causes' were small-scale agriculture, cattle ranching, logging, mining and urban growth. However, the paper also affirmed:

> ...government polices designed to open up Amazonia for human settlement and to encourage certain types of economic activity have played a key role in the deforestation process. In particular, massive road-building programmes carried out in the 1960s and 1970s made large areas of the region accessible by land for the first time and government-sponsored settlement schemes simultaneously attracted migrants from Brazil's north-east and south regions. Special fiscal incentives and subsidised credit lines encouraged land uses such as cattle raising, which allowed a relatively small population to have a large impact on the rain forest.[41]

---

38 This paper was initially issued by the Agriculture and Rural Development Department in 1987. A revised version was released under a different title by the Environment Department two years later (Binswanger, 1987; 1989).

39 More specifically, Binswanger observed that: (i) the virtual exemption of agricultural income from income taxation makes agriculture a tax shelter; (ii) rules of public land allocation provide incentives for deforestation because the rules used in determining the security of a claim and its land area encourage land clearing; (iii) the progressive land tax contains provisions that encourage the conversion of forest to crop land or pasture; (iv) the tax credit (i.e., fiscal incentive) scheme aimed toward corporate livestock ranches subsidises inefficient ranches established on cleared forest land; and (v) subsidised credit is available for SUDAM (Superintendency for the Development of Amazonia, which administered the 34/18–FINAM fiscal incentive programme in Legal Amazonia) approved ranching projects.

40 Binswanger (1989).

41 Mahar (1989), pp. 9–10.

Mahar concluded that government policies to develop Amazonia had, 'rarely been designed and carried out with due regard for their environmental consequences' and argued that a 'new policy should be developed for rain forest areas for which overland access does not yet exist'. He further proposed that one new instrument which should be used toward this end was agro-ecological zoning (see below). Changes in the prevailing policy framework for the region (similar to those proposed by Binswanger) were also recommended, specifically:

- Elimination of fiscal incentives for livestock projects (which later occurred).

- A moratorium on disbursements of fiscal incentives for metallurgical projects in the Greater Carajás area that use charcoal derived from native forest (some progress has also been made in this regard).

- INCRA (the federal colonisation and agrarian reform agency) should modify its policy of recognising deforestation as a form of land improvement. (INCRA now has a policy prohibiting the establishment of new settlements in virgin forests).

- The national forestry agency (formerly IBDF, now IBAMA) should abolish the rule requiring that 50 per cent of all individual landholdings in Amazonia be maintained under forest cover due to its unenforceability, instead requiring 'block reserves' equivalent to half the area in agriculture in a given region (only adopted in some new Bank-supported settlements in Rondônia).

- Improved collecting of rural land taxes (again some progress has been made).[42]

The 1990s: Sustainable Natural Resource Management, Rural Poverty Reduction and Biodiversity Conservation

Bank approaches to Amazonia shifted considerably in the 1990s, in part due to lessons drawn from the projects and studies undertaken during the previous decade, together with additional analytical work. While the road towards sustainable development continued to be bumpy, substantial

---

42 Mahar (1989), pp. 47–50. For a nearly contemporaneous Brazilian assessment, see Reis and Margulis (1991).

progress was made during the 1990s in terms of better integrating environmental (including global environmental) and social development concerns in Bank sector work, policy dialogue and lending operations. In addition, grant funding though the Rain Forest Pilot Programme (RFPP) and the Global Environment Facility (GEF), both established in the early 1990s, for forest management, biodiversity conservation and support to local communities has complemented Bank loans for infrastructure and rural development. Similarly, sub-national governments, civil society organisations and other development partners have played a much greater role in Bank programmes and projects in the region. These major changes have therefore been both in terms of substance and process.

Learning From Experience and Integrating Environmental Factors: Evaluation and Analytical Work

The Bank made a serious effort to learn from both the positive and negative aspects of its experience in Amazonia in the 1970s and '80s. An assessment by its autonomous Operations Evaluation Department (OED) of the environmental and social impacts of several large projects in Brazil, including Carajás and POLONOROESTE,[43] made a number of recommendations regarding the Bank's approach to development in the region and more generally. These included the need to:

- Better understand the ecological, socio-economic and political-institutional contexts (e.g., the complex political economy of the frontier) where the Bank was intervening.

- Maintain a spatial focus over a carefully determined geographical area of account (or project area of influence).

- Adopt a cross-sector and multi-disciplinary approach to complex projects such as Carajás and POLONOROESTE.

---

43   This study, which began in 1988, also evaluated Bank experience with urban-industrial pollution control in metropolitan São Paulo and power generation, involuntary resettlement and irrigated agriculture in the middle and lower São Francisco River valley in north-east Brazil. Another OED evaluation, on renewable resource management in agriculture, also contained a case study on Brazil (together with 11 other countries), which concluded that, with the notable exception of the north-west programmes (Bank) project lending has not used resource management as one of its themes (World Bank/OED, 1989).

- Systematically consider indirect and 'induced' project impacts.[44]

- Take interregional considerations into account.

- Assess unintended environmental and social consequences of public policies and programmes.[45]

Around the same time, a major sector study was undertaken, 'to improve the analytical and factual framework that underpins the Bank's approach to problems of economic development and environmental degradation in the Amazon'.[46] This review systematically examined the roles of the main 'actors' in the deforestation and environmental degradation process, specifically ranchers, loggers, small farmers and prospectors ('transient' activities), together with extractivists, large-scale miners and hydro-electric development ('geographically stable' activities). Its main findings, which for the first time in a Bank analytical piece on the region include a strong focus on global environmental concerns, were:

- Deforestation in the Amazon is occurring more slowly than is generally believed, and will probably continue at a slower pace for economic and demographic reasons.

- Even though the pressure for deforestation has declined, it will continue based on the economics of 'nutrient mining, the extraction through logging, annual cropping and ranching of the nutrients of the forest canopy and soil.

- Market forces will tend to promote nutrient mining, and prevent the emergence of sustainable agricultural techniques as long as new roads keep land abundant and cheap.

- Policies to restrict deforestation will be extremely difficult to implement due to lack of local support.

- While the economic opportunity cost to Brazil as a whole of reducing or eliminating further agricultural exploitation in the

---

44   The Bank has since October 1989, when Operational Directive (OD) 4.00, Annex A was adopted, had a formal requirement that all investment operations be submitted to an environmental assessment. It was later revised in October 1991 as OD 4.01 and converted into an Operational Policy (OP 4.01) in January 1999.

45   Redwood (1993).

46   World Bank (1992a), p. vi.

Amazon is very low, the cost of enforcing controls on deforestation would be very high.

The major reasons for reducing deforestation are: (i) to maximise the net benefits to society of the information embodied in the yet unknown numbers of threatened plant and animal species; (ii) to reduce greenhouse gas emissions from forest burning; (iii) to prevent problems of river silting and sedimentation; and (iv) to prevent possible climate change at the local level.

• Comparing the purchase and rental price of land in the Amazon with the carbon content of a hectare of dense tropical forests suggests that the north could contract with landowners in the Amazon not to burn. On a global scale, prevention of deforestation in the Amazon may be one of the lowest-cost ways of reducing greenhouse emissions. Thus, both donors and Brazil would benefit from transfers to reduce deforestation.[47]

The report concluded that an environmental and development strategy for the Brazilian Amazon should include the following elements: (i) a policy to regulate forest access;[48] (ii) elimination of policy-induced price distortions that favour deforestation (thus, reiterating similar recommendations previously made by Binswanger and Mahar); and (iii) a policy to identify and preserve special areas.[49] The latter would be partially developed and implemented with the assistance of the Bank-administered Pilot Programme to Conserve the Brazilian Rain Forest (PPG7) and two Global Environment Facility (GEF) grants (PROBIO/FUNBIO), discussed below.

47 World Bank (1992a), pp. vi–vii. On this latter point, see also Schneider (LATEN Discussion Note no. 2, 1993a), the principal author of the sector study, for further detail. See chapter 2 in this volume.

48 Similarly, another Bank sector study, on agriculture, rural development and natural resources in Brazil, undertaken at around the same time, contained a chapter entitled 'Conservation, Forestry and Biodiversity' which recommended for Amazonia: '...declare a moratorium on federal, state and municipal expenditure on road construction into areas zoned as not suitable for agricultural development. Develop enforcement mechanisms. Provide matching grants for strengthening environmental planning and enforcement at the state and municipal levels. Define a process for assigning any remaining *terras devolutas* (untitled lands under federal government oversight) to alternative uses within five years. If any areas are to be for private use, define a settlement policy that takes into account the full environmental impact of forest conversion.' (World Bank, 1994).

49 World Bank (1992a).

Before turning to these activities, two other seminal studies should be briefly highlighted. The first, by Robert Schneider, also the main author of the sector report briefly described immediately above, addressed the topic of government and economy on the Amazon frontier. Its main messages complement and reinforce many of those summarised above, particularly with respect to the need to better understand the political economy of the frontier and not to consider decentralisation (despite its potential benefits for environmental management) as a panacea in such areas:

- Settlers in the Amazon do appear to be improving their standard of living compared with people with the same education and skills outside the region.

- Transience and farm turnover on the frontier is due to powerful and fundamental economic forces. These forces can only be overcome by well-organised government policy.

- Transience, farm turnover and even apparent land abandonment are not necessarily linked to degradation of the agricultural resource base.[50]

- More attention needs to be given to the importance of reconciling the needs of local politicians with externally designed projects. Particularly important is the need to find ways of developing sustained support for the rural development services that encourage small farm stability.

- Creating a political coalition to support policies for orderly frontier development is difficult. Because the interests in more rapid development are largely local and regional, while the benefits from slower, more deliberate growth are national and global, greater political and economic autonomy at the local level may tend to undermine better settlement policies.

- Roads are the fundamental determinant of settlement. An extensive road network erodes incentives for sustainable agriculture and silviculture. An intensive network of farm-to-market roads is the most important determinant of economic viability of small farmer agriculture.

50   For further discussion on this subject, see Schneider (LATEN Dissemination Note no. 3, 1993b).

- Allocating land initially to small farmers is not only good policy from an equity standpoint, but in most cases it is the most efficient and orderly way to settle new lands.[51]

- National governments must define their objectives carefully with regard to establishing government beyond the economic frontier. Here also, local and national interests are unlikely to coincide.[52]

The second landmark study, based on two decades of empirical research on the sustainability of public and private rural colonisation in Amazonia, was completed in the mid-1990s while its principal author, Anna Luiza Ozório de Almeida, was a Bank staff member. The basic policy prescription emerging from this analysis was that, 'Amazonian deforestation can be reduced by inverting current economic rewards for speculation and inter-regional migration so that farmers are discouraged from selling their cleared land and moving on to clear forest further inland and from deforesting more extensively their current plots.' More specifically, in what the authors describe as 'a frontier poverty reduction programme that uses economic policies to raise agricultural incomes and reduce environmental aggression', the study recommended policies, ideally generated and enforced at the local level, to promote agriculturally sustainable frontiers combined with the 'judicious use' of pricing and fiscal policies in order to 'elevate agricultural productivity, punish speculation in land transactions and punish deforestation directly in the Brazilian Amazon.'[53]

Meanwhile Back in the North-west: PLANAFLORO and PRODEAGRO

Due in part to their timing, however, the findings and recommendations of the various project evaluations and policy-related research summarised above were only partly reflected in the next generation of Bank-supported investment operations in Amazonia. These took the form of two parallel natural resource management projects in Rondônia and Mato Grosso, better known as PLANAFLORO and PRODEAGRO. The former involved a Bank loan of US$167 million, approved in March 1992, the latter a loan of US$205 million, approved in June 1992.

---

51 On the important issue of property rights in frontier settlement in Amazonia, elsewhere in Brazil and North America, see Alston, Libecap and Schneider (1996a; 1996b; and 1996c)

52 Schneider (1994), pp. vi–vii.

53 Ozório de Almeida and Campari (1995), pp. 1–2.

The principal stated objective of these two operations is, 'to implement an improved approach to natural resource management, conservation and development.' In PLANAFLORO,[54] for example, this would be
achieved by assisting the federal and state governments to:[55]

- Institute a series of changes in policies, regulations and investment
  programmes, so as to provide a coherent incentive framework for
  the sustainable development of Rondônia.

- Conserve the rich biodiversity of the state, while creating the basis
  for the sustainable utilisation of its renewable natural resources for
  the direct economic benefit of the local population.

- Protect and enforce the borders of all conservation units,
  Amerindian reserves, public forests and extractive reserves, and
  control and prevent illegal deforestation, wood transport and forest
  fires.

- Develop integrated farming systems in areas suitable for permanent
  agriculture and agro-forestry, and systems for sustainable forest
  management and extraction of non-wood forest products in other
  areas, which should remain under natural forest cover.

- Support priority investments in socio-economic infrastructure and
  services to implement the state's agro-ecological zoning.

- Consolidate the technical operational capacity of state institutions,
  particularly those responsible for agriculture, forestry support services and the protection and management of forests and Amerindian
  reserves.[56]

The Staff Appraisal Report (SAR) for this highly ambitious new project included a brief discussion of some of the key lessons of
POLONOROESTE. The most important of these included:

- Public investments in frontier areas characterised by fragile natural
  resource conditions should be based on better technical knowledge

---

54   World Bank/SAR (1992), pp. 1–2.
55   The specific objectives and instruments utilised in PRODEAGRO were very
     similar.
56   The SAR also explicitly stated that, 'consolidation of agricultural development
     activities and infrastructure investments will only take place in areas already de-
     forested. No new settlements or new roads will be financed under the project.'

of the sustainable development potential than that which was available at the beginning of these projects. Agro-ecological zoning to guide public investment should be a *sine qua non* of future projects in such areas.

- The scope and content of project interventions should be sufficient to achieve project objectives. Beyond POLONOROESTE, agricultural projects supported actions only in parts of the state, without addressing the movement of populations and general state occupation patterns.

- Excessively centralised decision-making at the federal level is detrimental to efficient project implementation. Decentralisation in favour of the state and municipalities, including more control over budgetary resources, would result in greater accountability of project management to the community and facilitates implementation. Also, an enhanced role for NGOs in project implementation would enhance accountability to the ultimate beneficiaries and improve the responsiveness of project agencies.

- The physical demarcation of environmental conservation units and Amerindian reserves is a necessary, but not sufficient, condition for their protection. Financial disincentives, such as the absence of physical and social infrastructure in the surrounding areas and strong enforcement capacity to prevent and punish invasions, are also required.[57]

As these two projects are still under implementation, any attempt to fully assess their performance and results would be premature. It should, nevertheless, be noted that their execution has been far from smooth, with infrastructure (especially road improvements) moving ahead more rapidly than environmental and indigenous peoples components, mirroring (for many of the same reasons) the uneven implementation of POLONOROESTE. Both projects also underwent substantial restructuring following comprehensive mid-term reviews (MTRs) in 1996–97, including incorporation of new demand-driven community projects components with substantial NGO participation in their governance structures. PLANAFLORO, additionally, was the object of a formal complaint in

---

57   World Bank/SAR (1992b), pp. 13–4

1995 to the Bank's recently created Inspection Panel[58] by leading local
NGOs concerned with delays in the agro-ecological zoning and project financing in Rondônia.

An April 1997 press release following the Panel's review of progress in
implementing the action plan adopted by the Bank made in response to the
original complaint gives a sense of the issues at hand; '... (t)he Panel's report recognises the difficulties of carrying out such an ambitious, complex
project in the frontier areas of the Amazon... The report notes that, after
a delayed start of the project, "with Bank assistance significant improvements have taken place in PLANAFLORO's administration"...' It notes,
however, that deforestation has continued at high historical levels of nearly 450,000 hectares per year and recommends ongoing monitoring and
control of land clearing as a priority for the project. The report notes the
continuation of illegal timber extraction and settlement in protected areas,
and urges effective enforcement action against this infringement of defined borders. It also finds little progress in implementing a sustainable
health plan for indigenous people. Despite these problems, the review
noted that the local people affected by the project consider its continuation preferable to ending World Bank involvement.[59]

The MTR for PLANAFLORO was unusual in several respects.[60] It
took place fairly late during project implementation, at a time when the operation was on the verge of being cancelled because of poor performance.
The Inspection Panel experience had sharply reduced both the government's and the Bank's enthusiasm, and the MTR was really a high risk, last-
ditch effort to salvage the project. A number of innovations were also associated with the MTR. It was preceded by a comprehensive review of
project implementation, carried out by a multi-disciplinary team of independent Brazilian consultants. All relevant local, state, national and international stakeholders, including the main critics of the project (local ranching and logging interests, local civil society groups and international NGOs

---

58   The three-member Inspection Panel was established in September 1993 to help
      ensure that Bank lending operations adhere to the institution's operational poli-
      cies and procedures. Any group of individuals who feel they have been directly
      and adversely affected by a Bank-supported project can request the Panel to in-
      vestigate complaints that the Bank has failed to abide by its policies and proce-
      dures (see Shihata, 1994). On the Panel's response in the specific case of
      PLANAFLORO, see World Bank/Inspection Panel (1995).
59   World Bank/Inspection Panel (1997a; 1997b).
60   I am grateful to Dennis Mahar, the Bank's resident representative in Brazil at the
      time, for providing many of the details set out below on the MTR process.

such as Friends of the Earth and OXFAM) were invited to the review meeting in Porto Velho and all proceedings were open to the public. The meeting evolved into a constructive negotiation between the state government and the local NGO Forum, leading to restructuring of the project to accommodate both groups (for example, additional road improvements desired by the state government and the community-based development fund requested by the NGOs).[61] While the project continued to experience counterpart funding and other difficulties following the MTR, stakeholder dialogue and collaboration improved dramatically and implementation has been smoother as a result.

Two innovative aspects of PLANAFLORO and PRODEAGRO have been subjected to preliminary assessment by the Bank and deserve brief additional comment: agro-ecological zoning and civil society participation. While clearly improving the information base in relation to natural resource endowments, in the absence of consistent enforcement measures, zoning, as a largely technical exercise, has proven to be of limited effectiveness in stemming unsustainable occupation of the frontier. Ultimately, its greater effectiveness requires political will and a process that engages the major stakeholders in order to build consensus around desirable land use patterns, taking into account ecological and other constraints on agricultural and other primary production activities.[62] This is clearly reflected in the main conclusions drawn by the aforementioned assessment:

> The experience with land-use zoning (LZ) in ... Rondonia has been decidedly mixed. The main conclusion ... is that zoning is a valid instrument for guiding land use on tropical frontiers, although it is far from being a panacea...

> Farmers, ranchers and loggers have all, to some extent, reacted negatively to restrictions on land use, because many of the environmental and social benefits resulting from leaving the forest intact (for example, carbon sequestration, preservation of biodiversity and ensuring the rights of tribal peoples) accrue to stakeholders located outside the state and even the country ...

> The Rondônia experience underscores the fact that LZ is an inherently political process that will not work in the absence of broad public

61   At the end of the review meeting, furthermore, an unprecedented joint press release was issued by the Bank, Friends of the Earth and OXFAM that endorsed the agreements.
62   Mahar and Ducrot (1998); Mahar (2000).

support. Land-use planners frequently overemphasise the importance
of technical aspects of LZ ... While technical aspects are certainly crucial they should not be allowed to overshadow and obscure the politics
of zoning. By its very nature prescriptive LZ tends to polarise societies
into 'winners' and 'losers'. Typically, success in implementing a prescriptive zoning plan depends on the strength of the land users' incentives to challenge zoning relative to the capacity and incentive of the
government to enforce and maintain zoning laws.[63]

Despite the prescriptive nature of their zoning exercises, as indicated
above, PLANAFLORO and PRODEAGRO did introduce a much greater
level of NGO and other civil society participation in their decision and implementation processes than previous Bank-supported interventions in
these two states. A recent paper on this subject observes, for example:

> PLANAFLORO is a paradigmatic development project for the Bank
> because it involves many of the classic issues the Bank faces in social
> projects throughout the world: complex and layered social context;
> economic development versus environmental protection dilemma;
> weak government agencies beset by turf disputes and administrative
> discontinuity; low project ownership by government and other stake-
> holders; complex project design coupled with overly ambitious project
> goals; and lack of effective civil society participation mechanisms.[64]

Among the conclusions that can be drawn from PLANAFLORO in this
regard, especially following the mid-term review, are: [65]

- For participation to be successful there must be mutual acceptance
  by all sides.

- Effective stakeholder participation requires financial and institutional resources.

- Participatory approaches are essential in projects carried out in fragile ecosystems with complex social problems.

- PLANAFLORO exemplifies a growing trend in Bank lending operations in Brazil, which is to decentralise and streamline projects experiencing implementation problems in order to ensure that benefits more effectively reach their intended beneficiaries.

63   Mahar (2000), pp. 126–7.
64   Aparicio and Garrison (1999), p. 11.
65   See Burstyn (ed.) (1996). On the general political constraints facing
     PLANAFLORO, see Keck (1997).

- PLANAFLORO demonstrates how the Bank can significantly improve its funding and oversight roles by taking steps to ensure stakeholder participation.[66]

Fighting Deforestation and Forest Fires and Protecting Biodiversity: the G7 Pilot Programme, GEF and PROARCO

In addition to PLANAFLORO and PRODEAGRO, the 1990s witnessed several major new Bank-supported initiatives aimed at helping to stem deforestation and forest fires and protect Amazonia's rich biodiversity. Foremost among these is the Pilot Programme to Conserve the Brazilian Rain Forest ('Pilot Programme' or PPG7), which has also focused on the even more threatened Atlantic Forest in eastern Brazil.[67] This initiative had its origins at the summit of the heads of state of the Group of Seven (G7) industrialised countries in Houston, Texas in 1990, at which time the then German Chancellor Helmut Kohl called for a pilot programme to reduce

---

66 Aparicio and Garrison (1999), pp. 11–13. More specifically, the authors observe that: 'first, the Bank adopted a strategy that made ownership and accountability, especially by the government, preconditions for project renewal. Second, it assembled a multi-disciplinary team of economists, environmentalists, engineers and social scientists to oversee the restructuring process and hired outside consultants to promote consensus building. Third, it implemented a more decentralised 'hands-on' and collaborative approach to project supervision by appointing a locally-based task manager, carrying out more frequent and less formal supervision missions, and establishing and maintaining frequent contact with a variety of stakeholders such as CSOs (civil society organisations) and the private sector. In short, the Bank not only improved its project oversight, but also learned to exert a catalytic role in encouraging more constructive engagement between the government and key societal actors including CSOs and the private sector' (Aparicio and Garrison, 1999, p. 13).

67 For a history of the destruction of the *Mata Atlántica* since early colonial times, see Dean (1995). The Bank has also provided support to conservation in the Atlantic Forest through a specific component of the National Environment Project, approved in February 1990 and closed in December 1998. See World Bank/SAR, 1990; Ministério do Meio Ambiente(1997); and World Bank/ICR (2000) for details on this project which, through its matching grants component (Ministério de Meio Ambiente, 1998), also supported specific environmental projects in the states of Acre, Amapá, Maranhão, Pará, Rondônia and Roraima, among other states. All Amazonian states are also potentially eligible for matching grants under the Second National Environmental Project in Brazil, which was approved in December 1999 (World Bank/PAD, 1999).

the rate of deforestation of Brazil's rain forests. The programme was developed jointly by the Brazilian Government, the World Bank and the European Commission and was approved by G7 delegates and the European Union in December 1991. Together with the Netherlands, the G7 countries and the European Union pledged some US$250 million of grant funding for the PPG7, of which US$50 million was to go to a central Rain Forest Trust Fund.[68] The Bank was requested to coordinate the programme and administer the Trust Fund.[69] The programme's basic objectives are to:

- Demonstrate that sustainable economic development and conservation of the environment can be pursued at the same time in tropical rain forests.

- Preserve the biodiversity of the rain forests.

- Reduce the rain forests' contribution to the emission of greenhouse gases.

- Set an example of international cooperation between industrial and developing countries on global environment problems. (World Bank/Rain Forest Unit)

Since 1994, a total of 13 sub-projects has been approved with Pilot Programme resources and another is currently under preparation under five basic lines of action: (i) experimentation and demonstration — demonstration projects, forest resources management, floodplain resources management; (ii) conservation — extractive reserves, indigenous lands, ecological corridors; (iii) scientific research — science centres, directed research; (iv) institutional strengthening — natural resources policy, fire and deforestation control; and (v) lessons and dissemination — monitoring and evaluation. In addition to Brazilian federal and state governments and external donors, a broad range of NGOs have been key partners in the programme, particularly in the implementation of its demon-

---

68   Donor countries would provide the rest of the pledged resources bilaterally through supplementary funding of projects proposed for the programme and through direct technical cooperation.

69   Following a major institutional review in 1998–99, however, many coordination functions were strengthened within the Amazonian Secretariat of the Ministry of Environment, which oversees the programme on behalf of the Brazilian government (World Bank/Pilot Programme, 1999).

stration projects component.[70] Many of these organisations are members of the Amazon Working Group (GTA), a network of more than 600 community groups, associations of rubber tappers, rural workers unions and environmental organisations active in the region.[71] An independent International Advisory Group (IAG) composed of specialists from the various donor countries and Brazil monitors implementation and provides independent advice and evaluation of the programme.[72]

As with PLANAFLORO and PRODEAGRO, it is too soon to assess performance of the Pilot Programme in any comprehensive way, but several aspects of its implementation and early results merit attention. While its first projects took longer to prepare and disbursement of grant funds for its various component operations continue to be slower than expected, the programme has produced several major written outputs and had noteworthy results on the ground. True to its intention to generate and disseminate knowledge, the programme has published major studies on agro-forestry experiences,[73] forest fire management[74] and the use of economic instruments for sustainable development[75] in the region. It has also recently launched a series of 'success story' notes, the first of which indicating how a new environmental control system (using satellite remote sensing, GPS and GIS technology, together with effective enforcement of legal restrictions on forest clearing) in recent years has helped to reduce deforestation by one-third in the state of Mato Grosso. The second and third notes focus on the regular-

70   This component has allowed some 100 communities and organisations to experiment with new approaches to using and conserving natural resources in the Amazon and Atlantic forests through the establishment of agro-forestry systems, enrichment of forests with useful species, rehabilitation of degraded areas and reforestation, sustainable management of forests for timber and extraction of non-timber forest products, among other activities. See Programa Piloto (2001) for further details.

71   For a discussion of the early experience of GTA, see Berno de Almeida (2000).

72   Initially the IAG's role was understood by its members to be that of monitoring progress with the Pilot Programme. However, over time, the IAG's role has evolved towards performing a more general role advising the Brazilian government (and the Bank) on strategic issues, without becoming involved significantly in operational matters (personal communication from Anthony Hall).

73   Smith et al. (1998). See also Smith (2000) and on the topic of biodiversity and agricultural intensification, more generally, Srivastava, Smith and Forno (1996).

74   Nepstad et al. (1999).

75   Haddad and Rezende (2002).

isation of indigenous lands and fostering 'sustainable' cosmetics from the region through a partnership with the private sector.[76]

An Implementation Completion Report (ICR) for only one of the Pilot Programme projects (Science Centres and Directed Research — Phase One) has been issued thus far. This operation has helped modernise two important scientific institutions, the Emilio Goeldi Museum in Belém and the National Institute for Amazon Research (INPA) in Manaus. It also supported 23 research projects (out of 116 applications), the majority of which were concerned with sustainable natural resource management.[77] The ongoing indigenous lands project (PPTAL) has also achieved impressive results, with a total of some 45.4 million hectares (an area larger than Germany, the Netherlands and Switzerland) having been demarcated and another 9.5 million hectares of indigenous lands (an area slightly larger than Austria) having been identified to date.[78] Yet another project (RESEX) has resulted in the establishment and consolidation of four new extractive reserves in the states of Acre, Amapá and Rondônia, thus helping rubber tappers and Brazil-nut gatherers continue to earn their livelihoods through the harvesting of non-timber forest products.[79] However, long-term economic viability is still a long way off.[80]

State and municipal environmental management capacity is being strengthened in seven of the states in Legal Amazonia through the Natural Resources Policy Project,[81] while different models of sustainable economic production in the Amazon and Atlantic rain forests are being tested

76   World Bank/Rain Forest Unit (2002a, b and c).
77   World Bank/ICR (2001). The other approved research projects fell into the categories of Amazonian ecosystems and socio-economic and cultural systems.
78   For more on PPTAL and indigenous land demarcation under the Pilot Programme, see FUNAI (no date) and FUNAI/PPTAL/GTZ (1999) and World Bank/Rain Forest Unit, Success Story 2 (2002).
79   See the newsletter *Extrativismo na Amazônia* (Pilot Programme, 1997) for additional information. On the experience with extractive reserves and other community-based 'productive conservation' initiatives in the Brazilian Amazon region, see Hall (1997).
80   In addition to the harvesting of non-timber forest products, thought must be given to other forms of transfer payments that could be made for environmental services rendered within extractive reserves and what mechanisms might be appropriate for this.
81   Support to states in the region (and elsewhere in Brazil) to strengthen their environmental management capacity and protect priority environmental assets is also available through the World Bank financed Second National Environment Project.

through small demonstration projects. Another key component of the Pilot Programme is the proposal to establish a number of 'ecological corridors', five in Amazonia and two in the Atlantic Forest, in order to strengthen biodiversity conservation.[82] According to Hall, '... (t)he seven corridors would eventually link existing conservation zones (73 protected units and 116 indigenous areas), thus in theory covering 75 per cent of the region's biodiversity within 34 per cent of the forested area, permitting the greatest possible flow of species and genetic material throughout the region'.[83] Despite these important advances, however, deforestation rates in Amazonia remain high.

One interesting aspect of the PPG7 that has been initially assessed, however, is civil society participation. This takes various forms and connects with the overall programme and its various projects in different ways. At the broadest level, it has entailed creation and consolidation of NGO networks in both the Amazon (GTA, mentioned above) and Atlantic Forest (where a similar group has been established). In terms of project execution, civil society involvement has ranged from participation in formal project advisory commissions to direct responsibility for implementation, monitoring and evaluation. The aforementioned evaluation concludes that the Pilot Programme has 'indeed been exemplary in terms of the high level of participation of civil society organisations (CSOs) and beneficiary populations'.[84] Lessons and suggestions from this experience whose relevance extends well beyond the Pilot Programme are:

- Participatory processes have expanded to become mainstreamed into the PPG7 over the past decade.

- The ability of Pilot Programme activities to reach beneficiary populations has also increased over time, as has the breadth of their portfolio.

- Although there has been a wide range of participatory processes, over time civil society has generally gained decision-making power in the programme.

- Effective participatory processes contribute to improved project results.

82   World Bank/PAD (2001).
83   Hall (2000a), p. 102.
84   Abers et al. (2001).

- There is no universal recipe for participation in environmental projects.

- It is critical that appropriate institutional strengthening of CSOs and beneficiary groups be included in project design when they are given significant implementation responsibilities.

- The experience and capacity of government agencies to promote effective participation must also be evaluated and strengthened.[85]

The mid-term review of the Pilot Programme, in turn, has drawn attention to several persisting general implementation issues. After six years, the overall rate of disbursement stood only at around 30 per cent, suggesting poor executing capacity on the part of the government. Perhaps associated with this was the parallel finding that programme administration accounted for more than 40 per cent of total costs, which is excessively high. Thus, accelerating implementation and directing a greater share of its overall resources to grass-roots actions are continuing challenges for the programme. On the more positive side, however, the International Advisory Group (IAG), while recognising that the programme is unlikely to have a significant direct impact on the rate of deforestation, given its limited scale, has concluded that its indirect influence on policy-making for the region has been considerably greater.[86]

Finally, in terms of Bank interventions in Amazonia, more broadly, until very recently the problematic experiences with Carajás, POLONOROESTE, PLANAFLORO and PRODEAGRO had led the Bank to shy away from major new investment initiatives in the region. However, Bank involvement in the Pilot Programme is helping to change this (see the section on new initiatives below) in two important ways: first, by building up the Bank's image in Brazil as an effective partner for sustainable development and, second, by providing valuable lessons that can now be integrated into larger lending operations.

In addition to the Pilot Programme, grant funding for conservation activities in Amazonia has been mobilised by the Bank through the Global Environment Facility (GEF), more specifically the National Biodiversity Project (PROBIO) and the Brazilian Biodiversity Fund Project (FUNBIO), which were jointly approved in April 1996. The basic objective of these two closely interlinked projects (involving total GEF funding of

85   Lisansky and Sprissler (2002).
86   Personal communication from former IAG chairman, Anthony Hall.

US$30 million) is to 'promote and support partnerships among government, non-profit organisations, academic institutions and the private business sector in support of ... efforts to improve Brazil's conservation and sustainable use of biodiversity'. This objective would be achieved through a 'two-pronged' strategy, with the purpose of PROBIO being to 'assist the Government to initiate a programme for the sustainable conservation and use of biodiversity by identifying priority actions; stimulating the development of demonstration subprojects; and disseminating biodiversity information.' The second project would support establishment of a fund (FUNBIO), initially within the Getulio Vargas Foundation, to administer long-term grants to the private sector for the same objective.[87] The overall rationale for GEF support was Brazil's status as 'probably the most biodiversity-rich country in the world'.[88]

PROBIO, which co-finances Brazil's National Biodiversity Programme (PRONABIO) and is coordinated by the Ministry of Environment and FUNBIO has already produced notable results. These include undertaking a series of biome-level workshops to identify priority areas for biodiversity conservation in Amazonia, the Atlantic Forest, the savanna grass and scrublands (*cerrado*), Pantanal wetlands, xerophitic scrublands and dry forest (or *caatinga*) and the continental shelf.[89] A landmark publication by five Brazilian NGOs based on the biome workshop for Amazonia, held in Amapá in 1999, has recently been published.[90] 'Model

---

87 These projects, which are national in scope, were complementary to the Bank-supported National Environment Project that contained specific components for consolidation of federal conservation units and protection of fragile ecosystems, especially the Atlantic Forest, the coastal zone (see Ab' Saber, 2001) and the Pantanal wetlands (see Redwood, 2000; Swarts 2000).

88 More specifically, the project document noted: '... (w)ith more than 50,000 species of vascular plants (one-fifth of the world total), Brazil is the most plant-rich country, and areas such as the Atlantic Forest and western Amazon have been designated as biodiversity "hot spots" because of their floral diversity. One in eleven of all world mammals (394 species) are found in Brazil, together with one in six of all world birds (1,576), one in fifteen of all reptiles (468) and one in eight of all amphibians (502). Many of these species are unique to Brazil, with 68 endemic mammals, 191 endemic birds, 172 endemic reptiles, and 294 endemic amphibians' (World Bank/GEF, 1996, p. 4).

89 Biome-specific publications resulting from this process include Ribeiro, Lazarini da Fonseca and Sousa-Silva (eds.) (2001) on the *cerrado* and Ministério do Meio Ambiente (2002) on the coastal zone.

90 Capobianco et al. (2001, 2002).

biodiversity' projects in several parts of Amazonia are also being support-ed. FUNBIO, in turn, has funded private conservation projects, including assistance to communities within an extractive reserve (Pará), sustainable fisheries and forest management (Amazonas) and small productive enter-prises (Maranhão, Pará and Tocantins).

The other major focus of Bank activity in the late 1990s has been for-est fire management. During February/March 1998, large-scale wildfires burned some 40,000 square kilometres in the northern Amazonian state of Roraima, including more than 9,000 square kilometres of closed-canopy forest and extensive areas of savanna, agricultural fields and indian re-serves. It was feared that similarly damaging fires could occur during the June/July 1998 annual dry season throughout the southern part of Amazonia in an extensive zone nicknamed the 'Deforestation Arc' due to the abundance of highly flammable vegetation, exacerbated by the in-creasing extent of cleared, logged and previously burned (for agricultural/ ranching activities) areas.[91]

In response to this potential emergency, the Bank was requested to provide assistance to the federal (IBAMA), state and municipal govern-ments and local communities through a new Programme for Prevention and Control of Forest Fires in the Deforestation Arc in the Amazon (PROARCO), involving a loan of US$15 million, approved in September 1998, and a parallel US$2 million grant through the Pilot Programme (more specifically, its Fire and Deforestation Control Project — PRODESQUE).[92] PROARCO includes components for risk assessment and monitoring of critical areas, forest fire prevention and forest fire sup-pression. As the seasonal fires in southern Amazonia in mid-1998 proved not to be as extensive and damaging as originally feared, most of the re-sources under these two projects have been dedicated to monitoring, and with the help of many municipal governments and GTA, assisting local

91   See Nepstad, et al. (1999) for a more detailed discussion of the origins, impacts and alternatives to the use of fire for agricultural and ranching purposes in Amazonia. For more journalistic accounts of the role of fire, deforestation and land conflicts in the region, as associated with the highly publicised assassination of the rubber tapper and environmentalist Chico Mendes a decade earlier that focused international attention on the plight of the Brazilian rain forests and strongly contributed to creation of the Pilot Programme, see Revkin (1990) and Shoumatoff (1990).

92   Funds from the (first) National Environment Project were also reallocated to support emergency fire fighting activities in Amazonia while PROARCO and PRODESQUE were under preparation.

communities with fire prevention activities. These initiatives have been further supported through another PPG7 project for Amazon fire prevention, mobilisation and training (PROTEGER). The first PROTEGER project has trained over 13,000 people in more than 300 municipalities in Amazonia in fire prevention and control.[93] According to one recent assessment by a group of scientists, PROARCO's implementation in 2000 was associated with a two- to four-fold reduction in the number of fires registered by satellite images from 1999 to 2000 throughout most of the heavily settled eastern and southern portion of Amazonia.[94]

Starting the New Millennium: Towards the Sustainable Development of Amazonia

As the new millennium begins, the Bank together with its growing array of partners in government, the private sector and civil society, is stepping up its work on sustainable development in Amazonia through a number of projects that are currently under preparation, as well as through new analytical work on land use and deforestation, and support to the federal government on assessing the environmental impacts of proposed major regional infrastructure improvements. Since the mid-1990s, moreover, Bank concern with sustainable development in Amazonia, and Brazil more generally, has become increasingly explicit in its periodic Country Assistance Strategies.[95]

Country Assistance Strategies

Environment, together with supporting structural reforms, direct poverty reduction, infrastructure and portfolio management, was already one of the key elements in the Country Assistance Strategy (CAS) presented to the Bank's Board in June 1995. At that time, it was observed that 'development of the Amazon region and associated high rates of deforestation have attracted intense international attention because of the irreversible loss of biodiversity and its potential impact on global warming'. The 1995

---

93 Personal communication from Josef Leitmann, present Bank coordinator of the Pilot Programme.
94 Nepstad et al. (2002).
95 The CAS, which is normally redrafted every three years or so, reflects the Bank's agreement with national governments as to the priorities for Bank assistance over a multi-year time horizon. Increasingly, these strategies also involve extensive public consultations in the countries in question (see Bain and Gacitua-Mario, 1999; Senderowitsch and Cesilini, 2000).

CAS affirmed that 'in two innovative projects at the Amazon frontier, economic and ecological zoning, coupled with intensification of agriculture and agro-forestry development in areas zoned for development, are providing important first steps to helping reduce deforestation in Rondônia and Mato Grosso states'. It also mentioned the Pilot Programme and the two GEF biodiversity projects and that, '(i)n the Amazonian states of Mato Grosso and Rondônia, the Bank has strengthened projects by ensuring that NGOs have an active role in promoting environmental reforms'.[96]

The next CAS for Brazil, presented in June 1997, went further by focusing on the 'two basic objectives' of sustainable development and social development, understanding the former to include 'the structural fiscal fundamentals of stabilisation, measures to encourage private sector development, and measures to improve environmental sustainability, including water resource management'.[97] With respect to environmental sustainability, the 1997 CAS noted that Bank assistance has 'three overarching environmental objectives: (a) the protection and conservation of priority ecosystems; (b) the more efficient use and sustainable management of natural resources, such as water, forests and land; and (c) a renewed emphasis on the more effective management of pollution'.[98] It also affirmed 'the need to develop a model of environmentally sustainable development that balances the State's interests in growth with the conservation aspect of projects is increasingly apparent'.[99]

The current CAS, presented to the Bank's Board of Directors in March 2000,[100] stresses that '(e)nvironmental management needs to become an integral part of Brazil's overall development strategy, focusing in particular on those policies that help reduce poverty and contribute to, or are compatible with, renewed economic growth'.[101] This general concern is

---

96   World Bank/CAS (1995), p. 20.

97   World Bank/CAS (1997), p. 29.

98   For the Bank's assessment of urban-industrial pollution problems and priorities in Brazil, see World Bank (1998).

99   World Bank/CAS (1997), p. 23.

100   A series of 'policy notes', including one on environment and natural resource management, have been prepared by Bank staff for discussion with the new federal administration that took office in January 2003. They will also serve as important inputs for the next CAS.

101   World Bank/CAS (2000), p. ii. The CAS goes on to state: 'This includes the effective management of Brazil's natural resources and its pollution problems, which are severe in many urban areas, and the protection of important ecosystems. Important ecosystems include Brazil's rain forests, which are the largest repository of biodiversity in the world.'

further elaborated in a section on environment and natural resource management, which gives special attention to persisting deforestation. Here it is noted that deforestation rates in Amazonia fell in the early 1990s, rose sharply in 1995, fell again in 1996–97 and increased in 1998, with the highest rates occurring in the 'Deforestation Arc' in Rondônia, Mato Grosso and Pará. According to the 2000 CAS:

> … (d)eforestation is the result of a complex interplay of forces involving farming, ranching, logging, mining and others, and is closely related to economic factors, including inflation, capital availability and land prices. Solutions are equally complex and require a combination of protection of priority ecosystems with balanced measures to reduce poverty and develop sustainable alternatives for increasing the income of the local population. The government is experimenting with such alternatives through its Rain Forest Pilot Programme, in which the Bank plays a key coordination and secretariat role. Interest in the conservation of some of the country's environmental assets reaches beyond Brazil as these provide international externalities (e.g., biodiversity, carbon sequestration).[102]

New and Ongoing Evaluation and Analytical Work

One recent assessment, undertaken by the OED as part of its review of experience under the Bank's current forest strategy (adopted in 1991), includes a case study on Brazil[103] that weighs the delicate balance between conservation and development in the forest sector. Among its findings (again, some of which have applicability well beyond Brazil) are:

- The Bank's 1991 forest strategy gave particular attention to deforestation in the Amazon for reasons of global environment.

- Some of the pressures and causes of the loss of forest cover in Amazonia are the same as those encountered earlier in the Atlantic Forest, which is severely depleted and therefore currently in more urgent need of attention.

---

102 World Bank/CAS (2000), pp. 21–2.

103 Similar case studies were carried out in Cameroon, China, Costa Rica, India and Indonesia. For the overall results of this review see World Bank/OED (2000a).

- The synergistic relationship between plantation forestry and protection of natural forests has been ignored by Bank operations in Brazil.

- Plantation forests serve many of the same functions as natural forests, particularly with respect to carbon sequestration, soil and moisture conservation and other environmental services. But they are not efficient in other functions such as biodiversity conservation, cultural diversity and ethno-ecological knowledge (especially of traditional forest peoples).

- Although plantations are poorer in biodiversity, by relieving pressure on native forests, they can help conserve biodiversity.

- Brazil has vast tracts of degraded forest land [including in Amazonia] which are prime candidates for reforestation.

- The plantation sector in Brazil is among the most advanced in the world in research and technology and has a progressive, well-established private sector that is ready to address some of the problems in the natural forests.

- It may be possible, through improved policies and strategies, to slow the rate of deforestation in the Amazon and the consequent loss of livelihoods for the poor and indigenous peoples, but because selectivity, priorities and a focus on realistic targets for implementation are of utmost importance in conservation efforts, deforestation cannot be stopped altogether.

- The World Bank/WWF alliance [see below] poses a variety of problems. As currently conceived, it is unlikely to be a viable strategy for the protected areas by itself. But it can become an important part of an integrated land use strategy.

- A far more integrated strategy toward forest sector management is essential both in Brazil and in the Bank's interventions in Brazil.[104]

A second important recent study, carried out jointly with IMAZON, a prominent Brazilian NGO, focuses on constraints and opportunities for rural development in Amazonia. Based on rainfall and historical land-use patterns, this study concludes that there are severe natural (especially climate) limitations to the expansion of agricultural and ranching activities in

104 World Bank/OED (2000b), pp. 4–6.

vast areas within Legal Amazonia. More precisely, it is argued that the region can sustainably support such activities only in the roughly 17 per cent of its total area ('dry Amazonia') characterised by 'moderate' rainfall of under 1,800 mm/year. The most appropriate land-use in the rest of the region would be sustainable forest management. However, the study argues, if market forces are not controlled, predatory logging and extensive cattle ranching activities would tend to continue to dominate future land use which, because of its lack of ecological sustainability, would tend to lead to the same 'boom-bust' cycle typical of earlier agricultural frontier occupation elsewhere in Amazonia and other parts of Brazil.[105]

To avoid this undesirable cycle, the study suggests use of a set of 'economic and strategic' instruments, including charging stumpage fees for timber of 'predatory origin', payment for environmental services (including biodiversity conservation and carbon sequestration), and adopting incentives for sustainable forest management by the private sector.[106] The study likewise recommends expansion of the existing system of National Forests under federal government control (known as FLONAs in Brazil), which is considered to be, 'the most promising way to stabilise the logging sector and promote forest management in the new economic frontiers in the region'. Finally, it suggests that a sustainable development policy for Amazonia should place strong emphasis on intensive agriculture in those areas, roughly one-sixth of the total, which are environmentally suitable, and forest management in the remainder which is not suitable for agriculture. The recent establishment of a National Forest Programme by the Ministry of Environment,[107] which is seeking Bank financial and technical support for its implementation, is seen as an important step in this direction.[108]

---

105 Schneider et al. (2000). This is similar to the phenomenon labelled the 'hollow frontier' by geographer Preston James to describe the frontier settlement process in central Brazil in the 1950s and '60s. See James (1969); Redwood (1972); and Sawyer (1984).

106 Another potentially useful instrument consists of the value-added tax rebates to municipal governments for conservation and other environmental purposes (commonly referred to in Brazil as 'ICMS ecológico'); which have already been adopted in several Brazilian states, especially Paraná and Minas Gerais. See May et al. (2002) for details.

107 For the details of this programme, see Ministério do Meio Ambiente (2001b). See also Verissimo et al. (2002) on areas suitable for the establishment of new national forests in Amazonia and May and Veiga Neto (2000) on the critical issue of forest certification in the region.

108 Schneider et al. (2000, 2002), pp. vii-viii.

Other recent research by Kenneth Chomitz and Timothy Thomas of the Bank's Development Economics Department has focused on geographical patterns of land-use and land intensity in Amazonia. Echoing some of the results of the study by Schneider et al., cited immediately above, their principal findings include the following:

- Most agricultural land in the region yields little agricultural value. Nearly 90 per cent of agricultural land is in pasture (40 per cent stocking less than 0.5 cattle/hectare), abandoned, or in long fallow.

- Land distribution is highly skewed. Half of Amazonian farmland is located in the one per cent of properties that contain more than 2000 hectares.

- The wetter areas of Amazonia are inhospitable for agriculture. Ownership conversion rates and stocking rates decline with increasing rainfall (other things being equal).

- But the frontier is not hollow. Land-use has intensified over time in drier areas.[109]

Building directly on earlier research the Bank, together with the Amazonian Secretariat of the Ministry of Environment and the Pilot Programme, is also undertaking new analytical work on the agents and economic incentives driving deforestation in the region.[110] Preliminary results of this study suggest that the key factor explaining much of the deforestation that has occurred in the region in recent years is the profitability of cattle-raising.[111] This implies that deforestation results in clear eco-

---

109 Chomitz and Thomas (2001).
110 See Margulis (2001) for the basic design of this study and Faminow (1998) and Ministério do Meio Ambiente (2001a) for other recent non-Bank analyses of this important subject.
111 Chomitz, Thomas and Arima (forthcoming) in parallel research, find, for example, that within the Deforestation Arc, there is a very high correlation between the proportion of area deforested and the farmgate price of beef, suggesting that land value follows a similar gradient. As a result, they argue, '... (t)his suggests that a strategy of trading legal forest reserve obligations (i.e., the obligation to keep 80 per cent of each individual property under forest) could be effective in stabilising the frontier if public lands beyond the settlement frontier were placed in national forests. Noncompliant farmers (with less than 80 per cent forest) near towns could purchase forest reserve rights from a periphery of lower value land with remaining cover. Frontier stabilisation would benefit incumbent landholders, contributing to political sustainability' (Personal communication from Ken Chomitz).

nomic benefits, sometimes substantial, from a private standpoint (together with environmental costs from a social and global perspective) that are based on productive, rather than speculative activity. The agents that appropriate these benefits are loggers and intermediaries, who convert native forest into pasture, together with the ranchers themselves who often arrive later.[112]

All of this research has fed into a 'policy note' for the new federal administration of Luis Inácio 'Lula' da Silva on the subject of development and conservation choices for Brazilian forests, including the Mata Atlântica and *cerrado*, as well as Amazon forests. The main messages of this note highlight the need to:

- Develop a 'shared Brazilian vision' of the future of each forest region (or major biome) and to manage it accordingly.[113] Keep open options and stay clear of the threshold of irreversibility.

- Get ahead of the frontier by limiting open access to primary forests.

- Make standing forest more valuable by promoting its sustainable use, particularly by poor local communities.

- Promote and consolidate sustainable growth where the frontier has already passed.[114]

Much of the Bank's ongoing and future operational work in Amazonia (see the next section) is geared towards helping the Brazilian government implement these recommendations. Finally, the Bank is currently providing assistance to the Ministry of Environment, the Ministry of Planning and the National Economic and Social Development Bank (BNDES) regarding assessment of the environmental impacts of the proposed large-scale infra-

---

112 Personal communication from Sergio Margulis. He also notes that this research suggests that: (i) loggers are not the principal 'villains' of the story as is often alleged; (ii) land speculation is not a factor of primordial importance; (iii) the expansion of soybean and other grains in the region are not significant threats to the native forest; (iv) government incentives and subsidised credit can only explain a small share of the overall deforestation in the past, and today are of very little relevance; (v) because of the different occupation histories of different parts of the region, deforestation control policies have to take these local specificities into account; and (vi) accordingly, it is necessary to determine where to intervene and with which specific economic actors.

113 This strategy has been widely discussed among government ministries and agencies at federal, state and municipal levels, as well as with regional and national civil society representatives in Brazil.

114 Diewald (2002).

structure investments (roads, energy, waterways, etc.) that are included in the federal government's multi-year investment plan, *Avança Brasil*.

New Lending and Grant Operations under Preparation

Several new Bank-supported projects in Amazonia are presently at different stages of preparation, including one based on an innovative partnership between the GEF, the Pilot Programme,[115] a bilateral donor (KFW of Germany) and key international (WWF) and national (Brasil Connects) NGOs, to strengthen the protected area system in the region. This operation, better known as ARPA (for the Amazon Region Protected Areas Project), is also a major element in the World Bank/World Wildlife Fund (WWF) alliance that is seeking to place under formal protection ten per cent of the world's major forest biomes.[116] The project represents the first four-year segment of a three-phase programme that would place 18 million hectares in new protected areas, consolidate seven million hectares of existing protected areas, set up an endowment fund for protected areas and establish a biodiversity monitoring and evaluation system at both the individual protected area and broader regional levels. ARPA was approved by the Bank's Board of Directors in August 2002 and has GEF funding of US$30 million.[117]

A second project currently under preparation is for 'sustainable communities' in Amapá.[118] This would be the first stand-alone Bank operation

---

115   Pilot Programme funding would come from three existing projects, for Ecological Corridors, Extractive Reserves and Natural Resources Policy, respectively.

116   This alliance was formally established in April 1998 as a joint response to the continued depletion of the world's forest biodiversity and of forest-based goods and services essential for sustainable development. Its mission is to work with governments, the private sector and civil society to achieve three targets by 2005: (i) 50 million hectares of new forest protected areas; (ii) a comparable area of existing but highly threatened forest protected areas secured under effective management; and (iii) 200 million hectares of production forests under independently certified sustainable management. In Brazil, specifically, President Cardoso, in a speech on 28 April 1998, formally committed his government to protecting an additional 25 million hectares of Amazon rain forest (World Bank/WWF, 2000). The proposed ARPA project would make a major contribution toward this commitment.

117   World Bank/PAD (2002).

118   In May 2002, the Inter-American Development Bank approved a US$64.8 million loan to support sustainable development in the Amazonian state of Acre and is supporting eco-tourism activities in the region through the PROECO-TUR programme. The IDB has been previously involved in Acre through the Porto Velho-Rio Branco Highway Project and the associated Environmental and Indigenous Communities Protection Project (PMACI).

in this state. The project would aim to reduce poverty and promote sustainable rural development through economic efficiency, social equity and environmental conservation by financing a combination of demand-driven and targeted community subprojects.[119] Similarly the Bank has been asked to help fund a rural poverty reduction project, which would contain important aspects of sustainable natural resource management, in the state of Tocantins, thus extending to the environmentally sensitive Amazon region and expanding the decentralised approach to rural poverty alleviation that has been successfully developed over the past decade in north-east Brazil.[120] Preparation of this project is being carefully coordinated with that of another Bank operation for rural infrastructure improvements in that state.[121] These projects are both part of a broader Bank assistance strategy for Tocantins, which has applicability to other parts of Amazonia as well and seeks to: (i) establish decentralised, participatory and multi-sector planning processes for the improved delivery of public services; (ii) continue the agro-ecological zoning of the state and ensure its effective implementation; and (iii) promote environmentally, socially and economically sustainable activities to reduce poverty.[122]

Looking Ahead: Challenges for the Future

The World Bank's approach to development in the Brazilian Amazon region has evolved very significantly since the 1970s, both in terms of substance (from mining, transport infrastructure and 'integrated' regional development to rural poverty reduction, sustainable forest management and biodiversity conservation) and process (from top-down, technocratic operations through the federal government to demand-driven, decentralised projects with state and municipal governments involving ever-growing

119 World Bank/PCD (2002).
120 World Bank/PAD, draft (2001). A new generation of these north-east rural poverty reduction projects was approved in 2001–02 for the states of Bahia, Ceará, Pernambuco, Piauí and Sergipe, and similar operations are under advanced preparation for Alagoas, Minas Gerais, Rio Grande do Norte, Paraíba and Maranhão for Bank Board presentation in the second half of 2002 and 2003. For a recent independent evaluation of the north-east rural poverty reduction programme, see Van Zyl et al. (2000).
121 This was not the case, for example, with the earlier rural poverty and highway projects in the neighbouring state of Maranhão, both of which were approved in the mid-1990s.
122 Von Amsberg (2002).

participation on the part of civil society and other local stakeholders). This, of course, reflects the ways in which the Bank's, and its clients', approaches to poverty reduction and economic development have changed more generally over this period. It also took place in the general context of democratisation, empowerment of civil society and increasing fiscal and administrative decentralisation in Brazil.

In the case of Amazonia, moreover, it also reflects much greater knowledge and understanding, generated jointly with an increasingly broad array of local and other partners, about the environmental, social, institutional and political, as well as economic, realities and complexities of the region and of the sustainable development opportunities and constraints it faces. In this regard, the need to develop and/or consolidate strategic alliances, such as that being formed to support the ARPA project, and public-private partnerships more generally, in the region, as well as to continue to raise public opinion in Brazil, which has risen very significantly over the past decade, about the importance of sustainable development in Amazonia, cannot be overstressed.

In summary, the Bank has come a long way in its approaches to Amazonia since the 1970s. However, a number of key challenges remain, which the Bank can only effectively meet in close collaboration with local, regional and national stakeholders and development partners in both the public and private sectors. Among these challenges, which also represent significant opportunities, are the following:

- Both in Brazil and the Bank, there is a need to ensure greater coordination and coherence among its various current and future initiatives in the region. This includes learning and absorbing the lessons of experience of past and ongoing lending and grant operations, such as Carajás, POLONOROESTE, PLANAFLORO, PRODEAGRO, the Rain Forest Pilot Programme and others, and guaranteeing that future Bank, GEF and Pilot Programme projects are: (i) fully informed by and respond to the strategic directions and priorities set out in the Bank's analytical work; (ii) that their design fully considers the (positive and negative) experience of earlier projects in the region (and, as applicable, elsewhere); and (iii) that they are truly complementary such that the whole will, it is to be hoped, be greater than the sum of the parts.

- Both in Brazil and the Bank also, there is a persisting need to more fully integrate environmental and social with economic development concerns in Amazonia at the local, state, regional and federal levels.[123]

- Similarly, there is a need to elaborate a single (multi-stakeholder) sustainable development strategy for the region as a whole, ideally followed by similar strategies for each of its constituent states.[124] These should take into account ecological, institutional and political constraints and include, in a consistent and coordinated way, physical infrastructure and environmental and social development priorities both in rural and urban areas.[125]

- With respect to rural development, the approach outlined by Schneider et al. (2000, 2002) of intensifying agriculture and ranching activities in those areas where they can be ecologically and economically sustainable and focusing on sustainable forest management and biodiversity conservation in the rest appears to be a very appropriate starting point.

- In terms of urban development, it should not be forgotten that 70 per cent of the region's population resides in cities and towns, which have serious environmental and public health problems associated in part with significant deficits in basic sanitation services.[126] This

123 At the federal government level, for example, there is a need for greater coordination on regional strategy between the Ministry of Planning and Budget, which is responsible for national development planning (such as *Avança Brasil,* which includes important infrastructure investments in the region), the Ministry of Regional Integration, which is responsible for regional development policy in Amazonia, the Ministry of Environment, whose Secretariat for Amazonia coordinates the Pilot Programme, and other environment-related initiatives in the region and, ultimately, the Ministry of Finance, which controls fiscal policy.

124 Also, given their large territorial extensions, for specific sub-regions within states. Agro-ecological zoning, if carried out as both a technical and political process that involves all of the major (local and extra-local) stakeholder groups can, indeed, be a useful tool in this regard.

125 The earlier *Projeto Áridas* experience in north-east Brazil is a good model for this. After preparation of a regional sustainable development strategy, a number of the north-eastern states followed up with specific sustainable development strategies of their own.

126 A 28 March 2002 newspaper article in Belém, for example, citing recent data from the Brazilian Institute of Geography and Statistics (IBGE), highlighted the fact that Amazonia had the worst indicators of all the Brazilian regions in terms of the share of its residents having access to treated water, domestic sewage connections and storm drainage.

issue has been largely neglected by the Bank in the past, but needs to be an essential element in any sustainable development strategy for the region. Understandably, it is a priority for many state and local officials in Amazonia.

- The use of a number of emerging instruments of Bank assistance should be pursued in Amazonia, including support for sustainable forest management with independent certification in areas not formally designated as critical natural habitats (which would be eligible for Bank support under the proposed revised forest policy).[127] In addition are GEF funding for integrated silvo-pastoral ecosystem management[128] and payment for environmental services,[129] especially carbon sequestration, as in the proposed Plantar Project in Minas Gerais, under the recently established Prototype Carbon Fund.[130]

- Empowering local communities, building local social capital and strengthening local governance are also critical. However, excessive decentralisation in frontier areas can be risky as there is often a conflict between local short-term economic and associated political interests and broader long-term sustainable development objectives. Here, a delicate balance needs to be struck, with more effective central and state government intervention (as in the enforcement of regulations on deforestation, for example) being required on the active frontier until local institutions and incentives for more sustainable use and management of natural resources are in place.

- Finally, many of the problems, challenges and opportunities faced in the Brazilian Amazon region are by no means unique to Brazil. Thus,

127 The Bank's revised forest strategy and associated policy (see World Bank, draft, 2002) are expected to be formally considered by its Board of Directions later this year after a period of public consultation.

128 See World Bank/GEF/PAD (2002) for an innovative project of this sort in Colombia, Costa Rica and Nicaragua.

129 For an innovative recent Bank/GEF operation that involves payment for environmental services, see World Bank/PAD, Costa Rica (2000). See also Fearnside (1998; 1999; 2000).

130 On the Plantar Project, which involves payments for carbon sequestration in eucalyptus plantations (in substitution of native forest) to produce charcoal for the metallurgical industry in Minas Gerais, see World Bank/PCF/PAD (2002), and on the Prototype Carbon Fund, more generally, see World Bank/PCF (2001). The Plantar approach would also be directly applicable for the pig iron industries in the Carajás corridor.

there is also a need (through a multi-stakeholder process) to elaborate a broader multi-country sustainable development strategy for the Amazon Basin and to greatly expand the exchange of knowledge and experience among the countries that compose it. The permanent re-location to Brasília of the Secretariat of the Amazon Cooperation Treaty offers an excellent opportunity to begin to move forward on this with (if requested) support from the Bank, other development institutions and interested non-governmental organisations, as well as the member governments themselves.[131]

131 A Bank-supported meeting on sustainable development of the broader Amazon region with representatives of six of the eight Amazon Basin countries, hosted by President Fernando Henrique Cardoso in Brasília on 24–25 January 2002, made some of the same recommendations.

6

Political Reforms and Sustainability in the Bolivian Amazon: Decentralisation, *Participación Popular* and the Land Distribution Act

Martina Neuburger

Introduction

The concept of sustainability has been a central term in the international discussion of suitable development strategies for developing countries for many years. Conceiving and taking tangible steps for the realisation of the concept has hitherto posed the biggest problem. Due to difficulties in the planning process that emerged during the early phase of implementation, many development cooperation organisations have since begun to support the institutions involved in the planning process instead of directly aiding target groups such as peasants, women and indigenous peoples.

As a country in which great efforts are made towards sustainable development, Bolivia has received considerable international attention over the last few years.[1] Largely on this account, Bolivia is repeatedly mentioned as an example of good governance. Numerous analyses show that sustainability is the most basic concept in the integration of institutional reforms in Bolivia, and its most important fundamental principles such as participation and preservation of resources are carried over into practical planning processes as well as politics. However, scientific studies rarely investigate whether and how these undoubtedly notable reforms are executed at the local and regional level and what effects they have on the socio-economic framework.

It is with this very question that the present chapter will concern itself. The analysis will concentrate on the Bolivian Amazon region, essentially the departments of Beni and Pando, where the realisation of reforms is rendered difficult by the extremely weak presence of the State. The concept of new institutional economics is especially appropriate for this examination, as the interplay of formal and informal institutions will take

1   Nohlen (2001); Birle (1996); van Dijck (1998).

pride of place in the analysis. Here, the term 'institutions' includes not only all known formal rules (laws, regulations, etc.) but also all social value systems (traditions, habits, etc.) that determine the actions of individuals.[2] New institutional economics attempts to attribute the problems of development in the south to the weakness or incompatibility of different institutions.[3] Currently, the load-carrying capacity of this concept is being intensely and controversially discussed in the field of geographical development research.[4]

This analysis of current political reforms in Bolivia is intended to contribute to the recent discussion. For this purpose, the author will first of all outline the central elements of the political reforms in Bolivia. The political frameworks are especially important here, as the political surroundings throw light on the possible successes of implementation. After a brief introduction to the region under study, the Bolivian Amazon, the author will move on to the analysis of the effects of several reforms within the local and the regional contexts.

Political Reforms in Bolivia — Hollow Words or Drastic Change?

On the international stage, Bolivia has been known for its extremely unstable political conditions on the one hand and, on the other, for the great poverty that prevails in most regions of the country. Well into the 1990s, Bolivia had one of the highest indices of poverty and illiteracy and the lowest life expectancy in Latin America. Even though these indicators have improved within the last few years, Bolivia (along with Honduras) still comes last in the Latin American Human Development Index (HDI) ranking. Throughout the world, only the nations of Africa come lower down the scale that Bolivia.[5]

Moreover, the political climate for reform has been unfavourable. Political instability has prevailed since the Revolution of 1953 that manifested itself in the quick change of governments and presidents. From 1964 to the 1980s, a military dictatorship ruled in Bolivia. Over the decades, Bolivian politics has thus moved in circles between the interests of the political parties, the trade unions and the indigenous organisations. Confrontations between the leftist trade unions (in particular the largest,

2   Sen (2000); Dreze et al. (1995); North (1988; 1992); Mummert (1999).
3   Pritzl (1997).
4   *Geographica Helvetica* (2001).
5   PNUD (1998; 2000; 2002).

the *Central Obrera Boliviana* — COB as the trade union of the mineworkers) and the military, or the respective government, have been frequent. Therefore, speedy implementation of the revolutionary political reforms has been all the more astonishing.

The precondition for this was no doubt a climate of political change in the 1980s.[6] Democratisation in particular, which was supported equally by the military and *guerrilleros*, constituted the indispensable basis for policy reform. At the same time, the most influential political actors were caught up in a deep crisis so that traditional conflicts became less important. Specifically, the majority of miners were laid off due to economic recession and the closure of numerous mines. Thus, the COB lost its political vigour as the largest civil society organisation in Bolivia. Furthermore, the big political parties suffered a severe loss of credibility, as none of them were able to offer effective solutions for the economic crisis and political stagnation. As the political institutions operating in La Paz and maintaining order there for the entire nation lost some of their power, Cochabamba and Santa Cruz de la Sierra became more pivotal because of their economic success, thereby leading them to seek more political autonomy.

As members of a new generation of politicians and as representatives of a new economic policy, presidents such as Paz Estenzoro and Zamora benefited from the political vacuum of the mid-1980s. The reforms carried out since then can be divided into two different types. Essentially, first-generation reforms comprised the economic restructuring of the 1980s, which included economic stabilisation, structural adjustment and other neoliberal measures. Only the second-generation reforms of the 1990s brought about a realignment of the political landscape. While President Gonzalo Sánchez de Lozada retained his predecessors' neo-liberal economic policy, he implemented three large-scale reforms under the label 'Modernisation of the State'. These measures created the basic preconditions for the implementation of sustainable development policies.[7]

In this context, the laws of *Participación Popular* and of *Descentralización* must be mentioned first (*Ley No. 1551* of 20 April 1994 and *Ley No. 1654* of 28 July 1995). The essence of the two laws lies in the decentralisation of political decisions as well as the creation of the right to direct popular co-determination in decision-making processes at the municipal level. For this purpose, municipalities had to be created as new administrative units with their own administrative functions. Previously, only towns with more

6   Eróstegui (1996); Goedeking et al. (2001).
7   República de Bolivia (1997).

than 2,000 inhabitants had their own administrations. These, however, enjoyed a planning role for only their own town. The rest of the country remained under the direct control of central government (Figure 6.1).

Figure 6.1: New Political-Administrative Borders Resulting from Administrative Reform in Bolivia

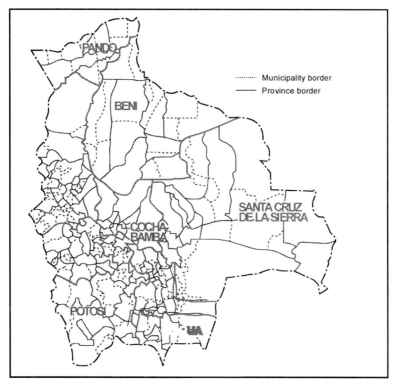

Source: INE (1999) *Atlas estadístico de municipios* (La Paz).

Since that time, these new administrative units have primary responsibility for healthcare, education and infrastructure. Even the public finance system was reformed in order to allow municipalities to come to terms with their new duties. In this context, a change in the allocation of funds by the central government was the most important element at the municipal level. Since 1994, municipalities have received funds according to the size of their populations and not, as happened previously, determined by their tax yields. This has led to an increase in funding for the municipalities of Bolivia's periphery, which until now have been the poorest. For example, allocations for the municipality of San Ignácio in the department of Santa Cruz de la Sierra rose from 2,900 B$ in 1993 to about 1.5 million B$ in 1999.

The offices of mayor and of local council members were created to institutionalise the political decision-making process at the municipal level, where the population directly elects all local officials. Since then, administrators and boards have made decisions concerning the use of municipal funds as well as political objectives for the municipality in general, an unprecedented change in Bolivia's political landscape. Furthermore, the population has the opportunity to control the municipal administration during its legislative period. In this context, the *Ley de Participación Popular* provides for the foundation for *Organizaciones Territoriales de Base* or OTBs. Every OTB represents the population of a certain area as a body of the civil society. Their chairpersons do not necessarily have to be elected democratically. Even traditional leaders such as chiefs, elders or shamans can take the chair of a territorially defined group.

OTBs enjoy the status of a legal entity and can thus take part in political activities. Each OTB of one municipality sends one representative to the *Comités de Vigilancia*. These control committees monitor the municipal administration in all its fields of responsibility, are involved in setting up a municipal development plan and have a say in the annual budgeting. The new legislation was adopted and implemented rather quickly at the local level. By 1998, a *Comité de Vigilancia* had been set up in 192 of the 311 municipalities, and about 13,000 OTBs were integrated within them. Another approximately 2,000 OTBs were still awaiting recognition as legal entities so that they also could bring their concerns to municipal politics.

Dramatic reforms were also realised at the next administrative level. Since the implementation of political reforms, administrative bodies at the level of the department, until then exclusively manned and controlled by the central government, have been subordinated to a department parliament which is elected by the mayors. The newly created body controls the executive of the department (the *Prefecto Departamental* and administration) and approves the regional development plan for the department. The regional development authorities, which had until then controlled this function, were dissolved and have been partially integrated into the departmental administrative machinery.

Thus, the *Ley de Participación Popular* and *Ley de Descentralización* generated progress for the realisation of sustainable development at the formal or institutional level in Bolivia. The participation of the people in the decision-making process was institutionalised as one of the most important preconditions. The shifting of numerous political decisions to the lower administrative levels is an indispensable precondition for locally adapted planning. The land distribution act (also known as the *Ley INRA*) is another body of laws which was enacted to fight one of Bolivia's greatest problems and to establish the necessary new institutionalised frame (*Ley No. 1715* of 18 October 1996). It was designed to help solve conflicts over access to land which had been caused both by increased migration to the cities from the Andes regions in the 1980s, and by colonisation of the *Oriente* rain forest. The old institutions (*Consejo Nacional de Reforma Agraria* — CNRA — and *Instituto Nacional de Colonización* — INC) were dissolved. The INRA (*Instituto Nacional de Reforma Agraria*) was created in their place. It was to take on the responsibilities of both institutions — from land surveys and the installation or renewal of the land register to the implementation of resettlement and agrarian reform projects.

An important legal advance contained in the *Ley INRA* allows for the disposal of land titles granted during the 1953 Agrarian Reform, which had hitherto been illegal. Thus, for the first time a liberalised land market, which existed only informally for many decades, was officially created. At the same time, the creation of collective land titles was meant to protect traditional indigenous forms of land use against the interests of private individuals. For this purpose, *Tierras Comunitarias de Origen* or TCOs were established. The TCO codifies an area as collective property under the jurisdiction of indigenous and other traditional groups.

Political reforms constitute the necessary formal basis for the reshaping of Bolivia's economy and society. The large-scale effects of the law have received international attention and recognition. Thanks to its participatory approaches to the development of anti-poverty strategies, Bolivia (along with only other two Latin American countries, Honduras and Nicaragua) was granted debt forgiveness at the Cologne G8-Summit in 1999.[8] Several governments such as those of the USA, Germany and the Netherlands have increasingly included Bolivia as an aid recipient within the last few years. At the same time, the expansion of NGO activities since the 1990s based on national and international cooperation testifies to a growing commitment within Bolivia's civil society.

8   Klauda (2001).

The Bolivian Amazon — the Effects of Institutional Reform on the Periphery

In the Amazon region of Bolivia, the departments of Beni and Pando, as well as the province of Iturralde in the department of La Paz, are extremely isolated. Road connections with the political and economic centres of the country have only existed for a few years and are passable only during the dry season. Flights between the biggest cities of the region (Trinidad, Cobija, Riberalta and Guayaramerin) and other department capitals are regularly cancelled due to heavy rainfall during the wet season which makes it impossible to land on the grass airstrips. Some airports are not even equipped with radar systems. Accordingly, the presence of the State in this region is weak. This situation is exacerbated by a low population density, scattered settlements and a low urbanisation rate.

However, the Bolivian Amazon region used to be of great importance. At the end of the nineteenth and at the beginning of the twentieth century, along with the neighbouring Brazilian forests, it was among the most dynamic regions of the country.[9] The extraction of natural rubber (*caoutchouc*) formed the basis of this dynamic activity, sustained by approximately 80,000 rubber collectors, controlled by three big 'caoutchouc barons'. Riberalta and Guayaramerin were the urban market centres. However, due to growing competition from the rubber plantations of Southeast Asia, production was declined substantially during the first half of the twentieth century. While the 'caoutchouc barons' left the region altogether, the rubber collectors migrated to the cities or kept the pot boiling under very poor conditions in staging areas in the forest. There, they carried on with extraction as a collective in so-called *comunidades libres* or they kept working in *barracas patronales* for a starvation wage after the area had been taken over by one of the former directors.

A new and at least modest boom as well as a diversification of the regional economy can be observed since the 1980s.[10] Besides rubber, goods such as Brazil nuts, palm hearts, and exportable exotic woods (principally mahogany) have become ever more important in the region. Moreover, extensive beef cattle farming continues to expand in areas near the cities. These developments are bringing about a shift in the regional structure.

The former economic centre of the region, areas of rubber production serving the markets of Riberalta and Guayaramerin, is becoming less im-

---

9   Stoian (2000); Roux (2000).
10   Henkemans (2001); Stoian (2000); Assies (1997).

portant. The southern part of the Beni department, because of its proximity to the booming department of Santa Cruz de la Sierra, as well as the
cities of Cobija and Trinidad, and due to their functions as capitals and
their administrative responsibilities in their departments, are gaining more
and more influence on politics in the Bolivian Amazon region. Moreover,
the border areas are evolving into the most dynamic parts of the region.
Cities such as Cobija and Guayaramerin, located on the international frontier, are becoming more important in cross-border and, above all, informal
commerce. At the same time, within the last few years, Brazilian settlers
have intruded into Bolivian territories along the border with Brazil to occupy and cultivate land, which is virtually inaccessible from the Bolivian
side and unnoticed by the State.

The shift in regional structures has created new migratory movements.
Migration to the cities is steadily on the increase so that the dynamic cities
in particular keep growing. Cobija, capital of the department of Pando,
grew from 8,000 inhabitants in 1986 to approximately 25,000 at the end of
the 1990s. The vast majority of the urban population lives in absolute
poverty on the outskirts without any prospect of acquiring decent living
conditions.[11] Only during the Brazil nut harvest from November to March
does a part of the population find work. Other than that, these marginalised groups cultivate small plots of land for subsistence production close
to their urban neighbourhoods. Except for informal commerce, even the
urban economy offers only few job opportunities that are accessible to the
formerly rural and often illiterate population.

It is within this regional context that the political reforms implemented by the government in the distant La Paz must be surveyed. As in all
other departments, the regional development authorities, which had formerly been appointed by the government in Beni and Pando, were dissolved and their personnel integrated into the new department administrations. The continuity in personnel, however, has created reluctance on
the part of the new administration to accept the control function of the
department parliaments. Moreover, the employees often show greater loy-
alty to the central government.[12]

Decentralisation measures brought about important changes in the
daily political life at the local level. Prior to the commencement of the
Participacion Popular law, there were only 12 cities with their own administrations in the Bolivian Amazon region. The remaining areas were con-

11   Henkemans (2001).
12   Urenda Diaz (1998).

trolled by a central government. It is likely that only a few of its members
have ever been to the Amazon region. Practically overnight and thanks to
the administrative reform, 36 municipalities came into existence in this region. They received political autonomy and thus the right to administer
their own territory and manage the municipal finances. In most cases,
however, the new administrations were not prepared for these extensive
responsibilities. Small rural municipalities in particular still have difficulty
in fulfilling their obligations.

**Figure 6.2: Human Resources in Municipal Administrations of the
Bolivian Amazon**

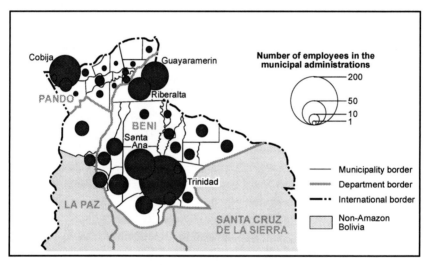

Source: Ministerio de Hacienda (1998) *Primer censo de gobiernos municipales* (La Paz).
Neuberger (2002)

One of the greatest obstacles is the lack of capable human resources, both
in numbers and qualifications (Figure 6.2). In some municipalities of
Pando department in particular, the public administration has only one
employee, presumably the mayor himself. With the exception of the municipalities of the department capitals, the administrative machinery hardly ever consists of more than ten employees. Lack of professional qualifications is also a common and almost insurmountable problem. The educational infrastructure in these settlements with several hundred families at
the most is extremely precarious and is just good enough to teach the population to read and write. At the same time, it is virtually impossible to re-

cruit qualified personnel from other municipalities or even departments. Qualified personnel from the big cities only rarely agree to move to such rural areas for professional reasons. Moreover, due to the former political practice, only a few municipalities have experience in the fields of management and planning. For a couple of years now, the central government has been offering schooling for administration employees in the hope of alleviating this problem.

The lack of human resources is especially acute at the moment because, as decentralisation measures and new participation opportunities take effect, central importance is given to the municipal administration. Equipped with a considerably higher budget, the main responsibility of the municipalities is the establishment and implementation of a local development plan, or *Plano de Desarrollo Municipal*. These plans codify development targets for the municipality over a few years. Only a few municipalities can properly perform this task. Due to the personnel situation, it is not surprising that most Amazon municipalities do not set up such a *Plano de Desarrollo Municipal*, let alone produce details in *Planos Directores*, *Planos de Manejo de Áreas Forestales*, and other plans (Figure 6.3).

Figure 6.3: Municipal Development Plans and OTBs in the Bolivian Amazon

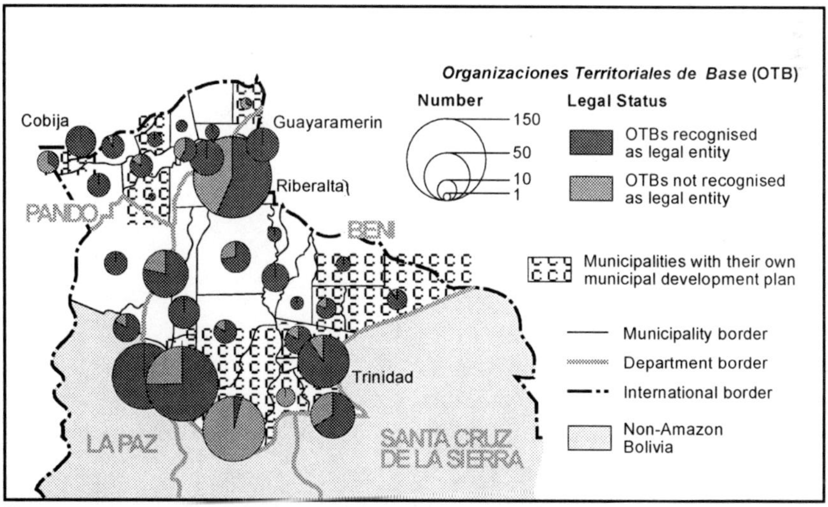

Source: Ministerio de Hacienda (1998) *Primer censo de gobiernos municipales* (La Paz). Neuberger (2002).

Neither is civil society prepared for its new participation opportunities. The population would have to join forces in *Organizaciones Territoriales de Base* (OTBs), as mentioned above, to take full advantage of their monitoring function within the municipal planning process. Although the UN suggests that the Bolivian population enjoys a high degree of organisation in general, this probably refers to the long-standing activities of trade unions in the highlands. With a population density of about four people per square kilometre in the Bolivian Amazon, the great distances between settlements make the setting up of OTBs difficult (Figure 6.3). Moreover, indigenous settlement areas often stretch across several municipality borders, so in many cases an OTB turns out to be an unsuitable instrument for the representation of the political interests of indigenous groups. At the same time, local elites often use their influence during the foundation of an OTB by standing up as founders themselves and recruiting their clientele to represent their interests without restrictions.

Over the last few years, the founding of OTBs has been increasingly supported by NGOs operating in the region — regional, national and international. Thus, an uneven spatial distribution of OTBs with the key aspects of their activities away from the department capitals has been created. This phenomenon can be explained by the preference of NGOs to locate in regions attracting national or international attention such as municipalities which own parts of national parks. However, the important functions of NGOs in the democratisation process and the shaping of political ideas must be viewed in the light of the fact that half of all NGOs are under non-Bolivian control and that the vast majority of the NGOs are not based in an Amazon department. In many cases, the cities of Santa Cruz de la Sierra or even La Paz serve as hubs of international activity. Thus, they can have an influence on local events as non-place-based-actors. In this case, as with many NGOs worldwide, their democratic legitimacy is questionable.

In spite of the relatively large number of OTBs working in the Bolivian Amazon, popular participation is still not taking place in many municipalities. On the one hand, many OTBs could not receive the status of a legal entity which grants them access to the *Comités de Vigilancia*. Due to the very high proportion of unrecognised OTBs, one must assume that their acknowledgement is not politically wanted and is thus delayed. On the other hand *Comités de Vigilancia*, the actual control bodies, have so far been founded in only 13 municipalities. An institutionalised form of participation is thus impossible.

The distortion of political structures reflected in the abuse of participatory instruments is well-documented by the conflicts over resources relating to the implementation of the *Ley INRA*. In this context, the introduction of collective land titles (*Tierras Comunitarias de Origen* or TCOs) is especially important for the Amazon. Indigenous groups of the Bolivian *Oriente* established this principle only after a long political struggle by founding the politically powerful umbrella organisation *Confederación Indígena del Oriente Boliviano* (CIDOB) in 1982 and though numerous spectacular campaigns. Among these, the march on La Paz in 1990 was probably the most sensational. They saw their rights to their own living space endangered by settlers who had invaded their territories from the highlands since the 1970s. With the adoption of the *Ley INRA* in 1996, indigenous groups finally gained legal protection for their settlements. A major concession for the extensive use of forests by these indigenous groups is that the collective land titles may exceed 250 hectares, the size of individual landed property as defined in the 1953 Agrarian Reform Law.

Endowed with this new right, the indigenous groups of the *Oriente* applied for recognition of a total of 30 TCOs (Figure 6.4). According to the new legislation, the law for the recognition of a TCO would have to be signed by the president and become final within six months of the application. Within this six-month period, the immediate *inmovilización* must be declared for the area of the future TCO; it is thus prohibited to change the land tenure and ownership structures in the affected territory. Then, until the law can finally be signed, the *saneamiento* has to be conducted, a study of the economic and cultural necessity for the recognition of the area within the borders.

Constitutional reality, however, looks quite different. By mid-2003, not a single one of the 30 TCOs had been legally recognised. On the contrary, after formal declaration of the *inmovilización*, the authorities have remained idle. Different actors hoping for high compensations or even rejection of the TCO have tried to assert a claim on the areas in question (Figure 6.4). Thus, owners of large estates as well as peasants have invaded the area. By assigning felling and mining concessions and allowing the construction of roads across the future TCOs, corrupt authorities contributed to endangering the legal process. Different claims for the resources of the TCO overlap. This leads to conflicts between the actors involved, in which the indigenous groups often suffer defeat.

Figure 6.4: Conflicts over Resources in the Bolivian Amazon

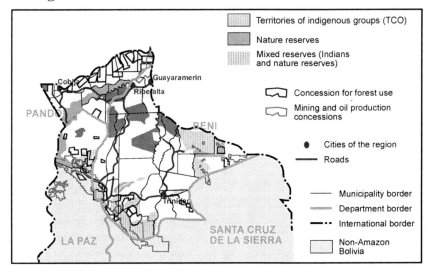

Source: INE (1999) *Atlas estadístico de municipios* (La Paz). Neuberger (2002).

The Forest Conservation Act of 1999 (*Ley Forestal*) brought another threat to indigenous groups' land rights. The new body of law allows among other things the granting of concessions to extract forest products. In the Bolivian Amazon this involves Brazil nuts, palm hearts and natural rubber. In this case also, political and economic elites abuse the underlying objective of the law, the promotion of sustainable forms of forest use. Former bosses of the rubber collectors, the *barraqueros*, have tried to bring the collection areas (especially in the department of Pando on the border with Brazil) under their control by filing applications for concessions. Thus they prevent the establishment of nature reserves or the recognition of TCOs.

However, indigenous groups also know how to use the new Forest Conservation Act for themselves. They also apply for forest use concessions with a view not towards promoting extractive products but rather for logging purposes. Through the marketing of exotic woods, they are trying to create a new source of income for themselves. As a reaction to new international market trends and in order to encourage long-term conservation of these forest areas they abide by the standards of sustainable timber extraction and apply for certification. Bolivia's largest area of certified timber extraction, located in the department of Santa Cruz de la Sierra and covering 80,000 hectares of forest, is cultivated by about 420 indigenous families living in 16 settlements. However, it could only be established with the help of a large NGO operating in the area and, even today, is still backed by international investors. On the basis of this constellation, the transferability of this example to other regions as well as its economic carrying capacity must be questioned.

These conflicts illustrate how many actors are involved in disputing Amazon space and resources. Traditional groups continue with their extractive production, or they secure their subsistence by cultivating their land. Along with marginalised urban groups of the cities, they use the Amazon as their retreat and habitat. Thus, the use of Amazon resources is of vital importance to their survival. This is quite unlike groups such as the owners of large estates, the timber industry or *barraquero*, who ruthlessly and illegally exploit existing resources to accumulate capital. Due to the weakness of public monitoring institutions, these groups do not have to fear any sanctions. They consider the Amazon region a vehicle for profit-oriented exploitation. Thus, economically and politically influential groups on the one hand and, for the most part, the marginalised population on the other, compete for the same resources. Only NGOs or municipal administrations could mediate between the involved actors in the subsequent disputes but even they only very rarely act as neutral parties. On the contrary, while NGOs often act on behalf of marginalised groups, municipal administrations are usually on the side of the economic elites. Constructive dialogue is thus rarely possible.

Approaches to Sustainable Development between Formal Institutions

The example of the Bolivian Amazon region shows how difficult it is to gear sustainable development from above. Within the last few years, far-reaching reforms have undoubtedly been made in Bolivia, which have attracted a great deal of international attention. The collapse of traditional socio-political structures and the formation of new political elites was the indispensable precondition for the adoption of new bodies of laws such as the *Ley de Participación Popular*, the *Ley de Descentralización*, and the *Ley INRA*. Weakening of the hitherto informal institutions through confrontation between trade unions and the government, and rivalries between and among parties, allowed for the implementation of formal institutions or laws which break with these 'old' bodies of legislation.

With the laws implemented at the regional and local levels, however, they quickly came up against obstacles. Although objectives such as democratisation, decentralisation and privatisation included numerous elements that could offer a suitable basis for sustainable development in Bolivia, they meet socio-political structures that are opposed to their underlying basic ideas (Figure 6.5). Unlike at the national level, the traditional social 'rules of the game' still work rather well in the Bolivian Amazon at the regional and local level, in spite of recent changes. Thus, formal and informal institutions with contrasting rationales overlap. One must fear that influential actors inside and from outside the particular region will abuse the evolving political vacuum, due to a lack of independent control, for their own purposes. In most cases, this causes a participation deficit for the marginalised population. Due to the weakness of the State on the one hand and a still weak civil society on the other hand, formal reforms with participatory and sustainable approaches at the local level can have contradictory impacts.

Figure 6.5: Political Reforms and Political Power Structures

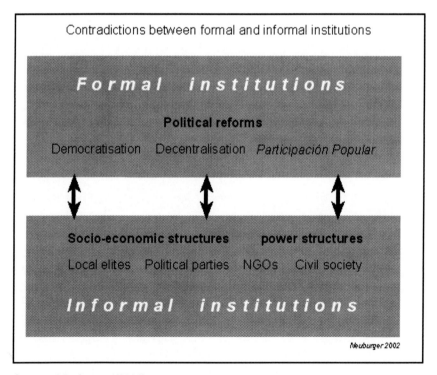

Source: Neuberger (2002).

In spite of these problems, however, the new laws offer great potential. On the one hand, they create the indispensable precondition that allows for participation of even marginalised groups. At the same time, political decision-making has shifted to the level of implementation. Therefore, conceptual design and planning lie in the hands of regional and local decision-makers who can set up adapted strategies of sustainable development based on their knowledge of regional problems and needs. The administrative structures and funds are certainly secured by the political reforms. Whether they achieve their goals depends ultimately on support for the democratisation process from national and international actors. Local power structures and the dynamics within civil society in the Amazon region are critical to the success of the reforms. Especially when the shaping of political ideas and the empowerment of the population develop dynamically, there is a good prospect for the implementation of sustainable development in the region.

7

Breaking the Tutelage of the State:
Indigenous Peoples in Brazil

Dan Pasca[*]

Introduction

The last 500 years of Brazilian history have above all been characterised by violence against indigenous peoples and by their spatial expulsion. Both access to land and the rights of natural resource use have been at the centre of conflict between indigenous and non-indigenous actors. Unlike for indigenous societies, which consider land their life-world, since it safeguards their physical, social and also cultural reproduction, within the logic of neo-Brazilian (i.e. all non-indigenous) actors land represents a good which should be accumulated and which promises prestige, influence and wealth. Moreover, natural resources are only useful once value has been attached to them and they have been extracted and marketed. Even today this conflict of world views and the perception of resources explains the individual actors' very different strategies especially in Amazonia, Brazil's most important indian living space in terms of area.

In the case of indigenous peoples, the close connections of space, knowledge and control of natural resources and social organisation becomes apparent. During contact with neo-Brazilian actors, indigenous peoples have realised that their survival depends strongly both on the preservation of their socio-cultural organisation and on the economic autonomy of their societies. Furthermore, it has become evident that access to natural resources is indispensable. Their primary struggle has been to secure recognition of their ancestral lands. However, they did not only have to submit to land losses but often also to the reduction and degradation of resources (i.e. through the clearing of woodland and economic activities) on their land. Consequently, indigenous societies are trying to

*   I would like to thank the Waiãpi and Dominique Gallois for their patience in answering my questions. I am especially grateful to Thorsten Suck, who provided the translation.

adapt their socio-economic systems to the new situation and to develop strategies for the reconstruction of their autonomy.

State actors thought that this contrast of world views and lifestyles would be temporary, as they never considered indigenous socio-economic organisational patterns on an equal footing, competing with western societies, but rather as primitive lifestyles which should be overcome. Thus, the Indian Protection Agency (FUNAI), after having placed indigenous peoples under its tutelage, attempted to encourage their incorporation into the dominant neo-Brazilian society and accelerate this process via development projects. The attraction of numerous indigenous communities, with their far-flung settlements and their redeployment to central locations were meant to clear their ancestral territories for private investors. The pressure created by powerful economic actors and the complicity of several state governments have led to regional conflicts, which the indigenous peoples cannot solve on their own. The altercations surrounding final recognition of the indigenous territory Raposa / Serra do Sol in the state of Roraima, and the severe conflicts between the Cinta Larga and thousands of diamond prospectors in Rondônia, for example, underline this development.

While in the regional context the implementation of indigenous rights has met with resistance and conflicts have become common, both indigenous rights and the ecological knowledge of these societies have increasingly gained recognition in political discourse and, above all, in the humanities at national and international levels.[1] The ideal of static communities living in perfect harmony with nature in an ecological and historical niche has gradually disappeared as a consequence of numerous ethnological studies. However, in the context of a more complex reality, indigenous peoples' role in the protection of biodiversity and the active management of what has previously been called intact nature was dignified.[2]

Thus a gradual strengthening of the indigenous communities' self-confidence in the composition of forces of local and regional actors has followed. This has led to a higher level of self-organisation and to the emergence of the indigenous movement. The increased recognition of their ecological knowledge, as well as their skills in the manipulation and management of natural resources in particular, have brought about a clear appreciation of their role in the policy of conservation of nature and resources. Considering the following facts and figures, it becomes evident

1   Posey and Overal (1990); Overal and Posey (1996); Cunha and Almeida (2002).
2   Posey (1987, 1996); Posey and Balée (1989); Diegues (2000); Capobianco et al. (2001); Bensusan (2002).

what an important task the indian territories fulfil, especially in protecting the tropical rain forest. Presently in the Brazilian Amazon, 30 per cent of the open rain forest *(floresta ombrófila aberta)* comprises indigenous territories, while only nine per cent is covered by nature reserves. As for the dense rain forest *(floresta ombrófila densa)*, 21 per cent falls within indigenous territories and only 14.5 per cent in nature reserves.[3]

At the same time, developments at the global level may be cited which go beyond the domain of environmental issues and already show important consequences for indigenous peoples. Thus, parallel to economic globalisation, a growing legalisation of international relations can be detected. The idea of a future, universally valid legal system based on human rights plays a major role. Increasing economic and political integration, as well as the expansion of international regimes in an ever-widening political realm, are a conspicuous sign of this tendency, which increasingly limits national sovereignty in favour of a future cosmopolitan law. The proceeding recognition of the indigenous peoples and their rights at the international level must be regarded in this context. Here protest and resistance movements, last but not least in Latin America, have played a major role. Worldwide support for the situation of indigenous peoples began in the 1970s. This process was institutionalised from the 1980s, when the Declaration of Indigenous Rights was prepared within the framework of the United Nations Working Group on Indigenous Populations. In 1989, the International Labour Organisation (ILO) adopted Convention 169 concerning indigenous and tribal peoples. In 1993, the UN proclaimed the international year of indigenous peoples, and 1995–2004 was declared the international decade of indigenous peoples. Finally, a permanent forum for indigenous issues was created within the framework of the UN Human Rights Commission.

Brazilian actors have displayed very different reactions to these developments. Indigenous organisations and their supporters may thus have an opportunity to overcome the regional constellations usually marked by conflicts with other, often more powerful actors. In the meantime, the former have come to enjoy a certain recognition as independent actors at the international level, and they have (albeit limited) access to crucial political forums, an opportunity they are often denied at the local or regional level. Hence they hope for a consolidation of public institutions and a further democratisation of the political process through international legalisation and the pressure for accommodation thus exerted at the national level. With consolidation and democratisation gradually expanding into the par-

3   Capobianco et al. (2001).

ticular region, constitutional indigenous rights could also be turned into political practice. Other actors who pursue economic and political interests in the regional and national context, which compete with those of the indigenous peoples, see their 'development model' jeopardised. While they use economic globalisation and the resulting market forces as powerful arguments for furthering their interests, they demonise the globalisation of civil rights as constituting interference with national sovereignty.

At the moment, advances and retreats characterise the process of recognising indigenous rights due to the different power constellations. Important progress has been made thanks to the mobilisation of indigenous organisations and their supporting civil actors, such as via the new Brazilian Constitution of 1988. This progress has been followed by regressive movements and blockades on the part of opponents, who have repeatedly delayed legal ratification of the Constitution.[4] The future of the Indian Agency (FUNAI) has also been left undefined. During its 36-year existence to August 2003, the agency had no fewer than 31 presidents. At the present time it is experiencing a downright 'implosion'.[5] Since the Constitution virtually abolishes tutelage of indigenous peoples, a redefinition of the role of the Indian Agency is long overdue.

In this legally and institutionally unsettled situation, indigenous organisations and supporting sectors of civil society play an even more important role, they perform ever more functions formerly fulfilled by the paternalistic State and strengthen their network with bi- and multilateral institutions of development cooperation. These, in turn, have directed their activity towards civil actors at the regional and local level, especially towards the indigenous peoples and their organisations, such as the institution of the so-called Indigenous Demonstration Projects *(Projetos Demonstrativos dos Povos Indígenas — PDPI)* within the framework of the Rain Forest Pilot Programme.[6] It is against this complex background that this chapter will investigate the changing relationship between indigenous peoples and the dominant Brazilian society.

Indigenous Peoples in Brazilian Society

Three major features characterise indigenous peoples in Brazil as well as their relationship to Brazilian society:

4   Carvalho (2000); Pasca (2004).
5   Lima and Barroso-Hoffmann (2002).
6   MMA (ed.) (2001).

- Its small size and its limited share of the total population respectively (approximately 0.3 per cent of a total of about 170 million Brazilians in 2000);

- Its great socio-cultural diversity (215 peoples with 180 different languages).

- The dramatic decimation of the indigenous population over the last 500 years.

At present the indigenous population consists of about 500,000 people. According to FUNAI, 345,000 live in indian territories and 100,000-190,000 in cities (Figure 7.1). Moreover, evidence points to the existence of another approximately 53 uncontacted indigenous groups. Today's indigenous population represents only a fraction of the peoples originally dwelling in Brazilian territory. The fact that these societies have survived underlines their will to resist oppression and coerced assimilation. However, the greater their decrease in numbers, the less attention they were given in public life. This vicious circle is a consequence of their rapid obliteration and of the increasing expulsion of indigenous populations until the last decades of the twentieth century. This is why indigenous peoples had hardly any political importance within party systems and the power constellations of the State until the mobilisation of civil society, which brought about the end of the military dictatorship and also had a decisive influence on debates within the constituent assembly.[7]

Another important issue in this context was the image of 'the indian' created as part of the nation-state ideology. The homogenisation of Brazilian society promoted by the political-administrative elite reinforced an ideology in which indigenous peoples hardly ever appeared as independent, historically important actors. They were portrayed, rather, as the passive bearers of certain Brazilian folkloristic traits.[8] This image of the indian was adopted by the indianist movement of Brazilian romanticism. It contrasted the dominant figure of the ignorant, brutal and irrational indian with the misty-eyed image of the noble and gentle savage, stereotypes which are still projected. As they both correspond to an essentialist definition of the 'nature of the indian' based on the attribution of fixed properties and immutable character traits, these extremes are responsible for perpetuating an ahistorical view of indigenous peoples that still prevails in Brazilian mainstream society. Similar motifs can also be found in the se-

7   Souza Filho (1999).
8   Lima (1995a, b).

mantic translation of certain key concepts. For example, the term 'discovery of Brazil' conceals the many wars of conquest with its millions of victims. State-run institutions have also enforced their power of definition in other areas; many different peoples were lumped together under the term 'indian', while their more than 180 languages were reduced to 'dialects'.

Figure 7.1: Development of Indigenous Populations in Brazil, 1500–2000

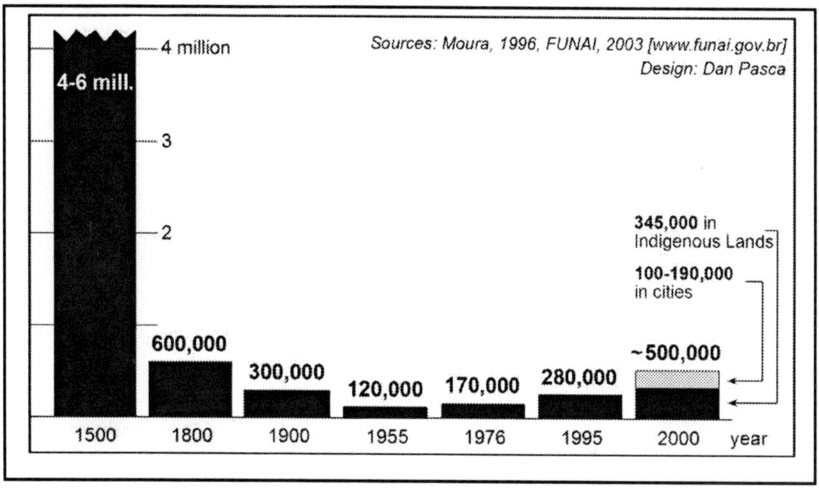

Legal and Institutional Issues

This image of 'the indian' marked the relationship between indigenous peoples and the Brazilian State until into the 1970s. The evolutionary and positivistic nation-state failed to realise that indigenous societies were not politically immature and irresponsible but simply culturally different. This reflected contempt for indigenous patterns of social organisation and their differentiated legal systems. The latter were ignored, and a legal system complying with nineteenth-century European civil law was imported in their stead. This system underlined the role of private property and allowed for no entity between the citizen and the State. Thus, no room was left for collective rights and jointly oriented jurisdiction. Eventually, this signified the substitution of various indigenous legal institutions with one universally applicable and supposedly consistent law.[9]

9   Souza Filho (1999).

At the same time, another substitution was promoted for the benefit of evolutionary progress. Indigenous societies were supposed to disappear into Brazilian society through assimilation and integration. However, in the meantime, 'white' law could not entirely ignore the indigenous population. Thus, in Brazil's civil code of 1916 (*Código Civil*) they were declared 'relatively immature' in respect of the understanding of their rights and duties alongside 16–21 year olds and 'eccentrics'. Until their integration into the 'civilisation of the country', the State would take charge of their tutelage, reflecting the provisional nature of indigenous identity. It was not intended that entire societies or peoples and their institutions should survive.

Thus, the first indian agency set up in 1910 was named the 'Service for Indian Protection and the Placement of National Labour' (SPILTN). It had military, frontier characteristics. Enlightened members of the government perceived the potential threat to the indigenous population and pleaded for their protection and the installation of indian reserves. At the same time, however, they were convinced that it was necessary to develop and educate indians to make them 'better people'. Thus, the reserves were meant to serve as spaces of transition. Both the new Indian Agency (FUNAI) and the Indian Statute (*Estatuto do Índio*), which came into being in 1967 and in 1973 respectively, followed this logic. As the 'primitive' indians were literally in the way of the economic modernisation project, FUNAI would contact them, pacify them, resettle and integrate them into 'civilised' society. The idea behind this plan was simple. With their loss of identity, the indians would also abandon their lands, which could then be 'turned into value'.

This strategy of incorporating new Amazonian spaces and natural resources into the neo-Brazilian economic mainstream, which emerged during the 1970s under the slogan 'land without people for people without land', was for indigenous societies a major assault on their territories. The spread of cattle-ranching, mining projects and dam construction, and especially the extension of highways granting more and more settlers, loggers and gold diggers access to Amazonia, led to devastating epidemics, violent conflicts and finally to the expulsion of the survivors into already existing reserves.[10]

10   Davis (1977).

Figure 7.2: Displacement and Return of Indigenous Peoples in Mato Grosso

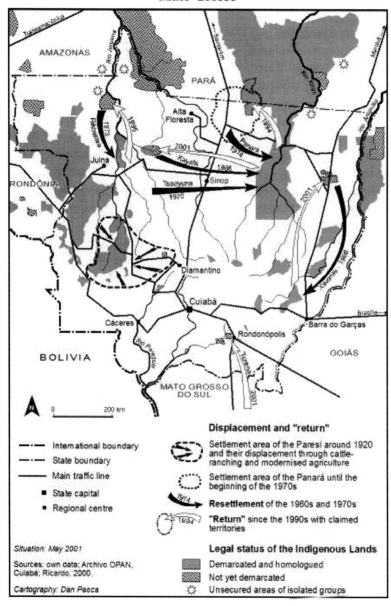

Using the state of Mato Grosso as an example, Figure 7.2 shows the reloca-tion of entire peoples, or what was left of them, in the context of settlement and road construction projects of the 1970s. Yet the new territorial dynam-ics that emerged in the mid-1990s are striking. How can we establish a link between these two scenarios? Contrary to expectations, indigenous peoples have not disappeared. They are, rather, trying to repossess their former terri-tories, as becomes apparent in the map of the latest migrations (Figure 7.2). These current tendencies have been made possible by the new Brazilian indi-an policy. The new Constitution of 1988, for the first time, refrained from co-erced integration and assimilation. It recognised the socio-cultural diversity of Brazilian society and the right of indigenous peoples to live and to maintain their own economic systems according to customary law and traditions, as well as the right to determine their own development. The end of the unequal relationship between indigenous peoples and the Brazilian State or the dom-inant society seemed closer.

However, the initial dynamic of the democratic process was repeatedly obstructed. Thus, the legal regulations of the progressive constitution have not yet been concluded. The civil code was finally adapted to the new legal situation in 2001, yet the adoption of a new Statute of Indigenous Peoples has so far been prevented by opponents of the indigenous movement. Debates over terms such as 'peoples', 'nations' or 'societies' is merely a pe-ripheral concern. The crucial issue is the degree of self-determination and effective control over their natural resources that indigenous peoples should be allowed to exercise.

Thus, several issues are clearly regulated in the new Constitution. Indian territories are the federal property of the Brazilian State, and in-digenous societies enjoy a permanent and exclusive right to possess and use the land and its natural resources according to their customs. However, for want of a clear legal position, other aspects are less precise. Can cus-toms and use change? Are indigenous societies thus allowed to introduce new strategies for the use of resources, such as commercial timber, miner-al or biogenetic resources? If they are denied this right, what sort of in-fluence over the use of these resources by a third party do they have, and what is their share of the profits?[11]

Territorial Issues

Recognition of the right of indigenous peoples to their ancestral territo-ries independent of current ownership was an important measure intro-

11   Posey (1998); Posey and Dutfield (1996); Santilli (2001).

duced by the new Constitution. It is for FUNAI to assess the continuity of settlement on the land or its use by indigenous communities on the basis of ethnological surveys. It is the responsibility of FUNAI to establish the borders of the territory in cooperation with the Ministry of Justice and to set boundary markers. Finally, the demarcation of the indigenous territory must be ratified by the president and officially recorded in federal and local land registries.

Here also practice has not kept pace with the legal momentum. Only a fraction of indian territories could be demarcated within the given five-year time limit before the constitutional deadline for demarcating all indigenous lands expired in 1993. Conflicts of interest with powerful regional actors, and especially inadequate funding of FUNAI, raised doubts about the government's commitment to solving this problem.

Table 7.1: Stage of Legal Recognition of Indigenous Lands in Brazil, October 2003

Status of the *Terras Indígenas* (TIs)	Number	Share of total Nr.	Area (million ha)	Share of total area
Demarcated and officially guaranteed for the exclusive usufruct of the Indians [1] *(TIs homologadas / reservadas / registradas)*	384	62.4 %	86.4	81.5 %
Declared as Indigenous Lands [2] *(TIs declaradas de posse permanente)*	53	8.6 %	14.1	13.3 %
Identified / Approved by FUNAI *(TIs identificadas / aprovadas)*	35	5.7 %	2.5	2.3 %
To be identified *(TIs a identificar / em identificação)*	143	23.3 %	~3.0 [3]	2.9 %
Total	614	100.0 %	~106.0 [4]	100.0 %

1 Ratified by presidential decree. 2 The minister of Justice declared the limits of the area and determined the beginning of its physical demarcation. 3 Their extensions have not been officially defined. 4 Representing about 12.4 per cent of the Brazilian state territory.

Source: Instituto Socioambiental [www.socioambiental.org/website/pib/english/whwhhow/where/sit_jurid.asp] last update: 08/10/2003.

Figure 7.3: Indigenous Lands in Brazilian Amazonia: Stage of Legal Recognition

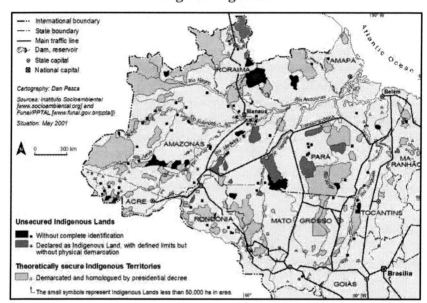

Due to growing pressure on the part of indigenous organisations, as well as national and international supporters, the demarcation process was finally recommenced in 1997. Financing within the framework of the international development cooperation was crucial. Thus, under the supervision of FUNAI and with mainly German funding, the Indigenous Lands Project (PPTAL), a component of the Rain Forest Pilot Programme, has supported the identification and demarcation of 160 Indian territories. In 54 cases (34 per cent), this process is complete.[12] If the present rapid implementation rate is maintained, we could soon see an end to the stage in which territorial integrity is the main aim (see Table 7.1 and Figure 7.4).

The fact that about 80 per cent of all indigenous lands are affected by illegal occupations and conflict with other actors (loggers, gold prospectors, ranchers, small farmers and pharmaceutical industry bio-prospectors) shows that legal recognition alone does not effectively protect their territories and resources.[13] In this current phase, strategies to safeguard in-

12   Gramkow (2002); Kasburg and Gramkow (1999).
13   Pasca (2000).

digenous socio-economic autonomy form the basis, requiring much more active role by indigenous actors at different levels. In the following section, this role will be examined more thoroughly.

The New Role of Indigenous Organisations

The prospect of the end of the military dictatorship and negotiations prior to the adoption of the 1988 Constitution gave new life to the indigenous movement. Reaffirmation of identity, territorial claims and the demand for public welfare took centre stage. While the State acted as a rival, a broad alliance with non-indigenous supporter organisations and representatives from different political parties as well as professional organisations was forged. The mediating function of these actors in the representation of indigenous interests beyond the local level during this phase should not be underestimated.[14] The Indigenist Missionary Council (CIMI) of the Brazilian Council of Bishops played an especially important role is this process.

A new dynamic has emerged within indigenous movements during the last decade. Between 1988 and 2000, the number of indigenous NGOs rose from eight to more than 250 in Brazilian Amazonia alone.[15] This impressive increase can be ascribed to the conjunction of different socio-political processes at national and international levels. Adoption of the 1988 Constitution played a major role in the national context, because it gave legal status to civil society organisations. At the same time, the State gradually withdrew from direct administration of the various indigenous needs and concentrated rather on territorial issues. As part of this development, FUNAI was politically and financially weakened. At the international level, discussion of environmental questions as well as minority rights played a crucial role. The Earth Summit (UNCED) of 1992 marked two important turning points in this context: intensified cooperation between environmentally and socially oriented NGOs and the decentralisation of development cooperation, which increasingly took civil society actors at the local level into consideration.

Bruce Albert (2000) identified the so-called 'project market' as the crucial engine for the current boom of indigenous NGOs. Against the legal backdrop of a progressive constitution, bi- and multilateral development cooperation, together with NGOs acting at the international level, have provided considerable project funding. Brazil's public authorities followed this trend and assigned increased tasks and funds to civil society. As

14   Carvalho (2000); Ramos (1998).
15   Ricardo (1996); Albert (2000).

a reaction to this shift, there was a change in the indigenous movement. A target-oriented ethnic movement has emerged out of the former ethno-political movement. Official indigenous organisations 'with boards of directors elected at meetings, registered by law and bank accounts'[16] are taking on more and more functions that the State no longer directly performs. Thus, a transfer of responsibilities for education and healthcare to the regional and local levels (either to states, municipalities or civil organisations) is evident. Moreover, the outsourcing of projects in order to safeguard the autonomy and sustainability of indigenous societies is striking. While the funding of such enterprises is ever more assured at the international level, either within the framework of bilateral or multilateral development cooperation or through trans-national NGOs, Brazil's civil society organisations and local indigenous NGOs are taking on the administration and implementation of these projects.

This new situation demands an adaptation of indigenous representation in the form of a differentiation between foreign and domestic policy. At the local level, the traditional political institutions of individual communities and peoples are still responsible for the regulation of external factors. Yet the founding of new indigenous organisations, based on political representation through delegation, is an attempt to empower indigenous peoples to negotiate with public and private institutions of the dominant society at national and international levels.[17]

The change from a conflict-driven movement characterised by informal ethno-political organisations and with the State as their counterpart, to the institutionalisation of a variety of organisations with diverse socio-economic functions and with international financial backers as their counterparts, has brought about a series of modifications:[18]

- The major indigenous actors have changed. The council of elders has often been replaced by young leader figures who are more and more familiar with organisation administration and project management.

- Consequently, the nature of the discourse has also gradually changed. The traditional speeches of charismatic tribal elders have given way to a practised ethnic discourse that incorporates the international rhetoric of 'sustainable development'.

---

16   Ricardo (1998), p. 89.
17   Ricardo (1998).
18   Following Albert (2000).

- Finally the functions of indigenous NGOs have changed. They take on an increasingly active role in projects to demarcate and secure their territories in the management of cultural, educational and healthcare projects as well as diverse market-oriented projects (arts and crafts, forest products and the like).

Thus, indigenous groups are gaining greater recognition as important actors in the regional development process, especially in social and ecological dimensions. This increasing legitimacy becomes evident through their participation in direct negotiations with public and private actors at national and international levels. Hence, following withdrawal of the State, indigenous peoples are now facing new challenges. A different kind of struggle has appeared alongside the old struggle to safeguard their territories; a battle to build up and preserve a complex network of partnerships at regional, national and global level. This network is designed to assure the funding of projects and, with it, the ecologically sensitive and economically efficient management of their natural resources. An examination of the Waiãpi will exemplify this situation.

The Waiãpi in a Complex Mesh of Actors

The Waiãpi live in the federal state of Amapá in north-eastern Amazonia. They have moved from total isolation to the mesh of actors described above within the last 30 years. The following highlights will briefly document this process and analyse the coping strategies that they have adopted. In conclusion, the current actor constellation in the conflict between mining and indigenous interests will be considered more closely (Figure 7.5).

At the beginning of the 1970s gold prospectors (*garimpeiros*) and road construction workers moved into the tribal area of the Waiãpi. During the years that followed, measles and flu epidemics decimated the Indian population. In 1973 FUNAI employees who accompanied the construction of the northern perimeter road in Amazonia (*Perimetral Norte*) finally established contact with the Waiãpi. A gold rush in the region was sparked by the publication of the results of investigations carried out by the mining department (*Departamento Nacional de Produção Mineral* —DNPM) and the ICOMI private group; gold, silver, manganese ore, tantalite, cassiterite and other metals stimulated the interest of mining companies.[19] The region's mineral deposits, however, at-

19   The *Perimetral Norte* was one of the road construction projects of the military government for Amazonia during the 1970s. It was meant to ensure the infrastructural development of the northern borderlands. Yet it was only partially completed. Its first segment leads from Macapá in the east, the capital of the state of Amapá, to the manganese ore mines around Serra do Navio and stretches into the territory of the Waiãpi (Figure 7.5).

tracted *garimpeiros* above all and smaller mining companies, which have been supported by politicians supporting the declaration of Amapá as a mining state. In 1987 at the height of the gold rush, mining licences registered with the DNPM covered nearly the entire Indian territory.[20]

Figure 7.4: Waiãpi Indigenous Lands and Current Conflicts

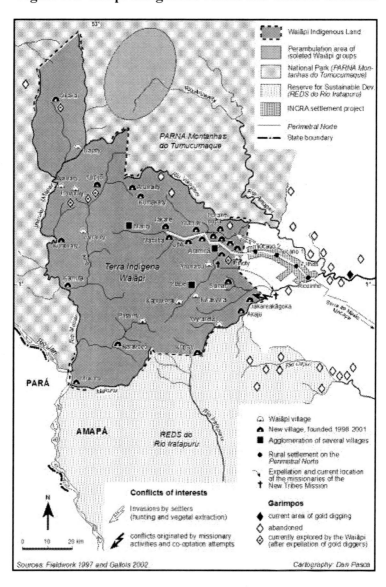

---

20   Raiol (1992); Gallois (1993).

Since contact with the Waiãpi was established, an ethnologist has been accompanying and investigating them. At the end of the 1970s she and other colleagues founded the *Centro de Trabalho Indigenista* (CTI) in São Paulo, one of the first non-indigenous support NGOs for Indians. Since then, the CTI has been preparing the Waiãpi for contact with Brazilian society. The desire of the Waiãpi to maintain their socio-cultural and economic autonomy and, at the same time, acquire new knowledge and skills, is at the forefront of this project. In 1994 indigenous communities founded the Council of Waiãpi-villages (Apina), an indigenous NGO. Its first task was to devote itself to the struggle for the demarcation of their territory. Until final recognition of the *Terra Indígena Waiãpi* in 1996, fierce conflicts with the *garimpeiros* took place, culminating in the eviction of gold miners from the territory.[21]

The Waiãpi's traditional system of land-use is characterised by long-term planning involving all members of local groups, and is based on a periodic relocation of their villages to areas rich in game. This form of land-use was greatly disturbed by the gold miners' invasion. The need to control invaded areas from time to time led the Waiãpi towards a gradual reversal of their spatial concentration and settlement by means of the establishment of new villages. During the 1970s missionaries from the evangelical North American New Tribes Mission as well as FUNAI employees had forced them to live in a few concentrated settlements. While there were only four villages in 1984, there were already 16 in 1997 and more than 40 by 2002.[22] When some invaders were expelled, several Indian groups which had become familiar with manual gold prospecting, decided both to occupy and to make use of the mineral deposits (Figure 7.4). Today, more than a third of the families mine for gold manually at certain times of the year. The marketing of these small amounts of gold, rarely more than five grammes, ensures the supply of sanitary products and metal implements. Gold mining was gradually accepted into the system of subsistence production and is one of several extractive activities.[23] Thus, vigilance, gold prospecting, vegetable extraction along with the spatial dispersion of villages comprise a set of measures to defend the area. Other precautions complement this strategy, including:

- The acquisition of knowledge and techniques in areas (such as education, healthcare, marketing, use of radio and video equipment)

21   Pasca (1997).
22   Gallois (1996; 2002).
23   Gallois (1993; 1996).

previously monopolised by social workers (FUNAI or missionaries). The Waiãpi took their first steps into this direction with support from the CTI.

- The systematic call for access to public discussion forums as well as information about projects and aid programmes which can contribute to the realisation of the other strategies.

These strategies are part of a long-term plan to achieve greater autonomy and better control over external relations. The Waiãpi face both invaders and paternalistic organisations with demonstrations of cultural, social and economic resistance, as illustrated by the following declaration:

> When the missionary (New Tribes Mission) began to work in the village, he brought the Waiãpi many things; hammocks, knives, fish hooks, ammunition and bullets, biscuits. When the Waiãpi went into the field, he brought fruit from there, brought pineapple, then the missionary bartered the hammock. He bartered sweet potatoes for soap and cloth, red cloth. When the Waiãpi went hunting, he bartered meat. We thought, will the missionary keep doing this, giving the Waiãpi things, or will he stop that? If the Waiãpi is already used to this, used to asking for things all the time, will he stay? We here, in the village, think this way; this missionary won't be like this anymore in the future. All of a sudden it will stop. Then the Waiãpi will ask and ask. But he will not have anything to give away. So we thought [...] and then we put together made a project (PD/A) application. Why have the Waiãpi done this? To be independent of FUNAI and to be independent of the government. To get along on our own, the Waiãpi, our community.[24]

The PD/A (demonstration project) mentioned in the above quote forms part of the Rain Forest Pilot Programme mentioned above (funded principally by the G-7, the EU and Brazil). It is meant to allow for a regeneration of the land degraded by gold-diggers. Moreover, it is designed to encourage ecologically sound gold mining.[25] This and similar projects supporting the sustainable use of natural resources and endogenous potential in order to strengthen people's livelihoods, show how development cooperation is increasingly directed toward civil society actors at the local level. In this case, the project application, support and competence of the non-

---

24   Kumaré, Aramirã village, 3 October 1997.
25   CTI (1997).

indigenous NGO as well as the indigenous organisation (Apina) were important preconditions for the granting of multilateral funding.

The demarcation of Waiãpi territory had already been carried out within the framework of the Rain Forest Pilot Programme mentioned earlier. As part of the Project for the Protection of Indigenous People and their Lands in the Amazon Region (PPTAL), the demarcation process was almost revolutionary. For the first time, the indigenous community was actively involved by the NGO in the process of defining and drawing territorial boundaries. The experience gained in this participatory demarcation was used and further developed in many other cases.[26]

The completed demarcation, however, did not stop influential politicians, linked closely to local gold mining interests, from torpedoing all the activities of indian-friendly groups. The Waiãpi's attempt to benefit from their small-scale extraction of gold in their own territory, and thus enhance their economic independence, enraged their opponents even further. Since 1966 they have intensified their attacks on indigenous organisations, especially the *Centro de Trabalho Indigenista* (CTI). Control over the regional press has enabled opponents to influence public opinion with accusations over the alleged 'illegal activities' of the CTI and foreign interest in the gold resources of the Waiãpi. This has taken place despite the fact that the CTI has set up projects in such fields as healthcare, education, regeneration of degraded areas and protection of indigenous territory, not only at the request of the Waiãpi community and in cooperation with their own organisation, but also within the scope of official cooperation agreements with FUNAI, the Ministry of the Environment, the state government of Amapá and international donors. A close examination of the opponents revealed an alliance of actors who had either an economic interest in the mineral resources of the Waiãpi or saw the future of their own institution endangered by the increased autonomy of the Waiãpi. This included local politicians and federal representatives from Amapá, officials of the regional FUNAI administration, the New Tribes Mission, as well as four indians co-opted by them.

The disinformation given out by these actors, as well as the political pressure, had an impact on the regional judicial system. Between 1996 and 1999 the Macapá public prosecutor ordered inquiries against the CTI as well as the anthropologist Dominique Gallois. In August 1997, a federal judge in Macapá followed the argument put forward by the public prose-

---

26   Gramkow (2002); Kasburg and Gramkow (1999).

cutor, who considered illegal the indians' gold mining activities on their own land and imposed an interim injunction against the institutions involved, including FUNAI, the Ministry of the Environment and the CTI, in order to prevent implementation of the PD/A project. Moreover, the anthropologist was prosecuted and CTI employees were denied access to Waiãpi territory. Consequently, all other projects were also stopped.[27] It was striking that neither the public prosecutor nor the federal judge ever gave the Waiãpi a hearing. Both the traditional chiefs of the individual village communities and the representatives of the indigenous NGO (Apina) tried in vain to apply to the authorities again and again in order to put forward their version in spoken or written form. Only when they appealed to the Federal Prosecutor's Office and sued the public prosecutor was the rule of law gradually re-established. What the Waiãpi called 'paper-warfare' slowly turned to good account. From 1999 the prosecution of CTI staff was dropped, the regional public prosecutor was removed from office and the earlier sentence was declared illegitimate and politically-ideologically motivated.[28]

Initially, only the four indians who were co-opted by the missionaries and local politicians, and who belonged to the village community of Ytuwasu which had a long-standing quarrel with all the other Waiãpi communities, were heard in court. Reassured by the attention paid to them and encouraged by local politicians, they founded their own NGO called API-WATA (*Associação dos Povos Indígenas do Triângulo do Amapari*) in 1998. At present, this NGO represents about 15 per cent of the Waiãpi population. When the occasion arises, those opposed to extensive autonomy for the indians use APIWATA as a vehicle to make their cases.

A look at the actors involved and their connected interests, as illustrated in Figure 7.5, throws light on just how complicated the situation has become. It is notable that homogenous groups of actors are rare. Thus, a careful consideration reveals that the State is divided into various individual actors with conflicting interests. A progressive local state government confronts individual and powerful federal representatives as well as all the regional offices of federal agencies, which exhibit clear involvement in particular mining interests.

27   Schwengber (2000).
28   *Ibid.*

Figure 7.5: Actors Involved in the Conflict between Mining and Indigenous Interests in the North-west of Amapá

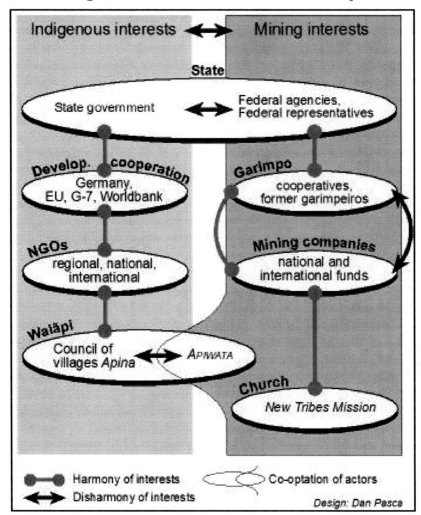

On one hand, the socially and ecologically dedicated state government under then Governor Capiberibe took advantage of the opportunity offered by the discourse of international sustainability and built up cooperation agreements with indigenous organisations, NGOs and international development cooperation actors. On the other hand, representatives of the gold-digging elite holding public office used the active and, above all, the unemployed *garimpeiros* as their political masses to be manipulated. The evangelical activists of the New Tribes Mission have had a lasting and destructive effect on the traditional, religious and socio-economic organisation of the Waiãpi. The missionaries try to break the Waiãpi's resistance movement, based on the perpetuation of their identity, on the grounds of a universalistic discourse of equality and the indians' integration into Brazilian society.[29] In so doing, they not only try to appease the indians so that they would not oppose mining interests, but they even exacerbate serious conflicts within Waiãpi society by co-opting single indians and by setting up relationships of dependence in one of the village communities.[30] The founding of the second, competing NGO (APIWATA) can be seen in this context.

By the end of the 1990s the conflict of interests between the mining lobby and the Waiãpi reached the national political level. A parliamentary fact-finding committee was installed in order to investigate the activities of FUNAI with regard to the cooperation with national NGOs as well as international actors. Conservative parliamentarians had eyed the CTI and especially the ethnologist who has been accompanying the Waiãpi for nearly 30 years now. Antônio Feijão, a federal representative from Amapá was the head of the committee and is known to be one of the most influential representatives of the gold-digger elite. He had also coordinated the defamation campaign against the CTI and exerted pressure on the regional judicial system.

Although attacks by those hostile to indians could be repelled, and the two indigenous organisations do not come into day-to-day conflict with each other, the actions of the various non-indigenous institutions have had dramatic consequences on the social, political and economic aspects of Waiãpi society. The exertion of influence and the often contradictory interventions of these actors have led to the division of indigenous society within the last few years. This could be observed during the so-called paper-war in particular, which was to have dramatic consequences. On the one hand, all projects for the improvement of territorial control and of environmental monitoring were delayed by five years. On the other hand, opponents of indigenous control over the natural resources of the Waiãpi Reserve could organise in the meantime. Thus, local politicians received open support from evangelical missionaries as well as from some officials of the regional FUNAI-administration. The campaign run by these actors,

---

29   Gallois and Grupioni (1999).
30   Ytuwasu, see Figure 7.4.

who have a basic aversion to the 'interference' of ethnologists and NGOs in indian issues, led to a reorganisation of existing socio-political factions Waiãpi society. They began to realign themselves according to the neo-Brazilian political scene in Amapá.[31] In this context, the new NGO API-WATA came into being in 1998, supported by local FUNAI officials and by evangelical missionaries. During the 'paper war' and the work of the parliamentary fact-finding committee, the new NGO attracted the attention of local politicians. The Council of Waiãpi villages (Apina) continued to be the counterpart to APIWATA. Apina represents the vast majority of village communities and it has supported the continuation of cooperation with the CTI. Moreover, it received nationwide support from numerous NGOs to fight the defamation campaign.

Furthermore, the introduction of individual wage payments and pensions from 1998 had a decisive influence on the settlement system. While Apina/CTI projects aimed at breaking with the policy of forced resettlement in central locations and with it the overuse of resources, wage labour introduced a type of occupation that is not modelled on sustainable use of local resources. On the contrary, it exhibits a strong dependence on exogenous actors. All these factors and interventions by outside actors had negative impacts on the settlement system and, generally, on the future prospects of the Waiãpi. Thus, the current situation can be summarised in three scenarios:[32]

- First, most family communities are willing to settle along the boundaries of their territory or in areas where natural resources secure a sustainable livelihood. They merely need support in the fields of communications, transport and the construction of community buildings.

- Second, many families choose to live close to the *karaiko*, the whites, i.e. near the road. They hope for support from various external actors such as the regional FUNAI administration, the mayor of Pedra Branca and other local politicians as well as the evangelical missionaries. They wish for financial help to allow them to purchase food and to construct buildings, etc.

- A third group, comprising families who, to some extent, participate in the settlement of the eastern border of the territory, takes an in-

31   Gallois (2002).
32   *Ibid.*

termediate position. However, they do not yet want to abandon the sites near the road or the FUNAI posts entirely.

One of the main problems the Waiãpi will have to face in the near future is the fact that the central settlements have become too old. Some have been inhabited for 20 years, although the quality of life at a site is only secure for five years. These settlements exhausted the natural resources in their hinterland long ago, and they face insurmountable rubbish-disposal problems. The population survives thanks to the accumulation of funds; wages for paramedics (*agentes indígenas de saúde*) and teachers, for services to the FUNAI post and cleaning personnel for the school or social welfare in the form of pensions for agricultural workers. The handling of these privately and individually acquired funds poses a second serious problem. Money is often spent on useless goods, on prostitutes or in the bars of Macapá. This not only promotes alcoholism, but it also helps to build a vast web of dependencies, culminating in settlements along the road. At present, ten out of 40 villages are located there (Figure 7.4). As pensions and wages are paid in the capital every month, and as the purchases are also made there, voyages to Macapá, which is 250 kilometres away, and the recreation periods between the journeys consume a good deal of the Waiãpi's time, leaving ever less time for other activities.

The Waiãpi have become more and more aware of these problems over the last few years. Discussions about the carrying capacity of their land and the sustainable use of their resources, which have been encouraged by Apina and CTI projects, have made clear the specific problems and prospects for the future of each and every single village community. Although every local community is traditionally autonomous and can independently determine the course of their development, the Waiãpi are currently realising that relations between the various village communities require better organisation. Most seem to agree that only better control of the inner, and above all, the outer relations with the various actors, which exert influence on their lives in the form of projects, wage labour or promises, will allow them to determine their own future.[33]

Even if there are a few local communities willing to accept dependence on wage labour, for the vast majority of the Waiãpi chiefs and for their local village communities, the safeguarding of their indigenous socio-economic autonomy is uppermost in their minds. With increased recognition of indigenous territories, the new strategies of the indigenous peoples aim

33   *Ibid.*

increasingly at safeguarding their economic and socio-cultural independence in order to regain control over their own development. Furthermore, the situation of the Waiãpi illustrates some other developments that are typical of a large proportion of Brazil's indigenous peoples. Four aspects are especially conspicuous:

- **Traditional clashes of interest display great inertia:** conflicts of interest amongst various actors, which can be traced back to the control of one particular resource, gold in this case, continue to exist even after a deposit is exhausted or the law denies non-indigenous actors access. This points to a dramatic ideological conflict between the different perceptions of resources, conceptions of progress and worldviews. For the more powerful actors, the development discourse serves as an instrument to disqualify indigenous forms of life and to marginalise these societies in political decision-making forums.

- **Formerly excluded actors link up to form a network of assertive alliances:** in order to be able to break through blockades at local and regional level, traditional and indigenous societies build up important alliances between each other. Moreover, they increasingly seek the assistance of civil society and international organisations. In this way, opportunities materialise for societies to secure their survival — and these opportunities can count on the long-lasting company of competent, well-organised supporter NGOs. However, conflicts with other actors in the new complex scenarios cannot be ruled out. What are the chances of other peoples who are less well prepared for altercations with a multitude of actors with conflicting interests?

- **Exogenous actors can strengthen or cause internal conflicts:** the often negative interventions of various non-indigenous actors influence the social, economic and political structure of indigenous society, bringing about internal conflicts. Finding a solution for this becomes a major challenge for the indigenous actors.

- **Standardised solutions for all indigenous societies will not work:** projects based on joint participation of the indians, aimed at the sustainable use of their territories and resources, must be adapted to the local context. Thus, it is not enough to strengthen capacity for territorial control of an indigenous people without solving, or at least considering, the contradictions mentioned above. It always has to be questioned whether, in the case of village communities which are politically and socio-economically autonomous, the 'community' actually exists, and to what extent participatory approaches have to be adapted to this situation.[34]

Current Tendencies and Prospects

The various actors involved demonstrate clear differences in their willingness to enter into dialogue with the indigenous peoples and to recognise their rights. In parallel with the gradual withdrawal of the State from indian policy, a growing autonomy of indigenous organisations is noticeable. Following the old struggle for the demarcation of their territories, they are now pursuing new strategies to safeguard their social and cultural independence within a complex political-ecological battlefield. Moreover, indigenous groups wish to be recognised as peoples with their own history, language and culture. They do not want to be regarded as the vestige of a civilisation that existed long ago and, in the eyes of many neo-Brazilians, has become almost extinct. This was the strongest demand made by indigenous delegates from Brazil at the world conference against racism, held in Durban, South Africa, in September 2001. Questions of self-definition and of legal status played a major role:

> We must be perceived as indigenous peoples, because we identify ourselves as indigenous peoples. [...] We do not want to be recognised as nations. [US] Americans have turned indigenous territories into nations, and then declared war on them right away. They won the war and they took everything the indians had. [...]. I like being Brazilian, and I want to stay Brazilian, without an autonomous territory. Yet I want my people's rights to be recognised.[35]

It becomes apparent that the Brazilian indigenous peoples' demands stand far behind those of their comrades-in-arms in Ecuador or Mexico. They call for far-reaching autonomy. The change from political ethnicity to pragmatic, target-oriented ethnicity presented above has led to an increased connection of the immediate local life-world of the indigenous communities with the national and global level. Moreover, it not only opened up opportunities for indian societies to gain access to various financial and technical resources but also to actors and decision-makers, reaching right to the

---

34   Gallois (2002); Schröder (1999).
35   Azelene Kaingang, Brazilian representative in Durban, *O Estado de São Paulo*, 3 Sept. 2001.

World Bank. It is now imperative to avoid creating new dependencies, that is, new mechanisms of clientelistic subordination.[36] The clientelism to be avoided refers to the relationships between funders and indigenous NGOs as well as between the latter and their indigenous bases.

The overall position of indigenous actors in Brazil has changed noticeably over the last decade. However, important aspects attest to the continuity of old conflicts and the weakened State–indigenous peoples relationship. Thus we cannot really speak of a definite recognition and institutionalisation of indigenous rights. Indigenous actors and their supporters have achieved individual successes in the recognition of their rights only thanks to the politicisation of the conflict situation and a massive mobilisation of national and international civil society and public opinion. Even in future, there is a need for constant mobilisation to repel rival attacks and to defend what has already been established.[37] As a matter of fact, attempts to limit indigenous rights have been observable under every government since the end of the military dictatorship. The Lula government, eagerly awaited by indigenous organisations, seems to be no exception.[38]

Yet all the signs had pointed to a positive change in indian policy. Only the coalition of President Lula, elected in October 2002, presented specific proposals for Amazonia, the environment and indigenous peoples within the scope of their electoral programme.[39] It announced a 'clear, democratic, objective and coherent' indian policy aiming at 'respect for and full guarantee of rights to land of indigenous peoples as well as their right of self-determination'. Besides many other measures, the programme promised that immediate steps would be taken to carry out the overdue demarcations and ratifications of indigenous territories. The government's commitment to the adoption of the new Statute of Indigenous Peoples was confirmed, and the complete restructuring and professionalisation of FUNAI was announced. The intended institutional support for indigenous groups and the strengthening of their autonomy, as well as a proposed national conference for the discussion of future indian policy, raised hopes that dialogue with indigenous organisations and civil society could be pursued on a much broader basis than in the past.

However, after the first year of Lula's government, disillusionment on the part of indigenous organisations and their supporters is overwhelming.

36   Albert (2000).
37   Carvalho (2000).
38   Santilli (2003).
39   www.lulapresidente 2002.org

The new government not only lacks the promised 'clear and coherent' indian policy, but it also seems to be sacrificing indigenous rights in favour of broad political support for their reform plans in the fiscal and social security sector. This has become especially apparent in Roraima, where the especially indian-hostile state political leadership agreed to support the Lula government, and governor Flamarion Portela even crossed over to the Workers Party (PT). The long overdue final recognition of six already demarcated indian territories in Roraima, awaiting only the president's signature, have been delayed. The president's office has asked a Senate committee, as well as the National Defence Council, for statements concerning the ratification of indigenous territories in the federal states of Roraima and Amazonia, which is completely unprecedented in the recognition process. The Commission for Constitution, Justice and Civil Rights of the Brazilian Senate has already declared itself against the recognition of five indigenous territories in Roraima.[40]

In view of this political manoeuvre, 56 members of Parliament have initiated a 'Parliamentarian Front for the Protection of Indigenous Peoples' with the help of civil society and the Indigenous Missionary Council (CIMI) in order to increase pressure on the government. Moreover, indigenous organisations, disappointed with the Lula government, have started a national and international campaign to defend indigenous rights. The campaign for 'Land, Justice and Autonomy', co-ordinated by the Coordination of Indigenous Organisations in Brazilian Amazonia (COIAB) was launched in November 2003 in Manaus. There, hundreds of indigenous representatives, participating in the First Permanent Forum of the Indigenous Peoples of Amazonia, burned the government's programme for indigenous peoples that Lula presented during the election campaign in order to remind him of the promises he made.[41] Clearly, there is still great need for constant vigilance and mobilisation if the indigenous rights embodied in the Constitution are to be defended.

The prospect of the end of the tutelage of indigenous peoples by the Brazilian State is provoking a strong backlash on the part of the actors whose economic interests are based on the extraction of natural, and par-

---

40   See Santilli (2003) and the statement of the Indian Council of Roraima *(CIR — Conselho Indígena de Roraima)* [www.amazonia.org.br/noticias/noticia.cfm?id=63915]. See the position of Governor Portela and other representatives of Roraima [www.amazonia.org.br/noticias/noticia.cfm?id=88906].

41   See the final document of the First Permanent Forum of the Indigenous Peoples of Amazonia [www.coiab.com.br/jornal.php?id=137] as well as [www.coiab.com.br/jornal.php?id=134] and [www.coiab.com.br/jornal.php?id=136].

ticularly mineral, resources on indian land. In this situation, strategic alliances with actors of the most different kinds become ever more important for indigenous peoples. The official indian agency FUNAI plays an increasingly less important role while other actors, such as anthropologists, national and international civil society or the institutions of development cooperation, gain in significance.

8

Fostering Change for Brazil's Indigenous People: The Role of the Pilot Programme

Judith Lisansky*

Introduction

This chapter analyses some of the effects of the Indigenous Lands Project (PPTAL),[1] part of the Pilot Programme to Conserve the Brazilian Rain Forest (PPG7) on Brazilian indigenous policies and institutions as well as highlighting some of the challenges for the years ahead. My contention is that, by combining new and improved methods with more effective indigenous participation and partnerships, this inter-

*   I am indebted for input to this chapter to FUNAI's PPTAL project team, in particular to Juliana Sellani and Luiz Nogueira and the PPTAL Annual Report for 2001, as well as comments and encouragement from Carola Kasburg and Marcia Maria Gramkow of GTZ, Artur Nobre Mendes, FUNAI, and to Graciela Lituma, Shelton Davis, John Redwood, Daniel Gross, Alberto Ninio and Loretta Sprissler of the World Bank. The findings, interpretations and conclusions expressed here are those of the author and do not necessarily reflect the views of the Board of Executive Directors of the World Bank or the governments they represent.

1   The Pilot Programme to Conserve the Brazilian Rain Forest (PPG7) is a joint undertaking of the Brazilian government, Brazil's civil society and the international community. It is financed by the G-7 countries, the European Union, the Netherlands and Spain as well as by Brazilian counterpart funds. For more information, please consult the website www.worldbank.org/rfpp. The Indigenous Lands Project (PPTAL) aims to improve the conservation of natural resources in indigenous areas and increase the well-being of indigenous people by regularising indigenous lands in the Brazilian Amazon and improving the protection of indigenous populations and areas. The project is supported by Germany (KfW and GTZ), the Rain Forest Trust (RFT) and Brazilian counterpart funds. For more information and analyses of various aspects of the project, as well as case studies, see the excellent two volume collection of articles, *Demarcando terras indígenas* I and II (Gramkow, 2002; Kasburg and Gramkow, 1999). To learn more in general about PPTAL, consult the web site www.gov.br/pptal.

nationally-financed project has not only made a major contribution toward securing the 20 per cent of Brazilian Amazon territory claimed by indigenous people but has also contributed to empowering indigenous people, altering national dialogue and perception of indigenous people as well as contributing to modernising the National Indian Foundation (FUNAI).

It would be misleading to overstate either the progress made over the past decade or the project's role in promoting such progress. Numerous issues pertaining to indigenous people remain unresolved in Brazil. These include an improved legal framework for the use and management of natural resources in indigenous lands, the ongoing need to protect indigenous lands from encroachment, invasions and illegal use and the as yet unrealised goal embodied in the recent National System of Conservation Units (SNUC) legislation (Law Number 9.985, 18 July 2000) to improve collaboration between environmental agencies and indigenous people. Yet if the changes that have occurred over the past decade are viewed in the light of the predominantly tragic and destructive 500-year history of indigenous people in Brazil with respect to their treatment by the national society, the achievements of the past decade are remarkable.

To mention only a few changes that will be discussed further below, in terms of securing indigenous lands, in 1990 only 37 per cent of all known indigenous lands in Brazil (526 areas) were demarcated and/or registered (just before the project began to be prepared), whereas today 64 per cent of the known 580 areas are demarcated and/or registered.[2] In the past, indigenous 'parks' or 'reserves' were declared by the president without consultation with indigenous people, or they were consulted primarily by an anthropologist during project identification. Today, however, indigenous people participate more actively in almost all phases of identification and demarcation. In the past, FUNAI was predominantly a paternalistic agency that operated on a model of tutelage of indigenous people who were viewed as minors and to whom the agency should provide assistance. Yet today one can say that this view is slowly being replaced by a sense of partnership.

It would be an exaggeration to attribute the cause of such changes entirely to the PPTAL project. Rather, one must view the project as having been uniquely positioned to take advantage of openings in the overall political climate in Brazil with respect to its tropical forests and the inhabitants of these forests. As such, the project has acted as a catalyst for change, leading the way in certain areas such as land regularisation meth-

---

2   For a map of the areas in question, please consult Fig. 7.3 in Chapter 7 above, p. 152

ods but always building upon changes occurring in the broader political context and among indigenous people themselves in Brazil.

The first section of the chapter will provide an overview of the history of indigenous people in Brazil with an emphasis on what has occurred in the Brazilian Amazon region since the turn of the century. I will also briefly summarise the history of the national society's attitude toward indigenous people, particularly in terms of its indigenous agencies, policies and the rather ineffectual progress in securing and protecting indigenous lands. The second section outlines the context for the genesis of PPTAL, as well as providing background on how it was negotiated during its preparation, some of the more contentious issues that arose and how they were addressed. It explains the project's basic components, its unusual 'open design' and procedural issues pertaining to regularising indigenous lands, including a discussion of the implications of the passage of a new decree (Decree 1775) in January 1996 that revised the process of indigenous land regularisation one month after the project was approved. The third section focuses on the accomplishments of the PPTAL project, particularly in terms of land regularisation, impacts on FUNAI and on indigenous participation, and examines some of the implications. The final section summarises some of the challenges for the future.

Historical Overview

Various scholars estimate that before European contact in 1500 the indigenous population of Brazil was probably somewhere between three to eight million. However, as a result of continuous territorial occupation, economic development, enslavement, land expropriation, warfare, disease and assimilation, Brazil's aboriginal population has been decimated. The brutality and devastating impact of the first 300 years are extensively documented in John Hemming's (1978) *Red Gold, the Conquest of the Brazilian Indians*. Darcy Ribeiro's (1970) landmark *Os índios e civilização* documented the extinction of some 80 different indigenous groups between 1900 and 1957. Other historical information and more recent accounts of adverse impacts of contact and national policies can be found in Shelton Davis (1977) *Victims of the Miracle: Development and the Indians of Brazil*; Alcida R. Ramos (1984) *Frontier Expansion and Indigenous People in the Brazilian Amazon*; Mercio P. Gomes (2000) *Indians and Brazil*; and numerous other publications.

In 1910 Brazil established the Indian Protection Service (SPI), which was charged with protecting the indigenous population. By the 1950s, however, Brazil's indigenous population appeared to have reached its nadir, when it is estimated that there were only about 200,000 left in the country, with approximately two-thirds in the Amazon region. The SPI was disbanded in 1967, when massive corruption in the agency was exposed, and the Brazilian Indian Foundation (FUNAI) was created in 1967. Both agencies, however, shared the dominant national view of indigenous people as exotic but somehow childlike people who were so different and uncivilised that they needed assistance to become more like everyone else; that is, non-indians. Furthermore, although Brazilian legislation and constitutions since 1934 recognised the rights of indigenous people to exist on their own lands, there was a deep-seated national ambivalence to recognising indigenous lands, especially as the number of indigenous people dwindled. Lack of comprehension about aboriginal cultures and the land-extensive livelihood adaptations caused many to question why so few 'deserved' so much land or why they should be allowed to 'stand in the way' of national development, particularly in the Amazon region. In view of Brazil's general policies favouring integration and assimilation of indigenous people into national society, the relative lack of progress in protecting or securing indigenous rights and lands, along with renewed national policies and programmes to 'integrate' and develop the Amazon from the 1960s onward, most observers over the past few decades predicted only the grimmest of futures for the remaining indigenous peoples of Brazil.

Nonetheless, over the last 30 to 40 years, despite previous negative trends, 'the indians have been experiencing a new, unexpected, and extraordinary development that we may unabashedly call "the indian demographic turn-around"'.[3] Today, the estimated indigenous population of Brazil is approximately 370,000. It is probably too early to understand fully what this means, but it is a highly promising development. In addition, since the 1970s there has been continuing growth of a pan-indian movement in Brazil and a proliferation of various types of indigenous non-governmental organisations, from local to national in scope and representation. Particularly during the past decade, as this chapter intends to demonstrate, there has been significant progress as regards regularising indigenous lands in the Amazon, as well as promoting changes in and debate about national policies for Brazilian indigenous people. There are definite signs that the relationship between the state and the aboriginal inhabitants of Brazil is changing in some important and fundamental ways, giving cause for some cautious optimism for the future.

---

3   Gomes (2000), p. 2.

Origins of the PPTAL

At the 1990 economic summit of the Group of Seven (G-7) industrialised countries in Houston, Texas, German Chancellor Helmut Kohl called for a pilot programme to reduce the rate of deforestation of Brazil's rain forests. Several months later, representatives of the Brazilian government, the World Bank and the European Commission worked together to outline such a programme. Approved in December 1991, it became known as the Pilot Programme to Conserve the Brazilian Rain Forest (PPG7), to which the G-7 countries, the European Commission and the Netherlands initially pledged some US$250 million. The goal was to create a new model of international partnership focused on environmental issues of global concern. The objectives aimed to help: (i) demonstrate that sustainable development and conservation of the environment can be pursued at the same time in tropical rain forests; (ii) preserve the biological diversity of the rain forests; (iii) reduce the rain forests' contribution to the world's emissions of greenhouse gases; and (iv) set an example of international cooperation between industrial and developing countries on global environmental issues.

The Pilot Programme included five thematic areas for financing: (i) experiments and Demonstration, which sought to promote practical experiences by local communities and governments in conservation, sustainable development and environmental education initiatives; (ii) conservation, to promote improved management of a wide variety of protected areas such as parks, national forests, extractive reserves and indigenous lands; (iii) institutional strengthening; (iv) scientific Research. (iv) learning and disseminating Lessons.[4]

Today it seems natural that indigenous lands should have been included in the Pilot Programme, but the acceptance of international funding for work on indigenous issues in Brazil was not a foregone conclusion at the time. The Brazilian government had long been reluctant to accept international financing for indigenous activities because indigenous issues were seen as a sensitive domestic concern that could easily generate international criticism and controversy. With international financing comes what could easily be construed by critics as international 'interference'. In addition, the World Bank had been asked to coordinate the programme and the Bank had in 1991 adopted its landmark Indigenous Peoples Policy,

---

4   Further information about Pilot Programme studies and publications can be found at www.worldbank.org/rfpp.

Operational Directive 4.20.[5] This policy emphasises respect for cultural diversity and self-determination by indigenous groups, with considerable attention to land tenure and natural resource issues, indigenous rights and participation. It contains guidelines to be followed for any activity affecting indigenous people with which the Bank is involved. Therefore, the Pilot Programme's proposed project with Brazilian indigenous people would also have to be screened and monitored for compliance with the Bank's policy. Hence, the first important hurdle was including an indigenous project in the Pilot Programme at all. That Brazil agreed to this was itself a significant development.

In 1988 Brazil adopted a new Constitution stipulating that all indigenous lands in the country would be demarcated by October 1993. However, despite this ambitious goal, less than 40 per cent of the country's indigenous areas had been demarcated by the deadline. Numerous experts agreed that, given the location of the majority of Brazil's remaining indigenous people in the Amazon region, together with frontier expansion occurring there ever more intensely over the previous decades, the most urgent priority was to work on guaranteeing indigenous people their lands. With respect to the Pilot Programme, with its focus on protecting the rain forests, one of the most salient facts about indigenous people was that they had long used the forest ecosystem without causing major environmental damage. Their specialised knowledge and stewardship of natural resources are considered by many scientists to be exemplary and could provide a foundation for the development of more sustainable approaches to rain forest use and management. Furthermore, satellite maps of the Amazon region clearly show that existing indigenous lands contain some of the most pristine and undisturbed forests in the region. Hence, a consensus emerged about the importance and urgency of securing indigenous lands for indigenous people in the Amazon region and the design of the PPTAL stemmed from this priority.

For regularising or legalising indigenous lands, Brazil already had a relatively comprehensive legal framework that stipulated the steps to be taken. In addition, Article 231 of the Brazilian Constitution states that indigenous people have primary, inherent and unalterable rights to the lands they (i) permanently inhabit (ii) use for productive activity, and which are necessary for (iii) the preservation of the natural resources on which they depend, and (iv) their cultural as well as physical wellbeing. 'Regularisation' of indigenous land in Brazil signifies official recognition (by the State) and

5   World Bank (1991).

demarcation of the areas where pre-existing rights of indigenous people pertain. In Brazil, indigenous lands are the property of the State; however, the regularisation process recognises and formalises indigenous rights and specifically guarantees perpetual usufruct by indigenous people of their lands. While theoretically these rights are not strictly dependent on land regularisation for their legitimacy, in practice it becomes vitally important that the State legalise indigenous areas.

Full regularisation consists of three main steps: (i) identification and delimitation; (ii) physical demarcation; and (iii) regularisation, which comprises land registration and a final presidential decree. The responsibility for regularising indigenous lands lies with FUNAI, although its parent agency, the Ministry of Justice, has the power to issue, or withhold, the *portaria declaratória*, which is a crucial step between the identification and delimitation stage and the actual demarcation itself. The *portaria declaratória* is a published decree in which the State recognises the legitimacy of the identification and delimitation, and hence is essential prior to any demarcation. Interestingly, during preparation of the project when timing was calculated for each task of each stage, only the issuing of the *portaria declaratória* had no timeframe and no deadline. It was also apparent that this was a point at which political pressure could be applied to slow down or stop the process and, in fact, many indigenous lands had been identified but never demarcated due to not having a *portaria declaratória*, sometimes for many years. During preparation of the PPTAL, the issue of putting a time limit on the issuing of the *portaria declaratória* came up repeatedly, but government at that time was unwilling to change the rules of the game.

Also during preparation of the PPTAL, the details of how all the tasks of the regularisation were carried out were discussed and examined with a view to improving them. One issue was that anthropologists who worked on identifications were unpaid volunteers, often busy with multiple activities and hence often delayed, sometimes for years, in delivering the essential identification reports necessary for delimitation. The project design team proposed professionalising this function and, under the PPTAL, members of the identification team are contracted and paid for their services. A second issue that was discussed at length focused on the need for environmental diagnostics of indigenous lands, especially during identification, to ensure complete understanding of the relationship of the indigenous people with their environment. This included, for example, areas used seasonally or areas vital to the ecosystem such as headwaters. Since environmental diagnostics were not part of traditional identification procedures, funds were set aside under PPTAL to develop an appropriate methodology, train environmental specialists and include them in future identification teams. A third issue that received attention was the traditional method for demarcating indigenous lands by cutting a wide swathe in the forest on the borders, which in remote areas is expensive and must be maintained due to forest regrowth. It was agreed that the PPTAL would commission a study on alternative methods of demarcation that would subsequently be tested in the project.

Three other issues were raised during project preparation for which satisfactory solutions were not agreed at the time: (i) indigenous participation and empowerment; (ii) protection of indigenous lands; and (iii) natural resource use and management. The first and second were particularly interrelated. Essentially, the regularisation method traditionally followed by FUNAI was to send outsiders to carry out the various steps of the regularisation. While an anthropologist was required to be part of the identification team, this did not ensure that the indigenous people fully participated in the process or in the subsequent demarcation. Demarcations were usually contracted out to specialist firms. Indigenous people might or might not be consulted by the firms and were occasionally hired as manual labourers. As such, there were cases of indigenous lands created where the aboriginal inhabitants were not even fully aware of the new borders of their land as recognised by the State. With respect to protection of the indigenous lands, based on available data it was obvious that FUNAI did not have the policing power, the budget or personnel to stop encroachment, and that other collaborating agencies (such as the forest police) often did not carry out these functions. The small project design team in FUNAI, in conjunction with the German donors (KfW and GTZ) and the Bank, in line with OD 4.20, were geared towards a policy of fundamentally altering regularisation and protection activities to ensure the full participation of indigenous people to encourage territorial control by the indigenous people of their lands.

However, in the early 1990s the Brazilian government, already uneasy about the involvement of international donors and agencies in indigenous affairs, clearly expressed its reservations about actions or language that might imply sovereignty of indigenous areas. At one point the World Bank received an official communication from the government requesting, for example, that it use the term in English 'indigenous people' rather than 'indigenous peoples' because the latter implied sovereignty. Hence, in project documentation the emphasis on participation was relatively light and the

term 'territorial control' was not used. Instead, the project proposed a series of studies of new methodologies which would subsequently be tested
under the project. The project thus 'opened the door' to more participatory and locally-based activities without forcing the issue or attempting to
predefine changes.

The third issue was related to the legal aspects of natural resource use
in indigenous areas and conflicts between conservation units (under
Brazil's environment agency IBAMA as well as state and municipal environmental agencies) and indigenous lands. During project preparation, an
NGO specialising in indigenous rights, the *Núcleo de Direitos Indígenas* (NDI
— Nucleus for Indigenous Rights), which later joined several other organisations to form the Socio-environment Institute-ISA, carried out a series of studies of existing pertinent legislation and regulations.[6] Numerous
issues were shown to be unclear or ambiguous due to inconsistencies in
Brazilian legislation such as the Constitution of 1988, the *Estatuto do Índio*
(the Indian Law of 1973) and the Forest Code of 1965, amongst others.
There was an underlying assumption in the legal framework that the
usufruct granted to indigenous people left them frozen in time insofar as
it was expected they would primarily subsist in their areas but never com-
mercially exploit natural resources. Usufruct did not extend to subsoil
rights, which belong to the State. The rules and regulations for third party
concessions, for example, for mineral rights and timber harvesting, were
not fully clear. In addition, in certain cases environmental conservation
units overlap with indigenous areas, raising unresolved questions about
how to settle possible conflicts between indigenous use and conservation
principles. Further compounding the difficulty was the problematic relationship between FUNAI and IBAMA that continues to this day.

Although the use and management of natural resources on indigenous
lands was the heart of the project, given the complexity of the issues involving legislative inconsistencies and multiple agencies, the project faced
limitations in terms of what could be addressed. As such, it allocated funds
to relevant studies and pilots, one for environmental diagnostics during
identifications and one for developing a methodology for ethnoecological
studies on indigenous lands. This was a compromise solution at best, as
will be discussed later in the section on challenges ahead.

Thus, the design of PPTAL included four components.[7] The first and
largest was 'Regularisation of Indigenous Lands', and included all the nec-

6   NDI (1993, 1994).
7   For further details, see World Bank (1995).

essary steps for regularising indigenous lands in the Amazon. The second component was entitled 'Surveillance and Protection of Indigenous Areas' and this was left somewhat open though oriented toward assisting indigenous people in developing protection activities for their lands (and not toward financing governmental policing actions). The third component was 'Studies and Capacity Building', and the fourth was 'Support to Project Management'. The total project costs were estimated at almost US$21 million, of which the central Rain Forest Trust Fund would provide US$2.1 million, Germany through the German Development Bank (KfW) would provide US$16.6 million (30 million DM at the time) and the government of Brazil would provide counterpart financing of US$2.2 million, or ten per cent. In addition, Germany pledged to provide technical cooperation as well via its Technical Cooperation Agency (GTZ).

One of the most relevant aspects of the PPTAL design was its designation as an 'open-ended project' insofar as it was agreed that the initial land regularisation targets could be reviewed and revised on the basis of the annual priority list of indigenous lands.[8] If funding permitted, more indigenous lands could then be added to the project's original targets. As will be described later, this open-ended aspect of the project has allowed it to expand its scope considerably over time.

Lastly, it is highly pertinent to note that in January 1996, only one month after the approval and signature of the PPTAL (in December 1995), Brazil adopted new legislation to revamp the process of indigenous lands regularisation. This was Decree 1775, which replaced the previous set of rules and regulations, Decree 22. Due largely to the addition of a civil administrative grievance procedure and 90-day period of contention for non-indians to challenge the identification and delimitation of indigenous lands (judicial grievance procedures were already in place and continue to be available), the majority of domestic and international NGOs concerned with indigenous issues in Brazil contested the new decree. Concerns focused primarily on the retroactive nature of the decree and the worry that already delimited indigenous lands, as well as new areas, might be reduced in size if non-indian claims were upheld. The World Bank, having signed a Grant Agreement predicated on Decree 22, carried out its own legal review of Decree 1775 and found that it did not contradict the project's legal contract insofar as the basic elements of regularisation were

8   Which is based on a system of prioritisation reflecting degrees of vulnerability and threats described in the Project's Memorandum of the Director, Annex 2, 1995.

consistent from one decree to the next. The German government went further and issued an official position that it would not finance any indigenous lands in the PPTAL that had been reduced in size due to the new contention procedure. However, the vast majority of claims and grievances against existing indigenous lands have so far been dismissed and the primacy of indigenous rights upheld. In the few cases where the Ministry of Justice used the new decree to mandate alterations in an indigenous area, Raposa Serra do Sol being the outstanding case (but not included in the PPTAL), these have also been subsequently challenged.

The positive aspects of Decree 1775 were somewhat overlooked in the storm of protest over the new grievance procedure. Most important among the new aspects of Decree 1775 were that it added an environmental diagnostic to the identification procedures, stipulated a set timeframe for the Ministry of Justice to issue the *portaria declaratória* for newly identified areas, and essentially opened the door for the revision and improvement of FUNAI's procedural manuals for all stages of indigenous land regularisation. Most importantly, the new decree created an opportune moment for the PPTAL to promote studies and pilots for improving indigenous land regularisation.

Achievements and Impacts of the PPTAL

Land Regularisation

Since 1996 the PPTAL has identified 9.5 million hectares of indigenous lands and demarcated 34 million hectares in the Amazon region of Brazil. Altogether (including all steps), the project has contributed to advancing regularisation of some 45.4 million hectares, which is an area slightly larger than Germany, Belgium and the Netherlands combined. More than 90 per cent of the original goal of 55 identifications and 58 demarcations has been reached. In line with the open nature of the project, targets have been reviewed and expanded annually until currently they stand at 101 identifications and 157 demarcations, more than double the original aims. Of these new targets, 45 per cent (45 indigenous lands) have been identified and 38 per cent (59 indigenous lands) have already been demarcated. A significant portion of the 59 indigenous lands already demarcated has already completed the final steps of land registry and finalisation by presidential decree. The project was due to close in 2000 but since the work programme expanded it has been extended to function until 2003 and possibly beyond. As such, PPTAL has made an enormously significant contribution towards securing approximately 20 per cent of the Brazilian Amazon region as indigenous lands.

The land regularisation progress has not been without problems, challenges and delays. Over the past seven years there have been highly productive periods, and other times when myriad problems combined to slow down the work. Problems and challenges have included securing the right experts to work on identifications, getting teams into the field in a timely manner, delays in report delivery and subsequent evaluations, myriad problems with contracting due to complex Brazilian rules which occasionally change, and the perpetual problem of organising work in remote locations and timing it with seasonal conditions. The PPTAL works closely with the FUNAI Land Department which, while one of the best departments in the organisation, still suffers from some of the institutional weaknesses of the agency, falling victim to bureaucratic, budgetary and contracting problems, and one year even temporarily losing 80 per cent of its staff. Sometimes local conflicts intervene, as in an area of Rondônia where neighbouring ranchers utilised scare tactics to stop the work of an identification team. In addition, as more participatory methodologies have been tested, it has been observed that these sometimes require more field time than traditional methods.

Nonetheless, the overall progress achieved by the PPTAL in regularising indigenous lands in the Amazon region is nothing short of astounding. Given the previous decades of slow progress, the leap forward during the past seven years signals that a number of positive factors are likely to be involved. These include the project itself with its additional budgetary resources and a dedicated team to push ahead as well as its high domestic and international visibility, a far more receptive domestic political climate than has ever been the case, general cooperation within FUNAI itself, and the growing voice of an indigenous constituency with stronger indigenous organisations that can successfully represent multiple ethnicities and dialogue with national society and government, for the first time in Brazilian history. Because of its relative success in meeting its objectives, the PPTAL has even been discussed periodically as a possible 'model' for reorganising FUNAI itself.

Improving Technical Standards and FUNAI

As stated previously, the PPTAL commissioned a series of studies designed to improve and test new regularisation procedures. These included the development of a methodology for rapid environmental diagnostics during the identification of indigenous lands, alternative methods to traditional demarcations, improved approaches to land tenure studies and resettlement issues pertaining to non-indian inhabitants of indigenous lands, the creation of a geo-referenced database on indigenous lands and the adoption of participatory methodologies. For example, the project developed a module for rapid environmental diagnostics and suggestions for how to integrate environmental specialists into identification teams that are now standard procedures at FUNAI. The study on demarcation alternatives led the way to alternative border marking methods such as the planting of perennials, new types of sign postings and the selection of only certain border sections for clearing, which has also helped reduce the cost of demarcations.

The net result of PPTAL's work is that it has improved technical standards of land regularisation procedures. For example, it is self evident that a better comprehension of indigenous definitions of their environment and their natural resource use patterns needs to be included in the identification of indigenous lands, since these are often fundamental to justifying the delimitation or selection of borders for a given area. Without an environmental assessment an identification team could easily overlook indigenous use of natural resources in a given location that perhaps may only occur in one season of the year and not during the visit of the outside team. While such environmental diagnostics are no substitute for natural resource management plans for indigenous lands, which are likely to be contemplated in the near future, they provide a foundation and important inputs for later management. Over the years, the PPTAL, in close collaboration with FUNAI's Land Department, has financed the development of a sophisticated geo-referenced database (Geographic Information System or GIS) on the indigenous lands in the project. The system is already functioning as an effective monitoring and mapping tool.

Not only has the PPTAL revised procedures and field-tested them but these innovations are being mainstreamed back into FUNAI. The PPTAL has contributed to the revision of internal procedural manuals that needed to be updated after the adoption of Decree 1775. As such, the PPTAL has contributed to raising standards for all indigenous land regularisation being carried out in Brazil. Furthermore, there are plans to extend the GIS database system agency-wide, so that FUNAI will at some time in the future have a GIS on all indigenous lands in Brazil. Such a system will be an essential tool for the improved protection of indigenous lands and perhaps some day, improved ethno-ecological management plans for natural resources. There may even be spillover effects to other Latin American countries as various indigenous agencies elsewhere have begun requesting study visits to FUNAI and the PPTAL.

Increasing Indigenous Autonomy and Territorial Control

As explained above, the participatory and empowering aspects of the PPTAL were not unduly emphasised during negotiation of the project. This was in part because of government concerns about the implications of ideas of indigenous sovereignty implicit in the term 'territorial control'. Another reason lay in the dominant organisational culture of FUNAI, which traditionally did not view indigenous people as partners but rather as *coitados* ('poor things') requiring protection and charitable assistance. Unsurprisingly, therefore, the PPTAL worked rather slowly at first to experiment with participatory methodologies.

The first experiments with more participatory approaches were undertaken with respect to demarcations in which communities, indigenous and indigenist organisations participated as partners. Most of the participatory demarcations were proposed and developed by indigenous organisations together with the PPTAL. In these demarcations, of which the Indigenous Land *Medio Rio Negro* is an outstanding example, not only were more communities mobilised, indigenous organisations were themselves also strengthened by the process. In a number of cases, indigenous participation corrected boundary errors. Some engineering firms and some parts of FUNAI were initially reluctant about participatory demarcations, but over time the approach has become more commonplace. Although the long-term implications of high indigenous involvement with the demarcation of their lands is not yet known, the short-term benefits include empowerment of indigenous communities, greater dissemination of information about the land and natural resources and the need to protect them, as well as increasing the quality of the work on the ground. In addition, it has been observed that when indigenous communities better understand the process of recognition of their lands by the State, they become more vigilant in trying to maintain and protect their territories.

The second area in which more participatory approaches were introduced was in the project component for surveillance and protection of indigenous lands. Rather than attempt to bolster the policing powers of governmental agencies (which were largely unsuccessful), this component focused on 'bottom-up' approaches such as local initiatives to help indigenous communities monitor and control their lands themselves. For example the PPTAL, in collaboration with indigenous organisations and the NGO Friends of the Earth, installed 73 radio systems in 63 villages and ten indigenous organisations. These radios have greatly improved communication among indigenous people and also to the outside, including with

FUNAI. Indigenous people have reported how the radios help in a wide variety of ways from planning meetings to informing about illegal invaders. Other typical protection activities supported by the PPTAL have including planning strategic locations for agricultural plots, support houses or sometimes even new villages near boundaries or in more vulnerable areas of the indigenous land. There is evidence that these activities have contributed to indigenous awareness about the importance of and the need to protect their lands and natural resources. The third area in which the PPTAL has supported greater indigenous participation is in identifications, a crucial stage during which the boundaries of an indigenous land are determined. This work is more incipient but includes attention to improved guidelines for identification teams and proposals for more time in the field.

Another significant achievement is that indigenous people have gradually gained a greater voice in the goals and methodologies of the project. For example, when the PPTAL began it included what was at the time an innovative approach, a project advisory commission composed of governmental and indigenous representatives, set up to supervise and provide oversight for the project. At the time the government insisted that this project commission should be only consultative and should have no decision-making powers. In 2001, the project commission officially requested that it be upgraded to have decision-making power, for example, for approving the project's annual work plan, priority list and protection activities to be financed. The government agreed and the commission was upgraded to become deliberative. Another example is that, during the project's mid-term review, indigenous representatives requested that a new subcomponent be added to strengthen indigenous organisations and provide training, technical assistance and capacity building. These new activities were subsequently incorporated into the project.

In summary, the PPTAL has helped to regularise a great many indigenous lands in the Amazon region, improve the way this is done, contribute to improving technical standards and techniques used by FUNAI, empower indigenous people and organisations and shift FUNAI's paradigm of working with indigenous people more toward a model of partnership. Despite these significant achievements, there are continuing challenges and difficulties. In particular, a major challenge of the future is how indigenous lands can be more successfully protected against outside encroachment and how indigenous people can successfully use and manage their natural resources not just to conserve them but also to facilitate the sustainable development necessary for indigenous wellbeing as cultures change, which is inevitably the case.

Challenges for the Future

Recognition by the State of indigenous lands is a necessary but not a sufficient condition for improving the conservation and sustainable development of natural resources and increasing the wellbeing of indigenous people in the Amazon region. Today the Amazon region, which covers about five million square kilometres, represents 61 per cent of Brazil's surface area, houses 30 per cent of the world's remaining tropical forests and contains some of the greatest genetic diversity on the planet. It is rapidly ceasing to be, as is amply shown by other chapters in this book, a highly remote, sparsely populated, under-utilised frontier. In 1970, when a major drought hit Brazil's north-eastern region, President Medici launched the first major Amazon development and colonisation initiative, the National Integration Plan (*Plano de Integração Nacional* — PIN), which he vowed would take 'people without land to a land without people'. Today, the Amazon region is home to 20 million, including indigenous groups, rubber tappers, nut gatherers, fishermen and small farmers as well as those engaged in soybean production, cattle ranching, mining, hydroelectric enterprises and other industries. This expanding pattern of economic and demographic occupation has major implications for use of the region's natural resources.

Hence, it is not enough that the region's indigenous lands have been regularised. The massive changes occurring in the region, including recent efforts to expand the amount of land in protected areas, will have impacts on the aboriginal population. Despite centuries of indigenous populations living in relative harmony with their natural environments, one cannot expect socio-cultural systems to remain frozen in time. In other regions of Brazil and elsewhere in Central and South America, indigenous people in contact with expanding national societies have become some of the poorest of the rural poor. If indigenous lands are not sufficiently protected from outside encroachment and invasion, if new cash needs lead to exploitative contracts with third parties who degrade the natural resource base, if new ways to use and manage natural resources in indigenous lands that allow for sustainable development are not put in place, the same process will take inexorable hold in Amazonia.

As stated previously, the legal framework for the use and management of natural resources on Brazilian indigenous lands continues to be inconsistent and poorly applied. A revised and updated version of the Indian Law, which regulates a significant portion of natural resource use on indigenous lands, has been under debate in Brazil for the past decade but has not yet been adopted. In 2002 a FUNAI president was dismissed for questioning the interests of mining companies seeking to exploit minerals on indigenous lands. As previously stated, the new National System of Conservation Units (SNUC) seeks to strengthen collaboration between environmental agencies, FUNAI and indigenous people, but so far this remains more of a goal than a reality.

The PPTAL has made an important beginning in this area by supporting the development and testing of a methodology for ethno-ecological studies on indigenous lands. Other non-governmental organisations, such as the Socio-environment Institute (ISA), the Amazon Conservation Team (ACT) and the Centre for Indigenous Work (CTI), amongst others, have also been working in this area and made major contributions; collaborating on specific projects with indigenous people, including on sustainable timber extraction, ethno-mapping and other initiatives. However, far more needs to be done if Brazilian indigenous lands are to be adequately protected and their natural resources sustainably managed and developed. This is the major challenge for the future.

9

Indigenous Peoples as Providers of Environmental Services in Amazonia:

Warning Signs from Mato Grosso

Philip M. Fearnside[*]

Introduction

Deforestation in Brazilian Amazonia is currently advancing at a rate that alarms many because of its potential damage to biodiversity and climate and to the indigenous peoples who depend on forest for their cultural and physical survival.[1] Planned infrastructure projects would further speed deforestation, logging and other forms of degradation in the coming decades.[2] The roles played by the forest in providing environmental services, such as avoidance of global warming, maintenance of the hydrological cycle and biodiversity, represent an opportunity to obtain financial and political support for preventing forest loss.[3] Currently, the role of Amazonian forest in the global carbon cycle is closest to providing the basis for monetary flows.[4] The July 2001 Bonn agreement rules out credit for avoided deforestation under the Kyoto Protocol's Clean Development Mechanism during the Protocol's first commitment period (2008–12), but inclusion of such provisions could occur for 2013 onwards

* I thank the Fundação Estadual do Meio Ambiente do Mato Grosso (FEMA–MT) for allowing me to accompany them in the field and both FEMA–MT and Tecnomapas, Ltda. for their information and patience. The Natural Resources Subprogramme of the Rain Forest Pilot Programme (RFPP–SPRN), within the Ministry of the Environment's Secretariat for Coordination of Amazonia (MMA–SCA) provided travel support. The author's work is supported by the National Council for Scientific and Technological Development (CNPq)(Proc. 470765/01–1).

1   Fearnside (2002c).
2   Laurance et al. (2001); Nepstad et al. (2001).
3   Fearnside (1997a).
4   Fearnside (1999a; 2001a, b).

depending on negotiations due to begin in 2005. Although the Convention on Biodiversity (CBD) lags behind the United Nations Framework Convention on Climate Change (UN–FCCC) as a potential source of financial flows, biodiversity concerns are sufficient to suggest that, with time, this role may also advance towards providing tangible rewards.[5]

Amazonian indigenous peoples have received almost no reward for the environmental services they provide by maintaining forests. An exception is the international funds that have been granted through the Rain Forest Pilot Programme (RFPP) that includes among its objectives the reduction of greenhouse gas emissions from deforestation.[6] As is also true for non-indigenous groups benefited by such funding sources, the recipients rarely understand the link between the benefits they receive and the environmental services of the forests they maintain, thus greatly reducing any strengthening effect that the funding might have on their motivation to maintain the forest.[7]

The state of Mato Grosso provides a unique view of the benefits and vulnerabilities of indigenous reserves as suppliers of environmental services. Mato Grosso is notorious as a state in which deforestation is most rapid due to its proximity to sources of population migration and markets for grains, beef and timber. The advance of soybean production and associated infrastructure has been especially strong in Mato Grosso due to climate and location factors.[8] Mato Grosso, together with adjacent areas in southern Pará, has accounted for a substantial portion of the total forest loss in Brazilian Amazonia as well as loss of non-forest ecosystems such as *cerrado* or central Brazilian savanna.[9] From 1999 to 2001, the Mato Grosso state environment agency (FEMA) undertook an unprecedented licensing and control programme to induce larger landholders to comply with federal legislation on land clearing.[10] The pattern of clearing rate changes over the 1996–2001 period in counties (*municípios*) with differing amounts of previous clearing and differing levels of enforcement effort indicates that the programme has had a significant effect on deforestation.[11] If constant clearing at the 1999 rate is assumed as the baseline for

5   Fearnside (1999b).
6   Brazil, MMA (2002).
7   Fearnside (2003a).
8   Fearnside (2001c; 2002a); Schneider et al. (2000).
9   Fearnside (1986; 1993).
10   Mato Grosso (FEMA, 2001).
11   Fearnside (2003b).

comparison, the decrease in clearing in Mato Grosso over the 2000-01 period avoided 43 million tons of carbon emission annually, equivalent to about half of Brazil's current emissions from fossil fuels.[12]

In October 2002 the election of Blairo Maggi as governor of Mato Grosso, the largest individual soybean entrepreneur in the world, made continued effectiveness of the FEMA programme unlikely. The widespread belief among large landholders that Maggi's electoral victory was assured may explain a generalised increase in clearing rates throughout Mato Grosso in 2002 (Figure 9.1). Regardless of the fate of the licensing programme in Mato Grosso under the Maggi administration, the response of deforestation rates at the county level over the 1999–2001 period offers an important demonstration that governments can control deforestation if they wish.[13]

Figure 9.1: Clearing of Forest, Transition and *Cerrado* in Mato Grosso

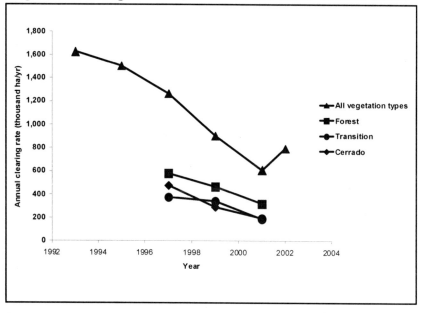

Source: FEMA (2004). At least a part of the decline from 1999 to 2001 can be attributed to the licensing and control programme. The upsurge in 2002 may be partly explained by expectation of a change of governor at the end of that year.

Controlling deforestation in private properties by enforcing environmental legislation, as in the FEMA programme, is only one of several approach-

12   Fearnside and Barbosa (2003).
13   Fearnside (2003b).

es to reducing forest loss. Establishment and protection of various kinds of parks and reserves is another strategy. Protected areas potentially provide more assurance that forest will be maintained over the long term, making them particularly important for biodiversity (as opposed to carbon). A different underlying conception of the importance of time, which affects the relative importance of short-term versus long-term conservation, is a critical difference between global warming mitigation and biodiversity conservation.[14] The location of higher biomass forests far from current deforestation frontiers and of threatened areas with high biodiversity near the frontiers also affects these priorities[15] as does the differing costs of forest protection and differing possible bases of comparison used in calculating environmental benefits.[16] Indigenous areas represent the most important category of protected and 'semi-protected' areas, despite their not being considered formal 'conservation units'.[17]

The Role of Indigenous Peoples

Indigenous reserves have a great potential role in avoiding deforestation for several reasons. Firstly, they cover about 20 per cent of Brazil's Amazon region. Secondly, their forests are generally much better conserved than those outside of reserves and protected areas. Thirdly, indigenous populations actively defend their areas against invasion. Yet although indigenous peoples have had a much better record of maintaining natural vegetation than have their non-indigenous counterparts, the data from Mato Grosso indicate that indigenous areas are not an automatic guarantee that clearing will be avoided.

The 2001 imagery interpreted by FEMA reveals large clearings in native vegetation (forest, 'transition' and *cerrado*) appearing in several indigenous reserves in Mato Grosso (Table 9.1 and Figure 9.2). The Maraiwatsede Reserve (Reserve no. 21 in Table 9.1 and Figure 9.2) had over 6,000 hectares cleared in a single two-year biennium (2000–01), including two clearings of about 1,800 hectares each. In the Bakairi Reserve (Reserve no. 5), approximately 6,000 hectares were cleared in 2000-01. This was in the form of large clearings of the type produced by large ranchers rather than small farmers. Several of the 56 reserves listed in Table 9.1 have very high clearing rates, expressed as a percentage of the re-

14   Fearnside (2002c, d); Fearnside et al. (2000).
15   Fearnside and Ferraz (1995).
16   Fearnside (1999a).
17   Fearnside and Ferraz (1995); Ferreira et al. (2001); ISA (1999).

serve area cleared in a single biennium (2000–01). It should be emphasised that most reserves have much fewer clearings. The most rapidly cleared reserve (Baikairi: Reserve no. 5) lost 11.3 per cent of its area in a single biennium, even more than the county with a similar record: Ipiranga do Norte with 8.4 per cent. Other reserves with dramatic deforestation surges in 2000–01 were Irantxe (Reserve no. 15) with 6.1 per cent cleared in the period, Juininha (Reserve no. 18) with 5.1 per cent, Maraiwatsede (Reserve no. 21) with 4.0 per cent, Parecis (Reserve no. 29) with 3.6 per cent and Perigara (Reserve no. 33) with 5.2 per cent.

Table 9.1: Clearing in Indigenous Areas in Mato Grosso(a)

Reserve number	Indigenous Area	Area of reserve	Clearing in the 2000–01 biennium		Cumulative total by 2001	
		(ha)	(ha)	(%)	(ha)	(%)
1	Apiaka-Kaiabi	109,245	219	0.20%	2,444	2.24%
2	Arara do Rio Branco	114,842	48	0.04%	390	0.34%
3	Areões	218,515	462	0.21%	1,132	0.52%
4	Areões Ii	16,650	6	0.04%	971	5.83%
4	Aripunã	750,649	439	0.06%	1,961	0.26%
5	Bakairi	61,405	6,922	11.27%	13,190	21.48%
6	Batovi	5,130	0	0.00%	109	2.12%
7	Capoto/Jarina	634,915	127	0.02%	3,243	0.51%
8	Chão Preto	8,060	8	0.10%	1,857	23.04%
9	Enawenê-Nawê	542,089	0	0.00%	0	0.00%
10	Erikbaktsa	79,936	74	0.09%		0.00%
11	Escondido	169,139	0	0.00%	27	0.02%
12	Estação Parecis	3,620	0	0.00%	2,852	78.77%

Table 9.1 continued

Reserve number	Indigenous Area	Area of reserve	Clearing in the 2000–01 biennium		Cumulative total by 2001	
13	Estivadinho	2,032	0	0.00%	430	21.14%
14	Figueiras	9,859	0	0.00%	622	6.31%
15	Irantxe	45,556	2,796	6.14%	5,115	11.23%
16	Japuira	152,510	262	0.17%	5,899	3.87%
17	Jarudore	4,706	10	0.22%	3,802	80.79%
18	Juininha	70,538	3,611	5.12%	19,965	28.30%
19	Kayabi	466,434 *	1,520	0.33%	3,861	0.83%
20	Lagoa dos Brincos	1,845	0	0.00%	0	0.00%
21	Maraiwatsede	168,000	6,645	3.96%	61,305	36.49%
22	Marechal Rondon	98,500	2,119	2.15%	27,300	27.72%
23	Mekragnoti	142,853 *	0	0.00%	6	0.00%
24	Menku	47,094	45	0.10%	427	0.91%
25	Merure	82,301	156	0.19%	3,718	4.52%
26	Nambikwara	1,011,961	4,824	0.48%	7,268	0.72%
27	Panará	132,593 *	222	0.17%	4,476	3.38%
28	Parabubure	224,447	120	0.05%	28,918	12.88%
29	Parecis	563,587	20,392	3.62%	60,449	10.73%
30	Parque Indígena Aripuanã	1,010,736 *	37	0.00%	10,893	1.08%
31	Parque Nacional do Xingu	2,642,004	0	0.00%	0	0.00%

Table 9.1 continued

Reserve number	Indigenous Area	Area of reserve	Clearing in the 2000–01 biennium		Cumulative total by 2001	
32	Pequizal	9,887	0	0.00%	968	9.79%
33	Perigara	10,740	555	5.17%	1,602	14.92%
34	Pimentel Barbosa	328,966	0	0.00%	40,901	12.43%
35	Pirines de Souza	29,580	20	0.07%	766	2.59%
36	Rio Formoso	19,749	34	0.17%	1,232	6.24%
37	Roosevelt	85,433 *	0	0.00%	450	0.53%
38	Sangradouro/ Volta Grande	100,280	27	0.03%	3,253	3.24%
39	Santana	35,471	19	0.05%	929	2.62%
40	São Domingos	5,705	86	1.51%	2,714	47.57%
41	São Marcos	168,478	10	0.01%	1,972	1.17%
42	Sararé	67,420	17	0.03%	4,232	6.28%
43	Serra Morena	148,300	318	0.21%	951	0.64%
44	Sete de Setembro	145,975 *	13	0.01%	2,331	1.60%
45	Tadarimana	9,785	0	0.00%	980	10.02%
46	Taihantesu	5,362	0	0.00%	369	6.88%
47	Tapirapé / Karajá	66,166	16	0.02%	2,492	3.77%
47	Tereza Cristina	25,694	0	0.00%	2,257	8.79%
48	Tirecatinga	130,575	150	0.12%	536	0.41%

Table 9.1 continued

Reserve number	Indigenous Area	Area of reserve	Clearing in the 2000–01 biennium		Cumulative total by 2001	
49	Ubawawe	51,900	4	0.01%	8,760	16.88%
50	Umutina	28,120	3	0.01%	5,617	19.98%
51	Urubu Branco	157,000	1,727	1.10%	1,727	1.10%
52	Utiariti	412,304	0	0.00%	934	0.23%
53	Vale do Guaporé	242,593	256	0.11%	7,195	2.97%
54	Wawi	149,900	329	0.22%	8,392	5.60%
55	Xingú	2,639,306	2,035	0.08%	12,973	0.49%
56	Zoró	355,790	0	0.00%	12,066	3.39%
TOTAL		**14,666,443**	**56,686**	**0.39%**	**395,366**	**2.70%**

(a) Data from FEMA. Clearing includes cutting of all classes of native vegetation: forest, 'transition' (forest-*cerrado* ecotones) and *cerrado*.
* Areas calculated by FEMA. All other areas are from decree creating the reserve.

In addition to clearing, logging is an important source of disturbance in indigenous areas. In the Cinta Larga tribe's Roosevelt Reserve near the border with Rondônia (Reserve no. 37 in Figure 9.2) a large logging scar appeared on the 2001 imagery, occupying the entire south-western portion of the reserve.

Purists in indigenous protection sometimes assert that indigenous peoples and their lands should be protected solely on the basis of human rights, rather than on the basis of any utilitarian benefits they provide to the rest of the world. The fear is raised that, if the utilitarian benefits that a group provides were perceived to have declined in importance, or if the value of converting the land to other uses were to be seen as more profitable, then the indigenous groups would be vulnerable if utilitarianism had become the only rationale for their maintenance. However, it is important to realise that human rights and utilitarian benefits are not mutually exclusive sources of motivation for support. Human rights concerns set a lower limit to support, but recognition of their importance should not serve as justification for foregoing the potentially much larger values implied by environmental services.

Figure 9.2: Principal Indigenous Areas in Mato Grosso (numbers correspond to the reserves in Table 9.1)

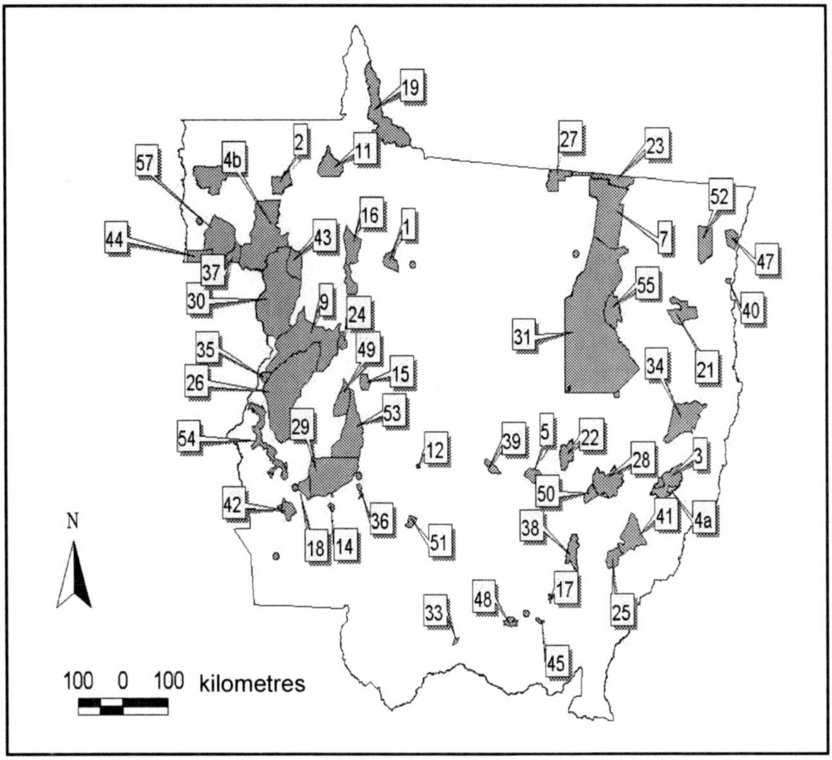

While some indigenous peoples inhabit desolate or degraded areas with little biodiversity, biomass carbon stocks and other features that are valued for their environmental roles, those who inhabit tropical rain forest have much to gain from tapping the value of environmental services. Furthermore, the magnitude of the resources is potentially much greater than can be expected from other options that are realistically available, including subsidies based on human rights concerns. Prior to the March 2001 decision of President George W. Bush to withdraw from negotiations over the Kyoto Protocol's 2008–12 first commitment period, carbon markets were expected to total over US$15 billion annually by 2010. While the US withdrawal greatly decreases this expectation for the first commitment period, and the July 2001 Bonn agreement rules out tropical forests altogether for that commitment period, markets from 2013 onwards could expand considerably above the previous expectations for 2008–12. Even a tiny fraction of these funds directed to indigenous peoples would eclipse other likely revenue sources.

From the perspective of the interests of indigenous peoples, the sustainable nature of forest maintenance, especially compared with non-forest uses such as cattle or soybean, together with the compatibility of this use with traditional indigenous lifestyles give this option tremendous advantages. Brazil's indigenous peoples support the inclusion of forest maintenance for carbon credit under the Kyoto Protocol's Clean Development Mechanism (CDM). The Coordination of Indigenous Peoples of Brazilian Amazonia (COIAB) signed a statement by Brazilian non-governmental organisations calling for such a provision in the CDM,[18] and has promoted a series of events and discussions of the issue in the region. It should be noted that no Brazilian indigenous peoples were represented in the Indigenous Peoples' Forum on Climate Change (an international association of indigenous groups led by South-east Asia) in its adoption of a contrary position.[19]

From the point of view of biodiversity conservation, the question of whether funds should be devoted to totally protected areas (areas without people) or to various forms of inhabited and/or managed areas, is a matter of continuing debate.[20] At one end of the spectrum, the future is seen as an inexorable march towards environmental degradation, with inhabited reserves only slightly postponing the time when these areas will arrive at their endpoint of virtually complete desolation.[21] The opposing view sees the creation of large areas under total protection as politically unviable and likely to cause injustices for traditional populations already living in the areas selected, ultimately offering less protection for nature because they lack the popular support of local inhabitants who can defend the forests from invaders more effectively than government-paid guards.[22] In

18   'Manifestação ...' (2000).
19   Indigenous Peoples' Forum on Climate Change (2000).
20   See the views in Kramer et al. (1997) and Brandon et al. (1998).
21   Terborgh (1999).
22   Schwartzman et al. (2000a, b); Terborgh (2000); Redford and Sanderson (2000).

Amazonian forests outside Brazil indigenous peoples have been important defenders of forest in many locations,[23] while adopting the destructive practices of non-indigenous settlers in others.[24] Although hunting and other activities by traditional peoples can reduce biodiversity compared to uninhabited forest, the convergence of many objectives between those seeking to secure the land rights of traditional peoples and those concerned primarily with biodiversity conservation offers great scope for mutually beneficial alliances.[25]

From the point of view of conservation, much better results can be achieved by using financial resources to pay directly for environmental services, rather than subsidising conservation indirectly by promoting ecotourism, agroforestry, sustainable forest management and other environmentally-friendly uses as compared to presumed alternatives.[26] Essentially, 'you get what you pay for' and the best way to conserve biodiversity, carbon stocks and other forest values is to pay for these functions directly. Credible monitoring arrangements would necessarily be a part of any system of direct payments for environmental services.[27]

Negotiation with indigenous peoples is a crucial area for Amazonian conservation policy, and one that has hardly begun. Indigenous lands represent much greater areas of natural ecosystems than do all types of conservation units combined and the future fate of indigenous lands will therefore be the dominant factor in the ultimate fate of these ecosystems. So far indigenous peoples have had a much better record of maintaining the natural ecosystems around them than have other populations in Amazonia. However, indigenous peoples are not inherently conservationist, as is sometimes assumed, and they can be expected to respond to the same economic stimuli that induce other actors to destroy and degrade forests. Indigenous areas are already a major source of illegally logged timber from Amazonia.[28]

Logging and clearing in indigenous areas not only sacrifice tropical forest but also damage what is perhaps the greatest asset of indigenous peoples for securing sustainable revenues in the future: namely, the credibility of these peoples as reliable forest guardians. Opting for short-term gains from environmental destruction would be a great error from the point of

23   Van de Hammen (2003) for Colombia.
24   Rudel and Horowitz (1993) in Ecuador.
25   Redford and Stearman (1993).
26   Ferraro and Kiss (2002).
27   Fearnside (1997c).
28   Cotton and Romine (1999).

view of the wellbeing of the indigenous groups themselves, in addition to its impact on global environmental concerns such as biodiversity and climate. It is precisely the ability of indigenous peoples to defend and maintain their forests that gives them an as-yet unremunerated role in providing environmental services.[29] In order to chart their future, they need to see that their conservationist role is valuable and is also the source of their support.

To date, indigenous peoples have been receiving no direct benefit from their environmental role as maintainers of the forest. This is also the case for non-indigenous Amazonians. Were environmental services to become a significant source of revenue, the economics of forest maintenance would be radically changed in favour of maintaining these areas.[30] Increasing forest loss within indigenous areas is an indication of the urgency of achieving progress on mechanisms to provide compensation for environmental services.

Conclusions

Indigenous areas have great potential importance for conservation of biodiversity and for maintenance of the climate stabilisation functions of tropical forest. Indigenous peoples have shown themselves to be much more able than non-indigenous groups at rain forest conservation. Capturing the value of these environmental services represents a vital opportunity to the indigenous peoples. Data from the state of Mato Grosso show that while indigenous reserves remain mostly intact (3.2 per cent of original vegetation lost by 2001), the rate of clearing in some reserves is alarmingly high. At the extreme, 11.3 per cent of one reserve was cleared in a single two-year period. Several clearings of over 1,500 hectares appeared in reserves in 2001, indicating that some groups are allowing outside farmers to exploit their land (for a fee). The presumption that indigenous peoples are inherently environmentalist is flawed and the events in Mato Grosso underline the importance of speedy integration of environmental services into the economies of the reserves and of the world.

29   Fearnside (1997a).
30   *Ibid.*

10

Extractivists, Indigenes and Protected Areas: Science and Conservation Policy in the Amazon

David Cleary

Introduction

A distinguishing, but often unrecognised, feature of the Amazon Basin is the abundance and variety of its protected areas, which on paper at least surpass anywhere on the planet in geographical extent; entirely appropriately, given the Amazon's status as the largest continuous tropical forest and greatest concentration of biodiversity in the world. No reliable percentage of area protected exists for the Basin as a whole, given definitional problems, but the national statistics are impressive.[1] The Brazilian Amazon, for example, which accounts for between 70 and 80 per cent of the total land area of the Amazon Basin, depending on which definition of the Basin is used, has around 22 per cent of its total area as demarcated indigenous lands and a further ten per cent as conservation units (see Table10.1).[2] The percentage of the Amazon Basin under some form of protection, however defined, far exceeds the percentage under formal protection in other large tropical or temperate landscapes such as the American West or the African savannas. That protection in the Amazon is often limited to designation on a map rather than reality in the field is unfortunate, but does not affect the Amazon's prominent place in global protected area statistics, much cherished by governments and international environmental organisations alike.

---

1   Cleary (2001).
2   For a detailed tabulation and mapping of protected areas in the Brazilian Amazon, far more accessible and useful than any governmental source, see the map and tables *Amazônia Brasileira 2000* (São Paulo: Instituto Socioambiental, 2000), available through the ISA website, www.socioambental.org.br.

**Table 10.1: Indigenous Lands versus Conservation Units,
Brazilian Amazon**

Conservation Unit Type	Number	Area (hectares)
Federal		
National parks	12	8,900,000
Biological reserves	8	3,000,000
Ecological stations	11	2,000,000
National forests	31	15,200,000
Extractive reserves	10	3,100,000
Environmental protection areas	3	439,000
Total	**75**	**32,639,000**
State		
State parks	17	4,200,000
State forests	13	2,700,000
Environmental protection areas	19	15,000,000
Total	**49**	**21,900,000**
Indigenous reserves		
'In identification'	90	4,000,000
'Under judicial review'	20	3,800,000
'Demarcated'	36	18,900,000
'Ratified'	43	17,100,000
'Confirmed and registered'	181	57,400,000
Total	**370**	**101,200,000**

Source: MMA (2002).

Protected areas in the Amazon fall for the most part into the two categories of indigenous areas and nature reserves, the latter usually called
conservation units in the technical and policy literature. In some countries
such as Venezuela and Colombia, protected areas may simultaneously be
both nature reserves and indigenous territory while other countries, such
as Brazil, make them mutually exclusive categories. This makes the task of
compiling comparative national statistics on protected and indigenous

areas in the Amazon a complicated exercise. There is an increasingly important third category of protected area, the extractivist or sustainable development reserve, which is aimed specifically at the non-indigenous Amazonian riverine peasantries known as *caboclos* in Brazil and *ribereños* in the Hispanic Amazon. This form of protected area began to appear in the 1990s and is so far restricted to the Brazilian Amazon, consolidating non-indigenous but low-impact forms of natural resource management, such as extractivism and artesanal fishing.

Nature reserves and indigenous territories are very distinct forms of protected area in the international conservation literature, but in the Amazon they often overlap. Several Amazonian countries assume that nature reserves may have indigenous populations and make special legal provision for them in national park legislation. Other countries are more dysfunctional in their protected area legislation. In the Brazilian Amazon approximately 18 million hectares, an area roughly the size of England, is demarcated as both indigenous land and conservation unit, a result of lack of coordination, shading into outright hostility, between federal indigenous and environmental agencies. Unfortunately, indigenous and national park legislation in Brazil is directly contradictory; any permanent human presence in a national park is technically illegal, indigenous or otherwise. Theoretically, this means that groups such as the Ingarikó, included within the Mount Roraima National Park without their knowledge when the park was created in 1989, are illegally present in their ancestral homelands. Their subsistence hunting and fishing would also make them liable to arrest by park rangers, since any form of economic activity is also barred in a Brazilian national park. Such absurdities have bedevilled relations between the indigenous and environmental communities in Brazil for a generation.

The Origins of Protected Areas in Amazonia

The formal creation of protected areas is a relatively recent historical phenomenon in all Amazonian countries outside the Guianas but its historical origins can be traced back to the nineteenth century. The first protected areas in the region were domesticated and heavily altered forest patches preserved for the enjoyment of urban populations the very earliest of which, later to evolve into the Museu Paraense Emílio Goeldi, was created in the Brazilian city of Belém in 1863. The urbanisation which accompanied the rubber boom also saw a number of initiatives to preserve forest cover in the watersheds of creeks used as a source of water by rapidly growing cities. These early protected area initiatives were of merely historical interest. Amazonian urbanisation, in practice, proceeded with little regard for the seemingly infinite reserves of water and wood available. Even before the large-scale expansion of national societies into the Amazon Basin from the 1960s onwards, the developmentalist lens through which governments in all Amazonian countries viewed the region was, on the surface at least, inherently hostile to the notion of areas by definition insulated from development. Latin American states in the twentieth century, irrespective of ideological persuasion and period, viewed their Amazonian territories as largely uninhabited wilderness. They were seen as demographic voids where the lack of an effective State presence and an industrial economy made national territory vulnerable to penetration by outsiders, either neighbouring countries, the United States or multinational companies. This is an extraordinarily persistent form of nationalist paranoia still regularly encountered on the more recidivist parts of the political spectrum to this day in all Amazonian countries.

Thus, the Amazonian regions of South American States lagged behind the rest of the country when governments set about the formal creation of national protected area systems. Beyond the Amazon, the first South American national parks and nature reserves were created as early as the 1920s, whereas the earliest protected areas in the Amazon date from the 1970s. In a sense it is surprising, given the apparent ideological hostility towards environmental protection, that any Amazonian protected areas were created even then. But there were two important motives pushing even developmentalist governments towards at least sporadic protection.

The first was the need in all Amazonian countries to separate territories reserved for the region's indigenous inhabitants from development corridors and areas of non-indigenous settlement. Environmental conservation was not a motive in this process, of course; the creation of indigenous territories was meant to facilitate development by radically reducing areas effectively controlled by indigenous peoples and the process routinely involved forced relocations and heavy indigenous mortality. Nevertheless, the end result was the creation of a regional network of indigenous territories whose legal status varied from country to country but which were functionally important as protected areas. Entry and exit was regulated and there was, at least theoretically, a legal obligation of stewardship for these areas laid upon the State and certain types of economic activity were either prohibited or heavily regulated. Obligations towards indigenous populations formed an increasingly specific part of international law and all Amazonian countries signed a series of international conventions in the latter part of the twentieth century which recognised indigenous rights, including the rights to effective protection of indigenous natural resources and intellectual property.[3]

On the ground, the degree of effective protection of indigenous lands varies from country to country, but throughout the Amazon Basin it has always been the case that ecosystems have tended to be more intact within indigenous areas than beyond them. Despite the many invasions of indigenous reserves across the Amazon over the years, as national indigenous movements have grown in scale these early, precariously maintained reserves became the basis of very significant national systems of indigenous territories, which now, in the Amazon Basin as a whole, cover a greater area and have greater biodiversity value than the conservation unit system.

The second motive driving the creation of protected areas systems had more to do with conservation *sensu strict*, the notion that 'wilderness' — a highly problematic concept much deconstructed by environmental historians — should be preserved by formally designating areas as national parks, biological reserves or ecological preserves.[4] Paradoxically, the importance of wilderness was also deeply bound up with certain strands within Latin American nationalism, even within developmentalism, which viewed a large area of relatively untapped natural resources as an important part of the national patrimony. Such areas had to be protected either for their own sake (romanticism and nationalism are natural bedfellows, after all) or because they constituted a valuable potential resource for the future, especially for comfortingly technocratic industries like biotechnology or pharmaceuticals. Ronald Foresta has traced out in fascinating detail how this process worked during the 1960s and 1970s in the Brazilian Amazon. A small group of dedicated conservationists, highly educated and with good connections at the highest levels of the military regime in power throughout the period, was able by a combination of astute lobbying, scientific argument and the exploitation of a strong but inchoate feeling among the Brazilian military that the Amazon was a valuable long-term geopolitical

3   Mackay (1999). See especially chapter 6, 'Medio ambiente, desarollo y participación' (pp. 277–325) for a useful summary of international law and State obligations in these areas.

4   Simon Schama's (1996) account is the most comprehensive deconstruction of the notion of wilderness and the historical processes underlying its manufacture in places once inhabited by indigenous people. See especially pp. 365–70, on the history of Yellowstone National Park.

asset, to create a significant conservation unit system in the Brazilian Amazon by the mid-1980s.[5]

Given the technocratic, developmentalist climate of the 1970s when this process began, it was inevitable that science should become intimately involved with the creation of Amazonian protected areas systems. The details are a fascinating example of the intersection between science and policy in the Amazon with consequences that have reverberated down to the present day. In the late 1960s, a small group of scientists attempted to synthesise available information about Amazonian biodiversity and come up with a general theory for its origins, its speciation dynamics and the modern distribution of flora and fauna. Their ideas came to be called refuge, or refugium theory. Refuge theory was a critical influence in the construction of conservation unit systems in the Amazon, since it appeared to offer a powerful methodology for defining the highest biodiversity areas which conservation units should protect, even given the fragmentary nature, then and now, of our knowledge of Amazonian biogeography. Yet while the research it stimulated greatly expanded our understanding of Amazonian biodiversity, like many productive scientific hypotheses it turned out to be wrong in virtually every detail. The story of the rise and fall of refuge theory is thus something of a scientific morality tale and deserves to be told in some detail.

Refuge Theory

Refuge theory was first formulated in the late 1960s by the German ornithologist Jürgen Haffer as a way of accounting for the geographical distribution of bird species in the Colombian Amazon and it suggested mechanisms through which speciation among forest birds took place.[6] He proposed what appeared to be a powerful model for explaining Amazonian biodiversity. If plant and animal species were isolated in the forest or savanna islands created by the fluctuating late Pleistocene and Holocene climate, they might well fission into a subspecies or evolve into a separate species before the forest or savanna refuge expanded again with a climate shift. It could now disperse over a much wider area until the next climate shift, when the new species and subspecies would be isolated again and the process of differentiation would repeat itself. The cumulative effect, over several climate shifts, would be exceptionally high biodiversity in

5   Foresta (1992).
6   Haffer (1969).

flora and fauna.[7] The importance of refuges for biodiversity formation was amplified in the Amazon, Haffer argued, since rivers also acted as significant geographical barriers and fractured the ranges of species.[8]

This hypothesis immediately caught the imagination of natural scientists working in the Amazon, since it offered a powerful ordering principle for the biogeography of the region. If the number and range of species of a particular kind of organism could be mapped out, the centres of high diversity, where the largest number of endemic species overlapped, must be the old refuge areas. They would be separated by intermediate zones of younger forest or savanna, across which species had spread more recently. The result would be a map marked by contour lines, with refuge areas marked out by a thick blur of species tapering out into relatively less biodiverse valleys between the old refuge areas. Thus, the 1970s became a vintage decade for scientific cartographers, suddenly charged with creating dozens of new biogeographical maps as regional specialists around the world rushed to apply refuge theory to their species lists and range maps. Refuges were swiftly defined for Amazonian lizards,[9] butterflies,[10] tree species[11] and other groups of organisms from all parts of the Amazon Basin.

This wave of research was combined with essays from geomorphologists and paleoecologists in two landmark volumes which were essentially extended manifestos for refugium theory, despite the presence of a couple of dissenting essays.[12] During the 1980s, refuge theory consolidated itself as the dominant paradigm for explaining the origins and present distribution of Amazonian biodiversity and was presented as established orthodoxy in the standard graduate textbook on regional biogeography and paleoecology, still in general use.[13] Ghillean Prance, the principal elaborator of refuge theory for the Amazon in the 1970s, gave institutional expression to its importance in the natural sciences by becoming successively director of the New York Botanical Garden and the Royal Botanical Garden at Kew, London. Most importantly, refuge theory became an explicit guiding principle in conservation policy in Amazon Basin countries and remains so. However, although

---

7 Haffer (1982).
8 *Ibid.*, p. 10. But more recent work suggests rivers may not be as important a factor in Amazonian speciation as has been thought. See Gascon et al. (2000).
9 Vanzolini and Williams (1970).
10 Brown et al. (1974).
11 Prance (1973; 1982).
12 Prance (1982a); Prance and Lovejoy (1986).
13 Whitemore and Prance (1987).

the scientific debate has moved on, many senior figures in national environmental ministries and parks authorities, trained when refugium theory was
dominant and subsequently without the time to keep up with the technical
debate, are still devotees of the concept.[14]

In retrospect, with the clarity of hindsight, this research consensus around
refuge theory seems hasty. As even proponents of refuge theory noted, once
composite maps of all the different species groups for which refuge areas
were posited were drawn up, it became rather difficult to find a part of the
Amazon Basin which had not been proposed as a refuge area at one time or
another.[15] There was also a worryingly tautological quality to a great deal of
refuge theory. Modern biogeographical data was being used as evidence for
past environmental change for which there was in fact only fragmentary evidence, but the paleoenvironmental data was nevertheless cited as further support for the interpretation of the distribution of Amazonian biodiversity in
the present.[16] This is inherently problematic, since a range of other factors
will always be relevant to modern species distribution as well.

Sampling biases and human impacts immediately spring to mind.
Sampling bias goes to the heart of a recurring problem of natural science
in the tropics, since it brings into focus not so much what we know but how
we know it, in a context of important knowledge gaps. Since many Amazon
plant species, for example, are rare and plant inventories in the Amazon are
far from complete, the more thoroughly local flora is studied the more it
will seem unique. Botanists in the field collect in areas where they think
there is a high likelihood of finding rare or endemic plant species. This
means, given a low knowledge base, there is an immediate danger that the
proposal of a high endemism area will become a self-fulfilling prophecy. In
other words, a location which is no more than averagely biodiverse is au-
thoritatively but wrongly endorsed by scientists as exceptional. Refuges proposed on the basis of high apparent endemism may simply be sampling
artefacts; there is a remarkable coincidence between the geographical density of botanical collecting and the occurrence of refugia.[17] It is also char-

---

14   A detailed account of the influence of refuge theory on conservation policy in
      Brazil in the 1970s and 1980s is given in Foresta (1992), chapter 2.
15   A point tellingly made by Foresta (1992), pp. 44–5, which reproduces different
      refuge maps drawn up by Haffer, Vanzolini, Prance and Brown.
16   Roosevelt (2000).
17   Nelson et al. (1990). Nelson's admonition that, 'with so many poorly collected
      species some presumed local endemics and disjuncts may actually have a wider
      distribution' (p. 715) should be framed on the office wall of every conservation
      planner in the Amazon.

acteristic of refugium theory to ignore possible human impacts and treat the Amazon as an entirely natural space. The modern distribution of edible mammals and birds is unlikely to be a reliable guide to paleoclimatic change, for example, nor is the distribution of dozens of palm species which have some utility to humans and have been intensively managed in some parts of the Amazon for millennia. In ignoring possible human impacts on species distribution, refugium theory often seemed naive and ahistorical to archaeologists and environmental historians.

One of the strongest initial attractions of refuge theory was that it appeared to be consistent with the emerging picture of Holocene and Pleistocene climatic instability. It at least had the cardinal virtue of making empirical forecasts about the paleoclimatic and paleoenvironmental patterns it expected to find, which could be directly tested as further paleoenvironmental research was done from the 1970s onwards. Refuge theory expected that the Amazonian climate would be shown to have been significantly colder and dryer, even arid, for much of the Pleistocene; that it would have been coldest and most arid during glacial periods; and that during these arid periods savanna would be the dominant Amazonian vegetation type. Associated with these predictions was the expectation that many currently forested areas would be shown to have been savanna in the past. In addition, refuge theorists expected that forests would be divisible into ancient refuge patches where savanna had never intruded, and much younger forest cover dating from the beginning of the current interglacial, with its warmer and wetter weather, when forests began to expand again from around 13,000 years ago.

But as evidence from lake cores and carbon isotope studies came in during the 1980s and 1990s, it became increasingly difficult to square with the predictions made by refugium theory. New, dated Pleistocene cores from the western Amazon, from Ecuador and Brazil, made that part of the Basin the most extensively studied by paleoecologists. The Ecuadorean section of the Amazon was an area which most refuge maps defined as a Pleistocene refuge, but pollen records from several cores showed it had not been a stable forest area. During cold periods it had resembled more a submontane Andean forest, with elements of lowland forest mixed together with submontane tree species advancing down to lower elevations with the cooling of the climate. This mixed forest could only have been supported by a wet climate, probably a seasonal one. Cooler temperatures, which are beyond doubt during glacial periods, did not mean a dry climate in this part of the Amazon, let alone an 'arid' one.[18] Another dated

18   Liu and Colinvaux (1985).

Pleistocene core from the western Brazilian Amazon was equally damaging to refuge theory. It showed that for 42,000 years, despite temperature and rainfall fluctuations which caused wide variations in lake depth and sedimentation rates, the study site had been continuously forested. Grasslands and savanna had never been present.[19]

The importance of this finding was twofold, and went well beyond refuge theory. It demonstrated for the first time that some parts of the Amazon Basin had been forested continuously for tens of thousands of years, long enough to approach the reliable limits of current dating technologies. This in itself was not damaging to refuge theory, since implicit in the latter was the notion that refuge areas would contain extremely ancient forest. The area from which these cores came, Lake Pata in the extreme west of Amazonas state, Brazil, near the Negro river, was not part of a postulated refuge, but that in itself was not the issue, given the characteristic elasticity of refuge mapping. The real damage to refuge theory was the demonstration that it was possible to have climatic fluctuations in a location, including shifts from hotter and wetter regimes to colder and dryer ones, and probably from seasonal to non-seasonal patterns and back again, without this having the slightest impact on the dominance of the area by forested ecosystems. The complete lack of evidence for savanna expansion at Lake Pata goes to the heart of refugium theory. Not a single dated Pleistocene core from anywhere in the Amazon shows a forested area remote from an existing forest-savanna boundary which had savanna periods in the past. By the end of the 1990s, the research consensus was growing that refuge theory was fundamentally flawed.[20]

Nevertheless, as Foresta documented in detail for the Brazilian Amazon, refuge theory was a crucial element in determining where exactly the boundaries of the new conservation units created in the 1970s and 1980s would be drawn. They were intended to cover as high a proportion of supposed Pleistocene refuges as possible. The collapse of refuge theory therefore removed an important element in the argument for their cre-

19   Colinvaux et al. (1996).
20   Others put it more harshly. Roosevelt, with her customary directness, notes, 'In refugium theory, modern Amazonian biogeography and undated geomorphological features were explained as the result of Pleistocene drying and became the evidence for late Pleistocene drying, in the absence of Pleistocene biological information … When intact Pleistocene pollen cores were finally collected, analysed for carbon isotopes and published, they held no evidence for the replacement of tropical rain forest by Pleistocene savannas, but this has not deterred refugium enthusiasts' (2000, p. 456).

ation, which had placed heavy emphasis on science's capacity to guide conservation strategies by identifying the most appropriate areas to be placed under protection. Yet, by the 1990s conservation units were literally part of the landscape, many of them of considerable biodiversity value whether or not they were forest or savanna in the late Pleistocene. Especially in Peru and Brazil, where a greater proportion of land was put under formal protection, Amazonian conservation unit systems played a prominent part in national strategies of environmental protection and even in efforts to attract multilateral funding to parts of the Amazon, as we shall see.

Protectionism, Livelihoods and Ecoregional Planning

Irrespective of the collapse of refuge theory, a silent and largely invisible process beyond academia gave rise to new scientific arguments to justify the creation of additional conservation units during the 1990s. However, these would now have to make their way in a political world which had undergone its own climate shift. Demands for Amazonian land for conservation would now have to contend with increasingly well articulated demands for Amazonian land by newly mobilised and powerful Amazonian social actors; indigenous peoples, the landless, small producers of various types and non-indigenous Amazonian peasantries. Central to this struggle, in which all the players routinely pay rhetorical homage to the importance of conservation and sustainable development despite having very different understandings of what the phrases mean, is the increasingly overt competition between conservation units and other forms of protected area, especially indigenous lands and extractive reserves. This is more than a straight political dispute; it also involves a struggle for dominance over definitions of Amazonian nature, where defenders of the wilderness model as its highest expression square off against those who emphasise the importance of human intervention in the evolution of Amazonian ecosystems. In terms of conservation policy, this has led to a fissure, often rancorous, between those who emphasise the reconciliation of human presence with biodiversity conservation, and those who see environmental protection as requiring the exclusion of humans. This dispute has been especially bitter in the technical literature of conservation biology where the policy implications are direct and very well understood by the participants.

During the 1990s the scientific substrate of conservation policy throughout Latin America, following similar trends in North American conservation, came to be known as 'ecoregional planning', initially a technical concept in conservation biology that assumed enormous importance for Latin American conservation in 1995 when it was adopted as an environmental planning tool by the World Bank.[21] Ecoregional planning divides continents into 'ecoregions', which are somewhat arbitrarily defined and redrawn every few years as new scientific information comes in, but which group together related ecosystem complexes and large landscapes into geographical units to serve as the basis for conservation planning. In the long term, the successful conservation of a 'portfolio' of sites within each ecoregion is imagined cumulatively to ensure the survival of regional biodiversity, even if much of the ecoregion is degraded or converted.

The standard map for Latin American and Caribbean ecoregions divides the southern section of the Americas into 200 ecoregions (compared to 80 for the United States), 34 of which fall within the Amazon (using a definition including the Guianas and the upper Orinoco). By the late 1990s, all the key institutional players in Amazonian conservation — environment ministries, the international conservation NGOs (The Nature Conservancy, Conservation International, WWF), bilateral and multilateral agencies, and including the development banks — were using standardised ecoregional maps to plan conservation actions, especially the setting of geographical priorities.[22]

Brazil, the Amazonian country with the most technically capable environment ministry, by far the highest volume of accumulated scientific research in its Amazonian region and the most systematically surveyed by the remote sensing technologies whose increasing sophistication was itself a driver of large-scale conservation planning, was the clearest example of integration between national and international conservation efforts based on ecoregional planning. In 1999, a programme within the Ministry of the Environment known as PROBIO (Project for the Conservation and Sustainable Use of Brazilian Biodiversity) organised a workshop of over 200 experts to define biogeographical conservation priorities for the Amazon, producing a map which classified the Brazilian Amazon into categories of conservation priority.[23] Overlaid on an ecoregional map of the Brazilian Amazon, this constitutes the standard geographical priority-set-

---

21   The key publication in this process was Dinerstein et al. (1995). A more detailed global ecoregional assessment is Bailey (1998).

22   A triad known in the trade as BINGOs — Big International Non-Governmental Organisations.

23   PROBIO's full title in the original is *Projeto de Conservação e Utilização Sustentável da Diversidade Biológica Brasileira.*

ting tool for all the relevant institutional actors.[24] By the time the PROBIO map was produced, however, important and very rapid changes were taking place within the protected area system in the Brazilian Amazon. The most significant of these was the astonishing expansion of the indigenous lands system. A number of factors underlay this development.

Expansion of Indigenous and Extractivist Areas

The 2000 census figures show a total Amerindian population of 351,500 in Brazil, 85 per cent of them in the Amazon. This represents an increase of some 20 per cent over the (less reliable) 1991 figure, in a context where the rest of the Brazilian population has stabilised and the rural population of the Amazon is falling steeply. This rapid growth in the Amerindian population is a sign of a new historical phase for Brazilian indians. Most groups are rebounding from the elevated mortality which followed upon the large-scale settlement of Brazilian society into the Amazon between the 1960s and the 1980s, the peak of the frontier cycle which is now almost at an end. Only a few isolated groups are still passing through, or are yet to pass through, the traumatic high mortality that was the general experience of indian groups for a generation. The typical indian group is today strikingly young, with a higher proportion of children than any other sub-group of the Brazilian population. Swarms of curious children are the first impression outsiders get of most indian villages. Projections are that rapid growth will continue for at least another two decades, before the Amerindian population stabilises at between 500,000 and one million during the period 2020 to 2030. It may go higher, since the demographic transition that is stabilising the general population may not operate in indigenous areas, or operate differently, due to cultural factors.

This demographic recovery is the most obvious sign of a cultural and ethnic renaissance among indigenous Amazonian peoples in Brazil, a critical expression of increasingly successful assertions of control over land, articulated by a growing indigenous movement with a network of strategic alliances in Brazilian civil society. International pressure played a vital role

---

24   MMA (2002). See pp. 120-1 for the PROBIO Amazon map. It is significant that the section on the Amazon is by far the most detailed and best quality, in terms of science. In Brazil as in other countries the Amazon attracts the best natural scientists, and in an inversion of the usual pattern this often means that the quality of conservation science is higher in Amazonian than in non-Amazonian biomes of South American states.

in supporting indigenous resistance to highly visible moments such as the early 1990s invasions of Yanomami lands by gold miners, intensive media coverage of which was highly embarrassing to the Brazilian government. It led directly to the demarcation and extraordinarily rapid ratification of almost ten million hectares as Yanomami reserve in 1993. Yet the most important international contribution was far lower profile. It comprised financial and technical support, especially from the German government, to a project within the Federal Indian Agency (FUNAI) known as PPTAL for the demarcation of indian lands. The chapter by Lisansky in this volume provides a detailed account of the PPTAL. Like Brazil's first extractive reserves for rubber tappers, the PPTAL forms part of the Pilot Programme to Conserve Brazil's Rain Forest (PPG7/RFPP). The move to legalise indian territories was aided by several factors, including firm political commitment to the demarcation of indigenous lands during the administration of Fernando Henrique Cardoso from 1995 to 2002 and advances in remote sensing and GPS technologies which automated much of what previously had to be laboriously carried out by field cartographers and surveyors.

The acceleration by the PPTAL project of the demarcation process lay behind a huge expansion of the indigenous lands system during the 1990s. Between 1990 and the end of 2000, the number of demarcated and ratified indigenous reserves in the Brazilian Amazon leapt from 45 to 217, involving an even more striking increase in land area covered from 12.3 million hectares to 74.5 million. By the end of 2002 indigenous reserves of all kinds covered just over a million square kilometres of 'Legal Amazonia' or about 22 per cent of its total area. To put this in context, the total area of land in indigenous reserves in the Brazilian Amazon, at slightly larger than the combined land areas of California, Arizona and Texas and roughly the same size as Colombia, is far larger than any European country. Over two-thirds of these reserves by land area, some 745,000 square kilometres, have now been ratified (*homologado*) and registered (*registrado*), the final stages in the complex process of legal confirmation of reserve boundaries. The remaining 400,000 or so square kilometres will follow in the next few years. This compares with 540,000 square kilometres of land in state and federal conservation units of all kinds.

Less spectacular, but still significant, growth occurred in the extractive and sustainable development reserve system, the roots of which go back to the mid-1980s and the founding of the National Council of Rubber Tappers (*Conselho Nacional dos Seringueiros* — CNS), the first attempt by extractivist populations of the Brazilian Amazon to found a regional organisation to press their claims to land. After the assassination of its leader Chico Mendes in 1988, the first extractive reserves were demarcated and ratified in 1990. By 2002 extractivist and sustainable development reserves accounted for just over eight million hectares, principally in the western Amazon. Although originally associated with extraction of non-timber forest products, the definition of extractivism has expanded to include artisanal fishing, both freshwater and marine, and a series of new extractive reserves shortly to be ratified will make them an important form of protected area on the Amazon floodplain and its ocean coastline.[25]

Although the original justification for the creation of extractive reserves was in defence of land rights, the advocates of extractive reserves were swift to make the argument that they were also an important contribution to environmental protection, since the complex livelihoods typical of long-established *caboclo/ribereño* populations in the Amazon have significantly fewer environmental impacts than the land-uses which threatened to displace them, especially cattle ranching. It is certainly the case, as with indigenous reserves, that ecosystems within extractive reserves tend to be much more intact than those outside them. The 1990s showed very clearly that the creation of an extractive reserve could be very successful in buffering what would otherwise certainly have been very environmentally destructive development. This was clearest in southern Acre, where the Chico Mendes extractive reserve was one of the first to be created, in 1990. During that decade, a series of road improvements between Rio Branco, Acre's state capital, and Assis Brasil on the Bolivian border, led to some deforestation along the highway corridor, in a familiar cycle of in-migration and development. However, the fact that the Chico Mendes reserve existed and was effectively functioning as a protected area, unlike many conservation units with stricter protection regimes, limited deforestation to a much narrower highway corridor than was typically the case in the Amazon in this situation. Even more importantly, it prevented the formation of a feeder road network off the main highway that is a prerequisite for the larger-scale highway corridor deforestation with a fish-

---

25 Interestingly, an ecoregional perspective is that the upland forests of the Amazon are not its most threatened ecosystem. Ecoregions containing upland forest are very large, and a great deal of deforestation needs to take place before the percentage of ecoregion converted rises significantly. It is the coastal ecoregions, geographically much less extensive, which present the highest levels of conversion and are the most threatened Amazonian ecosystems.

bone pattern seen time and again in the Brazilian Amazon in these circumstances since the 1960s.

While the indigenous and extractivist lobbies were waging their highly
effective campaigns for land during the 1990s, the defenders of a more traditionally scientific approach to environmental protection were making
their own adjustments to changing circumstances. Their bases of political
support in the 1990s were technical rather than originating in social movements, but were no less politically effective for that. They formed a loose
coalition of like-minded, highly educated individuals scattered between the
large international environmental NGOs, especially Conservation
International and the World Wildlife Fund, parts of the World Bank and
the protected areas bureaucracy within the federal Ministry of the
Environment. They tended not to be impressed by the growth of the indigenous and extractive reserves systems, believing that these were not as
effective for promoting a conservation strategy as expanding the strict protected area system, where there would be little or no human presence.
Although without the strong base of popular support in the Amazon itself
which the indigenous and extractivist movements could boast, the strict
protection lobby was extremely well connected politically at the federal
level, able to navigate bureaucratic jungles as confidently as rubber tappers
negotiated forest trails and was therefore much more skilled at identifying
opportunities for funding their goals.

The result was paradoxical. As the 1990s gave way to a new century, the
strict protected area system, much less important in terms of area and biodiversity value than the limited protection area systems, was set in the
Brazilian Amazon to receive considerably more financial and human resources for environmental protection than indigenous and extractive reserves. Indeed, the protectionist lobby had argued that it was precisely because strict protection areas represented a less geographically extensive
system that they should receive more resources, to increase their geographical coverage to match that of the other protected area systems.
Once again, scientific arguments were marshalled to support an increase in
the protected area system. Ecoregional analyses demonstrated that most
ecoregions in fact had insignificant percentages under strict protection,
and part of PROBIO's remit was precisely to suggest where new protected areas could most usefully be created.

From the mid-1990s all these arguments and subliminal political tensions coalesced around the Amazon Reserves and Protected Areas Project
(ARPA). This is a large-scale project to consolidate and expand the

Amazon's protected area system, for which the original initiative came from the World Wildlife Fund. WWF envisaged it as a means of increasing the percentage of the Brazilian Amazon under strict protection to ten per cent, and helped to co-ordinate the presentation of a proposal to the Global Environment Fund (GEF) with the World Bank as implementing agency. It was finally approved after years of negotiation in 2001. Through complex, co-financing arrangements between the Bank, the Brazilian government and NGO donors co-ordinated by WWF, it envisages the disbursement of $395 million over the decade from 2003, and began implementation in 2002.[26]

However, the version of ARPA that was finally approved was significantly different from its original formulation. What had begun as a project directed exclusively at strict protection emerged as a project with a heavy emphasis on strict protection but with significant components also directed at limited protection areas, especially extractive and sustainable development reserves. Quite simply, when the proposal emerged from the technical context in which it had originated and entered the political arena, institutional actors essential to its execution, such as the Secretariat for the Amazon within the federal Ministry of the Environment, or those with the capacity to create negative publicity if they were excluded, such as the *Conselho Nacional dos Seringueiros*, proved extremely impervious to ecoregional analysis. They insisted that such large financial resources directed exclusively at strict protection was unacceptable. They demanded that part of ARPA's resources should be directed towards limited protection areas, and they have been largely successful in achieving this reallocation of resources.

Conclusion

The fate of ARPA demonstrates how drastically the relationship between science and conservation policy has changed in the Amazon, with technical arguments increasingly marginalised by political realities in the design of protected area systems. A general overview of Amazonian protected area systems suggests that, with a few exceptions, they are largely complete. At least on paper, most Amazonian countries have a reasonable mix of strict and limited protected areas, on the whole representative of biodiversity at the regional level. A few more strict protected areas will be created, probably considerably more indigenous areas while extractive and

---

26 The ARPA documentation, including the full proposal, is available for download at the GEF website: www.gefweb.org.

sustainable development reserves will almost certainly spread beyond Brazil to other Amazonian countries. Ecoregional planning, like all conservation science, gravitates to the ideal. It is rather better at defining additional needs than indicating when enough is enough.

The protected area challenge for the Amazon is not so much the creation of new areas as the consolidation and strengthening of those which already exist. In particular, an overriding priority still not being systematically addressed is how to bring the considerable body of technologies and methodologies of environmental management of protected areas to bear on conservation and sustainable development in indigenous lands, still the poor relations of the Amazonian protected area system when it comes to external support. This problem has been recognised and finds expression in a companion programme to the PPTAL (known as the PDPI, or Indigenous Peoples' Development Programme), which is experimenting with ways of introducing income-generation and culture-strengthening initiatives to groups whose lands have been demarcated. Yet, as pointed out in several contributions to the present volume, achieving acceptable levels of economic, socio-political and environmental sustainability is a challenge facing all traditional groups in their quest to reconcile conservation with development.

11

Extractive Reserves in Rondônia:
The Challenge of Collaborative Management

Sérgio Rosendo*

Introduction: the Emerging Paradigm of Collaborative Management

The need to integrate conservation and development in tropical forests has been widely recognised and adopted, as demonstrated in a number of people-oriented approaches implemented in many parts of the world over the last twenty years. These approaches have evolved within the context of important changes in the political ecology of forest management. Globalisation places local forest use within the context of broader environmental issues such as biodiversity conservation and climate change, while localisation emphasises local and decentralised management solutions. The dual processes of globalisation and localisation are marked by a growing complexity of environmental management solutions involving collaboration and linkages between multiple stakeholders at different levels.

Approaches based on collaboration amongst actors at different levels have become an important means for addressing environmental problems and for managing particular resources or resource systems. 'Partnership' has gained currency as a concept in many areas of environmental management, both in the developed and developing world. In western Europe, for example, forming partnerships between various stakeholders has become central to government discourse not only in relation to environmental issues but also in other areas of policy such as health and trans-

* The author thanks the leaders and staff of the Organisation of Rubber Tappers of Rondônia (OSR) for facilitating the research presented in this chapter. This chapter was prepared within the Programme for Environmental Decision Making (PEDM) at the Centre for Social and Economic Research on the Global Environment (CSERGE), which is funded by the Social and Economic Research Council (ESRC). The views expressed here remain the sole responsibility of the author.

port.[1] In the environmental area, partnerships between communities, NGOs, the private sector and government (in variable combinations) have been implemented as a strategy to address waste management problems, rehabilitate degraded urban areas and manage conservation areas.[2]

In Latin America, local communities and other actors with an interest in environmental management (national and international NGOs, development agencies, research institutions and private sector companies) have formed partnerships for the implementation of specific projects and approaches aimed at generating income through sustainable forest management. The harvest and marketing of non-timber forest products has been one of the most widely promoted activities aimed at increasing income without threatening biodiversity, maintaining natural and cultural landscapes.[3] More recently, ecotourism, sustainable logging and carbon sequestration projects have also demonstrated great potential to integrate conservation and development.[4]

Extractive reserves are an important approach for integrating conservation and development in Brazilian Amazonia. The conceptualisation, creation, implementation and development of extractive reserves have been advanced through partnerships involving a wide range of actors and reflect the trends identified above. Extractive reserves are protected areas designated for the sustainable use of natural resources by the resident population.[5] They were planned as multiple-use areas that combine different elements of a sustainable system. These elements include biodiversity conservation, the satisfaction of the basic needs of the population through higher incomes and access to health and education as central goals, as well as participation in reserve management based on socio-political organisation.[6] Responsibility for implementing these elements is shared among the population of the reserve, grass-roots organisations and the government. NGOs, donors and research institutions are also important actors in overall extractive reserve implementation.[7]

Extractive reserves are based on two main forms of collaboration between actors. The first is co-management (*co-gestão*), which presupposes

1   Hamer (2002); Irvine (1997).
2   Taylor (2000); Stolton and Dudley (1999).
3   Neumann and Hirsch (2000); Richards (1993).
4   Anderson and Clay (2002); Pagiola et al. (2002); Wunder (2000); Gössling (1999).
5   Allegretti (1990); Schwartzman (1989).
6   CNS (1992).
7   IBAMA (1994).

shared management responsibilities between the government and organisations representing extractive reserve residents. The second is partnerships (*parcerias*), which may involve two or more stakeholders such as grassroots organisations, national and international NGOs, government, businesses and international donors. Within these multi-institutional arrangements, grass-roots organisations representing reserve residents at different levels (at the local, state and national levels) form the centre around which all other actors come together and projects are implemented. This is one of the key features of what Hall (1997, 2000) has called 'productive conservation', or conservation that requires the active participation of local populations and their collaboration with other institutions that can provide them with vital technical, financial and policy support.

Co-management and partnerships are emerging paradigms on a broader scale for promoting conservation and development in Brazilian Amazonia.[8] However, synergistic outcomes are often assumed rather than empirically demonstrated. The implementation and dynamics of these concepts have not been examined in depth. Collaborative processes and arrangements involve actors and institutions that are significantly different in terms of their interests, organisational capacity, the scale at which they operate and the organisational culture that shapes their responses and actions. Within this context, there is the ever-present danger of actors that are more powerful in terms of financial and political means, access to policy networks, organisational capacity and scope of action, having a greater influence over the goals of environmental management than local actors with much more limited resources and scope. Collaborative and participatory structures may even become strategies to manage the inclusion of local populations in order to avoid conflict and dissent and exert control over action.[9]

This chapter examines the interplay between rubber tappers and other key institutions involved in the creation, implementation and development of extractive reserves. It looks at the specific case of reserves established in the state of Rondônia, in Brazil's western Amazon region. The dynamics of institutional interplay are examined in terms of several dimensions: opportunities for grass-roots empowerment, barriers to effective integration between institutions within collaborative arrangements and requirements for better integration between institutions at different levels. The research presented here draws on insights from actor-oriented sociology[10]

8   World Bank (2000).
9   Few (2001).
10   Long (1992).

and the emerging fields of political ecology[11] and adaptive management.[12] These notions will be applied to analyse the evolution and outcomes of collaboration among key actors involved in extractive reserves within the frameworks of partnerships and co-management.

The Context of Extractive Reserves in Rondônia

Rondônia is located in western Amazonia, bordering Bolivia and the Brazilian states of Mato Grosso, Amazonas and Acre (Figure 11.1). Rondônia was given administrative autonomy as a federal state in 1982. The history of the region known as the Guaporé Territory, however, dates back to the colonial period. Portuguese armies built fortresses along the rivers Guaporé, Mamoré and Madeira to defend the territory from the Spanish and to promote settlement and commerce. Difficult access, hostile living conditions and frequent attacks by indigenous groups meant that settlement took place on a modest scale and only in areas surrounding military fortifications, and that commerce was confined to explorers looking for gold, precious woods and resins and indian slaves. This situation, however, changed dramatically in the late nineteenth century.

The expansion of the automobile industry in Europe and the United States created massive demand for a specific product found in abundance in Amazonian forests — rubber — used to manufacture car tyres. Rubber became a valuable commodity and attracted entrepreneurs that penetrated the headwaters of even the most remote rivers to claim large areas of forest as rubber estates or *seringais*. These individuals, known as *seringalistas* or rubber barons, recruited labour to work on their estates mostly from north-east Brazil, a region stricken by drought and poverty. Thousands of migrant peasants were brought to the region to work as rubber tappers or *seringueiros*. The operation of the rubber estates was based on the *aviamento* system under which the rubber barons advanced the tools, food and other provisions necessary to enable the rubber tappers to spend long periods of time in the forest extracting rubber. This constituted a loan that the *seringueiro* had to work hard to pay back. The rubber barons overpriced tools and provisions and offered a low price for rubber, which meant that the *seringueiros* were often unable to produce enough quantities of rubber to repay the loans. Thus, debt enslaved the *seringueiros*. They were not free to leave the rubber estate until they paid off their debts, which tended to increase rather than diminish.

11   Bryant and Bailey (1997); Peet and Watts (1996).
12   Berkes and Folke (1998); Pritchard et al. (1998).

Figure 11.1: Federal and State Extractive Reserves in Rondônia

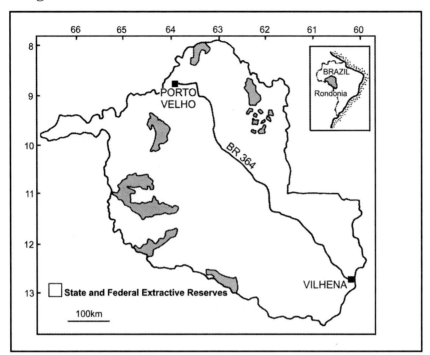

The rubber boom, however, was short-lived as plantations established by the British in colonial Malaya began producing rubber and supplying world markets at more competitive prices. The impressive structure that rubber supported in Amazonia collapsed and the region suffered economic decline. Nevertheless, it left a profound social mark. Indigenous populations were massacred when their territories were claimed for the establishment of rubber estates or they succumbed to the diseases brought by settlers. Surviving groups had to retreat further into increasingly remote areas to escape massacre and disease. The forest, however, did not become a demographic vacuum. Many of the migrants who came to the region to work as rubber tappers remained in the forest and gave rise to additional social groups such as the *ribeirinhos* or river dwellers. These groups were influenced by indigenous people through miscegenation and adopted many of their resource-use strategies. Demand for rubber to support emerging industrial development in Brazil still supported a population of rubber tappers in the forest, although on a far more reduced scale than during the peak of the rubber boom. Other groups lived off fishing, agriculture and the extraction of a range of forest products.

In World War II the Japanese took control of Malaya and other rubber producing colonies of the Allied nations. The need for an alternative source of rubber gave rise to a renewed and volatile boost in the extraction of rubber in Amazonia. Old rubber estates were reactivated and a new wave of migrants known as 'rubber soldiers' came from north-east Brazil to tap rubber. After the war ended the world economy was reorganised and the uncompetitive rubber estates in Amazonia ceased to be exploited on a large scale. In 1958, large tin-ore deposits were discovered in Rondônia, attracting local and migrant labour and boosting the territory's economy. Gold deposits were also discovered along the Madeira River and, especially in the 1980s, provoked a gold rush in Rondônia. Tin-ore mining declined in the 1970s as a result of conflicts between independent miners and mining companies and adverse international marketing conditions. Gold deposits were soon exhausted and their exploitation ceased to be economically viable.

In the 1960s Amazonia came to be considered by the Brazilian government as a strategic region that needed to be integrated into the national economy. Roads were viewed as a precondition for the development of the region and ambitious highway building programmes were initiated. The integration and development of Amazonia became a priority for the military regime that came to power in 1964. Integration was viewed as a matter of national security given the extensive borders of Amazonia with neighbouring countries and the operation of guerrillas and other threats to territorial sovereignty in those areas. The construction of more roads was prioritised including the Transamazon Highway. At the same time the government created incentives for the logging, mining and cattle ranching sectors to attract national and foreign investment to the region. Specific agencies and programmes were established to promote economic development in Amazonia, such as the Bank of Amazonia (BASA), the Superintendancy for the Development of Amazonia (SUDAM) and the National Integration Plan (PIN).

Roads made Amazonia accessible to thousands of small farmers, who settled along the Transamazon highway and other roads within the context of ill-planned government programmes that provided little assistance and virtually no infrastructure to support settlement. Road building, logging, mining, cattle ranching and agricultural settlement had massive environmental and social consequences. The establishment of these economic activities involved clearing vast areas of forest. There was little regard for the aptitude of certain areas for the activities implemented. This was especially true in relation to agriculture. Thousands of families were settled on poor soils that soon became exhausted, forcing farmers to abandon their plots in search of more productive areas.[13] Protection of the territories inhabited by indigenous populations was not effectively enforced and no measures existed to safeguard the land rights of traditional populations such as the *seringueiros*. Modern development displaced these populations on a large scale. Moreover, the struggle for land among small farmers, cattle ranchers, loggers, rubber tappers, miners and land speculators became intense and lead to a wave of rural violence.

In 1981 an innovative programme, for the north-west frontier zone or POLONOROESTE was launched to promote what was described as 'the orderly human occupation of the north-west region', which included Rondônia (see Chapter 5 in this volume). POLONOROESTE was funded by the World Bank and aimed to support the settlement of small farmers in areas suitable for agriculture and to develop suitable infrastructure, extension and social services to promote the viability of family farms. At the same time it included measures to avoid the invasion of indigenous reserves and indiscriminate deforestation. Major components also included the paving of the Cuiabá and Porto Velho highway (BR–364) and the extension of the feeder road network. However, serious implementation problems undermined many of the objectives of POLONOROESTE. Infrastructure (road building) was prioritised by the government, while productive, environmental and social objectives received less attention. In effect, POLONOROESTE contributed to some of the problems it had hoped to alleviate. Migration to the region occurred on a scale much larger than expected. Settlement became disorganised, lands were indiscriminately occupied, including indigenous areas, and deforestation reached unprecedented levels.

Criticism by international environmental NGOs and grass-roots movements exposing POLONOROESTE for its disastrous environmental and social impacts led the World Bank to re-evaluate its strategy for promoting development in Brazilian Amazonia.[14] The National Council of Rubber Tappers (CNS), set up in 1985, became one of the most vociferous critics of World Bank policies for Amazonia, using the case of Rondônia to draw national and international attention to the impacts that large-scale economic development projects could have on traditional populations. The

13   Martine (1990).
14   Rich (1994).

CNS lobbied for the inclusion of extractive reserves in future development strategies for Amazonia. In effect, the next project funded by the
World Bank in Rondônia, known as PLANAFLORO (Rondônia Natural
Resources Management Project), which replaced POLONOROESTE, included the creation and implementation of extractive reserves as one of its
key objectives.

The social movement for the creation of extractive reserves was strong
in Acre, where rubber tappers were politically active and determined to secure rights to land in the context of a similar process of land occupation
and deforestation prompted by road building, cattle ranching, logging and
other activities supported by economic development projects.[15] In
Rondônia, however, rubber tappers were not organised to defend land
rights and many were absorbed by the economic transformations happen-
ing in Rondônia. Some joined the urban labour force while others secured
plots on agricultural settlement projects and became farmers. Some families moved into forests not yet affected by the development frontier. The
rubber tappers who continued to live in the forest were largely unaware of
the movement for the creation of extractive reserves that had evolved in
neighbouring Acre. When plans for extractive reserves within
PLANAFLORO became known, environmental NGOs embarked upon a
campaign to secure these areas, the actual creation of which was by no
means guaranteed given the manifest lack of political will demonstrated by
the state government of Rondônia to implement protected areas.

NGOs took the initiative to mobilise and organise the rubber tappers
in Rondônia within the principles of the rubber tappers' movement led by
the CNS. However, as grass-roots leaders began to emerge in Rondônia,
the process of organising rubber tappers gained a dynamic of its own. In
1991, an organisation independent of the CNS, the Organisation of
Rubber Tappers of Rondônia (OSR) was established to represent the interests of rubber tappers. The OSR formed partnerships with international and national NGOs to enable the rubber tappers to participate in the
political and bureaucratic process of extractive reserve creation within
PLANAFLORO. Specific projects with NGOs also included building
community institutions and associations of rubber tappers to manage extractive reserves once these areas were created.

15   See Hecht and Cockburn (1989); Keck (1995).

The Institutional Landscape

Environmental management is becoming increasingly complex in terms of its goals, the actors involved and the processes they are involved in. Tropical forest management demonstrates this complexity. Tropical forests are increasingly managed for multiple goals that may include, for example, income generation for local communities, biodiversity conservation and watershed protection. The range of actors involved in environmental management is also much broader than before. The central role of the State is giving way to more decentralised approaches involving local communities, grass-roots organisations and NGOs. The processes of environmental management are also more sophisticated and cut across different levels of action. The inclusion of different actors requires novel approaches to planning and decision-making that lead to effective, efficient, legitimate and equitable outcomes. [16]

Extractive reserves have multiple goals and involve a wide range of actors within various configurations of interaction. These areas are co-managed by organisations representing the resident population and the government. Associations were the preferred extractive reserve management institutions established in Rondônia. There are seven associations in Rondônia, each concerned with the management of one or more reserves. In 2002 there were 22 extractive reserves in Rondônia ranging from small areas of 500 hectares inhabited by one single family to areas in excess of 300,000 hectares with over 50 families. Table 11.1 lists these extractive reserves, their location, area and population (expressed in numbers of families). In addition to the associations, the OSR also plays an important role in the management of extractive reserves in Rondônia. The OSR sits on government commissions and participates in policy-making processes at the state and national levels that impact on extractive reserves. It also mobilises funding and technical support from a range of national and international sources to support extractive reserves.

16   Adger et al. (2002); Brown (2002).

Table 11.1: Extractive Reserves in Rondônia

Name	Location	Area (ha)	No. of Families
Rio Cautário (S)	Costa Marques	146,400	60
Rio Cautário II (F)	Costa Marques	73.817	n/a
Curralinho (S)	Costa Marques	1,758	6
Rio Pacáas Novos (S)	Guajará Mirim	342,903	55
Rio Ouro Preto (F)	Guajará Mirim	204,583	107
Pedras Negras (S)	São Francisco	124,409	19
Rio Jaci-Paraná (S)	Nova Mamoré	191,324	23
Aquariquara (S)	Vale do Anari	18, 100	51
Seringueiras (S)	Vale do Anari	537	1
Itaúba (S)	Vale do Anari	1,758	2
Rio Preto Jacundá (S)	Machadinho	115,278	50
Maracatiara (S)	Machadinho d'Oeste	9,503	19
Ipê (S)	Machadinho d'Oeste	815	4
Jatobá (S)	Machadinho d'Oeste	1,135	2
Massaranduba (S)	Machadinho d'Oeste	5,556	4
Angelim (S)	Machadinho d'Oeste	8,923	3
Sucupira (S)	Machadinho d'Oeste	3,188	n/a
Mogno (S)	Machadinho d'Oeste	2,450	8
Freijó (S)	Machadinho d'Oeste	600	1
Roxinho (S)	Machadinho d'Oeste	882	3
Piquiá (S)	Machadinho d'Oeste	1,448	6
Castanheira (S)	Machadinho d'Oeste	10,200	6
Garrote (S)	Machadinho d'Oeste	802	3
Cuniã (F)	Porto Velho	95,000	45

(S) State Extractive Reserve; (F) Federal Extractive Reserve
n/a: information not available

Most extractive reserves in Rondônia were established by the state gov-
ernment within PLANAFLORO. This means that the government of
Rondônia is directly responsible for the co-management of these areas.
The government agency dealing with extractive reserves within the state

government is the State Secretariat for Environmental Development (SEDAM). There are, however, some instances where federal agencies intervene in extractive reserves in matters related to environmental protection, legalisation of land tenure and socio-economic development. The federal environmental control agency, IBAMA, applies and monitors environmental legislation that also relates to extractive reserves established by individual states. Within IBAMA there is an agency concerned with traditional populations and conservation, the National Centre for the Sustainable Development of Traditional Populations (CNPT). The colonisation and agrarian reform agency, INCRA, is involved in the land tenure legalisation of state extractive reserves, which were created on public lands under the domain of the federal government and on private lands that need to be expropriated from their owners. The Secretariat for Amazonia within the Ministry of Environment has considerable influence over policies for extractive reserves in general.

In Rondônia, NGOs were actively involved in the creation of extractive reserves and participate in various aspects of their management. Partnerships between national and international NGOs and the OSR were an important means through which the creation of extractive reserves was supported and it remains important in the implementation of projects to improve their social, economic and ecological viability. The World Wide Fund for Nature (WWF) has been a key partner of the rubber tappers in terms of providing financial support for specific projects, training and technical assistance. Small local environmental NGOs have also worked with the rubber tappers and have specialised in the implementation of income-generating projects funded by international NGOs and multilateral environmental conservation programmes. Ecological Action Guaporé (ECOPORÉ), for example, has mobilised funding from several sources for the implementation of community-based logging and ecotourism in extractive reserves. Networks of NGOs have also been important for articulating grass-roots interests within larger policy processes and on specific occasions when it has been necessary to join forces with other social groups to influence decisions at the national and international levels.

Multilateral agencies and programmes are key actors in environmental management in Brazilian Amazonia. Programmes financed by the World Bank such as the PLANAFLORO have not only provided funding for sustainable development activities in Amazonia but have also supported innovative approaches such as extractive reserves and processes such as the participation of civil society in policy-making and implementation. Although there are many ambiguities in the actions of the World Bank in Amazonia, its financial leverage over the Brazilian government has given an unprecedented impetus to the national environmental agenda. The same can be said of specific international programmes such as the Pilot Programme for the Conservation of the Brazilian Rain Forest (PPG7), funded by the Group of Seven industrialised countries, the European Union and the German government. The Pilot Programme is administered by the World Bank and implemented by the Brazilian government. It comprises objectives that range from demonstrating ways of protecting Brazil's rain forests and using them in a sustainable manner to strengthening public and civil society institutions which play a role in environmental management.[17]

Extractive reserves are set within a complex institutional landscape formed by organisations, legal frameworks, policies and projects. Researchers have devoted increasing attention to the way in which the broader institutional environment influences the success of initiatives aimed at integrating conservation and development, including the impacts of higher level institutions on local institutions.[18] The tendency, however, has been to examine how national and international level institutions and processes impinge on local actors and outcomes. Within these studies local actors are portrayed as being mainly impacted upon while their role in shaping such interactions is downplayed. Research set within a political ecology framework has begun to acknowledge the ability of local actors to scale-up their influence and access multiple political and institutional levels to further collective goals.[19] The following section combines perspectives from actor-oriented sociology of development and political ecology to examine the process leading to the creation of extractive reserves by the government of Rondônia. It examines strategies to articulate grass-roots interests within broader policy and institutional frameworks.

The Creation of Extractive Reserves

Plans for the creation of extractive reserves within PLANAFLORO represented a significant advance for various reasons. It demonstrated changes within World Bank policy in favour of sustainable development strategies that took into consideration the needs of local populations. It also illustrated the increasing responsiveness of the Brazilian government to in-

17   World Bank et al. (2002).
18   Berkes (2002); Gezon (1997).
19   Bebbington and Batterbury (2001); Perreault (2001).

ternational concerns over deforestation in Amazonia and loss of biodiversity. Although these conditions were supportive of the creation of extractive reserves, serious concerns emerged over the political will of the government of Rondônia to implement these areas. In a letter addressed to the president of the World Bank dated 13 October 1988, Francisco 'Chico' Mendes, the charismatic leader of the rubber tappers (who was assassinated later that year) clearly stated this concern when he wrote, 'We think that the extractive reserves included in POLONOROESTE II [PLANAFLORO] served only to give the government's proposal to the World Bank an ecological tone, lately so fashionable, and to guarantee such a voluminous loan'.[20]

This concern was shared by a number of NGOs working in the region. PLANAFLORO placed a strong emphasis on environmental conservation through the establishment of extractive reserves and other conservation areas of strict protection and sustainable use, support for indigenous communities and implementation of agro-forestry by small farmers. The adoption of land-use zoning as a planning instrument was another important objective of PLANAFLORO.[21] However, the project also included substantial infrastructure and public sector capacity-building components. The political structure of Rondônia was, and remains, dominated by economic groups associated with agro-industry, especially cattle ranching, dairy farming and logging. Politicians elected to the municipal, state and federal government are often directly involved in these economic activities. The establishment of protected areas was viewed by many politicians and segments of the business sector as an impediment to the economic development of Rondônia. There was a was strong conviction that any measures that placed restrictions on the exploitation of forests and their conversion to agriculture and other uses would act as a straightjacket for regional development.

The significance of PLANAFLORO in terms of opportunities to guarantee forest conservation in Rondônia attracted the attention of Brazilian and international NGOs, well aware of the fact that despite sounding impressive on paper, the project would not achieve stated goals in the absence of political will to implement its environmental components. The experience of POLONOROESTE was a clear indication of

20   Cited in Forum and FoE (1995), p. 24.
21   Land-use zoning (also known as socio-economic and ecological zoning or agro-ecological zoning) is a planning instrument that maps Rondônia into six macro-zones according to their suitability for different types of agriculture, forestry, extractivism or total environmental conservation. See Mahar (2000) for an analysis of the implementation of land-use zoning in Rondônia.

the monumental failures that apparently well-planned initiatives could result in because of poor implementation. These NGOs demanded the participation of civil society, especially of the direct beneficiaries (rubber tappers, indigenous populations and small farmers) in PLANAFLORO as a means of guaranteeing its effective implementation. The Bank responded to these demands with the establishment of co-management institutions within the project, comprising equal numbers of representatives from the government and civil society.[22] This opening for the participation of civil society provided a strong incentive for rubber tappers, indigenous populations and farmers to organise, since involvement in the co-management institutions of PLANAFLORO was reserved for organisations representing different sectors of civil society.

NGOs became actively engaged in assisting these groups not only to create organisations to represent their interests but also to enable their effective participation in PLANAFLORO through the provision of funding and specialised technical and legal support. Various NGOs came together to implement projects aimed at facilitating the creation of extractive reserves. These included local environmental NGOs already working with traditional peoples and international NGOs such as the WWF and the Ford Foundation. The WWF became a powerful driving force behind efforts to create extractive reserves in Rondônia. It established partnerships with local NGOs and the OSR to ensure that the objectives of PLANAFLORO regarding extractive reserves were not curtailed or that the process for the creation of these areas did not stagnate within the legal and bureaucratic apparatus of the state government.

In addition to the resistance that extractive reserves and other protected areas faced within state and municipal governments, the government agencies responsible for the creation and implementation of extractive reserves within PLANAFLORO had poor knowledge of the necessary legal and institutional procedures and lacked experience in working with traditional populations. In some cases their actions undermined rather than facilitated the process of reserve creation. Two state agencies were designated to deal with extractive reserves, the Rondônia Land Institute (ITERON)[23] and the Secretariat for Environmental Development (SEDAM). The demarcation of

---

22   See Millikan (1997) for an analysis of the effectiveness of the co-management
     institutions of PLANAFLORO.
23   ITERON was dissolved in the late 1990s and its responsibilities in relation to
     extractive reserves were transferred to SEDAM. However, during the imple-
     mentation of PLANAFLORO this agency was involved in the creation and im-
     plementation of extractive reserves.

extractive reserves was assigned to ITERON along with the implementation of specific physical infrastructure such as schools and health centres built with PLANAFLORO funding. SEDAM was entrusted with developing arrangements for the management of extractive reserves and implementing production infrastructure, for which PLANAFLORO also provided funding. This infrastructure consisted of vehicles, buildings and agricultural tools.

The creation and implementation of extractive reserves depended on concrete actions by ITERON and SEDAM. However, these agencies assumed a largely passive role in relation to key aspects of extractive reserve creation. The legal and institutional procedures for the creation of state extractive reserves were borrowed from the legislation and guidelines developed for federal extractive reserves. Government agencies in Rondônia were largely unfamiliar with such procedures and lacked the capacity and means to adapt them to the legal context of the state. The OSR and ECOPORE were forced to intervene constantly to keep the process of extractive reserve creation in motion. In some cases this involved helping government agencies to draft the necessary legal documentation. NGOs also produced most of the maps and surveys needed to support the request for creating reserves.

Despite these efforts, by 1995 none of the extractive reserves planned in PLANAFLORO had yet been created. In addition, there were serious concerns over the overall implementation of PLANAFLORO. NGOs and grass-roots organisations identified a number of problems including failure to establish land-use policies compatible with the objectives of sustainable development, delays in the institutionalisation of agro-ecological zoning and the creation of protected areas, inefficiency of government agencies in fulfilling environmental monitoring objectives, poor implementation of support for indigenous communities and the non-operation of PLANAFLORO co-management institutions for the participation of civil society in decision-making, monitoring and evaluation.[24]

Several attempts were made to alert the World Bank regarding failings in the implementation of PLANAFLORO. However, there was no prompt action by the World Bank to address these concerns. Although the effectiveness of the co-management institutions of PLANAFLORO proved questionable, the opportunity they represented at the onset for the participation of civil society led NGOs and grass-roots organisations to create a network to monitor project implementation and actively articulate the interests of the groups it represented. This network, known as the Forum of NGOs and

24   Forum and FoE (1995).

Social Movements of Rondônia (Forum), brought together a wide range of civil society organisations including environmental and research NGOs, popular education centres and organisations representing indigenous peoples, rubber tappers and small farmers. In 1995, the Forum began compiling evidence demonstrating the problems affecting the implementation of PLANAFLORO and the negative impacts this had on protected areas, indigenous and traditional populations. This evidence formed the basis of a request for the investigation of PLANAFLORO presented to the World Bank Inspection Panel in June 1995.[25]

The Forum was highly strategic for the rubber tappers because it enabled them to join forces with other sectors of civil society with an interest in PLANAFLORO. The collective mobilisation that resulted in the request for investigation had several consequences that were crucial for the creation and implementation of extractive reserves. Following the request for investigation, significant advances occurred in the creation and implementation of protected areas, including extractive reserves, which the government had failed to create. It also prompted negotiations between the government and project stakeholders to decentralise PLANAFLORO funding and make it more accessible to local communities. These negotiations resulted in a Programme for the Support of Community Projects (PAIC), which became an important source of funding for implementing innovative income-generating projects in extractive reserves such as ecotourism. Communities had to be organised in order to be eligible for funding, which involved complex project proposals and financial reporting. The rubber tappers, through their links and partnerships with NGOs, were in a strong position to propose community-based projects and satisfy financial reporting requirements.

Implementation Challenges

The creation of extractive reserves in Rondônia represents an important step towards environmental management consistent with the needs of traditional populations. However, the task of implementing these areas to fulfil their social, economic and environmental objectives is a major challenge. It requires reserve dwellers and their organisations to collaborate with actors that can assist them in improving the long-term sustainability of extractive

25   The World Bank Inspection Panel was created in 1993 to 'provide an independent forum to private citizens who believe that their interests have been or could be directly harmed by a project financed by the World Bank' (http://www.worldbank.org/html/ins-panel/overview.html).

reserves, including government at different levels, national and international NGOs, research institutions and donors. The process through which extractive reserves are implemented and managed represents no less of a challenge. These different actors view extractive reserves as a means to achieve quite different ends. The rubber tappers have a strong interest in extractive reserves as a means of guaranteeing land rights. Environmental NGOs support extractive reserves with the ultimate objective of conserving the forest and its biodiversity. The government is a heterogeneous actor with different levels and agencies, each with a particular view in relation to extractive reserves. Donors have multiple motives for supporting extractive reserves, which range from promoting equity to instrumental considerations. It is not necessary for actors to have exactly the same interests to collaborate. However, discrepancy between means, ends and views presents major challenges for successful and synergistic partnerships.

Legal Consolidation of Extractive Reserves

Extractive reserves imply the adaptation of traditional rights to land within the national legal framework. In extractive reserves, the government owns the land and in turn grants a concession of collective use to the association representing reserve residents. The residents, in turn, gain so-called usufruct rights to their traditional landholdings called *colocações*. However, the land tenure situation of most extractive reserves is complex. These areas were created on predominantly public lands, which are under the control of INCRA, the federal land reform agency. However, in many cases they also encompassed privately-owned lands. In order for rubber tappers to be issued with usufruct rights, the entire land area of the reserve must be brought under the control of the agency responsible for its management. This means that public lands must be transferred from the control of INCRA to this managing agency, private lands expropriated and their owners compensated.

When the government of Rondônia created extractive reserves it failed to clearly define the guidelines and procedures for their legalisation and inclusion in state legislation. The legal reference point used for the creation and legalisation of state extractive reserves was the same as that developed for federal extractive reserves. However, state extractive reserves were created without specific legislation being developed at the state level to support their legal consolidation. This situation was further complicated by a lack of communication between the federal and state governments. The federal government (through INCRA) controlled lands upon which the state government created extractive reserves. INCRA and the ITERON (the state agency dealing with the land tenure legalisation of state-administered protected areas) were unable to reach agreement for the transfer of land tenure from the federal to the state government. In effect, INCRA did not recognise the protected areas established by the state government and continued to create agricultural settlement projects and to issue private land titles within these areas.[26]

Rondônia's politicians are extremely interested in the transfer of jurisdiction from the federal to the state government of lands where state protected areas have been established. When the state of Rondônia was created in 1982, most lands remained under the control of the federal government through INCRA or the Brazilian army. The process of land transfer is therefore viewed as a means for the state government to gain greater administrative control over its territory. As one NGO activist remarked, politicians in Rondônia think that once the state government gains control over the lands occupied by protected areas it will be possible to manoeuvre the fate of these areas to accommodate economic interests associated with cattle ranching, logging, agricultural settlement and land speculation. Unsurprisingly, many politicians are openly or covertly involved in these activities. INCRA is also susceptible to the influence of interest-group politics. According to Millikan (1997), powerful politicians and businessmen orchestrate the appointment of INCRA officials at the local level as a means of defending their interests in land.

The involvement of ITERON and INCRA in extractive reserves reveals a number of important issues regarding inter-agency collaboration. Firstly, each of these institutions has its own institutional interests that are associated with territorial control. There is competition between them and this has stalled the process of land legalisation of extractive reserves. Secondly, both ITERON and INCRA serve political and economic interests that are generally not supportive of extractive reserves. Thus, these agencies are not committed to enabling the legal viability of state extractive reserves and their allegiance lies with such interests. Thirdly, there is an obvious lack of coordination between the actions of federal and state government agencies. This is evident in the way that INCRA ignores the existence of protected areas established by the state government. The implications of failing to complete the legal consolidation of state extractive reserves are significant. In particular, extractive reserves become vulnerable to political inter-

26   Millikan (1997); Forum and FoE (1995).

ests. OSR leaders comment that leading politicians have proposed reducing the area of some extractive reserves that they consider too large for the populations that inhabit them. It also facilitates the invasion of state extractive reserves by land speculators and loggers that use the fact that these areas not being recognised by INCRA to justify their actions.

Management of Extractive Reserves

Within the implementation of PLANAFLORO, SEDAM and ITERON were assigned responsibility for the co-management of state extractive reserves with the organisations representing the inhabitants of these areas. SEDAM was to lead the preparation and implementation of natural resource management plans, provide technical support for reserve communities and develop environmental monitoring activities. In addition to legalising land tenure, ITERON was to support community organisation on extractive reserves. Building the capacity of government agencies to implement PLANAFLORO was delegated to the United Nations Development Programme (UNDP). UNDP consultants were assigned to the job of implementing extractive reserves within PLANAFLORO and aimed to work closely with government officials and grass-roots organisations in various planning and community organisation activities.

Government agencies lacked the minimum necessary conditions to play an active role in extractive reserve implementation. According to one report, the agencies were understaffed and lacked the financial resources to accompany UNDP consultants to the reserves.[27] As a result, the work developed by UNDP consultants in extractive reserves progressed largely without the participation of government staff. Examples of this work included the preparation of resource use plans for extractive reserves as well as development plans. The resource use plan is a set of rules aimed at regulating the use of natural resources by reserve residents. The development plan is based on an assessment of existing problems in the reserve and proposes measures to address such problems. The preparation of both types of instruments was facilitated by UNDP consultants and was based on participatory methodologies.[28]

UNDP consultants had a closer working relationship with leaders and staff of the rubber tappers' grass-roots organisations than with government. There were significant advances in community organisation for the management of extractive reserves during the period UNDP consultants

27   GoR and UNDP (1997).
28   Weigand Jr and de Paula (1998).

worked in extractive reserves (1995–98). However, the intervention of the
UNDP was unable to create conditions for these advances to become self-
sustaining. When the project that supported these consultants ended, there
was no institution prepared to give continuity to the work they initiated.
The concept of collective organisation for the management of extractive
reserves had not yet matured sufficiently among communities and the
leaders and staff of the rubber tappers' grass-roots organisations lacked
the training, resources and time to improve community organisations.

The capacity of government actors to work with communities had also
not been strengthened. The agencies concerned with extractive reserve
management did not develop a coherent policy and methodology to work
in these areas and with local communities. For example, SEDAM assigned
only one of its employees to work with extractive reserves. One consult-
ant that worked for the UNDP noted that although this officer was interested in collaborating with the UNDP team, there was little institutional
support within SEDAM to support her involvement in community organisation and other initiatives in extractive reserves. Crucially, few resources
were made available to enable this officer to accompany UNDP consultants to the field. Collaboration between different actors for the implementation of extractive reserves, including co-management arrangements,
can easily be undermined when there is insufficient political will and flexibility to work in multi-institutional environments, as the case examined
above demonstrates. The UNDP, despite its good intentions, had a limited impact in terms of improving the participatory management of extractive reserves given a short time frame of involvement and lack of a clear-
er strategy to ensure the sustainability of its intervention.

The management of extractive reserves presupposes the implementation of actions to improve the incomes of reserve dwellers. Partnerships
between the OSR and environmental NGOs have been an important
means to implement projects aimed at developing extractive reserves.
Financial support for these projects has been obtained from international
NGOs (especially the WWF) and internationally funded programmes to
conserve tropical forests administered by the Brazilian government.
Examples of projects implemented through partnerships between the
OSR and NGOs include agro-forestry systems, production of a rubber-
coated fabric known as ecological leather (*couro vegetal*), community-based
logging and community-based ecotourism. Some of these are already providing a few communities with an alternative source of income, although
problems with their long-term economic viability remain unresolved. In

particular, there are concerns over their continuity once international funding to support their implementation terminates. The complexity of these
activities often means that continuous external technical support is needed, making partnerships vital with NGOs specialised in this kind of assistance to local communities and grass-roots organisations.

Community-based logging is among the most promising options for
improving the incomes of reserve dwellers. So far, logging projects have
been implemented in four state extractive reserves. These projects involve
collaboration between local communities and various actors. Community
logging in extractive reserves was initially developed by ECOPORE
through a partnership with the OSR and associations of rubber tappers on
two extractive reserves, with funding from WWF. At a later stage additional funding was obtained from the PPG7 Demonstration Projects
(PD/A) initiative, which enabled logging projects to be enhanced and expanded to other reserves. However, even this apparently successful initiative has experienced marketing and management difficulties. Community
logging was developed on the assumption that the timber produced would
be sold in niche markets for certified timber. However, accessing these
markets has been difficult and timber has been sold largely in regional markets at the same price as uncertified timber. Wider partnerships with
NGOs and the private sector are needed to enable the rubber tappers to
benefit from green certification. There have also been disputes over the
control of the project between the NGO, the associations and the communities, which have hindered logging operations.

Environmental monitoring and protection are further areas of extractive reserve management where collaboration between institutions is essential. The overall task of monitoring and protecting state extractive reserves belongs to SEDAM. However, these responsibilities are not clearly
defined because of overlaps with the federal environmental agency,
IBAMA. This overlap and lack of clarification between the attributes of
the two agencies and levels of government has been used as an excuse for
both agencies to disengage themselves from the monitoring and protection of state extractive reserves. Furthermore, these agencies are not generally effective at monitoring protected areas and lower level officials have
often been accused of facilitating illegal logging in these areas. The job of
protecting the reserves has largely been left to the rubber tappers and their
organisations. The rubber tappers' organisations, assisted by ECOPORE,
develop vigilance operations in the reserves. They confront invaders, gather evidence of their acts, demand that environmental agencies take action

and expose environmental crimes in the media. One of the most effective ways of protecting the reserves has been to liaise with public prosecutors, who have powers to indict environmental lawbreakers to answer accusations from individuals or civil society organisations.

Institutional arrangements based on collective action and collaboration are equally necessary to ensure that reserve residents use natural resources in a sustainable manner. Specific institutions called Reserve Protection Commissions were established as part of the management structure of extractive reserves. However, these commissions have so far been largely inactive. Rubber tappers have demonstrated the ability to unite against common external threats posed by invading loggers and land grabbers. However, in the longer term the legalisation of property rights, and the establishment of formal institutions to manage resources, signifies a move from individual-based, informally organised approaches to formal collective institutional arrangements that may require an extended period of social learning and adaptation as well as external facilitation.

The different rubber tappers' institutions demonstrate different levels of organisational capacity, which are reflected in the types of impacts they have on the management of extractive reserves. The OSR is a well-organised institution with access to financial and technical resources provided by NGOs and international programmes. Its capacity to participate in relevant policy-making and programmes has been crucial to enable the creation of extractive reserves and to mobilise financial support for their implementation. The achievements of associations of rubber tappers, however, have been less substantial. These organisations have experienced problems with the management of marketing for forest products. In addition, there is some lack of transparency and accountability regarding how association leaders manage funds, which has generated conflict and undermined the confidence of the grass-roots in these institutions.[29] In general, projects for extractive reserves are managed either by the OSR or by NGOs, since the associations do not have the necessary organisational capacity.

At the community level, social organisation for extractive reserve management is also deficient as demonstrated by problems with implementing mechanisms to monitor the use of natural resources. Attempts at improving community organisation were undertaken by UNDP consultants as part of their work with extractive reserve development plans. However, as discussed earlier, developing habits of co-operation can be a lengthy

29   Rosendo (2003).

process that requires long-term investment to become self-sustaining. Moreover, although the rubber tappers are able to co-operate in small informal groups (usually kinship-based groups), co-operation within formal participatory structures such as associations and commissions implies a different set of social relationships for which there is not a strong basis of social capital. It requires trust and reciprocity to develop within larger structures that cut across existing linkages, alliances and conflicts between individuals and families.[30]

The rubber tappers in Rondônia have formed a strong social movement by creating the OSR, associations and community-based institutions (*núcleos comunitários*). The internal consistency of social movements is rarely questioned. Yet social movements can bring together organisations with different priorities and organisational capacities. Although the rubber tappers' organisations in Rondônia can agree in relation to objectives that must be negotiated collectively, there is a strong dominance by the OSR on project management and strategic decisions. The organisational capacity of associations and communities is weak, which is often put forward as a justification for the sometimes heavy-handed intervention of the OSR. However, there are few measures readily available for strengthening the associations and extractive reserve communities. This undermines the role of the associations and extractive reserve communities, which are the institutions more directly concerned with extractive reserve management.

Conclusion

Local struggles for land rights and natural resources are increasingly played out within the broader context of biodiversity conservation and sustainable development.[31] This has created opportunities for collaboration among actors at different levels, from local to international. The need for collaboration and linkages between various stakeholders in environmental management has been increasingly emphasised in the literature.[32] This involves grass-roots, governmental and non-governmental institutions collaborating in a variety of arrangements such as co-management and multi-stakeholder bodies. These views assume synergistic relationships between the different institutions in ways that facilitate community empowerment and develop-

---

30   *Ibid.*
31   Escobar et al. (2002); Escobar (2001); Bryant and Bailey (1997); Peet and Watts (1996).
32   Berkes (2000; 2002); Hall (2000b).

ment. However, as the cases examined in this chapter demonstrate, barriers to effective integration between institutions in collaborative arrangements may emerge from internal and contextual factors at all institutional levels.

There are problems in dealing with and reconciling the interests of key actors, which range from the World Bank and international environmental organisations to grass-roots organisations. This mismatch has been referred to as problems of 'fit' between the different institutions involved in conservation and development.[33] The rubber tappers' organisations and NGOs have established partnerships with positive impacts on the political empowerment of extractivist populations even though this collaboration has so far been less successful in overcoming barriers to the improvement of household incomes.[34] Yet partnerships are also vulnerable to tensions and conflicts arising from the different interests of the parties involved and the power relationships that exist between them. Essentially, extractive reserves are seen as a means for achieving quite different ends by the different actors involved.

Other institutions, in particular government agencies at the state and federal levels, are more resistant to developing collaborative capacities and linkages. This is often rooted in conflicting interests, vague mandates and legislative frameworks, poor institutional capacities and lack of resources, inappropriate perspectives and lack of internal support. Donors, despite their apparent support for extractive reserves and other sustainable development strategies, have at times held contradictory positions. This is true of the World Bank which, having supported participatory approaches, failed to monitor their effective implementation.

Improved 'fit' between the institutions that are involved in extractive reserve implementation is essential. This may entail a fundamental change in the attitudes and worldviews of some institutions, especially of government agencies. Government institutions need to be willing and capable of dealing with the diversity and complexity of local communities, their institutions and the ecosystems in which they are situated. Encouraging examples of changes in government policy and behaviour can be found in the state governments of Acre and Amapá, where extractivism and other sustainable economic activities have been explicitly incorporated into official development strategies. It remains to be seen whether a similar political opening will take place in Rondônia to bring about change in government institutions.

---

33   Brown and Rosendo (2000a).
34   Brown and Rosendo (2000b).

12

Participatory Management Assessment:
A Framework for the Short-Term Evaluation of Locally Based Floodplain Resources Management in the Amazon *

Fábio de Castro

Introduction

The natural resource conservation agenda suffers from a dilemma of dual ecological and social demands at local and global levels. Ecosystem degradation is linked to local outcomes such as microclimate change and habitat destruction to global outcomes such as biodiversity decline and change in the biogeochemistry patterns. Ecosystems are used by multiple stakeholders who have differentiated interests with regard to resource use, such as sustaining livelihoods for local communities, generating profit for private companies, promoting economic development for the government, enhancing the knowledge base for scientists and maintaining global climate equilibrium. As a consequence, stakeholders vary on how they value and use the resource, how they perceive environmental change, how much decision power they have and how they are affected by those decisions.

Policy-makers have become aware of the multiple use problem of resource conservation, and designs of co-management systems have been proposed as an attempt to achieve multiple goals by giving voice to different stakeholders in the management process. Co-management systems are broadly defined as institutional arrangement with shared responsibilities between user groups and the government.[1] Therefore, the co-management paradigm accounts for users' participation in shaping policy strategies to combine resource conservation, conflict resolution and social justice. The

* This study was funded by the Rain Forest Pilot Programme (RFPP).
1 Pinkerton (1989).

management of natural resources in the Amazon is following a similar path that is relevant both locally and globally. At the local level, residents have gone through an empowerment process and in many cases have enjoyed the active position of defining community-based management systems to control access to and use of local resources.[2] At a global level, increasing concern over global environmental change has driven an international coalition to generate initiatives for sustainable resource use.[3] Along these lines, the participatory approach to management has become a key element on the agenda of international donors with respect to conservation and development projects.

The participatory approach represents a democratic solution for promoting power balance amongst stakeholders. However, any strategy to design a participatory management system must be based on reliable information about the potential and limitations of such an endeavour to achieve its multiple goals. Policy suggestions must derive from data on the ecological features of the natural resources and social relations underpinning their use decisions. An assessment of current co-management initiatives can, thus, yield important lessons to facilitate this process.

Many co-management initiatives have been developed in the Amazon over recent decades, such as the well known Rubber Tappers' Council[4] and Mamirauá Sustainable Reserve.[5] Yet, several other less conspicuous examples have sprung up along the Basin, based on different institutional arrangements, levels of user participation and performances. These different co-management models have flourished depending on the regional demands of resource conservation and conflict resolution. However, little has been done to assess the lessons from those experiences to help to inform new initiatives of participatory management systems.

In this chapter I present an analytical framework for assessing the participatory management of floodplain resources in the Brazilian Amazon, with a focus on fisheries, in order to propose basic guidelines for the co-management of floodplain resources in the Amazon. This framework represents an effort to provide theoretical and methodological support to short-term assessment that fits both the political demand for a rapid local-global solution to floodplain resource problems and the scientific demand for coherent and accurate data collection and analysis that may be used to describe patterns of resource use.

2   Hecht and Cockburn (1989); Castro (2002).
3   Kolk (1996).
4   Allegretti (1990).
5   Lima-Ayres (1999).

The Theory of Participatory Management

The theory of participatory management has evolved from a community-based approach to an internalisation of a broader social and ecological context. In the 1980s many authors reacted to the 'tragedy of the commons' approach to management[6] by citing numerous cases in which local populations were able to craft collective, ecologically sound mechanisms to avoid resource depletion.[7] However, while emphasising the social aspects of local groups and the ecological features of the managed resources, this focus on community-based management systems overlooked some fundamental problems. Firstly, commoners were usually assumed to be homogeneous, harmonious groups with similar interests. Secondly, it overlooked other stakeholders of equal importance in the resource management system. Thirdly, the State and the market usually appeared in the analysis as major negative pressures, underestimating their potential role as collaborators. In other words, the efficiency of a community-based management system should not be taken for granted. This will depend on a set of factors embedded in social relationships at the local and regional levels. Since the 1990s, the ability of local management to respond efficiently to broader influences and to integrate successfully into a broader institutional arrangement system has been recognised as a fundamental issue in the co-management approach.

The co-management approach recognises that local management systems have a strong potential to conserve natural resources.[8] However, it also acknowledges the fact that resources are used by multiple stakeholders and that the government must play a key role in the conflict resolution process.[9] User groups are heterogeneous and sometimes conflictive. Thus, the need for collaboration between local users and other actors is a major factor that must be taken into account in the development of a co-management theory. In addition, the focus on the fit between ecosystem, resources, users and institutions, which is inherent to the co-management approach, has broadened the analysis of interconnections between human action and resource sustainability.

The co-management dimension has improved the management theory in many aspects. Firstly, while conventional resource management systems

---

6   Hardin (1968).
7   McCay and Acheson (1987); Berkes (ed.) (1989); Ostrom (1990); Bromley (ed.)(1992).
8   Jentoft (2000).
9   Jentoft (1989); Pinkerton (1989); Pomeroy and Berkes (1997).

based on bio-economic models have consistently failed to promote conservation, community-based management systems have enjoyed some success, although this has been limited to small areas and specific resources.
A co-management system is expected to integrate successful local initiatives
into broader management schemes. Through users' participation in decision-making processes, local knowledge and rule compliance are expected to
improve. The centralised structure of conventional management systems
creates an unequal power relationship among users, leading to marginalised
local communities. In contrast, a totally decentralised management system
overemphasises the role of local communities and fails to resolve conflicts
between local residents and other users. However, in a jointly managed system, empowerment of marginalised actors and social justice can be achieved
in a well-balanced fashion. Finally, conventional management systems are
usually based on specific resources (sometimes a single species), while ignoring interconnected factors affecting the resource base. Local management often focuses on a system, yet this is often within a limited area and involves few users. A co-management system would broaden the sector-based
approach into a systemic approach including other actors and processes related to the conservation of the managed resource.

Yet the promise of the co-management approach must be treated with
caution. The term 'co-management' applies to any institutional arrangement
in which government and user groups participate in the management design.
However, 'user participation' may take different forms, ranging from users
merely being informed by the government about its decisions to communities simply informing the government about their decisions.[10] Assessment of
co-management experiences around the globe reveals that, in general, user
participation is higher in developed countries, revealing the importance of a
more stable institutional structure to support long-enduring systems of
community-based management and in promoting integration of such institutions into broader co-management systems.[11] Therefore, it is crucial to ensure that a co-management initiative is not just a cosmetic exercise but rather
a dynamic process of reshaping social relations regarding the managed resource.[12] Only through a careful analysis of the ecological, social and historical dimensions of the resource use and management system will a co-
management initiative have chance to flourish and survive.

10   Jentoft and McCay (1995); Sen and Nielsen (1996).
11   Sen and Nielsen (1996).
12   Jentoft et al. (1998).

The Socio-environmental Context of the Amazon Floodplain

The user strategies of natural resources in the Amazonian floodplain are complex and involve a range of driving forces influencing their management. The spatial and temporal variation in the landscape is reflected in a myriad of resources distributed in four main subsystems: river channels, lakes, flooded forest and lowlands. Patterns of flooding and rainfall as well as local technologies, ecological knowledge and social relations are local factors that have been influencing management strategies across generations. At a broader level, geopolitics, market demands, urbanisation and global environmental concerns have driven large-scale land use patterns such as the establishment of settlements, mining, commercial timbering and fisheries, cattle ranching and, more recently, conservation policies. Today, the Amazon has become a major ecological icon, bringing new actors into the picture and linking more directly local communities to global society. As a result, local actions lead to global outcomes as much as global actions lead to local outcomes. This dialectic process has placed local communities at the centre-stage in the conservation debate.

The role of community-based management in the conservation agenda of the Amazon started as a reaction to mainstream, technocratic management schemes.[13] From villains, who were destroying the natural resources, local populations became potential collaborators and guardians. In the 1990s many projects in the category of 'conservation and development' were delivered by major international donors such as the WWF, ODA, USAID and World Bank. As part of this trend, the G7 Pilot Programme to Conserve the Brazilian Rain Forest — PPG7 (now the Rain Forest Pilot Programme — RFPP) was launched in 1993 as part of an effort by the Brazilian government and the international community to design appropriate strategies for Amazonian natural resources and its populations.[14] Amongst other goals, the RFPP aims to provide subsidies for designing a co-management system of natural resources including all stakeholders. In particular, the ProVarzea floodplain management sub-programme has a specific research project on the participatory management aquatic resources. Taking into account the socio-environmental complexity of the region and the lack of current data, this project has been designed to assess the few initiatives in the region that have been able to integrate local management systems into broader institutional designs. Although most of these initiatives are informal, they are real experiments that provide valuable information about the opportunities and constraints upon co-management endeavours in the Amazon Basin.

13   McGrath et al. (1999).
14   Kolk (1996).

Participatory Management of Floodplain Resources in the Amazon

The local management of aquatic resources is a long-standing practice in the Amazon.[15] In the 1960s, however, a new management system to control access to lakes emerged as part of social changes in the production systems, technological innovations and local political organisation.[16] Community-based management in the floodplain takes many forms, but its organisation is genuinely local. Recently, many of these local institutions have increasingly been connected to regional-based organisations. In this study, I analyse a few examples that illustrate some of the diversity of situations in the Basin. Six examples have been selected based on four main criteria: 1) management stage; 2) level of ecological and social complexity; 3) geographic location; and 4) data availability/logistics. Cases of participatory management systems vary in stage of execution, ranging from incipient to intermediate or advanced. Without presuming any linearity in management dynamics, static patterns or performance this criterion is used as an analytical starting point to place the institution in a temporal context. These cases also vary in the complexity of their management system, from small areas and a single user group to large areas including several resources and stakeholder groups. By considering different levels of socio-environmental complexity, one can identify emerging characteristics resulting from increased complexity. Socio-environmental diversity in the Amazon is striking, as will be the solutions for tackling environmental problems. Finally, the rapid assessment nature of the methodology relies heavily on existing secondary data sources and on logistics for collecting primary data. Thus, cases were selected based on the degree of collaboration with NGOs already present in the study areas.

The six case studies are located along the River Amazon in or nearby the following municipalities: Tefé, Silves, Parintins, Oriximiná, Santarém and Gurupá (Figure 12.1). Tefé is located in the Upper Solimões and the lake management system, established in the 1970s, is one of the oldest in the Amazon. It is based on a zoning system divided into maintenance, subsistence and preservation lakes. The Catholic Church has played a major role in organising and supporting this process but currently other local and regional organisations are involved. Silves is situated in the Middle Amazon and its local management system is connected to an eco-tourism business. This initiative, carried out by a local organisation with support

15   Castro (2002).
16   Castro and McGrath (2003).

from an international NGO and the municipal government, has approximately ten years of experience. Parintins is also located in the Middle Amazon and lake management is combined with other product systems such as stilt-bed gardens. The management systems sometimes meet resistance from cattle ranchers, who control a large part of the floodplain. Oriximiná, in the Lower Amazon, is the fourth case study. This area is highly influenced by a mining company, which directly influences local politics and, in turn, the management initiative. Santarém has the first participatory management initiative, launched in 1995 by the national environmental control agency (IBAMA). This system is based on a fishing council comprising many stakeholders such as local residents, the commercial sector and policy makers. Finally, Gurupá is located in the Amazon estuary and is strongly influenced by tidal patterns. The management system is also one of the oldest in the Amazon and is part of a long-term organisational process, supported by a national NGO since the 1960s. A recent demand for the establishment of a reserve has been debated among local residents and supporting actors from the region.

Figure 12.1: The Amazon Basin showing the six case studies: (1) Tefé; (2) Silves; (3) Parintins; (4) Oriximiná; (5) Santarém; (6) Gurupá.

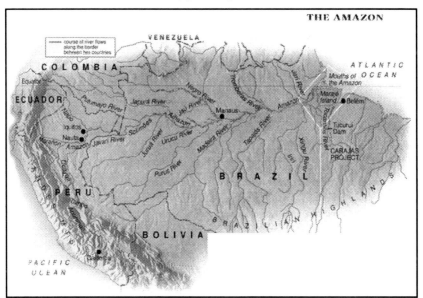

The six cases represent a glimpse of the socio-environmental variability in the Basin. The participatory management assessment aims at shedding light on major factors influencing the dynamics of social and ecological interactions regarding resource conservation, social conflicts and welfare.

The Participatory Management Assessment Framework (PMA)

Studies of co-management have shown that patterns of use and management of natural resources take place in a scenario encompassing four major components. Two concern the ecological features of the target resources, the landscape and its natural resources, and two have to do with the social characteristics of the users, direct and indirect (Figure 12.2). The landscape encompasses the ecosystem in which the resources are spatially and temporally distributed and used. Its boundaries are arbitrary, depending on the spatial scale of the co-management exercise. Natural resources are the central target of management. They may correspond to the whole landscape or those that connect parts of the landscape. Direct users are groups of individuals who extract direct benefit from the resource. Indirect users are those who extract benefits indirectly or play an intermediary role amongst users. The four components are tightly connected through ecological and social processes. In the Amazon floodplain, the landscape is a product of the floodplain system, while target resources may vary including fish, flooded forest, game, natural grassland and palm trees. Direct users are local residents, commercial fishers, ranchers, loggers and farmers, while indirect users include NGOs, grass-roots organisations, governments, timber companies and scientists.

Relationships between the components are determined by the structure of incentives faced by the users, which affects the opportunities and constraints related to the resource use at different decision levels (the household, community, municipality, region, national and international). Thus, a focus on ecological and social relations as a basis for understanding stakeholders' decision-making towards resource use and management is fundamental to revealing how diverse factors influence the performance of management systems. Three main dimensions of the management system will be assessed: 1) the production system; 2) the resource use purpose; and 3) the rules of use and social interaction.

Figure 12.2: Participatory Management Assessment Framework

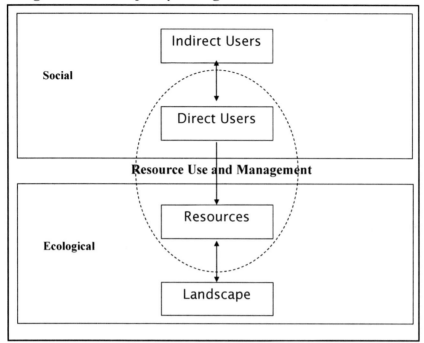

Production system. The ecological heterogeneity of the landscape floodplain provides a myriad of resources and, in turn, generates a complex use of aquatic and terrestrial resources. Yet variations in the distribution of different resources as well as differences in the social features of users (such as economic options, household structure and land tenure) influence the variability of resource use strategies. The assessment of the production system will help to reveal distinct patterns of resource use and how they are related to the management system.

Use purpose. Natural resources are used for many purposes. Despite the commercial importance of many resources, other factors such as their subsistence value, aesthetics, sense of security and identity are other factors governing resource use that must be considered in the analysis of how individuals make management. Assessment of the resource value for each stakeholder is crucial to reveal conflictive interests and potential common interests.

Rules of use and social interaction. Resource-use strategies are filtered by rules that are consciously or unconsciously crafted by users. Commonly, user groups defined rules instinctively according to their interests, generating a variety of outcomes. Rules may be the result of a social process that no longer operates and, consequently, their original goal may no longer exist. Thus, effective and non-effective rules to the management goal should be sorted out in order to assess the degree of fit and effectiveness for achieving the multiple goals of a co-management endeavour. Rules reflect social interactions. Individuals interrelate through norms of behaviour, which may facilitate or constrain cooperation. Assessment of cooperative and conflictive interactions experienced by users is important for assessing the social capital and social costs upon which a co-management system can be built.

Assessment of participatory management systems is based on a comparison of three major aspects: 1) performance; 2) the scale of relationships; and 3) regional variation.

Performance. Comparison of incipient, promising or unsuccessful cases of local management systems will explore forces supporting and constraining the emergence of collective management systems. It is important to note that a 'promising' case may not represent a robust institutional arrangement, just as an 'unsuccessful' case may not represent a failed institutional arrangement. These instances must be treated as transitional phases in a dynamic process of institutional crafting. In short, while considering the current moment to define performance, a process approach to compare performance based on institutional change throughout its history will be the ultimate analytical strategy.

Scale of relationships. Comparison across different degrees of social and ecological complexity of participatory management will explore the emerging features of scaling up from relatively simple to more complex systems. This analysis will be useful for providing information on how to build up simple, successful management systems into more complex co-management systems for multiple users. Geographical extension (for example, from one lake to a lake system), social expansion (from one single community to several stakeholders), resource spread (from one single resource to the floodplain landscape) and institutional arrangements (from incipient rules to formal documentation) will be included in the analysis as much as possible.

Geographic variation. Comparison across large regions will explore the role of ecological landscape, social organisation and occupational history along the Basin. Variations in the landscape structure have resulted from different inundation and rainfall patterns, creating a distinct set of resources and spatial and temporal distribution. By the same token, variations in the history of human occupation are reflected in different forms of user social organisation and social interactions among stakeholders. By sampling case studies along the Amazon River, from the Upper Solimões to the estuary, this analysis will take account of the diversity of situations and response patterns and, in turn, avoid generalisations and blueprint models for co-management designs.

Research Strategy

The methodology of participatory management assessment is based on the analysis of the relationships between four components of co-management — landscape, resources, direct users and indirect users, as defined below.

Subproject 1: Assessment of the degree of influence of the management system in the ecological structure and ecological functions of the managed area.

Subproject 2: Socio-economic assessment of the resource use strategies by the direct users and their relationship with the local management system.

Subproject 3: Assessment of the social relations of direct users, evaluating the potential and limitations for cooperative and conflictive behaviour.

Subproject 4: Assessment of the compatibility between the local management system and the local social system.

Subproject 5: Assessment of the compatibility between interests by direct and indirect users and the institutional relations in different scales of decisions of the management system.

Subproject 6: Elaboration of models of participative management of aquatic resources according to regional specificities, level of environmental complexity and stage in the participative process.

Subproject 1 focuses on the biophysical features of the landscape and its respective resources. The assessment of ecological relations will provide information on how the local management system influences (and is influenced by) ecological functions such as biological productivity, ecosystem resilience, habitat integrity and landscape heterogeneity. Subproject 2 deals with the socio-economic strategies and resource uses employed by direct users. Assessment of economic alternatives, household composition and production systems carried out by different user groups are some of the topics explored in this subproject. Subproject 3 is related to the social relations among individuals of the same group, such as the history of co-existence, kinship, common understanding and social organisation. Information on ecological and social structure and change in the managed area will help to assess the potential and limitations for cooperation in each group. Subproject 4 focuses on the institutional arrangements of the management system, including the local management itself and its supporting institutions such as such as patron-client relations, cooperatives and local associations. Such an analysis will provide insights on the degree of dependence of the local management system with regard to other local institutions that may facilitate or block the development of a co-management system. A broader institutional analysis of the decision-making process of indirect users towards the management system such as the policy-making process, market structure, research agendas and conservation ethics is made for subproject 5. Organisational limitations, the negotiation process, conflicts of interest and conflict resolution are some of the topics touched upon in this subproject. The last subproject aims to join the pieces into a single picture by developing an integrative analysis of the different case studies and formulating theoretical and policy models of participatory management based on regional idiosyncrasies. In order to ensure a reliable dataset, collection and analysis of data must be carried out by a research team with an interdisciplinary training in ecological and social theories and familiarity with the Amazonian environment in order to be able to carry out a short-term assessment effectively. In addition, the research team must be heavily committed to interacting in all phases of the project, from fieldwork scheduling to data analysis and report writing, in order to enable information cross-fertilisation and bridge the gap between the social and ecological dimensions of the resource management. Joint fieldwork, workshops and the development of an integrated database fed by information from all subprojects will facilitate dialogue among researchers during the research development.

Final Comments

Participatory management assessment (PMA) is based on a short-term, comparative, interdisciplinary-oriented methodology. Similar analysis will be carried out in a set of cases with differences based on a pre-defined set of criteria. Six case studies, selected along the Basin, will help to maximise the coverage of socio-environmental diversity. The PMA framework is an effort to provide a research strategy integrating social and ecological dimensions of resource use and management with similar data collection, enabling cross-comparative analysis. It also aims to reveal variability across cases in order to avoid any blueprint approach. Due to the dual demand of scientific and policy questions, the PMA framework enables a rapid strategy to gather reliable data to inform policy strategies. Its conceptual breadth in the inclusion of diverse components may enable extrapolation to other areas.

13

Fire Use and Prevention in the Brazilian Amazon: A Conceptual Household Behaviour Model

Larissa Chermont

Introduction

Fire is a natural phenomenon with its own ecological role. Natural fires are important for the sustainability of ecosystems. They influence plant community development, soil nutrient availability and biological diversity. Fire has also been used for centuries as an important agricultural tool. Since Palaeolithic times fire has helped people to interfere with the natural habitat in order to survive. Nowadays, slash-and-burn agriculture is a generalised practice. Regarded as a cheap and efficient technique, fire is used in different countries to clear forest and secondary vegetation for agriculture, to improve grazing land and to kill or drive away predatory animals and other pests. This practice is especially common where shifting agriculture remains a predominant land-use strategy. The system used in Latin America comes from the Maya. Land preparation starts with the felling of the forest, letting the debris dry in the hot season, and burning it before the beginning of the rainy season. 'Fires are an important means by which humans have transformed their environment.'[1]

Conversely, destruction by uncontrolled fires may cause serious or even irreversible damage to ecosystems as well as contribute to decreases in the levels of human health and welfare. The frequency of such fires has increased substantially in recent decades, due mainly to a combination of climatic conditions and human activities.[2] During the most recent *El Niño* years the dry conditions persisted long enough for standing forests to be burned as fires started for land-clearing activities spread out of control. A study in Indonesia has estimated that during the period between 1997 and

---

1   Goudie (2000).
2   Levine et al. (1999).

1998 the costs from fire damage reached US$9 billion, or 2.5 per cent of the country's GDP.[3] In the Brazilian Amazon, the key consequence of the *El Niño* drought has been frequent and widespread forest fires. In 1998 an average of 10,000 square kilometres of primary forests were burned by accidental fires in Roraima state,[4] while another 4,000 square kilometres were affected in the south of Pará state.[5]

From this discussion emerges the most important distinction between intentional and accidental fires. Whereas intentional fires are a culturally determined land-use tool, accidental fires are considered hazardous events that depend on extraneous factors such as landscape fragmentation, climatic conditions and road network density. This study focuses on human activity in the Brazilian Amazon as the main source of fire ignition. More specifically, it is our intention to present a conceptual model that assesses rural household decisions linked to the use and/or prevention of fire. Agriculture and extensive cattle ranching are the activities to be assessed in order to reveal the rationale that lies at the roots of Amazonian household behaviour with respect to fire.

Most of the related literature is focused on the trajectories of small settlers that have grown up along the boundary between existing agricultural land and the virgin forest. Fire use is normally considered an outcome of the land-use decisions of individual households.[6] While the value of this research is widely acknowledged, it is also important to assess fire use and prevention as a primary decision within the production dynamics of Amazonian households. Furthermore, in addition to small settlers, this study will also assess both medium-sized farms and large-scale commercial farms and consider their influence on local and regional socio-economic development.

This chapter aims to put into perspective the household decision-making process that regards fire as a production tool as well as a hazard to be prevented. The main challenge is to develop a conceptual model that interrelates the experience and information available within the household with the physical and environmental characteristics of their property (i.e. the piece of land they manage). I start with a contextualisation of land-use and fire use/prevention in the Brazilian Amazon. Section three describes two case studies and presents the survey design. The conceptual model is set out in the fourth section, in which a preliminary sample characterisation is also offered. The conclusion suggests the need for further appro-

---

3   WRI (2000).
4   Kirchhoff and Escada (1999).
5   Nepstad et al. (1999).
6   Sorrensen (1998).

priate public policies for this sector and points out the potential usefulness of the proposed model.

Fire Use in the Brazilian Amazon

Fire destruction in the Amazon region is causing serious negative impacts on the proper functioning of its ecosystems. This is due mainly to its effects on land cover, land use, biodiversity, climatic change and forest ecosystems. Economic impacts and effects on human health are also important issues to be addressed when dealing with fire within this regional context. Forest destruction caused by fire has an increasing significance in terms of Amazonian development, since it is closely linked to environmental losses, economic activity and land use systems in the region. Among its main causes are land clearing, logging, road construction and accidental fires.

Fire is used regularly in the Amazon to deforest and to clean agricultural land and pasture. Due to its low cost and straightforward procedure, fire is strongly linked to land-use patterns adopted in the region. Paradoxically, fire itself is also one of the greatest threats to Amazon ecosystems when, having escaped from human control, it burns forests, animals and material goods. As gross deforestation reached the mean rate of 18,226 square kilometres per annum in 2000[7] accidental fire is believed to be the greatest threat to the Amazon forest. In 1998 drought increased the fire-vulnerable area in northern Brazil to an area of over one million square kilometres.[8] Nevertheless, little is known about the impacts of accidental ground fires on carbon stocks, forest metabolism, forest hydrology, human welfare and the prospect of sustainable forest management.

Data collected by the NOAA-12 satellite has identified a fire belt along the south of the region that is approximately 1.2 million square kilometres in size.[9] Data regarding fire events in the Amazon is still dramatic. The Brazilian Ministry of the Environment (MMA) has announced that the number of hot pixels in the region has increased from 67,461 in 2000 to over 100,000 in 2001, our survey year. The states of Mato Grosso and Pará, where our study sites are located, retain the highest levels of hot pixels in the region; in 2001 Mato Grosso registered over 33,000 and Pará 28,500.[10] In agriculture burning has been used mainly to clear land for planting and for transforming areas of pasture as part of a process of gen-

7   INPE (2002).
8   Wood and Walker (1999).
9   Moran et al. (1996); Schwartzman (1997).
10   IBAMA (2001).

erating productive land. Additionally, soil conditions and 'the presence of numerous invasive and sometimes toxic plant species necessitates repeated
burning to control them…'[11] This reinforces the need to consider burning as
one of the most important variables within the land-use system framework.

Figure 13.1: RisQue98 Model Map: Forest Flammability and
Agricultural Burning

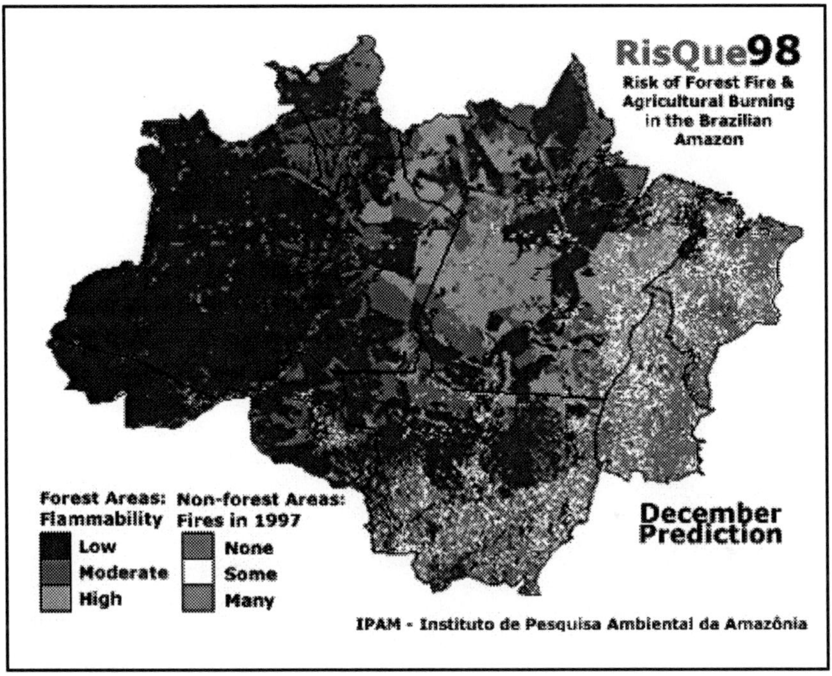

Source: (IPAM, 2001)

A predictive model called RisQue98 has been developed by a group of researchers at the Instituto de Pesquisa Ambiental da Amazonia (IPAM).
Considering forest flammability as a function of both drought and logging activity, the model ranks the vulnerability to fire of the different areas of the
Amazon forest. Field data from forest flammability studies was used in order
to classify the Amazon areas according to their vulnerability to fire. Figure 13.1
shows the December 1998 prediction for forest flammability, the RisQue98.
The final map shows flammability levels for forest areas in the region as well
as a quantification legend for fires in non-forest areas during 1997.

11   Walker et al. (2000).

Three distinct types of fires occur in the Amazon:[12]

(i)   'Deforestation Fires' linked to clear-cutting activities on primary forest vegetation.

(ii)   'Forest Surface Fires' caused accidentally, occurring either in primary or logged forests.

(iii)   'Fire on Deforested Land' resulting from the burning of pasture or secondary vegetation. This can be divided into: intentional, for pasture and land management, and accidental, that has spread onto cleared land.

Considering the fact that human activities such as slash-and-burn agriculture and extensive cattle ranching are the main sources of environmental degradation and economic loss generated by fire, it is also important to recognise these agents as primary sources of ignition. In addition to the size of a property, other elements need to be considered when performing a categorisation of producers in the region. These elements include location, cropping system, level of capital and technology as well as and cultural and economic background. Adopting a preliminary standard classification, we attempt to relate the size and nature of production units:

- Small producers: less than 100 hectares

- Medium producers: 100–500 hectares

- Commercial producers: over 500 hectares

It is important to point out that these categories will need to be related to the land-use system adopted by each unit to better reflect the differences between producers and to explain their dynamics. It is our intention to identify different land-use patterns, always focusing on the use of fire as a management tool. Fallow period extension, burning intensity and type of output will act as determinant factors.

One important factor related to traditional techniques of land-use is that upon arrival, newcomers do not possess satisfactory knowledge of local specificities and environmental characteristics. This is one of the main factors responsible for degradation and burning in the initial period of activities. Another factor is related to these producers' lack of capital, since burning can be completely replaced by the use of appropriate equipment.

---

12   Nepstad et al. (1999).

Diversification is another important element when analysing land use in the Amazon. Small farmers tend to diversify more than large ranchers. In general, manioc is widely used after all fallow periods. The planting of rice is more frequent after long fallow periods, while beans are used in fields previously covered with a light cover of herbaceous vegetation. In addition, there is a strong tendency for cultivated fields to be converted to pasture. Annual crops are closely linked with frequent burning while perennials are a strong incentive for reducing this activity.

As well as being active agents of the use of fire, Amazonian farmers also suffer from the negative consequences of uncontrolled accidental fires. The loss of both pasture and permanent crop areas, as well as possible asset losses, has become a constant in the region. Consequently, there is a growing tendency among landholders to invest in fire prevention. The use of adequate equipment and firebreaks has increased over the years in order to protect properties from accidental fires.

It was estimated from a survey study of the area known as the Amazonian 'Arc of Deforestation' that approximately 48 per cent of forest fires are caused by pasture fires which have burned out of control, while 13 per cent are caused by deforestation fires.[13] In 1998, fire was used to convert approximately 18,000 square kilometres of clear-cut forests into soil-fertilising ash through deforestation.[14] Even in the absence of logging, forests stressed by long dry seasons can burn rapidly if ignited by agricultural fires.[15]

Although there are many disadvantages arising from the use of fire, it remains a constant feature of rural production. For many years people have been facing the consequences of accidental fires, either indirectly due to their effects on the environment, or more directly as a result of financial losses. Economic and environmental losses faced by farmers as a result of accidental fires increase every year. Risk of destruction caused by accidental fire, however, has contributed to perpetuate this extensive model. There were few incentives to invest in perennials or any other fire vulnerable activity due to the high risk imposed by accidental fire. This situation is described as a feedback cycle, where frontier occupation and extensive production systems contribute to increasing accidental fire, which will, in turn, cause more agroforestry losses, leaving the vegetation even more vulnerable to fire.[16]

---

13   Nepstad et al. (1999).
14   INPE (2000).
15   Negreiros et al. (1997); Nepstad (1995).
16   Nepstad et al. (2002).

Fire evolved as a solution to human survival but with inevitable harmful effects as a land-use tool. The frontier expansion process in the
Brazilian Amazon has intensified this scenario, where land was the single
cheapest and most abundant resource. In the face of labour and capital
shortages, an extensive land-use model has been implemented in which fire
is one important element. This has contributed to a win-lose situation, in
which high private benefits are associated with high social costs as a consequence of this frontier expansion process.

The Survey

In order to obtain household data, a formal survey was undertaken during
the Amazonian dry season of 2001. In total, 349 interviews were conducted with rural producers of the chosen study sites located in four
Amazonian municipalities along the corridor formed by the
Cuiabá–Santarém highway (BR–163): Santarém and Belterra in the state of
Pará; and Guarantã do Norte and Matupá in Mato Grosso. These municipalities are identified in Figure 13.2.

This survey was designed to assess households' endowments, primary
portfolio dimension, cultural background and land-use decisions, by means
of a formal questionnaire. The aim was to obtain property-level data that
could not be obtained from any other primary or secondary source.
Although aggregated data, available from the Brazilian Agrarian Census
for 1998,[17] were used for a preliminary description and survey design,
these data do not provide any information at the household level as their
unit of analysis is the municipality as a whole.

The population surveyed for this study was drawn from communities
of rural producers in the Amazon region. Due to a number of constraints,
a complete survey of this population was not a feasible goal for the study.
Instead the target has been to use a case study approach, focusing on the
two chosen study sites, from which inferences on household behaviour
based on empirical evidence can be obtained with reasonable confidence.
The absence of reliable household information for our case study areas
prevented the use of the stratified random selection process that we initially intended to employ. As a second best option, based on the only available source of information on the target population, it was decided that
the area sample frame method was the best methodological procedure
available for selecting the sample of households to be studied.[18]

17   IBGE (1998).
18   Deaton (1997).

Figure 13.2: Study Sites Locations

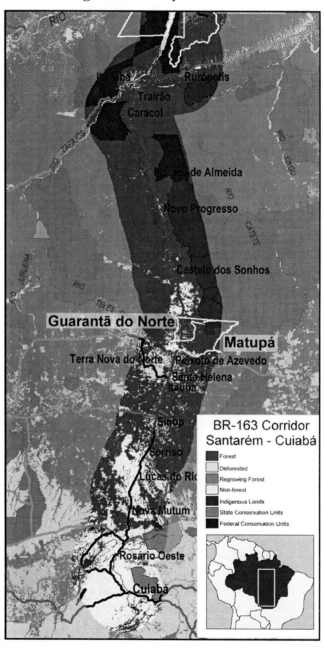

Source: Woods Hole Research Center, 2001

The lack of information on rural households remains the main obstacle for socio-economic surveys within both the Amazon and Brazil in general. The official census tract data possessed by the federal government are not made public in order to guarantee the confidentiality of respondents' replies. In rural areas, information is an especially complex issue as land registry data are frequently out of date and suffer from bureaucratic inefficiency. Land conflicts have at the same time contributed to the maintenance of this obsolete system and suffered its perverse consequences. It is still very common for rural landholders to remain on the waiting list for their titles for more than 20 years.

It was possible to consider the use of the area frame method because of the availability of satellite images from 1999 as well as additional GIS information. This material was obtained through cooperation with IPAM and with a research team from Indiana University undertaking fieldwork in the same areas. A 60-kilometre long area alongside the BR–163 Highway was defined as the vertical axis of the frame for both case studies. In the Santarém site, the boundaries were completed by covering all secondary roads on either side of the main axis. The lateral boundaries were imposed by physical limits: the Tapajós River on the western side; and on the eastern side either the Curuá-Una River or the ends of the secondary roads themselves, approximately 30 kilometres from the highway. In the Mato Grosso site, a similar 60-kilometre stretch of the highway was defined as the vertical axis of the frame while the lateral boundaries were set either by the ends of the secondary roads or by the points at which they reached an average of 30 kilometres either side of the main road. Definition of these boundaries was chosen to be consistent with the available satellite images that covered the two study sites.

The Study Sites

The opening of the Amazon as a development frontier has occurred in many different areas of the region. Each of these areas has its own specific characteristics and dynamics. The two sites chosen for primary data collection are substantially representative of the general land occupation process, as well as of the specific factors such as types of landowners and farm characteristics. Settled in different periods of the occupation history of this region, the two study sites belong to the corridor formed by the settled areas along the Cuiabá-Santarém highway (BR–163), which is paved on the Mato Grosso side and in very poor condition on the Pará side.

The BR–163 highway was conceived initially as an export corridor both for industrial products from the Manaus free trade zone heading south to the main Brazilian population centres, and for grain production from the centre-west of the country heading north to the port of Santarém for export. Government planning neglected most of the socio-economic or environmental impacts of this opening. Inevitably this resulted in disorganised settlement alongside the highway of small landholders who today face difficulties because of the poor infrastructure and lack of technical assistance.

The choice of these sites for the case studies was due mainly to their importance as Amazonian agricultural frontiers and to their geographical location in terms of both the regional economy and fire risk. They are both in strategic but very distinct stretches of the BR–163 corridor. The specific characteristics considered in the selection process were:

- Property size diversity

- Frontier age

- Settlement type (government induced or spontaneous)

- Fire vulnerability

- Regional economic magnitude

A decisive factor for choosing these sites was their degree of susceptibility to fire. Santarém and Belterra are located in an area of relative fire susceptibility and classified as an intermediary zone by the RisQue98 map.[19] Although not yet a problematic area this study site has experienced high rates of deforestation and landscape changes. Recent changes in its economic dynamics as well as in its perspectives for the future have made this area a priority for further research. Guarantã do Norte and Matupá, however, are located in an area of high fire vulnerability, known as the Deforestation Arc, on the same RisQue98 map. This location and the predominant activity of extensive cattle ranching were the most important criteria for the choice of this area as a case study site.

In order to make a brief comparison of the four municipalities reached by our survey, population, occupation and average farm size of each municipality are shown in Table 13.1. However, it is important to emphasise that while the Brazilian Census adopts the municipality as its unit of analysis, our case study areas, which focus on the micro level, are formed by smaller areas within those municipalities. Furthermore, differ-

19   IPAM (2001).

ent settlement patterns, among other factors, have influenced the predominance of larger farms in both Guarantã do Norte and, more extensively, Matupá. This is easily detected by observing the data on the average size of farms on the same table.

Table 13.1: Municipalities Area, Population and Farm Size

Municipality	Area (km²)	Total Population	Rural Population (% of total)	Average size of farms (ha)
Santarém	24,314	262,538	76,241 (29%)	42
Belterra	2,629	14,594	9,468 (65%)	59
Guarantã do Norte	2,756	28,200	8,835 (31%)	164
Matupá	7,127	11,289	2,503 (22%)	603

Source: *Population Census, 2000* (IBGE, 2002)

Santarém is an important and traditional municipality of the state of Pará. Its capital, of the same name, is the third largest city in the Amazon region and occupies a strategic location in the confluence of two important rivers, the Amazon and the Tapajós. The farms surveyed in this case study are located along the rural corridor, which borders the BR–163 highway, and is shared by the municipalities of Santarém and Belterra. This area is an interfluvial plateau and has a piedmont, rolling uplands topography that is locally referred to as *interfluvial terra firme* or *plano alto*. The native vegetation has been classified as dense rain forest and dense *terra firme* forest.[20]

The municipality of Belterra was created from part of Santarém municipality in 1997. Belterra village itself is located 20 kilometres south of Santarém on the BR–163 highway. Its origins are linked to a large rubber tree plantation which the Ford Motor Company maintained in the area between 1924 and 1945. During this time Ford invested in village infrastructure for their workers and in one ten-year period planted more than three million trees. Traditional spontaneous settlement is the predominant pattern of land occupation in this study site and, in general, the majority of the properties

20   Scatena et al. (1996).

consist of small and medium sized farms. There is a long tradition of both agriculture and agro-forestry in the area. Nevertheless, some settlements have been organised by the federal government institution for land reform (INCRA). These are found mainly in the south of this area, where more recent government induced occupation has been taking place. This study site is experiencing an intense process of land aggregation. There has also been a substantial increase in private investments in rural production.

The second study site lies in that part of the north of Mato Grosso state known locally as *Nortão*. Situated in the southern part of the Legal Amazon, this area is made up of six neighbouring municipalities: Terra Nova; Nova Guarita; Peixoto de Azevedo; Matupá; Guarantã do Norte; and Novo Mundo. These municipalities occupy a total area of 19,289 square kilometres, with the focal point being the junction of the BR–163 federal highway with the state highway MT–080. Guarantã do Norte and Matupá are the two municipalities on which our field activities took place. Typical of the peripheral areas of the Amazon Basin, this study site is considered an ecological tension transition area, strongly influenced by its hot and humid climate and the fragmented landscape. Several types of vegetation such as savanna, *cerrado*, ombrofilous forest and dense forest, occur simultaneously in this heterogeneous landscape. This natural landscape has been substantially modified by human intervention in the form of an intense and rapid process of occupation.

Guarantã do Norte is one of the younger municipalities of Mato Grosso. It emerged simultaneously with the opening of the BR–163, during the late 1970s and early 1980s, with an influx of families of small settlers from the south of the country, who were attracted by both the government and private settlement schemes which were being promoted in the region at that time. The first 20 families arrived in 1980 and were settled mainly with the support of a subsidiary of the *Southern Cooperativa Tritícola de Erechim* (COTREL). They were offered plots of 45 hectares and peri-urban plots of three hectares for their houses. The legal forest reserve area, required by federal law, was located in a collective reserve in the area of the Serra do Cachimbo. The Cooperativa de Guarantã has recently replaced the original COTREL and its members have been strongly inclined towards cotton and fruit production.[21]

The federal government's agrarian reform institution (INCRA) started its activities in the area in 1980. Its main task was to support and provide reasonable living for the families already settled by providing infrastruc-

21   Soares Filho (1998)

ture, food and legalising titles. In addition to the southern families of COTREL, there was also a group of families that had been removed from the area of the Machadinho dam, as well as a large number of Brazilian families that had been expelled from Paraguay, who were supported by a group of Dominican Sisters.

The families from Paraguay, known as *Brasiguaios*, numbered 550 in 1981, with 300 more arriving in 1982. Most had their plots alongside the BR–163 highway legalised as properties of 50 hectares and had, in addition, the right to an equivalent area in a collective forest reserve. With the support of the federal government a cooperative was founded for the acquisition of machinery and the production of grain. Today this cooperative is bankrupt and the producers are facing serious difficulties in maintaining its activities.

In 1984 the village of Guarantã became a district of the Colider municipality. It gained administrative autonomy in 1986 when Guarantã do Norte became a municipality of Mato Grosso state.[22] Today, 33 per cent of its total area is occupied by rural establishments, most of which are dedicated to rural activities. The capital of the municipality, also named Guarantã do Norte, is located alongside the BR–163 highway and suffers, among other problems, from uncontrolled growth caused by rural exodus and intense air pollution caused by burning activity in neighbouring rural areas.

Matupá, however, was originally a private colonisation area belonging to the Ometto group, a large family enterprise from São Paulo state. Their Agropecuário Cachimbo project was established in the mid-1970s with an initial area of 300,000 hectares. Encouraged by fiscal incentives from the Amazon Regional Development Agency (SUDAM), the firm started extensive cattle ranching activities as well as rural and urban colonisation. Although Matupá gained the status of municipality in 1987, the Agropecuário Cachimbo project remains operational with its cattle ranching activities on a property of 100,000 hectares.

Originally designed as a planned settlement, Matupá has a continuous grid-structure of regular plots of 100 and 200 hectares. The pattern of properties in this area has suffered intensive change. Today large farms are a major feature of the area. In addition, invasions of private and public forest reserves have became a permanent source of conflict. The most significant example of this activity is that of the original 300,000 hectares of the Agropecuário Cachimbo project, some 200,000 hectares of which have been invaded by squatters and the area intensely deforested.[23] Although

22   Prefeitura de Guarantã do Norte (1999).
23   Soares Filho (1998).

similar to the other study site, there have been substantial changes in the dynamics of the economy and in the organisation of property in this municipality, mainly as a result of the agribusiness-induced production of grains further south in Mato Grosso. The economy is based on rice production, in which Matupá ranks first in the region.

In the 1990s, the Brazilian federal government launched the *Avança Brasil* (Forward Brazil) programme, a large-scale investment scheme for infrastructure, economic and social projects, which is designed to almost triple the Amazonian paved road network from the current 6,300 kilometres to 18,145 kilometres. The programme includes investments in rail network construction, dam building, port enlargement and river transportation. In the specific cases of our two study sites, this federal programme encompasses both the paving of the Pará section of the BR–163 highway and expansion of the port of Santarém.[24] These investments will complete an integrated scheme to provide this corridor with the infrastructure needed to stimulate the export of the rural produce from the centre-west.

The Model

Our main hypothesis is that the propensity of a land user to use fire decreases, and their investment in fire prevention increases, as agriculture becomes more intensive and permanent. An additional hypothesis is that fire prevention is directly related to the diversification of the household portfolio. The goal is to investigate and estimate how diverse sets of conditions interact to determine household behaviour with respect to fire.

Our conceptual model aims to describe the decision-making process experienced by Amazonian landholders involved in agriculture and cattle ranching activities. In view of the fact that that different kinds of land-use lead to different technological choices, our point of departure is to argue that a farmer's decision to use fire as an agricultural management tool, or to prevent damage from accidental fire, is the result of a sequential decision-making process. Assuming that households behave in an economically rational way, they should always select the alternative with the highest utility. These decisions will be assessed in the model as an output of empirically observed explanatory variables within the household decision context. Household endowments, as a general measure of the physical and financial initial conditions, are the constraints used for this model. These constraints determine the feasibility of the choices made. Both fire use and prevention decisions should

24   IPAM (2001).

result from the same labour, capital and environmental constraints that determine a household's capacity to bring land into production.[25]

Figure 13.3 is an attempt to describe the fire use/prevention decision-
making process at the micro-level within the region. Ultimately, this
process is the output of a household's revealed perceptions and preferences, which are in turn determined by both the experience and information contexts of the household. The two alternatives to be considered are
the decisions to use fire as an agricultural management tool and the decision to invest in fire prevention. As illustrated, these technological options
are regarded as a result of the household's assessment of the feasibility of
the alternatives given their budget and physical constraints.

**Figure 13.3: A Micro-level Conceptual Framework of the
Household Decision-making Process Regarding Fire Use and
Prevention in the Brazilian Amazon**

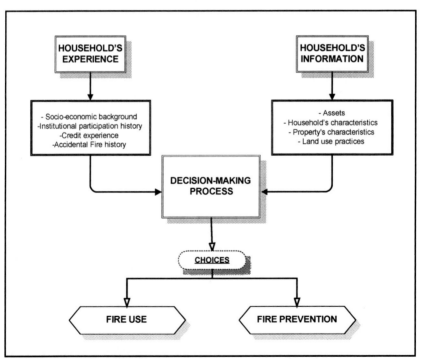

Adapted from: McFadden (2000).

25   Pérez and Walker (2002).

It is necessary to point out the importance of the decision-maker's experience in determining the preferences and perceptions that will lead to a choice. As shown in Figure 13.3, experience and information were the criteria for selecting the explanatory variables to be included in this conceptual model. The household's experience block is formed by a group of four subsets of variables: namely, socio-economic background; institutional participation history; credit experience; and accidental fire history. Four other groups of explanatory variables form the household's information block: assets; household characteristics; the property characteristics; and land-use practices.

Households are considered to be economic agents that aim to optimise their welfare functions. In this case the choices of adopting a fire-intensive technology option and/or investing in fire prevention will be valued by attributes of the respective alternatives. In other words, households will base their choices regarding fire use and fire prevention on both their experience and their information. Considering that empirical research which addresses the relationship between land use systems and fire activity in the Brazilian Amazon is limited, this study focuses mainly on the use of primary data analysis to assess household behaviour regarding fire activity.

Two independent empirical models will be presented in order to assess the two different decisions made by farmers; using fire as a management tool and investing in fire prevention. In both models, household decisions will be determined by specific exogenous variables. The two dependent variables will consist of binary variables regarding fire use (Model 1) and fire prevention (Model 2).

Since Amazonian rural households use fire intensively as a management tool in agricultural production, Model 1 will address the decision-making process for this type of practice. In this model the dependent variable is the household's decision as to whether to use fire as an agriculture management tool. As can be seen in Table 13.2, the explanatory variables are grouped by household experience and information. These outcome variables allow us to address the question of what factors influence the decision as to whether, and with what intensity, fire will be employed as a land use tool.

On the other hand, fire prevention efforts are increasing every year among Amazonian households. Firebreaks and community organisation were identified as the most commonly used prevention activities. In Model 2, household fire prevention efforts will be assessed as the binary dependent variable. Similarly to Model 1, all the explanatory variables will appear in two different groups, depending on the data surveyed. The aim is to explain the decision-making process that leads to the fire prevention decision, and to assess the household's effort in this regard. Table 13.2 summarises the explanatory variables from Figure 13.3 and presents the respective labels and operational definitions for both empirical models. The next section presents a preliminary survey data analysis and a brief household description using some of the variables referred to above.

Table 13.2: Household Choice Models Variables

Dependent Variables	= 1, if household uses fire-intense technology = 0, if household does not use fire = 1, if household prevents from fire = 0, if household does prevent from fire		

Explanatory Variables		Variable Label	Measurement
Household's Experience			
• Household's head age		AGE	Years
• Household's head region of birth		NATIVE	Amazon = 1 Others = 0
• Household's head education level		EDUCATION	Years of schooling
• Household's head previous activity		BACKGROUND	Agriculture = 1 Others = 0
• Time working on property		TIME ON PROPERTY	Years
'Institutional history'	• Participation in rural organisation	ORGANISATION	Years as member
	• Participation in Producers' Cooperative	COOPERATIVISM	Years as member
	• Tenure security	TITLE	Yes = 1 No = 0
	• Settlement type	SETTLEMENT	Government=1 Spontaneous= 0

Table 13.2 continued

Explanatory Variables		Variable Label	Measurement
'Credit experience'	• Has received official Credit at least once	CREDIT	Yes = 1 No = 0
	• Indebtedness	INDEBTED	Yes = 1 No = 0
'Fire History'	• Previous experience with accidental fire	FIRE IN PROPERTY	Yes = 1 No = 0
	• Community Organisation for Fire	ORG FIRE	Yes = 1 No = 0
	• Usage of Official License for burning	LICENSE	Yes = 1 No = 0
	• Fire Brigade in the area	BRIGADE	Yes = 1 No = 0
	• Non-Official Organisation in the area	NGOS	Yes = 1 No = 0
'Property Characteristics'	• Property size	SIZE	Hectares
	• State	STATE	PA = 1 MT = 0
	• Public Electricity	ELECTRICITY	Yes = 1 No = 0
	• Public School	DISTANCE TO SCHOOL	km
	• Public Health	DISTANCE TO HEALTH	km
Household Information			
'Assets'	• Fence in property	FENCE	km
	• Corral on property	CORRAL	Number of Corrals
	• Equipment	TRACTOR	Number of Tractors
	• Private Roads in property	ROADS	km
	• Other Rural Properties	OTHER RURAL	Hectares
	• Urban Properties	URBAN	Number of properties

Table 13.2 continued

Explanatory Variables		Variable Label	Measurement
'Household Characteristics'	• Household size	RESIDENTS	No. of persons
	• Household's head presence in farm	HEAD RESIDENT	Yes = 1 No = 0
	• Family Working force	FAMILY LABOUR	No. of Persons
	• Hired labour	HIRED LABOUR	No. of workers
	• Retirement Income	HEAD RETIRED	Yes = 1 No = 0
	• Monthly Income	INCOME	Reais R$
	• Portfolio Diversification	DIVERSIFICATION	Yes = 1 No=0
'Land Use Practices'	• Perennials	PERENNIALS	Hectares
	• Natural Pasture	NAT PASTURE	Hectares
	• Planted Pasture	PLAN PASTURE	Hectares
	• Annuals	ANNUALS	Hectares
	• Fallow	FALLOW	Hectares

Preliminary Sample Description

Considering the explanatory variables listed in Table 13.2 and using some of the survey data, this section will describe the households interviewed in 2001. The total sample consists of 349 households, of which 165 are located in the Santarém site and 184 in the Guarantã do Norte site. The origin of the household head is an important variable. As with most Amazonian settlers, 87 per cent of household heads surveyed come from other regions. In the Santarém sample, outsiders make up 73 per cent, while in Guarantã do Norte this number rises to 99.5 per cent. The vast majority of settlers arrived in the 1970s and 1980s, attracted by a strong government campaign and investments to colonise the region. Santarém is a relatively older frontier area, in which 35 per cent of its settlers arrived during the 1970s, with most of them settling spontaneously following the gold boom. Guarantã do Norte, however, is a newer frontier area in which 60 per cent of households arrived during the 1980s, attracted mainly to government-induced settlements.

The vast majority of the household heads interviewed (81 per cent) come from agricultural backgrounds, attracted by government programmes. They are mostly from rural families in the south of the country, where land had become scarce and expensive. This new generation came to the Amazon searching for a chance to keep their agricultural traditions. For instance, in Guarantã do Norte the Italian traditions are kept in the same way as they are by the older generations of immigrants in southern Brazil.

A mixture of government-induced and spontaneous types of settlement was verified as the source of land acquisition, with 60 per cent of the plots being bought on the private market. A substantial 30 per cent share comprises settlers that received their plot directly from the federal government's agrarian reform institution (INCRA), which is consistent with the indication that 42 per cent of them have worked on their properties for up to 20 years. The average age of household heads is considered young, with 78 per cent of the sample being under 60 years of age. Nevertheless, following the patterns of other Brazilian rural areas, education levels are very low. Only 16 per cent of interviewed household heads had completed primary school, while 57 per cent had two years or less of schooling.

Regarding the sample households' portfolio diversification and total income, the survey reveals that 72 per cent receive less than US$270 per month. These data are even more significant when it emerged that most households with this level of income are those that benefit from retirement pensions. The majority of the landholders interviewed (78 per cent) live on rural properties and rural production is their main economic activity, given that 73 per cent of them reported that they live exclusively from their farms and just 29 per cent have urban properties.

Land tenure security is another crucial issue for Amazonian landholders, since a formal land title is essential in order to obtain credit and security of tenure acts as an incentive for investments in the farms. However, only 45 per cent of the sample properties have formal documentation. Most of the remaining households have precarious documentation, while 12 per cent do not have any documentation at all. Property size is another important explanatory variable used in the model. Table 13.3 shows the distribution of property size for the total surveyed population of 349 households.

Table 13.3: Sample Property Size

Size (ha)	Santarém	Guarantã	Total	%
<100	133	121	254	73
100-500	27	48	75	22
>500	5	15	20	6

Household production in the study sites is based strongly on annual crops and cattle ranching. Although most households engage in subsistence activities, only 17 per cent are exclusively subsistence units. Market sales remain their main source of income, with 11 per cent selling their products directly in the local market. As in the rest of the region, most rural produce is commercialised through intermediaries. In the case of the survey sample this represents 63 per cent of total sales. Family members continue to make up the principal labour force for the sample settlers, with 88 per cent of the sample using this kind of production factor.

Agriculture is the main activity of the sample settlers. Among the 349 households interviewed, 93 per cent reported that they engage in some kind of agricultural production, with 34 per cent having opened up new areas for this activity in the previous year. Among the most common crops are rice and perennials such as coffee and black pepper. Cattle ranching is the other main economic activity carried out by Amazonian landholders. In addition, the possession of cattle plays an important role as a form of asset saving. Sample households reported that 62 per cent have between ten and 1,000 head of cattle. Another 33 per cent have fewer than ten head but most have stated their willingness to increase their herd size as a retirement plan. Credit is used mainly for cattle acquisition and capital investment. Of the sampled households, 52 per cent reported having received rural credit at least once. Levels of indebtedness are very high and most of the associations formed to facilitate credit are suffering from corruption and mismanagement.

Fire was found to be a common tool among the interviewed settlers, of whom 64 per cent reported using it annually in order to prepare the land for cultivation. Yet prevention efforts were also heavily reported, given that 87 per cent of landholders use at least one type of fire prevention technique. Finally, at both study sites accidental fire was shown to be a constant feature of people's lives. A substantial number (66 per cent) have had a fire invade their properties at least once and 46 per cent have had losses from accidental fires. These losses involve mainly the burning of plantations and pasture as well as losses of constructions and machinery.

Discussion and Conclusions

Preventing deforestation is not a sufficient condition for eradicating the fire problem in the Brazilian Amazon. The design of public policies in this regard has necessarily to deal with a combination of regional development and conservation strategies. Fire is intrinsically linked both to land-use practices and natural resource-use. Therefore, efficient public policies should manage collective interests and individual ambitions. Land tenure, infrastructure planning, protected areas and credit programmes are important options to be considered.

Historically, public policies regarding fire in the Brazilian Amazon officially intensified after1998 when the federal programme PROARCO was designed as an emergency initiative to fight large-scale fires in the state of Roraima which raged out of control for weeks. During this period the Brazilian Environment Ministry (IBAMA) used funding from the United Nations Programme for the Environment (PNMA) and from the Pilot Programme to Conserve the Brazilian Rain Forest (PPG7) which was initially intended to fund another federal programme for mobilisation campaigns for fire prevention targeting small producers.

Nevertheless, there is little tradition within the region with integrated public policies meant to combat the true causes of the fire problem. The conceptual model presented in this paper is intended to contribute to debates aimed at promoting behavioural change policies. This tool will be useful for the implementation of media and educational campaigns, community organisation, legislative and economic approaches aimed to either discourage fire-use or encourage fire prevention. Bearing in mind the fact that the solution resides in behavioural change and education, fire prevention needs to be encouraged through media campaigns, social mobilisation and monitoring. A complete technological change that eradicates fire use would be the desirable target for public policies in the region. However, it is faster and more feasible to focus on the encouragement of prevention techniques. In this respect, the anticipated contribution of this conceptual model is to influence rural production and forest protection policy-making in order to contain fire damage. This result emerges when potential fire ignition sources are reduced by lower production costs and or increased landholders' profits.

Integrated public policies, aimed at supporting an agricultural intensification model from which old frontier zones benefit from government investments in infrastructure, would prevent new frontier opening and the expansion of extensive land-use practices. A more sedentary population would enjoy better survival conditions and benefit from increased earnings and productivity. Some legislative and economic approaches should be implemented in order to deal with long-term behaviour change regarding fire use and prevention. This target could be achieved through the inclusion of fire prevention techniques and equipment as financed items, thus reducing prevention costs for households. Existing credit policies such as the Constitutional Fund for the North (FNO), the Programme for Supporting the Agrarian Reform (PROCERA) and the National Programme for Family Production (PRONAF) could be used in this regard, linking the timing of credit with the agricultural calendar to avoid burning during the dry season in order to have the money in time for planting. Adopting community fire agreements as a precondition for government investments in local infrastructure and including fire maps as criteria for ecological and economic zoning would prove to be effective initiatives to avoid accidental fire in the region.

The relationship between economic and ecological issues is particularly crucial for understanding those new perspectives. It is now clear that Brazilian society expects a new approach and new priorities from policy makers and planners in relation to the region's future. In general, the work that has been done on Amazonian land-use has neglected fire activity and household behaviour. Theoretical discussion and empirical analysis need to be linked in order to obtain a more complete diagnosis of public policies for the Amazonian rural sector.

BIBLIOGRAPHY

Ab'Saber, Aziz Nacib (2001) *Litoral do Brasil/Brazilian Coast* (São Paulo: Metavideo SP Produção e Comunicação Ltda.).

Abers, Rebecca, Millikan, Brent, von Bulow, Maria and Little, Paul (2001) *Civil Society Participation in the Pilot Program to Conserve the Brazilian Rain Forest*, consultants' report (Brasília: World Bank).

Achard, F., Eva, H., Stibig, H., Mayaux, P., Gallego, J., Richards, T. and Malingreau, J. (2002) 'Determination of Deforestation Rates of the World's Humid Tropical Forests,' *Science*, vol. 297, pp. 999–1002.

Adger, N. and Brown, K. et al. (2002) 'Governance for Sustainability: Towards a "Thick" Understanding of Environmental Decision Making,' *CSERGE Working Paper EDM 02–04*.

Albert, B. (2000) 'Associações indígenas e desenvolvimento sustentável na Amazônia brasileira,' in C.A. Ricardo (ed.), *Povos indígenas no Brasil 1996–2000* (São Paulo: Instituto Socioambiental), pp. 197–207.

Allegretti, M.H. (1990) 'Extractive Reserves: an Alternative for Reconciling Development and Environmental Conservation in Amazonia', in A.B. Anderson (ed.), *Alternatives to Deforestation: Steps towards Sustainable Use of the Amazon Rain Forest* (New York: Columbia University Press), pp. 252–64.

Almeida, Alfredo Wagner (2000) 'Mapas temáticos ou mapas situacionais? A reconceituação dos conflitos sócio-ambientais e os fatores étnicos como delineadores de novos procedimentos técnicos de zoneamento,' in *Anais do Seminário Sobre o ZEE na Amazônia Brasileira* (Manaus).

Alston, Lee J., Libecap, Gary D. and Schneider, Robert (1996a) 'The Determinants and Impact of Property Rights: Land Titles on the Brazilian Frontier,' *The Journal of Law, Economics & Organization*, vol. 12, no. 1.

Alston, Lee J., Libecap, Gary D. and Schneider, Robert (1996b) 'The Demand and Supply of Property Rights on the Frontier: The Cases of North America and Brazil,' in Terry L. Anderson and

Peter J. Hill (eds.), *The Privatization Process: A Worldwide Perspective* (London: Rowman & Littlefield Publishers).

Alston, Lee J., Libecap, Gary D. and Schneider, Robert (1996c) 'Violence and the Assignment of Property Rights on Two Brazilian Frontiers,' in Michelle R. Garfinkel and Stergios Skaperdas (eds.), *The Political Economy of Conflict and Appropriation* (New York: Cambridge University Press).

Amigos da Terra (1994) *Sound Public Policies for the Amazon Region* (São Paulo: Friends of the Earth).

Anderson, Anthony B. (1990) 'Smokestacks in the Rainforest: Industrial Development and Deforestation in the Amazon Basin,' *World Development*, vol. 18, no. 9, pp. 1191–1205.

Anderson, A. and Clay, J. (eds.) (2001) *Esverdeando a Amazônia: Comunidades e empresas em busca de práticas para negócios sustentáveis* (São Paulo: IEEB).

Andrade, Manoel Correia de (1996) 'Territorialidades, desterritorialidades, novas territorialidades: os limites do poder nacional e do poder local,' in M. Santos et al. (eds.) *Território Globalização e Fragmentação* (São Paulo: Hucitec–ANPUR), pp. 213–20.

Aparício, Teresa and Garrison, John (1999) 'The Challenges of Promoting Sustainable and Participatory Development in the Amazon,' *Thinking Out Loud: Innovative Case Studies on Participatory Instruments*, Latin America and the Caribbean Region (Washington, DC: World Bank).

Aragón, Luis (1994) *The Amazon as a Study Object: Building Regional Capacity for Sustainable Development*, Monograph 28 (Stockholm: Institute of Latin American Studies, University of Stockholm).

Arima, Eugênio, Thomas, Timothy and Chomitz, Kenneth (forthcoming) 'Policy Options for Encouraging Efficient Land Use in the Amazon,' Development Economics Department (Washington, DC: World Bank).

Arnell, N., Cannell, M., Hulme, M., Kovats, R., Mitchell, J., Nichols, R., Parry, M., Livermore, M. and White, A. (2002) 'The Consequences of CO_2 Stabilisation for the Impacts of Climate Change,' *Climatic Change*, vol. 53, pp. 413–46.

Arnt, R. (ed.) (1994) *O destino da floresta: Reservas extrativistas e desenvolvimento sustentável na Amazônia* (Rio de Janeiro: Relume Dumará).

Assies, W. (1997) *Going Nuts for the Rainforest, Non-Timber Forest Products, Forest Conservation and Sustainability in Amazonia* (Amsterdam: Thela Publishers).

Associação de Universidades Amazônicas (UNAMAZ) (1998) *Amazonia 21: uma agenda para um mundo sustentável* (Brasília: FINEP).

Bailey, R. (1998) *Ecoregions: The Ecosystem Geography of the Oceans and Continents* (New York: Springer–Verlag).

Bain, Katherine and Gacitua-Mario, Estanislao (1999) 'Promoting a Participatory Country Assistance Strategy: Lessons Learned from Colombia, El Salvador and Peru,' in *Thinking Out Loud: Innovative Case Studies on Participatory Instruments*, Latin America and the Caribbean Region (Washington, DC: World Bank).

Bebbington, A.J. and Batterbury, S.P.J. (2001) 'Transnational Livelihoods and Landscapes: Political Ecologies of Globalization,' *Ecumene*, vol. 8, no. 4, pp. 369–80.

Becker, Bertha (2001) 'Síntese do processo de ocupação da Amazônia. Lições do passado e desafios do presente,' in Ministério do Meio Ambiente (ed.), *Causas e dinâmica do desmatamento na Amazônia* (Brasília: Ministry of the Environment), pp. 5–28.

Beder, S. (1999) 'Corporate Hijacking of the Greenhouse Debate,' *The Ecologist*, vol. 29, no. 2, pp. 119–22.

Bensusan, N. (ed.) (2002) *Seria melhor mandar ladrilhar? Biodiversidade como, para que, por quê* (Brasília: University of Brasília and Instituto Socioambiental).

Berkes, F. (2000) 'Cross-Scale Institutional Linkages: Perspectives from the Bottom Up,' paper presented at the International Association for the Study of Common Property Conference, Idiana University, June.

Berkes, F. (2002) 'Cross-Scale Institutional Linkages for Commons Management: Perspectives from the Bottom Up,' in E. Ostrom, T. Dietz, N. Dolsak et al., *The Drama of the Commons* (Washington, DC: National Academy Press), pp. 293–321.

Berkes, F. (ed) (1989) *Common Property Resources: Ecology and Community-Based Sustainable Development* (London: Belhaven Press).

Berkes, F. and Folke, C. (1998) 'Linking Social and Ecological Systems for Resilience and Sustainability,' in F. Berkes and C. Folke, *Linking Social and Ecological Systems: Management Practices and Social Mechanisms for Building Resilience* (Cambridge: Cambridge University Press), pp. 1–25.

Berno de Almeida, Alfredo Wagner (2000) 'The Growing Pains of an Unprecedented Civil Society-Government Partnership in the Brazilian Amazon: The Case of the Amazon Working Group (GTA),' *Thinking Out Loud II: Innovative Case Studies On Participatory Instruments* (Washington, DC: World Bank).

Bierregaard, Richard O., Gascon, Claude, Lovejoy, Thomas E. and Mesquita, Rita (2001) *Lessons from Amazonia: The Ecology and Conservation of a Fragmented Forest* (New Haven, CT: Yale University Press).

Binswanger, Hans (1987) 'Fiscal and Legal Incentives with Environmental Effects on the Brazilian Amazon,' Agriculture and Rural Development Department (Washington, DC: World Bank).

Binswanger, Hans (1989) 'Brazilian Policies that Encourage Deforestation,' Environment Department Paper No. 16 (Washington, DC: World Bank).

Birle, P. (1996) 'Interne und Externe Rahmenbedingungen der Bolivianischen Reformpolitik,' *Lateinamerika, Analysen — Daten — Dokumentation*, vol. 13, no. 31, pp. 15–26.

Blanco, J. and Forner, C. (2000) 'Expiring CERs: A Proposal for Addressing The Permanence Issue For LUCF Projects in the CDM,' unpublished manuscript, Economic and Financial Analysis Group, Ministry of the Environment, Bogotá, Colombia. 4 pp. FCCC/SB/2000/MISC.4/Add.2/Rev.1, 14 September, http// www.unfccc.de.

Brandon, K., Redford, K. and Sanderson, S. (eds.) (1998) *Parks in Peril: People, Politics and Protected Areas* (Covelo, CA: Island Press).

Brazil (1995) *Os ecosistemas brasileiros e os principais macrovetores de desenvolvimento: subsidios ao planejamento do gestão ambiental* (Brasília: Ministry of the Environment).

Brazil (1997) *Agenda Amazônica 21: bases para discussão* (Brasília: Minsitry of the Environment).

Brazil (1998) *Programa Piloto para a Proteção das Florestas Tropicais do Brasil*, vol. II (Brasília: Secretariat for Amazonia, Ministry of the Environment)

Brazil (1999) *Plano Pluianual 2000–2003: Mensagem ao Congreso Nacional* (Brasília: Ministério do Planejamento, Orçamento e Gestão).

Brazil (2002) *Programa Piloto para a Proteção das Florestas Tropicais do Brasil, PPG7* (Brasília: MMA) http://www.mma.gov.br/port/sca/faze-mos /ppg7/apresent.html

Brazil (2003a) *PPA 2004–2007, Lista geral de projetos de infra-estrutura* (Brasília: Ministério do Planejamento, Orçamento e Gestão).

Brazil (2003b) *Plano Amazônia Sustentável — PAS* (Brasília: Ministério da Integração Nacional, Ministério do Meio Ambiente).

Brazil (2003c) *Plano de ação para a prevenção e controle do desmatamento na amazônia brasileira* (Brasília: Grupo Permanente de Trabalho Interministerial Sobre o Desmatamento da Amazônia).

Brazilian NGO Declaration (2000) 'A Brazilian NGO Declaration on Forests and Climate Change within the Scope of the Clean Development Mechanism of the Kyoto Protocol' (São Lourenço da Serra, São Paulo: Vitae Civilis).

Bromley, D.W. (ed.) (1992) *Making the Commons Work: Theory, Practice and Policy* (San Francisco: ICS Press).

Browder, John O. (1989) 'Lumber Production and Economic Development in the Brazilian Amazon: Regional Trends and a Case Study,' *Journal of World Forest Resource Management*, vol. 4.

Browder, John O. and Godfrey, Brian J. (1997) *Rainforest Cities: Urbanization, Development and Globalization of the Brazilian Amazon* (New York: Columbia University Press).

Brown, K. (2002) 'Innovations for Conservation and Development,' *The Geographical Journal*, vol. 168, no. 1, pp. 6–17.

Brown, K. and Rosendo, S. (2000a) 'The Institutional Architecture of Extractive Reserves in Rondônia, Brazil,' *Geographical Journal*, 166 (1), pp. 35–48.

Brown, K. and Rosendo, S. (2000b) 'Environmentalists, Rubber Tappers and Empowerment: The Politics and Economics of Extractive Reserves,' *Development and Change*, 31, pp. 201–28.

Brown, K., Sheppard, P. and Turner, J. (1974) 'Quaternary Refuges in Tropical America: Evidence from Race Formation in *Heliconius*

Butterflies,' *Proceedings of the Royal Society, London*, Series B, no. 187, pp. 369–78.

Bryant, R.L. and Bailey, S. (1997) *Third World Political Ecology* (London: Routledge)

Bukes, G. (2000) *Der Zusammenhang von wirtschaftlicher Entwicklung und Demokratisierung, das Beispiel Bolivien* (Hamburg: Institut für Iberoamerika-Kunde).

Bunker, Stephen G. (1985) *Underdeveloping the Amazon* (Chicago: University of Chicago Press).

Burstyn, Marcel (ed.) (1996) *Avaliação de meio termo de Planafloro* (Brasília: United Nations Development Programme).

Cantanhêde, E. (2000) 'Brasil quer manifestar repúdio a Fujimori,' *Folha de São Paulo*, 29 July, p. A12.

Capobianco, J.P.R. (2001) 'Representatividade das unidades de conservação e terras indígenas em relação às fitofisionomias da Amazônia Legal,' in J.P.R. Capobianco et al. (eds.), *Biodiversidade na Amazônia brasileira: avaliação e ações prioritárias para a conservação, uso sustentável e repartição de benefícios* (São Paulo: Estação Liberdade, Instituto Socioambiental), pp. 263–67.

Capobianco, J.P, Veríssimo, A., Moreira, A., Sawyer, D., dos Santos, I. and Pinto, L.P. (eds.) (2001) *Biodiversidade na Amazonia brasileira: avaliação e ações prioritárias para a conservação, uso sustentável e repartição de benefícios* (São Paulo: Editora Estação Liberdade/Instituto Socioambiental). A summary of this publication has also been issued by the Ministry of Environment under the title *Avaliação e identificação de ações prioritárias para a conservação, utilização sustentável e repartição dos benefícios da biodiversidade na amazonia brasileira*, Brasília, 2002.

Cardoso, Fernando Henrique and Muller, Geraldo (1977) *Amazonia: expansão do capitalismo* (São Paulo: Editora Brasiliense).

Carvalho, B. (1992) 'Conferência Preparatória: EUA rejeitam acordo sobre CO_2 e jogam mais "água fria" na reunião,' *Folha de São Paulo*, 26 March.

Carvalho, G.O. (2000) 'The Politics of Indigenous Land Rights in Brazil,' *Bulletin of Latin American Research*, no. 19, pp. 461–78.

Castro, F. (2002) 'From Myths to Rules: The Evolution of Local Management in the Lower Amazonian Floodplain,' *Environment and History*, vol. 8, no. 2, pp. 197–216.

Castro, F. and McGrath, D. (2003) 'Community-Based Management of Lakes and Sustainability of Floodplain Resources in the Lower Amazon,' *Human Organization*, vol. 62, no. 2, pp. 123–33.

Chomitz, Kenneth and Thomas, Timothy (2001) 'Geographic Patterns of Land Use and Land Intensity in the Brazilian Amazon,' *World Bank Policy Research Working Paper 2687* (Washington, DC: World Bank).

Chomitz, Kenneth, Thomas, Timothy and Arima, Eugenio (forthcoming) 'Price and Profitability of Cattle Products and Amazonian Deforestation,' Development Economics Department (Washington, DC: World Bank).

Cleary, D. (2001) 'Towards an Environmental History of the Amazon: From Prehistory to the Nineteenth Century,' *Latin American Research Review*, vol. 36, no. 2, pp. 65–96.

Clüsener-Godt, Miguel and Sachs, Ignacy (eds.) (1995) *Brazilian Perspectives on Sustainable Development of the Amazon Region* (Paris/New York: UNESCO, The Parthenon Publ. Group) Man and Biosphere Series, no. 15.

CNS (1992) *Parameters for An Extractive Reserves Program in Amazonia* (Rio Branco: Conselho Nacional dos Seringueiros).

Colby, G. and Dennett, C. (1995) *Thy Will Be Done — the Conquest of the Amazon: Nelson Rockefeller and Evangelism in the Age of Oil* (New York: Harper Collins).

Colinvaux, de Oliveira, P., Moreno, J., Miller, M. and Bush, M. (1996) 'A Long Pollen Record from Lowland Amazonian Forest: Cooling in Glacial Times,' *Science*, 274/5284, October 4, pp. 85–8.

Costa, Wanderley M. da (1999) 'Políticas territoriais brasileiras no contexto da integração sul-americana,' *Território*, vol. IV, no. 7, pp. 199–218.

Cotton, C. and Romine, T. (1999) *Facing Destruction: A Greenpeace Briefing on the Timber Industry in the Brazilian Amazon.* (Amsterdam: Greenpeace International).

Council on Foreign Relations Independent Task Force (2001) 'A Letter to the President and a Memorandum on US Policy toward Brazil' (New York: Council on Foreign Relations), 13 pp., http://www.cfr.org

Cowell, Adrian (1990) *The Decade of Destruction: The Crusade to Save the Amazon Rainforest* (New York: Henry Holt & Co.).

Cox, P., Betts, R., Collins, M., Harris, P., Huntingford, C. and Jones, C. (2003) *Amazonian Dieback under Climate-Carbon Cycle Projections for the 21st Century.* Hadley Centre Technical Note no. 42 (Wallingford, UK: Hadley Centre), http://www.meto.gov.uk/research/hadley-centre/pubs/HCTN/HCTN_42.pdf

Cox, P., Betts, R., Jones, C., Spall, S. and Totterdell, I. (2000) 'Acceleration of Global Warming Due to Carbon-Cycle Feedbacks in a Coupled Climate Model,' *Nature,* vol. 408, pp. 184–7.

Coy, M. (1988*) Regionalentwicklung und Regionale Entwicklungsplanung an der Peripherie in Amazonien. Probleme und Interessenkonflikte bei der Erschließung einer jungen Pionierfront am Beispiel des Brasílianischen Bundesstaates Rondônia*, Tübinger Geographische Studien 97, Tübingen.

Coy, M. (1990) 'Pionierfront und Stadtentwicklung. Sozial- und wirtschaftsräumliche Differenzierung der Pionierstädte in Nord-Mato Grosso,' *Geographische Zeitschrift*, vol.78, no. 2, pp. 115–35.

Coy, M. (1996) 'Periphere Stadtentwicklung und Planung zwischen Ökonomie und Ökologie — das Beispiel der Regionalmetropole Cuiabá,' in P. Gans (ed.), *Regionale Entwicklung in Lateinamerika. Erfurter Geographische Studien 4*, pp. 297–315.

Coy, M. (1997) *Stadtentwicklung an der Peripherie Brasiliens. Wandel lokaler Lebenswelten und Möglichkeiten nachhaltiger Entwicklung in Cuiabá (Mato Grosso)*, Habilitationsschrift, Geowissenschaftliche Fakultät der Universität Tübingen, Tübingen.

Coy, M. (1998) 'Sozialgeographische Analyse raumbezogener nachhaltiger Zukunftsplanung,' in G. Heinritz, R. Wiessnerand M. Winiger (eds.), *Nachhaltigkeit als Leitbild der Umwelt- und Regionalentwicklung in Europa. 51*, Deutscher Geographentag Bonn 1997, vol. 2, pp. 56–66, Stuttgart.

Coy, M. (1999) 'Städtischer Strukturwandel und Planung an der brasilianischen Peripherie. Das Beispiel Cuiabá,' *Trialog — Zeitschrift für das
Planen und Bauen in der Dritten Welt*, vol. 61, no. 2, pp. 37–43.

Coy, M. and Krings, T. (2000) 'Umweltveränderungen und Politische
Ökologie in Entwicklungsländern. Einleitung,' in H. Blotevogel, H.
Ossenbrüggeand G. Wood (eds.), *Lokal Verankert — Weltweit
Vernetzt, 52*. Deutscher Geographentag Hamburg 1999.
Tagungsbericht und wissenschaftliche Abhandlungen, Stuttgart, pp. 396–99.

Coy, M. and Lücker, R. (1993) *Der brasilianische Mittelwesten. Wirtschafts- und
sozialgeographischer Wandel eines peripheren Agrarraumes*, Tübinger
Geographische Studien 108, Tübingen.

Coy, M. and Neuburger, M. (2002a*) Aktuelle Entwicklungstendenzen im
ländlichen Raum Brasiliens*, Petermanns Geographische Mitteilungen,
vol. 156, no. 5, pp. 74–83.

Coy, M. and Neuburger, M. (2002b) *Brasilianisches Amazonien. Chancen und
Grenzen nachhaltiger Regionalentwicklung*, Geographische Rundschau,
vol. 54, no. 11, pp. 12–20.

CTI (ed.) (1997) *Consolidação do Projeto: recuperação ambiental e despoluição de
áreas da TI Waiãpi degradadas por garimpo* (São Paulo: Centro de
Trabalho Indigenista).

Cunha, M. Carneiro da and Almeida, M. Barbosa de (eds.) (2002)
Enciclopédia da floresta. O Alto Juruá: O conhecimento das populações (São
Paulo: Companhia das Letras).

Daly, H. and Cobb, J. (1989) *For the Common Good: Redirecting the Economy toward Community, the Environment and a Sustainable Future* (Boston,
MA: Beacon Press).

Davies de Freitas, Maria de Lourdes (ed.) (1998) *Amazonia: Heaven of a New
World* (Rio de Janeiro: Editora Campus).

Davis, S.H. (1977) *Victims of the Miracle: Development and the Indians of Brazil*
(Cambridge: Cambridge University Press).

Dean, Warren (1995) *With Broadaxe and Firebrand: The Destruction of the
Brazilian Atlantic Forest* (Berkeley, CA: University of California Press).

Deaton, A. (1997) *The Analysis of Household Surveys: A Microeconometric
Approach to Development Policy* (Washington, D.C.: Johns Hopkins
University Press).

den Elzen, M. and de Moor, A. (2001) *Evaluating the Bonn Agreement and Some Key Issues*, RIVM Report no. 728001016/2001 (Bilthoven, Netherlands: National Institute of Public Health and the Environment — RIVM).

Deutscher Bundestag (1990) *Protecting the Tropical Forests: A High-Priority International Task*, Referat Öffentlichkeitsarbeit (Bonn, Germany: Deutscher Bundestag).

Diegues, A.C. (ed.) (2000) *Etnoconservação: novos rumos para a proteção da natureza nos trópicos* (São Paulo: NUPAUB/USP).

Diewald, Christoph (forthcoming) 'Development and Conservation Choices for Brazilian Forests,' draft policy note (Brasília: World Bank).

Dinerstein, E., Olson, D., Graham, D., Webster, L., Primm, S., Bookbinder, M. and Ledec, G. (1995) *A Conservation Assessment of the Terrestrial Ecoregions of Latin America and the Caribbean* (Washington, DC: WWF/World Bank).

Dourojeanni, Marc and Pádua, Maria Tereza (2001) *Biodiversidade, a hora decisiva* (Curitiba: Editora da UFPR).

Dreifuss, R. (2000) 'Strategic Perceptions and Frontier Policies in Brazil,' in A. Hall (ed.), *Amazonia at the Crossroads: The Challenge of Sustainable Development* (London: Institute of Latin American Studies, University of London), pp. 205–32.

Dreze, J. and Sen, A. (eds.) (1995) *The Political Economy of Hunger*, 3 vols (Oxford: Clarendon Press).

Dutschke, M. (2002) Fractions of Permanence — Squaring the Cycle of Sink Carbon Accounting,' *Mitigation and Adaptation Strategies for Global Change*, vol. 7, pp. 381–402.

Edward, J. (2003) 'Mato Grosso: O trator no governo,' *Veja*, 10 December, pp. 84–6.

Eglin, Jean and Théry, Hervé (1982) *Le pillage de l'Amazonie* (Paris: Livrairie François Maspero), Petit Collection Maspero no. 266.

Environment Ministers of the Amazonian Countries (1999) 'Meeting of the Ministers of Environment and Forestry of the Amazonian Countries on Clean Development Mechanism (CDM),' held in Cochabamba, Bolivia, 14–15 June 1999.

Eróstegui, R. (1996) Die bolivianischen Gewerkschaften: Krisen und Perspektiven, *Lateinamerika, Analysen — Daten – Dokumentation*, vol. 13, no. 31, pp. 37–42.

Escobar, A. (2001) 'Culture Sits in Places: Reflections on Globalism and Subaltern Strategies of Localization,' *Political Geography*, vol. 20, no. 2, pp. 138–74.

Escobar, A., Rocheleau, D. et al. (2002) 'Environmental Social Movements and the Politics of Place,' *Development*, vol. 45, no. 1, pp. 28–36.

ESP (2004a) 'Agricultura em Santarém: progresso ou ameaça?' *Estado de São Paulo*, 1 February.

ESP (2004b) 'Amazônia: desmatamento aproxima-se de recorde,' *Estado de São Paulo*, 4 March.

Eva, H., Achard, H.-J., Stibig, H. and Mayaux, P. (2003) 'Response to Comment on "Determination of Deforestation Rates of the World's Humid Tropical Forests",' *Science*, vol. 299, p. 1015b.

Faminow, M.D. (1998) *Cattle, Deforestation and Development in the Amazon: An Economic, Agronomic and Environmental Perspective* (Oxford: Oxford University Press).

Fearnside, P.M. (1986) 'Spatial Concentration of Deforestation in the Brazilian Amazon,' *Ambio*, vol. 15, no. 2, pp. 72–9.

Fearnside, P.M. (1986a) *Human Carrying Capacity of the Brazilian Amazon* (New York: Columbia University Press).

Fearnside, P.M. (1993) 'Deforestation in Brazilian Amazonia: The Effect of Population and Land Tenure,' *Ambio*, vol. 22, no. 8, pp. 537–45.

Fearnside, P.M. (1994) 'Biomassa das florestas Amazônicas brasileiras,' in *Anais do seminário emissão × seqüestro de CO_2* (Rio de Janeiro: Companhia Vale do Rio Doce — CVRD), pp. 95–124.

Fearnside, P.M. (1996a) 'Amazonian Deforestation and Global Warming: Carbon Stocks in Vegetation Replacing Brazil's Amazon Forest,' *Forest Ecology and Management*, vol. 80, nos. 1–3, pp. 21–34.

Fearnside, P.M. (1996b) 'Socio-economic Factors in the Management of Tropical Forests for Carbon,' in M.J. Apps and D.T. Price (eds.) *Forest Ecosystems, Forest Management and the Global Carbon Cycle* (Heidelberg: Springer–Verlag), pp. 349–61.

Fearnside, P.M. (1997a) 'Environmental Services as a Strategy for Sustainable Development in Rural Amazonia,' *Ecological Economics*, vol. 20, no. 1, pp. 53–70.

Fearnside, P.M. (1997b) 'Monitoring Needs to Transform Amazonian Forest Maintenance into a Global Warming Mitigation Option,' *Mitigation and Adaptation Strategies for Global Change*, vol. 2, nos. 2–3, pp. 285–302.

Fearnside, P.M. (1997c) 'Greenhouse Gases from Deforestation in Brazilian Amazonia: Net Committed Emissions,' *Climatic Change*, vol. 35, no. 3, pp. 321–60.

Fearnside, P.M. (1999a) 'Forests and Global Warming Mitigation in Brazil: Opportunities in the Brazilian Forest Sector for Responses to Global Warming under the "Clean Development Mechanism",' *Biomass and Bioenergy*, vol. 16, no. 3, pp. 171–89.

Fearnside, P.M. (1999b) 'Como o efeito estufa pode render dinheiro para o Brasil,' *Ciência Hoje*, vol. 26, no. 155, pp. 41–3.

Fearnside, P.M. (1999c) 'Biodiversity as an Environmental Service in Brazil's Amazonian Forests: Risks, Value and Conservation,' *Environmental Conservation*, vol. 26, pp. 305–21.

Fearnside, P.M. (2000a) 'Effects of Land Use and Forest Management on the Carbon Cycle in the Brazilian Amazon,' *Journal of Sustainable Forestry*, vol. 12, nos. 1–2, pp. 79–97.

Fearnside, P.M. (2000b) 'Global Warming and Tropical Land-Use Change: Greenhouse Gas Emissions from Biomass Burning, Decomposition and Soils in Forest Conversion, Shifting Cultivation and Secondary Vegetation,' *Climatic Change*, vol. 46, nos. 1–2, pp. 115–58.

Fearnside, P.M. (2000c) 'Greenhouse Gas Emissions from Land-Use Change in Brazil's Amazon Region,' in R. Lal, J.M. Kimble and B.A. Stewart (eds.), *Global Climate Change and Tropical Ecosystems. Advances in Soil Science* (Boca Raton, Fl.: CRC Press), pp. 231–49.

Fearnside, P.M. (2000d) 'Environmental Services as a Strategy for Sustainable Rural Development in Rural Amazonia,' in Clovis Cavalcanti (ed.), *The Environment, Sustainable Development and Public Policies: Building Sustainability in Brazil* (Cheltenham: Edward Elgar).

Fearnside, P.M. (2001a) 'Saving Tropical Forests as a Global Warming Countermeasure: an Issue That Divides the Environmental Movement', *Ecological Economics*, vol. 39, no. 2, pp. 167–84.

Fearnside, P.M. (2001b) 'The Potential of Brazil's Forest Sector for Mitigating Global Warming under the Kyoto Protocol,' *Mitigation and Adaptation Strategies for Global Change*, vol. 6, nos. 3–4, pp. 355–72.

Fearnside, P.M. (2001c) 'Soybean Cultivation as a Threat to the Environment in Brazil,' *Environmental Conservation*, vol. 28, no. 1, pp. 23–38.

Fearnside, P.M. (2002a) 'Avança Brasil: Environmental and Social Consequences of Brazil's Planned Infrastructure in Amazonia,' *Environmental Management* vol. 30, pp. 748–63.

Fearnside, P.M. (2002b) 'Greenhouse Gas Emissions from a Hydroelectric Reservoir (Brazil's Tucuruí Dam) and the Energy Policy Implications,' *Water, Air and Soil Pollution*, vol. 133, nos. 1–4, pp. 69–96.

Fearnside, P.M. (2002c) 'Time Preference in Global Warming Calculations: A Proposal for a Unified Index,' *Ecological Economics*, vol. 41, no. 1, pp. 21–31.

Fearnside, P.M. (2002d) 'Why a 100-year Time Horizon Should be Used for Global Warming Mitigation Calculations,' *Mitigation and Adaptation Strategies for Global Change*, vol. 7, no. 1, pp. 19–30.

Fearnside, P.M. (2002e) 'Amazonia, Deforestation of,' in A.S. Goudie and D.J. Cuff (eds.), *Encyclopedia of Global Change: Environmental Change and Human Society*, vol. I (New York: Oxford University Press), pp. 31–8.

Fearnside, P.M. (2003a) 'Conservation Policy in Brazilian Amazonia: Understanding the Dilemmas,' *World Development*, vol. 31, pp. 757–79.

Fearnside, P. (2003b) 'Deforestation Control in Mato Grosso: A New Model for Slowing the Loss of Brazil's Amazon Forest', *Ambio*, vol. 32, no. 5, pp. 343–45.

Fearnside, P.M. (2003c) 'Environmentalists Split over Kyoto and Amazonian Deforestation,' *Environmental Conservation*, vol. 28, no. 4, pp. 295–9.

Fearnside, P.M. (2004a) 'A água de São Paulo e a floresta amazônica,' *Ciência Hoje*, 34 (203), pp. 63–5.

Fearnside, (2005), 'Mitigation of climatic change in the Amazon,' in W.F. Laurance and C.A. Peres (eds.), *Emerging Threats to Tropical Forests* (Chicago, IL: University of Chicago Press).

Fearnside, P.M. and Barbosa, R.I. (1998) 'Soil Carbon Changes from Conversion of Forest to Pasture in Brazilian Amazonia,' *Forest Ecology and Management*, vol. 108, nos. 1–2, pp.147–66.

Fearnside, P.M. and Barbosa, R.I. (2003) 'Avoided Deforestation in Amazonia as a Global Warming Mitigation Measure: The Case of Mato Grosso,' *World Resource Review*, vol. 15, no. 3, pp. 352–61.

Fearnside, P.M. and Barbosa, R.I. (2004) 'Accelerating Deforestation in Brazilian Amazonia: Towards Answering Open Questions,' *Environmental Conservation*, vol. 31, no. 1, pp. 7–10.

Fearnside, P.M. and Ferraz, J. (1995) 'A Conservation Gap Analysis of Brazil's Amazonian Vegetation,' *Conservation Biology*, vol. 9, no. 5, pp. 1134–47.

Fearnside, P.M. and Guimarães, W. (1996) 'Carbon Uptake by Secondary Forests in Brazilian Amazonia,' *Forest Ecology and Management*, vol. 80, nos. 1–3, pp. 35–46.

Fearnside, P.M. and Laurance, W.F. (2003) 'Comment on "Determination of Deforestation Rates of the World's Humid Tropical forests",' *Science*, vol. 299.

Fearnside, P.M. and Laurance, W.F. (2004) 'Tropical Deforestation and Greenhouse Gas Emissions,' *Ecological Applications*, vol. 14, no. 4, pp. 982–86.

Fearnside, P.M., Lashof, D.A. and Moura-Costa, P. (2000) 'Accounting for Time in Mitigating Global Warming through Land-Use Change and Forestry,' *Mitigation and Adaptation Strategies for Global Change*, vol. 5, no. 3, pp. 239–70.

Fearnside, P.M., Leal Filho, N. and Fernandes, F. (1993) 'Rainforest Burning and the Global Carbon Budget: Biomass, Combustion Efficiency and Charcoal Formation in the Brazilian Amazon,' *Journal of Geophysical Research* vol. 98, no. D9, pp. 16, 733–43.

Ferraro, P. and Kiss, A. (2002) 'Direct Payments to Conserve Biodiversity,' *Science*, vol.298, pp. 1718–9.

Ferreira, L.V., de Sá, R.L., Buschbacher, R., Batmanian, G., da Silva, J.M.C., Arruda, M.B., Moretti, E., de Sá, L.F.Sn., Falconer, J. and Bampi, M.I. (2001) 'Identificação de áreas prioritárias para a conservação de biodiversidade por meio da representatividade das unidades de conservação e tipos de vegetação nas ecorregiões da Amazônia brasileira,' in Indigenous Peoples' Forum on Climate Change 'Declaration of the First International Forum of Indigenous Peoples on Climate Change,' Lyon, France, September.

Few, R. (2001) 'Containment and Counter-Containment: Planner/Community Relations in Conservation Planning,' *The Geographical Journal*, vol. 167, pp. 111–24.

Folha de São Paulo (2000) 'Itamaraty atuou nos bastidores para tentar evitar isolamento do presidente Fujimori no cenário internacional: Governo brasileiro tentou legitimar "rerreeleição",' (28 May), p. A23.

Foresta, R. (1992) *Amazon Conservation in the Age of Development* (Gainesville: Florida University Press).

Forum and FoE (1995) *Pedido de investigação apresentado ao Painel de Inspeção do Banco Mundial sobre o Plano Agropecuário e Florestal de Rondônia* (Porto Velho: Forúm de ONGs e Movimentos Sociais que Atuam em Rondônia and Friends of the Earth, Programa Amazônia).

Friedrich, M. (1995) 'Hidrovia Paraná — Paraguai. Wirtschaftliche, soziale und ökologische Konsequenzen für das Pantanal und den Einzugsbereich des Oberen Rio Paraguai,' in G. Kohlhepp (ed.), *Mensch-Umwelt-Beziehungen in der Pantanal-Region von Mato Grosso/Brasilien. Beiträge zur angewandten geographischen Umweltforschung*, Tübinger Geographische Studien, Tübingen, no. 114, pp. 125–56.

FUNAI (2001) *PPTAL Annual Report for 2001* (Brasília: FUNAI).

FUNAI (n.d.) *PPTAL: Protection of Indigenous People and their Lands in the Amazon Region of Brazil* (Brasília: National Indian Foundation).

FUNAI/PPTAL/GTZ (1999) *Demarcando terras indígenas: experiências e desafios de um projeto de parceria* (Brasília).

Gallois, D.T. (1993) 'Jane Karakuri — o ouro dos Waiâpi: a experiência de um garimpo indígena,' in A.C. Magalhães (ed.), *Sociedades indígenas e transformações ambientais* (Belém: NUMA), series Universidade e Meio Ambiente, no. 6, pp. 25–46.

Gallois, D.T. (1996) 'Controle territorial e diversificação do extrativismo na Área Indígena Waiãpi,' in C.A. Ricardo (ed.), *Povos indígenas no Brasil 1991–1995* (São Paulo: Instituto Socioambiental), pp. 263–71.

Gallois, D.T. (2002) 'Vigilância e contrôle territorial entre os Waiãpi: desafios para superar uma transição na gestão do coletivo,' in M.M. Gramkow (ed.), *Demarcando terras indígenas II: experiências e desafios de um projeto de parceria* (Brasília: PPG7/GTZ/FUNAI/PPTAL), pp. 95–112.

Gallois, D.T. and Grupioni, L.D.B. (1999) 'O índio na Missão Novas Tribos,' in R.M. Wright (ed.), *Transformando os deuses: os múltiplos sentidos da conversão entre os povos indígenas no Brasil* (Campinas: UNICAMP), pp. 77–129.

Garay, Irene and Dias, Braulio (eds.) (2001) *Conservação da biodiversidade em ecossistemas tropicais. Avanços conceituais e revisão de novas metodologias de avaliação e monitoramento* (Petrópolis: Vozes).

Gascon, C. et al. (2000) 'Riverine Barriers and the Distribution of Amazonian Species,' *Proceedings of the National Academy of Science USA*, vol. 97, no. 25), pp. 13672–7.

Gasques, José Garcia and Yokomizi, Clando (1986) 'Resultados de 20 anos de incentivos fiscais na agropecuária da Amazonia,' *XIV Encontro Nacional de Economia*, ANPEC.

Gazeta de Cuiabá (2004) 'Desmatamento: Amazônia sofre a maior devassa dos últimos 10 anos,' 1 April.

Geographica Helvetica (2001), vol. 56, no. 1. (Themenheft: Institutionelle Regelungen im Entwicklungsprozess).

Gezon, L. (1997) 'Institutional Structure and the Effectiveness of Integrated Conservation and Development Projects: A Case Study from Madagascar,' *Human Organization*, vol. 54, no. 4, pp. 462–70.

Goedeking, U., CONDEPA und UCS (2001) Zwei Parteien und ihre Erbfolgeprobleme. Eins Hoffnungsträger vieler nicht-weißer Bolivianer, befinden sich beide Parteien nach dem Tod ihrer *caudillos* in der Krise, *Lateinamerika, Analysen — Daten — Dokumentation*, vol. 17, no. 45, pp. 24–32.

Gomes, Gustavo Maia, Ramos de Souza, Hermino and Magalhães, Antonio Rocha (eds.) (1995), *Desenvolvimento sustentável do Nordeste* (Brasília: IPEA).

Gomes, M.P. (2000) *The Indians and Brazil*, translated by John W. Moon. (Gainesville, Fl.: University of Florida Press).

Gonçalves de Almeida, José Maria (ed.) (1986) *Carajás: desafio político, econômico e desenvolvimento* (São Paulo: CNPq and Editora Brasiliense).

Goodland, Robert J.A. (1980) 'Environmental Ranking of Amazonian Development Projects in Brazil,' *Environmental Conservation*, vol. 7, no. 1.

Goodland, Robert J.A. and Irwin, H.S. (1975) *Amazon Jungle: Green Hell to Red Desert?* (Amsterdam: Elsevier).

Goodman, D. and Hall, A. (eds.) (1990) *The Future of Amazonia: Destruction or Sustainable Development?* (London: Macmillan).

GoR and UNDP (1997) *Avaliação do subcomponente RESEXs* (Brasília: Governo de Rondônia and United Nations Development Programme).

Gössling, S. (1999) 'Ecotourism: a Means to Safeguard Biodiversity and Ecosystem Functions?' *Ecological Economics*, vol. 29, no. 2, pp. 303–20.

Goudie, A. (2000) *The Human Impact on the Natural Environment* (London: Blackwell).

Goulding, Michael, Smith, Nigel J.H. and Mahar, Dennis J. (1986) *Floods of Fortune: Ecology and Economy along the Amazon* (New York: Columbia University Press).

Governo do Estado de Rondônia (1998) *Projeto Úmidas: uma estratégia de desenvolvimento sustentável para Rondônia, 1988–2020*, 3 vols. (Porto Velho, RO).

Gramkow, M.M. (ed.) (2002) *Demarcando terras indígenas II: experiências e desafios de um projeto de parceria* (Brasília: PPG7 / GTZ / FUNAI / PPTAL).

Greenpeace (2004) 'Desmatamento na Amazônia é emergência national,' press release (Greenpeace Brasil, São Paulo).

Greenpeace International (2000) *Cheating the Kyoto Protocol: Loopholes and Environmental Effectiveness*. (Amsterdam: Greenpeace International), 16 pp.

Haddad, Paulo and Rezende, Fernando (2002) *Instrumentos econômicos para o desenvolvimento sustentável da Amazonia* (Brasília: Ministério do Meio Ambiente, Secretaria de Coordenção da Amazônia).

Haffer, J. (1969) 'Speciation in Amazon Forest Birds,' *Science* 165, pp. 131–7.

Haffer, J. (1982) 'General Aspects of the Refuge Theory,' in G. Prance (ed.), *Biological Diversity in the Tropics* (New York: Columbia University Press), pp. 6–24.

Hall, A. (1989) *Developing Amazonia: Deforestation and Social Conflict in Brazil's Carajás Programme* (Manchester and New York: Manchester University Press).

Hall, A. (1997) *Sustaining Amazonia: Grassroots Action for Productive Conservation* (Manchester and New York: Manchester University Press).

Hall, A. (1997a) 'A New Agenda for Research, Policy and Action in Brazilian Amazonia,' *Revista Europea de Estudios Latinoamericanos y del Caribe*, vol. 62, June, pp. 9–31.

Hall, A. (ed.) (2000a) *Amazonia at the Crossroads: The Challenge of Sustainable Development* (London: Institute of Latin American Studies, University of London).

Hall, A. (2000b) 'Environment and Development in Brazilian Amazonia: From Protectionism to Productive Conservation,' in A. Hall (ed.), *Amazonia at the Crossroads: the Challenge of Sustainable Development* (London: Institute of Latin American Studies, University of London), pp. 99–114.

Hamer, L. (2002) *Planning across the Local Strategic Partnership (LSP): Case Studies of Integrating Community Strategies and Health Improvement* (London: Health Development Agency).

Hardin, G. (1968) 'The Tragedy of the Commons,' *Science*, vol. 162, pp. 1243–8.

Hecht, S.B. (1984) 'Cattle Ranching in Amazonia: Political and Ecological Considerations', in Marianne Schmink and Charles H. Wood (eds.), *Frontier Expansion in Amazonia* (Gainesville, Fl.: University of Florida Press), pp. 366–98.

Hecht, S.B. and Cockburn, A. (1989) *The Fate of the Forest: Developers, Destroyers and Defenders of the Amazon* (London, New York: Verso).

Hemming, J. (1978) *Red Gold: The Conquest of the Brazilian Indians* (Cambridge, MA: Harvard University Press).

Henkemans, A.B. (2001) *Tranquilidad and Hardship in the Forest, Livelihoods and Perceptions of Camba Forest Dwellers in the Northern Bolivian Amazon* (Utrecht: PROMAB).

Herzog, H., Caldeira, K. and Reilly, J. (2003) 'An Issue of Permanence: Assessing the Effectiveness of Temporary Carbon Storage,' *Climatic Change*, vol. 59, pp. 293–310.

Hicks, James, Daly, Herman, Davis, Shelton and Davies de Freitas, Maria de Lourdes (1990) *Ecuador's Amazon Region: Development Issues and Options*, World Bank Discussion Paper No. 75 (Washington, DC: World Bank).

Houghton, J., Ding, Y., Griggs, D., Noguer, M, Van der Linden, R. and Xiausu, D. (eds.) (2001) *Climate Change 2001: The Scientific Basis* (Cambridge: Cambridge University Press).

Houghton, R., Lawrence, K., Hackler, J. and Brown, S. (2001) 'The Spatial Distribution of Forest Biomass in the Brazilian Amazon: A Comparison of Estimates,' *Global Change Biology* vol. 7, pp. 731–46.

IBAMA (1994) *Roteiro para criação e legalização das reservas extrativistas portaria no. 51–N de 11 de Maio de 1994* (Brasília: Instituto Brasileiro do Meio Ambiente e dos Recursos Naturais Renováveis).

IBAMA (2001) *Monitoramento e avaliação do risco de incêndios florestais em áreas críticas* (Brasília: IBAMA).

IBGE (1998) *Censo agropecuário 1995/1996* (Rio de Janeiro: IBGE).

Indigenous Peoples' Forum on Climate Change (2000) 'Declaration of Indigenous Peoples on Climate Change,' The Hague, 11–12 November, available from http://www.klimabuendnis.org/kb-home/cop6_decl.htm

INPE (2000) *Monitoring the Brazilian Amazon Forest by Satellite* (São José do Campo: INPE).

INPE (2002) *Monitoring the Brazilian Amazonian Forest by Satellite* (São José do Campo: INPE).

INPE (2003) *Taxas nos períodos 2000–2001 e 2001–2002 para 50 cenas críticas* (São Paulo: Instituto Nacional de Pesquisas Espaciais), http://www.obt.inpe.br/prodes/prodes_2002_2002.htm.

Instituto Socioambiental (2000) *Povos indígenas no Brasil, 1996–2000: Porto Inseguro* (São Paulo: ISA).

IPAM (2001) *Fire in the Amazon* (Belém: IPAM). Indigenous Peoples' Forum on Climate Change (2000a) available from: http://www.yvwiiusdinvnohii.net/Articles2000/IFOIP000913De claration.htm#English.

IPEA (1990) 'O desempenho ambiental do governo brasileiro e do Banco Mundial em projetos co-financiados pelo Banco', *Textos Para Discussão* no. 194 (Rio de Janeiro: Instituto de Pesquisa Econômica Aplicada).

Irvine, K.N. (1997) *Underground Revolution: Modernizing London Underground through Public-Private Partnerships* (London: Adam Smith Institute).

Instituto Socioambiental (ISA) (2000) *Povos indígenas no Brasil, 1996–2000: Porto Inseguro* (Sao Paulo),

ISA (2004) 'Sociedade civil consolida propostas socioambientais para a area de influência da BR–163' (São Paulo: Instituto Socioambiental).

ISA (Instituto Socioambiental), IMAZON (Instituto do Homem e do Meio Ambiente da Amazônia), IPAM (Instituto de Pesquisa Ambiental da Amazônia), ISPN (Instituto Sociedade, População e Natureza), GTA (Grupo de Trabalho Amazônico) and CI (Conservation International) (1999) *Seminário Consulta de Macapá 99: avaliação e identificação das ações prioritárias para a conservação, utilização sustentável e repartição dos benefícios da biodiversidade da Amazônia* (http://www.isa.org.br/bio/index.htm) (São Paulo: ISA).

ISTOÉ (1997) 'A versão do Brasil,' 15 October, p. 98.

James, Preston (1969) *Latin America* (New York: Odyssey Books).

Jentoft, S. (1989) 'Fisheries Co-Management: Delegating Government Responsibility to Fishermen's Organizations,' *Marine Policy*, vol. 13, no. 2, pp. 137–54.

Jentoft, S. (2000). 'The Community: The Missing Link of Fisheries Management,' *Marine Policy*, vol. 24, pp. 53–9.

Jentoft, S. and McCay, B. (1995) 'User Participation in Fisheries Management: Lessons Drawn from International Experiences,' *Marine Policy*, vol. 19, no. 3, pp. 227–46.

Jentoft, S., McCay, B. and Wilson, D.C. (1998) 'Social Theory and Fisheries Co-Management,' *Marine Policy*, vol. 22, nos 4–5, pp. 423–36.

Kaimowitz, D., Mertens, B., Wunder, S. and Pacheco, P. (2004) *Hamburger Connection Fuels Amazon Destruction: Cattle Ranching and Deforestation in Brazil's Amazon* (Jakarta: CIFOR).

Kasburg, C. and Gramkow, M.M. (eds.) (1999) *Demarcando terras indígenas: experiências e desafios de um projeto de parceria* (Brasília: PPG7/GTZ/FUNAI/PPTAL).

Katzman, Martin T. (1977) *Cities and Frontiers in Brazil* (Cambridge, MA: Harvard University Press).

Keck, M.E. (1995) 'Social Equity and Environmental Politics in Brazil: Lessons from the Rubber Tappers of Acre,' *Comparative Politics*, vol. 27, no. 4, pp. 409–24.

Keck, M.E. (1997) 'Planafloro in Rondônia: The Limits of Leverage,' in J. Fox and L.D. Brown (eds.), *The Struggle for Accountability: The World Bank, NGOs and Grassroots Movements* (Cambridge, MA: MIT Press).

Kimmerling, J. (2000) 'Oil Development in Ecuador and Peru: Law, Politics and the Environment,' in A. Hall (ed.), *Amazonia at the Crossroads: the Challenge of Sustainable Development* (London: Institute of Latin American Studies, University of London), pp. 73–98.

Kirchoff, V.W. and Escada, P.A. (1999) *O megaincêndio do século–1998* (São Paulo: Transtec Editorial).

Klauda, F. (2001) 'Bolivien auf dem Weg zum HIPC-Schuldenerlass,' in R. Sevilla and A. Benavides (eds.), *Bolivien. Das Verkannte Land?* (Bad Honnef: Horlemann), pp. 258–72.

Kohlhepp, G. (1987) 'Wirtschafts- und sozialräumliche Auswirkungen der Weltmarktintegration Ost-Amazoniens. Zur Bewertung der regionalen Entwicklungsplanung im Grande Carajás-Programm in Pará und Maranhão,' in G. Kohlhepp (ed.), *Brasilien Beiträge zur regionalen Struktur- und Entwicklungsforschung*, Tübinger Geographische Studien 93, Tübingen, pp. 213–54.

Kohlhepp, G. (ed.) (1995) *Mensch-Umwelt-Beziehungen in der Pantanal-Region von Mato Grosso/Brasilien. Beiträge zur angewandten geographischen Umweltforschung*, Tübinger Geographische Studien 114, Tübingen.

Kohlhepp, G. (1998a) 'Regenwaldzerstörung im Amazonasgebiet Brasiliens. Entwicklungen — Probleme — Lösungsansätze,' *Geographie Heute*, vol. 162, pp. 38–42.

Kohlhepp, G. (1998b) 'Das internationale Pilotprogramm zum Schutz der tropischen Regenwälder Brasiliens. Globale, nationale, regionale und lokale Akteure auf dem Weg zu einer Strategie der nachhaltigen Entwicklung?' in G. Kohlhepp and Coy, M. (eds.), *Mensch-Umwelt-Beziehungen und nachhaltige Entwicklung in der Dritten Welt*, Tübinger Geographische Studien 119, Tübingen, pp. 51–86.

Kohlhepp, Gerd (2001) 'A Amazônia frente a um novo desafio: o desenvolvimento sustentável e o programa Avança Brasil,' *Cadernos Adenauer II*, no. 4, September, pp. 9–38.

Kolk, A. (1996) *Forests in International Environmental Politics: International Organizations, NGOs and the Brazilian Amazon* (Utrecht: International Books).

Kramer, R., van Schaik, C. and Johnson, J. (eds.) (1997) *Last Stand: Protected Areas and the Defence of Tropical Biodiversity* (Oxford: Oxford University Press).

Laurance, W.F., Cochrane, M.A., Bergen, S., Fearnside, P.M., Delamônica, P., Barber, C., D'Angelo, S. and Fernandes, T. (2001) 'The Future of the Brazilian Amazon,' *Science*, vol. 291, pp. 438–9.

Leggett, J (ed.) (1990) *Global Warming: The Greenpeace Report.* (Oxford: Oxford University Press).

Levine, J.S., Bobbe, T., Ray, N., Singh, A. and Witt, R.G. (1999) *Wildland Fires and the Environment: A Global Synthesis* (Nairobi: UNEP).

Lima, A.C. de Souza (1995a) 'Um olhar sobre a presença das populações nativas na invenção do Brasil,' in A. Lopes da Silva and L.D. Benzi Grupioni (eds.), *A temática indígena na escola: novos subsídios para professores de 1° e 2° graus* (Brasília: MEC, MARI, UNESCO), pp. 407–19.

Lima, A.C. de Souza (1995b) *Um grande cerco de paz. Poder tutelar, indianidade e formação do Estado no Brasil* (Petrópolis: Vozes).

Lima, A.C. de Souza and Barroso-Hoffmann, M. (2002) 'Questões para uma política indigenista: etnodesenvolvimento e políticas públicas. Uma apresentação,' in A.C. de Souza Lima and M. Barroso-Hoffmann (eds.), *Etnodesenvolvimento e políticas públicas: bases para uma nova política indigenista* (Rio de Janeiro: Contra Capa, LACED), series Territórios Sociais, 6, pp. 7–28.

Lima-Ayres, D. (1999) 'Equity, Sustainable Development and Biodiversity Preservation: Some Questions on the Ecological Partnership in the Brazilian Amazon,' in C. Padoch, J.M. Ayres, M. Pinedo-Vasquez and A. Henderson (eds.), *Várzea: Diversity, Development, and Conservation of Amazonia's Whitewater Floodplain* (New York: The New York Botanical Garden Press), pp. 247–63.

Lisansky, Judith (1990) *Migrants to Amazonia: Spontaneous Colonization in the Brazilian Frontier* (Boulder, CO: Westview Press).

Lisansky, Judith and Sprissler, Loretta (2002) Lessons from the Rain Forest: Participation in the First Decade of the Pilot Program to Conserve the Brazilian Rain Forest,' in *Thinking Out Loud III: Innovative Case Studies on Participatory Instruments*, Latin America and the Caribbean Region (Washington, DC: World Bank).

Liu, C. and Colinvaux, P. (1985) 'Forest Changes in the Amazon Basin during the Last Glacial Maximum,' *Nature*, vol. 318, pp. 556–7.

Long, N. (1992) 'From Paradigm Lost to Paradigm Regained? The Case for an Actor-Oriented Sociology of Development,' in N. Long and A. Long (eds.), *Battlefields of Knowledge: The Interlocking of Theory and Practice in Social Research and Development* (London: Routledge), pp. 16–46.

Lovejoy, Thomas E. (2000) 'Amazon Forest Degradation and Fragmentation: Implications for Biodiversity Conservation,' in A. Hall (ed.), *Amazonia at the Crossroads: The Challenge of Sustainable Development* (London: Institute of Latin American Studies, University of London), pp. 41–57.

McFadden, D. (2000) *Disaggregate Behavioral Travel Demand's RUM Side: a 30-Year Retrospective* (Brisbane: International Association of Travel Behavior Analysts).

Mackay, F. (1999) 'Medio ambiente, desarollo y participación,' *Los derechos de los pueblos indígenas en el sistema internacional* (Lima: APRODEH/FIDH), pp. 277–325.

Mahar, D.J. (1978) *Desenvolvimento econômico da Amazonia: uma análise das políticas governamentais*, Relatório de Pesquisa no. 39 (IPEA: Rio de Janeiro).

Mahar, D.J. (1979) *Frontier Development Policy in Brazil: A Study of Amazonia* (New York: Praeger).

Mahar, D. (1988) *Government Policies and Deforestation in Brazil's Amazon Region* (Washington, DC: World Bank).

Mahar, D.J. (1989) *Government Policies and Deforestation in the Brazilian Amazon* (Washington, DC: World Bank). Also reproduced as 'Deforestation in Brazil's Amazon: Magnitude, Rate and Causes,' in G. Schramm and J.J. Warford (eds.) *Environmental Management and Economic Development* (Baltimore, MA: Johns Hopkins University Press).

Mahar, Dennis J. (2000) 'Agro-Ecological Zoning in Rondônia, Brazil: What Are the Lessons?' in A. Hall (ed.), *Amazonia at the Crossroads: the Challenge of Sustainable Development* (London: Institute of Latin American Studies, University of London), pp. 115–28.

Mahar, Dennis J. and Ducrot, Cecile E.H. (1998) 'Land-Use Zoning on Tropical Frontiers: Emerging Lessons from the Brazilian Amazon,' *EDI Case Studies* (Washington, DC: World Bank).

Manifiestação (2000) *Manifestação da sociedade civil brasileira sobre as relações entre florestas e mudanças climáticas e as expectativas para a COP–6, Belém, 24 de outubro de 2000* (Belém: Instituto de Pesquisa Ambiental da Amazônia, IPAM), 2 pp. http://www.ipam.org.br/polamb/man-belem.htm

Margulis, S. (2001) 'Who Are the Agents of Deforestation in the Amazon, and Why Do They Deforest?' (Brasília: World Bank).

Margulis, S. (2003) *Causas do desmatamento na Amazônia brasileira* (Brasília: World Bank).

Martine, G. (1980) 'Recent Colonization Experiences in Brazil: Expectations versus Reality,' in F. Barbira-Scazzocchio (ed.) *Land, People and Planning in Contemporary Amazonia* (Cambridge: Cambridge University Press), pp. 80–94.

Martine, G. (1990) 'Rondônia and the Fate of Small Farmers,' in D. Goodman and A. Hall (eds.) *The Future of Amazonia: Destruction or Sustainable Development?* (London: McMillan), pp. 23–48.

Mato Grosso, Fundação Estadual do Meio Ambiente (FEMA) (2001) *Environmental Control System on Rural Properties in Mato Grosso* (Cuiabá, Mato Grosso, Brazil: FEMA).

May, Peter and Veiga, Fernando Neto (2000) *Barreiras à certificação florestal na Amazônia brasileira: a importância dos custos* (Rio de Janeiro: Pronatura).

May, Peter, Veiga, Fernando Neto, Denardin, Valdir and Loureiro, Wilson (2002) *The Ecological Value Added Tax: Municipal Responses in Paraná and Minas Gerais, Brazil* (Rio de Janeiro: Pronatura).

McCay, B J. and Acheson, J.M. (eds.) (1987) *The Question of the Commons: The Culture and Ecology of Communal Resources* (Tucson: The University of Arizona Press).

McGrath, D., Castro, F., Câmara, E. and Futemma, C. (1999) 'Community Management of Floodplain Lakes and the Sustainable Development of Amazonian Fisheries,' in C. Padoch, J.M. Ayres, M. Pinedo-Vasquez and A. Henderson (eds.), *Várzea: Diversity, Development and Conservation of Amazonia's Whitewater Floodplain* (New York: The New York Botanical Garden Press), pp. 59–82.

MCT (2002), *Degravação do workshop: utilização de sistemas automáticos de monitoramento e medição de emissões de gases de efeito estufa da qualidade da água em reservatórios de hidrelétricas*, Centro de Gestão de Estudos Estratégicos do MCT, Brasília DF, 6 February (Brasília: Ministério da Ciência e Tecnologia), http://www.mct.gov.br/clima/brasil/doc/workad.doc.

Meinshausen, M. and Hare, B. (2000) *Temporary Sinks do not Cause Permanent Climate Benefits* (Amsterdam: Greenpeace International), 7 pp. www.carbonsinks.de

Mello, Neli A. (1999) 'Amazônia: questão regional, nacional e global,' *In RA'E GA: o espaço geográfico em análise* (Curitiba: Departamento de Geografia), volume 3, no. 3, pp. 121–48.

Mello, Neli A. (2002) *As políticas públicas territoriais na Amazônia brasileira: conflitos entre conservação ambiental e desenvolvimento. 1970–2000*, PhD thesis (São Paulo: Faculdade de Filosofia Letras e Ciências Humanas da USP, and Paris: Université de Paris X –Nanterre).

Merrick, Thomas and Graham, Douglas (1979) *Population and Economic Development in Brazil: 1800 to the Present* (Baltimore, MA: Johns Hopkins University Press).

Millikan, B. (1988) *The Dialectics of Deforestation: Tropical Deforestation and Degradation and Society in Rondônia, Brazil*, Masters thesis (Berkeley, CA: University of California).

Millikan, B.H. (1997) *Políticas públicas e desenvolvimento sustentável em Rondônia: problemática e desafios para sua implementação* (Porto Velho: Forum das Organizações Não-Governamentais e Movimentos Sociais que Atuam em Rondônia).

Ministério do Meio Ambiente (2001a) *Causas e dinâmica do desmatamento na Amazônia* (Brasília: MMA).

Ministério do Meio Ambiente (2001b) *National Forest Program* (Brasília: MMA). Also available in Portuguese.

Ministério do Meio Ambiente (2002) *Avaliação e ações prioritárias para a conservação da biodiversidade das zonas costeira e marinha* (Brasília: MMA).

Ministério do Meio Ambiente, dos Recursos Hídricos e da Amazonia Legal (1997) *Conservação ambiental no Brasil: Programa Nacional do Meio Ambiente, 1991–1996* (Brasília: MMA).

Ministério do Meio Ambiente, dos Recursos Hídricos e da Amazonia Legal (1998) *Projetos de execução descentralizada: relatorio final* (Brasília: MMA).

Ministry of Planning and Budget (1995) *Projeto Áridas: A Strategy for Sustainable Development in Brazil's Northeast* (Brasília: MPO).

MMA (2002) *Biodiversidade brasileira: avaliação e identificação de áreas e ações prioritárias para conservação, utilização sustentável e repartição dos benefícios da biodiversidade brasileira* (Brasília: Ministério do Meio Ambiente).

MMA (ed.) (2001) *PDPI — Projetos demonstrativos dos povos indígenas: informações básicas e formulário para apresentação de projetos* (Ministry of the Environment, Brasília).

Molin, Nilson (2001) *L'Amapá un Nord pour le Brésil, Entretiens avec le gouverneur João Alberto Capiberibe* (Montpellier: Centre de Documentation Tiers Monde).

Monzoni, M., Muggiatti, A. and Smeraldi, R. (2000) *Mudança climática: tomando posições* (São Paulo: Friends of the Earth/Amigos da Terra, Programa Amazônia), 41 pp. http://www.amazonia.org.br/ef/Mudanca%20Climatica.pdf

Moran, Emilio F. (1984) 'Colonization in the Transamazon and Rondônia,' in Marianne Schmink and Charles H. Wood (eds.), *Frontier Expansion in Amazonia* (Gainesville, Fl.: University of Florida Press), pp. 285–303.

Moran, E.F., Packer, A., Brondizio, E.S. and Tucker, J. (1996) 'Restoration of Vegetation Cover in Eastern Amazon,' *Ecological Economics*, vol. 18, pp. 41–54.

Moura, R. (1996) *Expectativa de vida dos povos indígenas brasileiros* (Manaus: unpublished report).

Mueller, Charles C. (1990) 'Recent Frontier Expansion in Brazil: The Case of Rondônia,' in F. Barbira-Scazzocchio (ed.) *Land, People and Planning in Contemporary Amazonia* (Cambridge: Cambridge University Press).

Mummert, U. (1999) Wirtschaftliche Entwicklung und Institutionen. Die Perspektive der Neuen Institutionenökonomik, in R.E. Thiel (ed.), *Neue Ansätze zur Entwicklungstheorie*, Themendienst, vol. 10 (Bonn: DIE), pp. 300–11.

Myers, N. (1989) *Deforestation Rates in Tropical Forests and their Climatic Implications* (London: Friends of the Earth).

Myers, N. (1990) 'Tropical Forests,' in J. Leggett (ed.), *Global Warming: The Greenpeace Report* (Oxford, UK: Oxford University Press), pp. 372–99.

Nascimento, H. and Laurance, W.F. (2002) 'Total Aboveground Biomass in Central Amazonian Rainforest: A Landscape-scale Study,' *Forest Ecology and Management*, vol. 168, pp. 311–21.

Negreiros, G. H., Nepstad, D. C., Sandberg, D., Alvarado, E., Hinckley, T. and Pereira, M. (1997) 'Fire Along the Transition between the Amazon Forest and the Cerrado Ecosystems,' *13th Conference on Fire and Forest Meteorology*, Lorne, Australia.

Nelson, B., Ferreira, C., da Silva, M. and Kawasaki, M. (1990) 'Endemism Centres, Refugia and Botanical Collection Density in Brazilian Amazonia,' *Nature*, vol. 345, pp. 714–6.

Nepstad, D., Capobianco, J.P., Barros, A.C., Carvalho, G., Moutinho, P., Lopes, U. and Lefevebre, P. (2000) *Avança Brasil: os custos ambientais para a Amazônia* (Belém: IPAM, ISA, WHRC).

Nepstad, D., Capobianco, J.P., Barros, A.C., Carvalho, G., Moutinho, P., Lopes, U. and Lefebvre, P. (2002) *Roads in the Rainforest: Environmental Costs for the Amazon* (Belém: IPAM/ISA).

Nepstad, D.C., Carvalho, G., Barros, A.C., Alencar, A., Capobianco, J.P., Bishop, J., Moutinho, P., Lefebvre, P., Silva Jr., U.L. and Prins, E.

(2001) 'Road Paving, Fire Regime Feedbacks, and the Future Of Amazon Forests,' *Forest Ecology and Management,* vol. 154, no. 3, pp. 395–407.

Nepstad, D., McGrath, D., Alencar, A., Barros, A.C., Carvalho, G., Santilli, M. and Vera Diaz, M. del C. (2002) 'Frontier Governance in Amazonia,' *Science,* vol. 295, January 25.

Nepstad, D. C., Moreira, A.G., and Alencar, A.A. (1999) *Flames in the Rain Forest: Origins, Impacts and Alternatives to Amazonian Fire,* Pilot Program to Conserve the Brazilian Rainforest (Brasília: World Bank, PPG7).

Nepstad, D.C., Moutinho, P.R., Negreiros, G.H., Vieira, S. and Rapport, D. (1995) *Evaluating and Monitoring the Health of Large-Scale Ecosystems* (New York: Springer–Verlag).

M. Neuburger (2002) 'Pionierfrontentwicklung im Hinterland von Cáceres (Mato Grosso, Brasilien),' *Ökologische Degradierung, Verwundbarkeit und kleinbäuerliche Überlebensstrategien,* Tübinger Geographische Studien, vol. 135 (Tübingen).

Neumann, R.P. and Hirsch, E. (2000) *Commercialisation of Non-Timber Forest Products: Review and Analysis of Research* (Bogor, Indonesia: CIFOR and FAO).

Nitsch, Manfred (2000) 'The Future of the Amazon: Critical Issues and Scenarios,' Lecture at the German-Brazilian Workshop on Neo-Tropical Ecosystems (revised version), Hamburg, Germany, September.

Nohlen, D. (2001) Die politische Entwicklung Boliviens in den letzten zwei Dekaden. Eine Bilanz,' in R. Sevilla and A. Benavides (eds.), *Bolivien. Das Verkannte Land?* (Bad Honnef: Horlemann), pp. 26–42.

North, D.C. (1988) *Theorie des institutionellen Wandels. Eine neue Sicht der Wirtschaftsgeschichte* (Tübingen).

North, D.C. (1992) *Institutionen, institutioneller Wandel und Wirtschaftsleistung* (Tübingen).

Núcleo de Direitos Indígenas (NDI) (1993) *Indigenous Populations Legal Rights to their Lands and Natural Resources: Part I and II* (Washington, DC: unpublished manuscript in World Bank project files, Part I November 1993, Part II September 1994).

Ostrom, E. (1990) *Governing the Commons: The Evolution of Institutions for Collective Action: The Political Economy of Institutions and Decisions* (Cambridge: Cambridge University Press).

Overal, W.L. and Posey, D.A. (1996) 'Práticas agrárias dos índios Kayapó do Pará: subsídios para o desenvolvimento da Amazônia,' in C. Pavan (ed.), *Uma estratégia latino-americana para a Amazônia*, vol. I (Brasília and São Paulo: UNESP), pp. 183–200.

Ozório de Almeida, Anna Luiza (1992) *Colonização dirigida na Amazonia* (Rio de Janeiro: IPEA 135). Later published in English as *The Colonization of the Amazon* (Austin, Texas: University of Texas Press).

Ozório de Almeida, Anna Luiza and Campari, João (1995) *Sustainable Settlement in the Brazilian Amazon* (New York: World Bank and Oxford University Press).

Pagiola, S., Bishop, J. and Landell Mills, N. (eds.) (2002) *Selling Forest Environmental Services: Market-Based Mechanisms for Conservation* (London: Earthscan).

Pasca, D. (1997) *Situação do setor garimpeiro no Amapá e conflitos entre garimpeiros e Waiãpi. Relatório técnico da missão de avaliação do projeto 'Entorno Waiãpi'* (Tübingen, Eschborn/GTZ: unpublished report).

Pasca, D. (1998) 'Nachhaltige Ressourcennutzung versus nachhaltiger Verlust von Ressourcen: Die Rückzugsräume der Indianer in Mato Grosso, Brasilien,' in G. Kohlhepp and M. Coy (eds.), *Mensch-Umwelt-Beziehungen und nachhaltige Entwicklung in der Dritten Welt* (Tübingen: Geographical Institute Press), series Tübinger Geographische Studien 119, pp. 167–94.

Pasca, D. (2000) 'Nutzungskonkurrenz um Raum und Ressourcen: indigene Gesellschaften und Garimpeiros in Brasilien,' in H.H. Blotevogel et al. (eds.), *Lokal verankert — weltweit vernetzt. (Tagungsbericht und wissenschaftliche Abhandlungen des 52. Deutschen Geographentags Hamburg 2.–9.10.1999)* (Stuttgart: Springer), pp. 415–22.

Pasca, D. (2002) 'Indigene Völker in Brasilien — von der Bevormundung zur Selbstbestimmung,' *Petermanns Geographische Mitteilungen*, vol. 146, no. 1, pp. 22–3.

Pasca, D. (2004) *Ressourcennutzungskonflikte und Strategien zur Sicherung indigener Räume an der brasilianischen Peripherie* (Tübingen: Geographical Institute Press).

Pasca, D. and Friedrich, M. (1998) 'Wasserstraßen gefährden indigenen Lebensraum,' *Pogrom*, vol. 199, pp. 41–3.

Peet, R. and Watts, M. (1996) *Liberation Ecologies: Environment, Development, and Social Movements* (London: Routledge).

Pérez, S. and Walker, R. (2002) 'Household Life Cycles and Secondary Forest Cover among Small Colonists in the Amazon,' *World Development*, vol. 30, pp. 1009–27.

Perreault, T. (2001) 'Developing Identities: Indigenous Mobilization, Rural Livelihoods, and Resource Access in Ecuatorian Amazonia,' *Ecumene*, vol. 4, no. 4, pp. 381–413.

Pinkerton, E. (ed.) (1989) *Co-operative Management of Local Fisheries: New Directions for Improved Management and Community Development* (Vancouver: University of British Columbia Press).

PNUD (Programa de las Naciones Unidas para el Desarrollo) (1998) *Informe de Desarrollo Humano en Bolivia 1998* (La Paz).

PNUD (Programa de las Naciones Unidas para el Desarrollo) (2000) *Informe de Desarrollo Humano en Bolivia 2000* (La Paz)

PNUD (Programa de las Naciones Unidas para el Desarrollo) (2002) *Informe de Desarrollo Humano en Bolivia 2002* (La Paz)

Pomeroy, R.S. and Berkes, F. (1997) 'Two to Tango: The Role of Government in Fisheries Co-management,' *Marine Policy*, vol. 2, pp. 465–80.

Posey, D.A. (1987) 'Manejo da floresta secundária, capoeiras, campos e cerrados (Kayapó),' in D. Ribeiro (ed.), *Suma etnológica brasileira*, vol. 1 (Petrópolis: Vozes), pp. 173–85.

Posey, D.A. (1996) 'Os povos tradicionais e a conservação da biodiversidade,' in C. Pavan (ed.), *Uma estratégia latino-americana para a Amazônia*, vol. 1 (Brasília, São Paulo: UNESP), pp. 149–57.

Posey, D.A. (2000) 'Biodiversity, Genetic Resources and Indigenous Peoples in Amazonia: (Re)Discovering the Wealth of Traditional Resources of Native Amazonians,' in A. Hall (ed.) *Amazonia at the Crossroads: The Challenge of Sustainable Development* (London: Institute of Latin American Studies, University of London), pp. 188–204.

Posey, D.A. and Balée, W. (eds.) (1989) *Resource Management in Amazonia: Indigenous and Folk Strategies* (New York: The New York Botanical Garden), series Advances in Economic Botany, no. 7.

Posey, D.A. and Dutfield, G. (1996) *Beyond Intellectual Property: Toward Traditional Resource Rights for Indigenous Peoples and Local Communities* (Ottawa: IDRC).

Posey, D.A. and Overal, W.L. (ed.) (1990) *Ethnobiology: Implications and Applications. (Proceedings of the First International Congress of Ethnobiology, Belém 1988)*, 2 vols (Belém: MPEG).

Pouyllau, Michel (1997) 'Environnement et gouvernance. Mariage de raison ou concubinage forcé? (a partir d'exemples latino-américains),' in Jean-François Baré (ed.), *Regards interdisciplinaires sur les politiques de développement* (Paris/Montréal: L'Harmattan), pp 283–328.

PPG7 (1991) *Progress Report of October 1991* (Geneva: mimeo.).

PPG7 (1993–2001) *Reports of the First to Fifteenth Meetings* (Brasília: International Advisory Group — IAG, mimeo.).

PPG7 (1996) *Report on the Third Meeting of the Participants* (Bonn: 10–12 September).

PPG7 (1997) Rain Forest Pilot Program. Discussion Paper for Donors' Meeting in Paris. *The Brazil Rain Forest Pilot Program Transition to a Phase Two* (Paris: World Bank).

PPG7 (1999) *Review of Institutional Arrangements* (Brasília: Pilot Programme to Conserve the Brazilian Rainforest, Ministry of the Environment).

PPG7 (2000a) *Outputs by Complementary Lines of Action* (Cuiabá: Pilot Programme to Conserve the Brazilian Rainforest, Ministry of the Environment).

PPG7 (2000b) *Annual Report 1999–2000* (Brasília: Pilot Programme to Conserve the Brazilian Rainforest, mimeo.).

PPG7 (2001a), *Open Letter of the IAG and IAG Comments on the Mid Term Review Report* (Brasília: Pilot Programme to Conserve the Brazilian Rainforest, mimeo.).

PPG7 (2001b) *Reunião dos participantes. Relatórios da primeira (1994) à sexta (2001) reuniões* (Cuiabá: mimeo.).

Prance, G. (1973) 'Phytogeographic Support for the Theory of Pleistocene Forest Refuges in the Amazon Basin: Evidence from Distribution Patterns in Caryocaraceae, Chyrsobalanaceae, Dichapetaleceae and Lecythidaceae,' *Acta Amazonica*, vol. 3, no. 1, pp. 5–28.

Prance, G, (1982a) 'Forest Refuges: Evidence from Woody Angiosperms, in G. Prance (ed.) *Biological Diversity in the Tropics* (New York: Columbia University Press), pp. 137–58.

Prance, G. (1982b) 'A Review of the Phytogeographic Evidences for Pleistocene Climate Changes in the Neotropics,' *Annals of the Missouri Botanical Gardens*, vol. 9, pp. 594–624.

Prance. G. and Lovejoy, T. (eds.) (1986) *Amazonia: Key Environments* (Oxford: Pergamon Press).

Prefeitura de Guarantã do Norte (1999) *Esta terra vale ouro* (Guarantã do Norte — MT: Polo de Desenvolvimento do Nortão).

Price, David (1989) *Before the Bulldozer: The Nambiquara Indians and the World Bank* (Washington, DC: Seven Lochs Press).

Pritchard, L., Colding, J. et al. (1998) *The Problem of Fit between Ecosystems and Institutions* (Bonn: International Human Dimensions Programme on Global Environmental Change).

Pritzl, R.F. (1997) '"Property rights", Rent-Seeking und "institutionelle Schwäche" in Lateinamerika. Zur institutionenökonomischen Analyse der sozialen Anomie,' *Ibero-Amerikanisches Archiv*, vol. 23, no. 3/4 (1997), pp. 365–407.

Programa Piloto para Proteção das Florestas Tropicais do Brasil (1997) *Extrativismo na Amazonia*, Boletim No. 1, August 1997.

Programa Piloto para Proteção das Florestas Tropicais do Brasil (2001) *PDA 5 Anos: uma trajetória pioneira* (Brasília: Ministério do Meio Ambiente).

Raiol, O. (1992) *A utopia da terra na fronteira da Amazônia: a geopolítica e a posse da terra no Amapá* (Macapá: Editora Gráfica O Dia).

Ramos, A. R. (1984) 'Frontier Expansion and Indigenous People in the Brazilian Amazon,' in Marianne Schmink and Charles H. Wood (eds.), *Frontier Expansion in Amazonia* (Gainesville, Fl.: University of Florida Press).

Ramos, A.R. (1998) *Indigenism: Ethnic Politics in Brazil* (Madison: The Univesity of Wisconsin Press).

Redford, K.H and Sanderson, S.E. (2000) 'Extracting Humans from Nature,' *Conservation Biology*, vol. 14, pp. 1362–64.

Redford, K.H. and Stearman, A.M. (1993) 'Forest-Dwelling Native Amazonians and the Conservation of Biodiversity: Interests in Common or in Collision?' *Conservation Biology*, vol. 7, pp. 248–55.

Redwood III, John (1972) *Internal Migration, Urbanization and Frontier Region Development in Brazil Since 1940*, Masters thesis, Department of City and Regional Planning (Berkeley, CA: University of California).

Redwood III, John (1979) *Implicit and Explicit Regional Policies in Brazil: The Impact of the Public Sector on Spatial Development Disparities since the Second World War*, PhD dissertation, Department of City and Regional Planning (Berkeley, CA: University of California).

Redwood III, John (1993) *World Bank Approaches to the Environment in Brazil: A Review of Selected Projects* (Washington, DC: World Bank).

Redwood III, John (1996) *The Carajás Metallurgical Pole: Perspectives and Energy Options*, Environment Department, unpublished monograph (Washington, DC: World Bank).

Redwood III, John (1998) 'Social Benefits and Costs of Mining: The Carajás Iron Ore Project,' in *Mining and the Community: Results of the Quito Conference*, Energy, Mining and Telecommunications (EMT) Occasional Paper no. 11 (Washington, DC: World Bank).

Redwood III, John (2000) 'The World Bank and the Pantanal', in F.A. Swarts (ed.) *The Pantanal: Understanding and Protecting the World's Largest Wetland* (St. Paul, Minn: Paragon House).

Reis, Eustaquio J. and Margulis, Sergio (1991) 'Options for Slowing Down Amazon Jungle-Clearing,' in R. Dornbusch and J.M. Poterba (eds.), *Global Warming: Economic Policy Responses* (Cambridge, MA: MIT Press).

República de Bolivia — Ministerio de Desarrollo Humano Secretaría Nacional de Participación Popular (1997) *El pulso de la democracia, Participación ciudadana y descentralización en Bolivia* (Venezuela: Nueva Sociedad).

Revkin, Andrew (1990) *The Burning Season: The Murder of Chico Mendes and the Fight for the Amazon Rain Forest* (Boston, MA: Houghton Miflin).

Ribeiro, José Felipe, Lazarini da Fonseca, Carlos Eduardo and Sousa-Silva, José Carlos (eds.) (2001) *Cerrado: caracterização e recuperação de matas de galeria* (Brasília: Planaltina).

Ricardo, C.A. (ed.) (1996) *Povos indígenas no Brasil 1991–1995* (São Paulo: Instituto Socioambiental).

Ricardo, C.A. (1998) 'Indigenous Social Diversity in Brazil Today,' in M.L. Davies de Freitas (ed.), *Amazonia: Heaven of a New World. A Collection of Articles on Science and Life in the Brazilian Amazon* (Rio de Janeiro: Campus), pp. 83–104.

Ricardo, C.A. (ed.) (2000) *Povos indígenas no Brasil 1996–2000* (São Paulo: Instituto Socioambiental).

Rich, B. (1994) *Mortgaging the Earth: The World Bank, Environmental Impoverishment and the Crisis of Development* (London: Earthscan; Boston: Beacon Press).

Richards, M. (1993) 'The Potential of Non-Timber Forest Products in Sustainable Natural Resource Management in Amazonia,' *Commonwealth Forestry Review,* vol. 72, no. 1, pp. 21–7.

Roosevelt, A. (2000) 'The Lower Amazon: A Dynamic Human Habitat,' in D. Lentz (ed.) *Imperfect Balance: Landscape Transformations in the Precolumbian Americas* (New York: Columbia University Press), pp. 455–92.

Rosendo, S. (2003) 'Adapting Institutions to Social Context: Rubber Tappers' Associations and Extractive Reserves in Brazilian Amazonia,' *CSERGE Working Paper Series,* University of East Anglia.

Rossi, Georges (1997) 'Voulons-nous la participacion ? Essai critique sur l'environnement et le développement,' in Jean-François Baré (ed.), *Regards interdisciplinaires sur les politiques de développement* (Paris/Montréal: L'Harmattan), pp. 329–48.

Roux, J.C. (2000) *La Bolivie Orientale, confins inexplorés, battues aux Indiens et économie de pillage* (Paris: L'Harmattan).

Roux, J.C. (2001) 'De los límites a la frontera: o los malentendidos de la geopolítica amazónica,' *Revista de Índias,* vol. LXI, no. 223, pp. 514–39.

Rudel, T.K. and Horowitz, B. (1993) *Tropical Deforestation: Small Farmers and Land Clearing in the Ecuadorian Amazon* (New York: Columbia University Press).

Runyan, Curtis (1999) 'Ação na Linha de Frente,' *World-Watch* [s.l.], November–December, pp. 12–21.

Santilli, J. (2001) 'Biodiversidade e conhecimentos tradicionais,' in J.P.R. Capobianco et al. (eds.), *Biodiversidade na Amazônia brasileira: avaliação e ações prioritárias para a conservação, uso sustentável e repartição de benefícios* (São Paulo: Instituto Socioambiental), pp. 235–43.

Santilli, M. (2003) *Cem dias a espera de uma política indigenista* (Especial Mês do Índio, abril de 2003), Homepage of the Instituto Socioambiental [www.socioambiental.org/website/especiais/mesdoindio/index. shtm].

Santos, J. V. Tavares dos (1993) *Matuchos: exclusão e luta: do Sul para a Amazônia* (Petrópolis: Vozes).

Sawyer, Donald R. (1984) 'Frontier Expansion and Retraction in Brazil,' in Marianne Schmink and Charles H. Wood (eds.), *Frontier Expansion in Amazonia* (Gainesville, Fl.: University of Florida Press).

Scatena, F.N., Walker, R., Homma, A.K., Conto, A.J.D., Ferreira, C., Carvalho, R., Neves da Rocha, A., Moreira dos Santos, A. and Mourão de Oliveira, P. (1996) 'Cropping and Fallowing Sequences of Small Farms in the "terra firme" Landscape of the Brazilian Amazon: A Case Study From Santarém, Pará,' *Ecological Economics*, vol. 18, pp. 29–40.

Schama, S. (1996) *Landscape and Memory* (New York: Columbia University Press).

Schmink, Marianne and Wood, Charles H. (eds.) (1984) *Frontier Expansion in Amazonia* (Gainsville, Fl.: University of Florida Press).

Schneider, R.R. (1993a) *The Potential for Trade with the Amazon in Greenhouse Gas Reduction*, LATEN Dissemination Note # 2 (Washington, DC: World Bank).

Schneider, R.R. (1993b) *Land Abandonment, Property Rights and Sustainability in the Amazon*, LATEN Dissemination Note # 3 (Washington, DC: World Bank).

Schneider, R.R. (1994) *Government and the Economy on the Amazon Frontier* Latin America and the Caribbean Technical Department, Regional Studies Program, Report no. 34 (Washington, DC: World Bank). Later issued under the same title as World Bank Environment Department Paper no. 11, August 1995.

Schneider, R.R., Arima, E., Veríssimo, A., Barreto, P. and Souza Junior, C. (2000) *Amazônia sustentável: limitantes e oportunidades para o desenvolvimento rural* (Brasília: World Bank and Belém: IMAZON).

Schneider, R.R., Platais, G., Rosenblatt, D. and Webb, M. (1993) *Sustainability, Yield Loss and Imediatismo: Choice of Technique at the Frontier*, LATEN Dissemination Note # 1 (Washington, DC: World Bank).

Schneider, Robert R., Arima, Eugenio, Veríssimo, Adalberto, Barreto, Paulo and Souza, Carlos (2002) *Sustainable Amazonia: Limitations and Opportunities for Rural Development*, World Bank Technical Paper No. 515 (Washington, DC: World Bank). A Portuguese version of the same document was previously published as *Amazônia Sustentável: Limitantes e Oportunidades para o Desenvolvimento Rural* (Brasília: World Bank/IMAZON), 2000.

Scholz, F. (2002) 'Die Theorie der "fragmentierenden Entwicklung",' in *Geographische Rundschau*, vol. 54, no. 10, pp. 6–11.

Schröder, P. (1999) 'Os índios são participativos? As bases sócio-culturais e políticas da participação de comunidades indígenas em projetos e programas,' in C. Kasburg and M.M Gramkow (eds.) (1999), *Demarcando terras indígenas: experiências e desafios de um projeto de parceria* (Brasília: PPG7/GTZ/FUNAI/PPTAL), pp. 233–64.

Schwartzman, S. (1989) 'Extractive Reserves: The Rubber Tappers' Strategy for Sustainable Use of the Amazon Rainforest,' in J.O. Browder (ed.), *Fragile Lands of Latin America: Strategies for Sustainable Development* (Boulder, CO: Westview Press), pp. 150–63.

Schwartzman, S. (1997) *Fires in the Amazon — an Analysis of NOAA–12 Satellite Data 1996–97* (Washington, DC: EDF).

Schwartzman, S., Moreira, A. and Nepstad, D. (2000a) 'Rethinking Tropical Forest Conservation: Perils in Parks,' *Conservation Biology*, vol. 14, pp. 1351–57.

Schwartzman, S., Moreira, A. and Nepstad, D. (2000b) 'Arguing Tropical Forest Conservation: People Versus Parks,' *Conservation Biology*, vol. 14, pp. 1370–74.

Schwengber, A.M. (2000) 'Waiãpi e CTI: uma parceria ameaçada,' in C.A. Ricardo (ed.), *Povos indígenas no Brasil 1996–2000* (São Paulo: Instituto Socioambiental), pp. 387–90.

Secretaria Especial do Meio Ambiente, International Waterfowl Research Bureau and Companhia Vale do Rio Doce (1987) *Desenvolvimento econômico e impacto ambiental em areas de trópico úmido brasileiro; a experiência da CVRD* (Rio de Janeiro: SEMA, IWRB, CVRD).

Sen, A. (2000) *Ökonomie für den Menschen. Wege zu Gerechtigkeit und Solidarität in der Marktwirtschaft* (München).

Sen, S. and Nielsen, J.R. (1996) 'Fisheries Co-Management: A Comparative Analysis,' *Marine Policy*, vol. 20, no. 5, pp. 405–18.

Senderowitsch, Roberto and Cesilini, Sandra (2000) 'The Country Assistance Strategy in Argentina; How to Make a Consultative Process Work,' *Thinking Out Loud II: Innovative Case Studies on Participatory Instruments*, Latin America and the Caribbean Region (Washington, DC: World Bank).

Sheehan, M. (2001) *City Limits: Putting the Brakes on Urban Sprawl*, Worldwatch Paper no. 156 (Washington, DC: Worldwatch Institute).

Shihata, Ibrahim F.I. (1994) *The World Bank Inspection Panel* (New York: Oxford University Press).

Shoumatoff, Alex (1990) *The World is Burning: Murder in the Rain Forest* (New York: Avon Books).

Sistema Nacional de Unidades de Conservação (SNUC) (2000) *Lei No. 9.985 de 18 de julho de 2000* (Brasília: Government of Brazil).

Skillings, Robert F. and Tcheyan, Nils O. (1979) *Economic Development Prospects of the Amazon Region of Brazil*, Occasional Paper no. 9, Center for Brazilian Studies, School of Advanced International Studies (SAIS) (Washington, DC: John Hopkins University).

Smeraldi, R. and Veríssimo, A. (1999) *Acertando o alvo: consumo de madeira no mercado interno brasileiro e promoção da certificação florestal* (São Paulo: Friends of the Earth. Piracicaba: IMAFLORA. Belém: IMAZON).

Smith, Nigel J.H. (1982) *Rainforest Corridors: The Transamazon Colonization Scheme* (Berkeley, CA: University of California Press).

Smith, Nigel J.H. (1999) *The Amazon River Forest: A Natural History of Plants Animals and People* (New York: Oxford University Press).

Smith, Nigel J.H. (2000) 'Agroforestry Development and Prospects in the Brazilian Amazon,' in A. Hall (ed.), *Amazonia at the Crossroads: the Challenge of Sustainable Development* (London: Institute of Latin American Studies, University of London), pp. 150–70.

Smith, Nigel J.H., Dubois, Jean, Current, Dean, Lutz, Ernst and Clement, C. (1998) *Agroforestry Experiences in the Brazilian Amazon: Constraints and Opportunities*, Pilot Program to Conserve the Brazilian Rainforest (Brasília: World Bank).

Smith, Nigel J.H., Serrão, Emanuel Adilson S., Alvim, Paulo T. and Falesi, Italo C. (1995) *Amazonia: Resiliency and Dynamism of the Land and People* (New York: United Nations University Press).

Soares Filho, B. S. (1998) *Modelagem da dinâmica de paisagem de uma regiao de fronteira de colonização amazônica* (São Paulo: University of São Paulo).

Sorrensen, C.L. (1998) 'Contributions of Fire Use Study to Conceptualizations of Deforestation and Land Use/Cover Change in the Brazilian Lower Amazon,' *Meeting of the Latin American Studies Association*, Chicago, Illinois.

Souza Filho, C.F. Marés de (1999) *O renascer dos povos indígenas para o direito* (Curitiba: Juruá).

Srivastava, Jitendra P., Smith, Nigel J.H. and Forno, Douglas (1996) *Biodiversity and Agricultural Intensification: Partners for Development and Conservation*, Environmentally Sustainable Development Studies and Monographs Series no. 11 (Washington, DC: World Bank).

Stoian, D. (2000) Variations and Dynamics of Extractive Economies: The Rural-Urban Nexus of Non-Timber Forest Use in the Bolivian Amazon (Freiburg: im Breisgau).

Stolton, S. and Dudley, N. (1999) *Partnerships for Protection: New Strategies for Planning and Management for Protected Areas* (London: Earthscan).

Swarts, Frederick A. (ed.) (2000) *The Pantanal: Understanding and Protecting the World's Largest Wetland* (St. Paul, Minn: Paragon House).

Taylor, M. (2000) 'Communities in the Lead: Power, Organisational Capacity and Social Capital,' *Urban Studies*, vol. 37, no. 5–6, pp. 1019–1035.

Teniere-Buchot, Pierre-Frédéric (2001) 'Decision, expertise, arbitraire et transparence: éléménts d'un développement durable', *Le Courrier de l'environement de l'INRA*, no. 44, October, pp. 41–52.

Terborgh, J. (1999) *Requiem for Nature* (Washington, DC: Island Press).

Terborgh, J. (2000) 'The Fate of Tropical Forests: A Matter of Stewardship,' *Conservation Biology*, vol. 14, pp. 1358–61.

Théry, Hervé (1995) *Pouvoir et territoire au Brésil: de l'archipel au continent* (Paris: Éditions de la Maison des Sciences de l'Homme).

Théry, Hervé (ed.) (1997) *Environnement et développement en Amazonie brésilienne* (Paris: Éditions Belin).

UN–FCCC (1992) *United Nations Framework Convention on Climate Change*. Available in English at http://www.unfccc.de and in Portuguese at http://www.mct.gov.br.

UN–FCCC (1997) *Kyoto Protocol to the United Nations Framework Convention on Climate Change*, Document FCCC/CP/1997;7/Add1, available in English at http://www.unfccc.de and in Portuguese at http://www.mct.gov.br.

UNAMAZ (1998) *Amazonia 21: Uma Agenda para um mundo sustentavel* (Brasília: UNAMAZ).

Urenda Diaz, J.C. (1998) *La descentralización deficiente* (La Paz: Los Amigos Del Libro).

van der Hammen, M.C. (2003) *The Indigenous Resguardos of Colombia: Their Contribution to Conservation and Sustainable Forest Use* (Amsterdam, Netherlands: Netherlands Committee for IUCN).

van Dijck, P. (ed.) (1998) *The Bolivian Experiment: Structural Adjustment and Poverty Alleviation* (Amsterdam: CEDLA).

Van Vliet, O., Faaij, A. and Dieperink, C. (2003) 'Forestry Projects under the Clean Development Mechanism? Modelling of the Uncertainties in Carbon Mitigation and Related Costs of Plantation Forestry Projects,' *Climatic Change*, vol. 61 nos. 1–2, pp. 123–56.

Van Zyl, Johan, Sonn, Loreta and Costa, Alberto (2000) *Decentralized Development, Enhanced Community Participation and Local Government Performance: Evidence from Northeast Brazil*, draft consultants' report, Pretoria, South Africa.

Vanzolini, P. and Williams, E. (1970) 'South American Anoles: The Geographic Differentiation and Evolution of the *Anolis chrysolepis* Species Group (Sauriae, Iguanidae),' *Arquivo Zoológico de São Paulo*, vol. 19, pp. 1–298.

Verrísimo, Adalberto, Cochrane Mark A., Souza, Carlos and Salomão, Rodney (2002) 'Priority Areas for Establishing National Forests in the Brazilian Amazon,' *Conservation Ecology*, vol. 6, no, 2.

Von Amsberg, Joachim (2002) 'Tocantins Strategy,' internal memorandum (restricted document) (Washington, DC: World Bank).

Walker, R., Moran, E. and Anselin, L. (2000) 'Deforestation and Cattle Ranching in the Brazilian Amazon: External Capital and Household Process,' *World Development*, vol. 28, pp. 683–99.

Weigand Jr, R. and de Paula, D. (1998) *Reservas extrativistas em Rondônia: dando poder ás comunidades através da elaboração e implantação participativa do Plano de Desenvolvimento* (Porto Velho: SEPLAN, SEDAM, PLANAFLORO, PNUD).

Whitemore, T. and Prance, G. (eds.) (1987) *Biogeography and Quaternary History in Tropical America* (Oxford: Oxford Science Publications).

Wiens, Thomas and Guadagni, Maurizio (1998) *Designing Rules for Demand-Driven Rural Investment Funds: The Latin American Experience*, World Bank Technical Paper no. 407 (Washington, DC: World Bank).

Wilson, E.O. (1992) *The Diversity of Life.* (Cambridge, MA: Belknap, Harvard University Press).

Wilson, John F. (1985) *Ariquemes: Settlement and Class in a Brazilian Frontier*, PhD dissertation (Gainseville, FL: University of Florida).

Wilson, John F. and Alicbusan-Schwab, A. (1991) *Development Policies and Health: Farmers, Goldminers and Slums in the Brazilian Amazon*, Environment Department, Divisional Working Paper no. 1991–18 (Washington, DC: World Bank).

Wood, C. and Walker, R. (1999) 'Saving the Trees by Helping the Poor — A Look at Small Producers along Brazil's Transamazon Highway,' *Resources*.

Wood, Charles and Wilson, John (1984) 'The Magnitude of Migration to the Brazilian Frontier,' in Marianne Schmink and Charles H. Wood (eds.), *Frontier Expansion in Amazonia* (Gainesville, FL.: University of Florida Press).

World Bank (1982) *Tribal Peoples and Economic Development: Human Ecologic Considerations* (Washington, DC: World Bank).

World Bank (1983) *Brazil: Integrated Development of the Northwest Frontier*, World Bank Country Study (Washington, DC: World Bank).

World Bank (1991) *Operational Directive 4.20, Indigenous People* (Washington, DC: World Bank).

World Bank (1992a) *Brazil: An Analysis of Environmental Problems in the Amazon*, Report no. 9104–BR (Washington, DC: World Bank). Restricted document.

World Bank (1992b) *World Development Report 1992: Development and the Environment* (New York: Oxford University Press).

World Bank (1992c) *Rain Forest Trust Fund Resolution, Background note, Part I, Introduction and Objectives* (Washington, DC: World Bank), http://www.worldbank.org.

World Bank (1994) *Brazil: The Management of Agriculture, Rural Development, and Natural Resources*, Report no. 11783–BR (Washington, DC: World Bank), restricted document.

World Bank (1995) *Memorandum of the Director (MOD), Brazil: Indigenous Lands Project, Report Number 13048–BR*, (Washington, DC: World Bank).

World Bank (2000) *Brazil: Forests in the Balance: Challenges of Conservation with Development* (Washington, DC: World Bank, Operations Evaluation Department).

World Bank (2001) *Making Sustainable Commitments: An Environmental Strategy for the World Bank* (Washington, DC: World Bank).

World Bank (2002) *Pilot Program to Conserve the Brazilian Rain Forests: An Innovative Experience in International Cooperation for Sustainable Development* (Brasília: Ministry of the Environment).

World Bank (2002a) *A Revised Forest Strategy for the World Bank* (Washington, DC: World Bank). Restricted document.

World Bank (2002b) *Reaching the Rural Poor: An Updated Strategy for Rural Development* (Washington, DC: World Bank). Restricted document.

World Bank (2002c) *World Development Report 2003: Sustainable Development in a Dynamic World: Transforming Institutions, Growth and Quality of Life* (New York: Oxford University Press).

World Bank / CAS (1995) *Country Assistance Strategy for the Federative Republic of Brazil*, Report no. 14569–BR (Washington, DC: World Bank). Restricted document.

World Bank / CAS (1997) *Country Assistance Strategy for the Federative Republic of Brazil*, Report no. 16582–BR (Washington, DC: World Bank). Restricted document.

World Bank/ CAS (2000) *Country Assistance Strategy for the Federative Republic of Brazil*, Report no. 20160–BR (Washington, DC: World Bank). Restricted document.

World Bank/Global Environment Facility (1996) *Brazil — National Biodiversity Project, Brazilian Biodiversity Fund Project*, Project Document (Washington, DC: World Bank).

World Bank/Global Environment Facility/Project Appraisal Document (2002) *Integrated Silvopastoral Approaches to Ecosystem Management Project in Colombia, Costa Rica and Nicaragua*, Report no. 21869–LAC (Washington, DC: World Bank).

World Bank/Implementation Completion Report (2000), *Brazil — National Environment Project*, Report no. 20344 (Washington, DC: World Bank). Restricted document.

World Bank/Implementation Completion Report (2001) *Brazil — Science and Technology Subprogram: Science Centers & Directed Research — Phase I and Emergency Assistance*, Report No. 22533 (Washington, DC: World Bank). Restricted document.

World Bank/Inspection Panel (1995) *Recommendation of the Inspection Panel: Request for Inspection: Rondônia Natural Resources Management Project*. Loan no. 3444–BR (Washington, DC: World Bank).

World Bank/Inspection Panel (1997a) *Review of Progress in Implementation of the Rondônia Natural Resources Management Project*. Loan no. 3444–BR (Washington, DC: World Bank).

World Bank/Inspection Panel (1997b) 'Inspection Panel Finds Mixed Results in Brazilian Amazon Project,' press release (Washington, DC: World Bank), 10 April.

World Bank/OED (1988) *Rural Development: World Bank Experience, 1965–86*, Operations Evaluation Department (Washington, DC: World Bank).

World Bank/OED (1989) *Renewable Resource Management in Agriculture*, Operations Evaluation Department (Washington, DC: World Bank).

World Bank/OED (1991) *Dynamics of Rural Development in Northeast Brazil: New Lessons from Old Projects*, Operations Evaluation Department (Washington, DC: World Bank).

World Bank/OED (1992a) *World Bank Approaches to the Environment in Brazil — Volume III: The Carajás Iron Ore Project*, Report no. 10039, Operations Evaluation Department (Washington, DC: World Bank). Restricted document.

World Bank/OED (1992b) *World Bank Approaches to the Environment in Brazil — Volume V: Polonoroeste*, Report no. 10039, Operations Evaluation Department (Washington, DC: World Bank). Restricted document.

World Bank/OED (2000a) *The World Bank's 1991 Forest Strategy and its Implementation*, Operations Evaluation Department (Washington, DC: World Bank).

World Bank/OED (2000b) *Brazil — Forests in the Balance: Challenges of Conservation with Development*, Operations Evaluation Department (Washington, DC: World Bank).

World Bank/PAD (2001) (World Bank/Project Appraisal Document/ Rainforest Trust Fund Grant) *Brazil — Ecological Corridors Project*, Report No. 23514 (Washington, D.C.: World Bank).

World Bank/PAD (2001, draft) *Project Appraisal Document for the Tocantins Rural Poverty Reduction Project*, Report No. 22595–BR (Washington, D.C: World Bank), dated November 12, 2001.

World Bank/PAD (2002) *Brazil — Amazon Region Protected Areas (ARPA) Project*, Report No. 23756, project appraisal document (Washington, DC: World Bank).

World Bank/PCF (2001) *World Bank, Prototype Carbon Fund: A Public/Private Partnership to Mitigate Climate Change — Annual Report 2001* (Washington, D.C., World Bank.

World Bank/PCR (1992) *Project Completion Report for the Amazonas Agricultural Development Project*, Report No. 10553 (April 22).

World Bank/PCR (1997) *Project Completion Report for the Amazon Basin Malaria Control Project*, Report No. 16482 (April 10).

World Bank/Pilot Programme to Conserve the Brazilian Rain Forest (1999) *Review of Institutional Arrangements* (Washington, DC: World Bank). Unpublished consultants' report.

World Bank/Project Appraisal Document (1998) *Brazil — Amazon Emergency Fire Protection and Control Project (PROARCO)*, Report no. 18365–BR (Washington, DC: World Bank). Restricted document.

World Bank/Project Appraisal Document (1999) *Brazil — Second National Environmental Project*, Report no. 19875–BR (Washington, DC: World Bank).

World Bank/Project Appraisal Document (2000) *Costa Rica — Ecomarkets Project*, Report no. 20434–CR (Washington, DC: World Bank).

World Bank/Project Concept Document (2002) *Brazil — Amapá Sustainable Communities Project* (Brasília: World Bank).

World Bank/Prototype Carbon Fund (2001a) *Prototype Carbon Fund: A Public-Private Partnership to Mitigate Climate Change — Annual Report 2001* (Washington, DC: World Bank).

World Bank/Prototype Carbon Fund (2001b) *Brazil — PCF Minas Gerais Plantar Project*. Project appraisal document (Brasília: World Bank). Restricted document.

World Bank/Rain Forest Unit (no date) *Pilot Program to Conserve the Brazilian Rain Forest* (Washington, DC: World Bank).

World Bank/Rain Forest Unit (2002a) 'New Environmental Control System Helps Reduce Deforestation by One-third in Mato Grosso,' *Brazil Rain Forest Pilot Program Success Story 1* (Brasília: World Bank).

World Bank/Rain Forest Unit (2002b) 'Innovative Project Contributes to Regularizing Indigenous Lands in the Amazon,' *Brazil Rain Forest Pilot Program Success Story 2* (Brasília: World Bank).

World Bank/Rain Forest Unit (2002c) 'Fostering "Sustainable" Cosmetics from the Amazon: A Private Sector Partnership to Conserve the Rain Forest,' *Brazil Rain Forest Pilot Program Story 3* (Brasília: World Bank).

World Bank/Rainforest Trust Fund Grant (2001) *Brazil — Ecological Corridors Project*, Report no. 23514, project appraisal document (Washington, DC: World Bank).

World Bank/Staff Appraisal Report (1990) *Brazil — National Environmental Project*, Report no. 8146–BR (Washington, DC: World Bank). Restricted document.

World Bank/Staff Appraisal Report (1992a) *Brazil — Mato Grosso Natural Resource Management Project*, Report no. 10402–BR (Washington, DC: World Bank). Restricted document.

World Bank/Staff Appraisal Report (1992a) *Brazil — Rondônia Natural Resource Management Project*, Report No. 8073–BR (Washington, DC: World Bank). Restricted document.

World Bank/WWF (2000) *World Bank WWF Alliance for Forest Conservation and Sustainable Use — Annual Report 1999* (Washington, DC: World Bank).

World Commission on Environment and Development (1987) *Our Common Future* (New York: Oxford University Press, New York).

WRI (2000) *The 1997–98 Forest Fire in Indonesia: Impact, Costs And Causes* (Washington, DC: World Resources Institute).

Wunder, S. (2000) 'Ecotourism and economic incentives,' *Ecological Economics*, vol. 32, no. 3, pp. 465–79.

WWF Climate Change Campaign (2000) *Make-or-break the Kyoto Protocol* (Washington, DC: World Wildlife Fund–US), http://www.panda.org/climate.

CPSIA information can be obtained at www.ICGtesting.com
Printed in the USA
266224BV00002B/10/A